CONFLICTS

Conflicts

THE POETICS AND POLITICS OF PALESTINE-ISRAEL

Liron Mor

FORDHAM UNIVERSITY PRESS NEW YORK 2024

Cover art: Raida Adon, still from *Strangeness*, 2018, digital video, 33:30 mins.

Fordham University Press also publishes its books in a variety of electronic formats. Some content that appears in print may not be available in electronic books.

Visit us online at www.fordhampress.com.

Library of Congress Cataloging-in-Publication Data available online at https://catalog.loc.gov.

Printed in the United States of America

26 25 24   5 4 3 2 1

First edition

for Rania

Contents

NOTE ON TRANSLITERATION AND TRANSLATION ix

Introduction 1

1 *Conflict* (Judgment/*Ishtibāk*) 25

2 *Levaṭim* (Disorienting Dilemmas) 68

3 *Ikhtifā'* (Anti/colonial Disappearance) 108

4 *Ḥoḳ* (Mediating Law) 153

5 *Inqisām* (Hostile Severance) 195

Postscript 243

ACKNOWLEDGMENTS 251

BIBLIOGRAPHY 255

INDEX 277

Note on Transliteration and Translation

This book employs a simplified version of the Library of Congress transliteration system for Hebrew: to parallel Arabic romanization, the silent final letter "He" is everywhere dropped and titles are capitalized as they would be in English. The book also follows the International Journal of Middle Eastern Studies (IJMES) transliteration system for Arabic, with three exceptions: diacritical dots were preserved in press names and titles for clarity and for maintaining continuity with Hebrew romanization; names of authors already published in English are transliterated as they appear in their published works; and names of characters and places are generally transliterated as they appear in existing translations for the sake of consistency. I rely on published translations when available; my own translations and modifications are specified. When texts in the original languages are cited, page numbers in the original follow the page numbers in the English translation.

CONFLICTS

Introduction

It is nearly impossible to find an English-language discussion of Palestine-Israel that does not invoke the term "conflict." Yet, public discussions seem to take the meaning of the word for granted. Scholars who explore current conditions in Palestine-Israel—investigating their causes, implications, or representations—also rarely explain what they mean by "conflict," as though its definitions were transparent, universal, and unproblematic. Following three decades of Israeli adoption of "conflict management" as a mechanism of control, papered over by a protracted charade of negotiations over an eternally postponed "conflict resolution," it is clear that the meaning of "conflict" is neither objective nor neutral and that understanding it is ever more pressing.

Conflicts takes on the task of reconsidering this central political paradigm. What is conflict? Do we accept a normative definition of conflict as a zero-sum game between two opposing sides, or do we err in the opposite direction by conceiving of political communities as chaotic multitudes? What is the history of this twin conception of conflict, and what colonial effects might it conceal? What is to be gained by substituting specific conflictual concepts for the universality of a singular conflict, and how might literary works from Palestine-Israel concretize, defy, and hone our perceptions of conflict?

Critical of a universalizing, Western conception of conflict, the following study breaks it apart and contests its adequacy to the Palestinian-Israeli context. It turns to literature to articulate instead locally specific modes of theorizing the antagonisms and mediations, colonial technologies, and anti-colonial practices that make up the fabric of this site. The book combines political and rhetorical theory with a comparative study of Hebrew and Arabic literature, thus challenging the separation between the conceptual and the poetic, the universal and the local. The literary archive explored, which ranges from the 1930s to the present and from prose and poetry to film and television, includes works by both canonical writers and less recognized, more contemporary figures. I engage these works on their own terms to assess the specific mechanisms of conflict that they themselves detect or suggest. This study moves from naming and complicating common conceptions of conflict to revealing and analyzing less familiar or obvious ones. It thus offers five figurative concepts of conflict that are derived from the poetics of the works—*conflict* (judgment/ *ishtibāk*), *levaṭim* (disorienting dilemmas), *ikhtifāʾ* (anti/colonial disappearance), *ḥok* (mediating law), and *inqisām* (hostile severance). Transcending the language of conflict resolution or management, these models gradually defamiliarize the meaning of "conflict" and build toward a more complex framework for considering the specificities of Palestine-Israel—a framework whose theoretical components might nonetheless echo other colonial contexts.

Insisting that literature is not separate from but rather essential to understanding and reimagining conflicts, I use the lens of poetics to reassess conflict and its manifestations in this particular colonial setting. Precisely because existing scholarship takes the definition of conflict for granted, it tends to examine the literature of Palestine-Israel as a record of real or phantasmatic relations that predate and exceed the separation between the two cultures. By showing that such cultural relations are neither primary nor necessarily harmonious, *Conflicts* aims to delineate their specific forms and the histories of their often-violent construction. Treating literature not as a case study or a social document but rather as a culturally embedded formal material that questions the very distinction between theory and case, *Conflicts* draws conceptual insights from poetic elements. Specifically, it studies the operation of rhetorical figures (such as litotes or metaphors) and literary affects (such as melancholic hesitation, irony, or humor) by putting the canon of literary theory in contact with cultural production from Palestine-Israel and with Muslim and Jewish traditions of rhetorical theory (such as *ʿilm al-bayān* or *pilpul*). In so doing, the book aims to generate a historically and geographically situated mode of theory-making that departs from universalizing categories. It thus joins an emergent body of scholarship that pushes the bounds of contemporary critical theory by putting it in challenging conversations with non-Western literatures, cultures, and thought.

Why Conflicts Now?

In the past few decades, conflict has elicited renewed interest from scholars of political theory. Major works such as Jean-François Lyotard's *The Differend* (1989 [1983]), which posits discursive conflict as necessary for political ontology, and Michel Foucault's *"Society Must Be Defended"* (2003 [1997]), which famously rearticulated the modern perception of politics as "the continuation of war by other means," have paved the way to a distinctly twenty-first-century engagement with conflict and civil war as paradigmatic forms of politics. Such studies include Étienne Balibar's "What's in a War? (Politics as War, War as Politics)" (2008), Jacques Rancière's *Dissensus* (2010), Chantal Mouffe's *Agonistics* (2013), and Giorgio Agamben's *Stasis* (2015), amongst others. Perhaps in dialectical response to this concern with antagonism and war, an interest in impasse and stillness has also emerged, as exemplified by Emily Apter's elaboration of a micropolitical vocabulary for commonplace political impasses in *Unexceptional Politics* (2018). (The concept of "peace," meanwhile, was deserted, left in the hands of political scientists and centers for peace and conflict studies.)

There are two crucial reasons for reopening the conversation on conflict, dissensus, stasis, "politics as the continuation of war," and all that discordant jazz. First, these theories have largely neglected the racial and colonial implications of conflict and focused on Europe (or, sometimes, the United States) as the main model for understanding it. This study joins a handful of scholars of literary and political theory who have begun to displace the discussion of conflict to non-Western contexts, exploring its political and discursive effects from the perspective of the colonized. Nasser Mufti's *Civilizing War* (2017), for instance, traces the discursive transformation of civil war from a "civilized" affair characteristic of the West alone in the early Victorian era to an "uncivil" crisis that becomes synonymous with the colonial and postcolonial periphery and justifies imperial intervention. From a different angle, George Ciccariello-Maher's *Decolonizing Dialectics* (2017) seeks to reclaim the combative rupture of the dialectic by closely engaging with the anticolonial writing of Frantz Fanon and Enrique Dussel. While sharing some of Ciccariello-Maher's concerns, I reject the recuperation of antagonisms in dialectics. Instead, I am interested in exploring concrete modes of conflict that produce effects or movement and are nonetheless irreducible to either dialectics or sheer chaos, thus destabilizing foundational political categories.

Second, we have ultimately failed to adequately deal with conflict in general and with the so-called Israeli-Palestinian conflict, in particular. In committing to examining this topic, I depart from current works in Palestine Studies, whose authors aim to decenter what is known as the Israeli-Palestinian conflict. They rightfully foreground instead Palestinian culture, economy, society, and politics without subordinating their investigations to the consideration of Zionism.[1] The advantage of this approach, as the historian Sherene Seikaly

1. For instance, Adnan Mohammed Abu-Ghazaleh, *Arab Cultural Nationalism in Palestine during the British Mandate* (Beirut: Institute for Palestine Studies, 1973); Ami Ayalon, *Reading*

observes, is its refusal of colonial epistemologies in which the Palestinian either appears as a shadow figure of the colonizer—forever reacting to colonial actions—or is recovered "into the light" in an attempt to overcome all that is wrong with the Palestinian present.[2] While the scholarly shift away from Zionism is vital, I believe that it might be premature (especially for me, as a Mizrahi Jewish scholar originally from Israel) to move beyond this problem space, whose very concrete effects and mechanisms are yet to be surpassed or even understood. While insisting on the urgency of reexamining the Palestinian-Israeli context, however, I heed Seikaly's call for formulating new questions beyond such colonial frameworks. Starting just before the 1948 solidification of Zionism into a state, this study refuses to recover or dwell in nostalgia for an authentic or harmonious past preceding colonization and focuses instead on understanding forms of antagonistic settings and techniques that are shaping the present. In examining cultural production by both Palestinians and Jews, this book does not subordinate the study of one to that of the other, nor does it equate, unite, or even compare them. Instead, it explores the various ways in which literary works diagnose, respond to, and intervene in a colonial reality, which is shared, albeit in ways that are radically different and inequitable, neither agreeable nor agreed upon.

As a point of departure, I would like to offer three axiomatic statements about the construct known as "the Israeli-Palestinian conflict": first, it does not take place between two; second, it is not separate from its literatures; and, third, it is not, in fact, a conflict. Through these provisional statements, I introduce here the main terms of the book, which also form its title—Palestine-Israel, poetics and politics, and conflict. Three questions about conflict more broadly correspond to these negative statements: What is conflict? What does it involve, and what might it obscure? And how is poetics related to conflicts and to the possibility of thinking them otherwise? Subsequent chapters flesh out concrete sites of conflict that provide constructive yet circumscribed answers to these questions.

Palestine: Printing and Literacy, 1900–1948 (Austin: University of Texas Press, 2004); Rana Barakat, "Writing/Righting Palestine Studies: Settler Colonialism, Indigenous Sovereignty and Resisting the Ghost(s) of History," *Settler Colonial Studies* 8, no. 3 (2018): 349–63; Sarah Graham-Brown, *Palestinians and Their Society, 1880–1946* (London and New York: Quartet, 1980); Rashid Khalidi, *Palestinian Identity: The Construction of Modern National Consciousness* (New York: Columbia University Press, 2009); Sherene Seikaly, *Men of Capital: Scarcity and Economy in Mandate Palestine* (Stanford, Calif.: Stanford University Press, 2015); Salim Tamari, *Mountain against the Sea: Essays on Palestinian Society and Culture* (Berkeley: University of California Press, 2008).

2. Seikaly, *Men of Capital*, 20.

This Conflict Is Not between Two

The language of "conflict" implies a symmetrical relationship between two opposed sides. In the case of Palestine-Israel, however, both the assumed symmetry and the dyadic form are false yet carry far-reaching repercussions. First, then, it is crucial to stress the deeply asymmetric nature of the relations between Jewish Israelis and Palestinians. Born of the nationalist movements that swept Europe during the nineteenth century, Zionism emerged as a settler colonial project that sought to construct a Jewish nation state in Palestine with the aid of Western powers, while drawing ideological support from a secularized scriptural notion of "return" to the Holy Land. Zionists consolidated the colonization of Palestine during the 1948 War, establishing the State of Israel and displacing most of the indigenous Palestinian population—a development known in Arabic as *al-nakba* (the catastrophe). Palestinian nationalism, born in response to seismic economic and political changes in the Ottoman Empire and to European and Zionist colonial intrusions, is—by contrast—the galvanizing force of the colonized. It further intensified after 1948, despite the political crisis and societal fragmentation unleashed by the *nakba*. Thus, the first and most pressing reason for reconsidering the operation of "conflict" in Palestine-Israel is the need to push against a discursive framework that views a settlement movement and a colonized people as equivalent competitors over a single strip of land.

Second, this "conflict" does not in fact take place solely between two. In Palestine, in the late nineteenth and first half of the twentieth centuries, the two national movements—as well as their societies, economies, and cultures—developed in relation not only to one another but also to both the Ottoman Empire and the West (specifically, after World War I, in close contact with British imperialism). Zionism must be understood in the context of its European origins, as both a defensive reaction to historic nationalistic anti-Semitism in Europe and the brainchild of the European national idea. Palestinian nationalism developed not only in relation to imperial powers and Western political thought but also through intellectual and cultural interactions with neighboring countries and with longer literary and philosophical traditions of the Arab world. Both also arose as Palestine was undergoing rapid integration into the global capitalist market. This entanglement is indeed reflected in literature. The Arabic and the Hebrew modern literary revivals—the *nahḍa* and the *teḥiya*, respectively—developed not only by "rediscovering" their own past traditions but also through exchanges with other literary corpuses and through fraught colonial relations, mainly with Europe.[3]

3. These relations were more explicitly colonial in the case of Arabic literature. By contrast, in its European context, Hebrew literature was caught in what could be portrayed, following

The "two parties" narrative also erases the particular functions and circumstances of Mizrahi Jews in Palestine-Israel. Jews who originated from the Arab and Muslim world, as well as the indigenous Jewish population of Palestine, have come to be known in Israel as "Mizrahi" ("Oriental" or "Eastern" in Hebrew)—a homogenizing sociopolitical category that obscures highly diverse histories and cultures. Mizrahi Jews are also known as Sephardi (*sefaradim*; lit., Spanish), a term that historically strictly referred to Jews who were expelled from Iberia and, later, came to be used more broadly to designate non-Ashkenazi liturgical practices, thus increasingly becoming in recent decades the name of a religious traditionalist ethnic identity. They were also officially termed Jews "of the lands of the Orient" or "descendants of the communities of the Orient" (*bne ʿedot ha-mizraḥ*)—ethnicizing terms used by "special departments and programs meant to deal with the 'Levantine element. . . .'"[4] Finally, some *mizraḥim* refer to themselves as "Arab Jews," often as a politically oppositional claim. All of these, however, are misnomers, or partial frames, eliding the fact that many *mizraḥim*, such as Iranian and Kurdish Jews, are not Arabs, while others have never passed through Spain, and still others are in fact from the *maghreb*, the West.

As the intricacy of naming suggests, Mizrahi Jews tend to complicate given categories, troubling the dividing line between colonizer and colonized, colonial and postcolonial. Largely, *mizraḥim* migrated to Israel in the early years of the State because of Zionist campaigns to actively encourage their emigration or because their living conditions became untenable as a result of Israel's wars with Arab countries. Following this displacement, most *mizraḥim* were unable, and are still unable, to return to their lands of origin. Today, Mizrahi Jews are still discriminated against in most aspects of economic, political, and cultural life, even though they constitute about half of the Jewish population in Israel.[5] In fact, as this book demonstrates, the mechanisms that sanctioned

---

Michel Foucault, as "internal colonialism," born as a boomerang effect of external colonialism; Foucault, *"Society Must Be Defended": Lectures at the Collège de France, 1975–1976*, trans. David Macey (New York: Picador, 2003), 103. In depicting these relations as colonial, however, I do not mean to suggest that they were simply forced or unilateral; rather, I wish to stress their initiation by colonial intrusions and their uneven power relations. On the complexity of the colonial encounter in literature, see Shaden M. Tageldin, *Disarming Words: Empire and the Seductions of Translation in Egypt* (Berkeley: University of California Press, 2011).

4. ". . . just as special departments were formed to deal with '*hamiʿut haʿaravi*' (the 'Arab minority')—that is, the Palestinians." See Ella Shohat, "Rupture and Return: The Shaping of a Mizrahi Epistemology," *Hagar: International Social Science Review* 2, no. 1 (2001): 66.

5. The numbers of Mizrahi Jews in Israel are elusive. Until 2022, the Israeli Central Bureau of Statistics recorded as "Mizrahi" only those born in Asia or Africa or those whose father was

Zionism's occupation of Palestine and its subjugation of Palestinians are deeply imbricated with the Zionist marginalization of *mizraḥim*, who were similarly perceived as Oriental. Thus, Mizrahi Jews are colonizers who, at the same time, suffer something akin to a "semi-colonial" condition[6]—they, too, were subjected to the forced population transfer, violent social engineering, and cultural suppression dictated by the colonial interests of a settler state.[7] However, their Jewishness, a religious marker turned racial difference, allows them a path to settlerhood and to hegemonic Jewish Israeli society that is completely foreclosed to Palestinians. Indeed, while most *mizraḥim* were reluctant colonizers at first, many now support the nationalist political camp, insisting on the exclusivity of their path (a transformation examined in detail in Chapter 5).[8] Thus, available concepts—such as "colonizer" and "colonized," "colonial" and "postcolonial," and perhaps also "settler colonialism"—do not seem to fully capture this history and its contemporary effects. Likewise, "the Israeli-Palestinian conflict" cannot be adequately comprehended without adding two more dimensions to the dyad implied by this phrase, marking

born in Asia or Africa. The bureau thus discounted third- and fourth-generation *mizraḥim*, as well as offspring of women born in Asia or Africa whose partners were born elsewhere. Estimates nonetheless suggest that *mizraḥim* account for about half of Israel's Jewish population. See Noah Lewin-Epstein and Yinon Cohen, "Ethnic Origin and Identity in the Jewish Population of Israel," *Journal of Ethnic and Migration Studies* 45, no. 11 (2019): 2,118–37.

6. The term is borrowed from Ella Shohat, who writes that Mizrahi Jews, "as a Jewish Third World people, form a semi-colonized nation-within-a-nation." See Shohat, "Sephardim in Israel: Zionism from the Standpoint of Its Jewish Victims," *Social Text*, no. 19/20 (1988): 2.

7. On these processes and Mizrahi resistance to them see, for instance, Yali Hashash, *Bat shel Mi At: Drakhim le-Daber Feminizem Mizraḥi* (Tel Aviv: ha-Ḳibuts ha-Me'uḥad, 2022); Ella Shohat, *Israeli Cinema: East/West and the Politics of Representation*, rev. ed. (London and New York: I. B. Tauris, 2010); Erez Tzfadia and Haim Yacobi, *Rethinking Israeli Space: Periphery and Identity* (London and New York: Routledge, 2011).

8. On the complex identity of Mizrahi Jews in Israel and its history see, for example, Aziza Khazzoom, "The Great Chain of Orientalism: Jewish Identity, Stigma Management, and Ethnic Exclusion in Israel," *American Sociological Review* 68, no. 4 (2003): 481–510; Amnon Raz-Krakotzkin, "Zionist Return to the West and the Mizrachi Jewish Perspective," in *Orientalism and the Jews*, ed. Ivan Davidson Kalmar and Derek J. Pensler (Waltham Mass.: Brandeis University Press, 2005), 162–81; Ella Shohat, "The Invention of the Mizrahim," *Journal of Palestine Studies* 29, no. 1 (1999): 5–20; Yehouda Shenhav, *The Arab Jews: A Postcolonial Reading of Nationalism, Religion, and Ethnicity* (Stanford, Calif.: Stanford University Press, 2006). On Mizrahi integration into Zionist settler society and for Palestinian critiques of it, see Joseph Massad, "Zionism's Internal Others: Israel and the Oriental Jews," *Journal of Palestine Studies* 25, no. 4 (1996): 53–68; Lana Tatour, "The Israeli Left: Part of the Problem or the Solution? A Response to Giulia Daniele," *Global Discourse* 6, no. 3 (2016): 487–92.

Western influences on this context and acknowledging the specific, if sometimes ambiguous, role of Mizrahi Jews within it, which is still understudied.

Since the separation between "Arabs" and "Jews" is itself the result of processes initiated by Zionism, these categories, moreover, are neither given, complete, nor stable.[9] A case in point is that of Palestinian Jews who, deep into the 1920s and even beyond, largely viewed themselves, and were viewed by their Muslim and Christian neighbors, as Palestinians.[10] Thus, any consideration of these volatile categories must acknowledge that they do not exist independently of the colonial forces that have constituted them and continue to shape them—that is, Zionism, as well as the Orientalist European notions of "the Arab" and "the Jew."

Indeed, who are the two parties, exactly? What should they be named? Speaking of "Jews" and "Muslims" not only overlooks other religious affiliations in the region but also erroneously suggests that the complexity of Palestine-Israel is reducible to religious differences. Speaking of "Israelis" and "Palestinians" creates the false impression of two symmetrical, autonomous nations and overlooks the existence of Palestinians who are citizens of Israel. Finally, the commonly used categories "Jew" and "Arab" do not even share a semantic field: while "Jew" designates a religious or cultural affiliation (but what culture exactly do Jews from different continents share?), "Arab" is a generic "ethnic" category, which discounts the national identification of Palestinians and obscures the specific history and cultures of Palestine. It at best refers to a broad linguistic affiliation and at worst is an immutable racial category. Official Israeli discourse utilizes this dominant pair, allowing the state, as Gil Anidjar observes, to discriminate based on "nationality" (Jew or Arab) as distinguished from "citizenship" (Israeli), which both Jews and Palestinians share within 1948-borders Israel. Presenting the two as complementary, moreover, racializes the category of "the Jew" while detheologizing the category of "the Arab," so that both become racial categories, out of which, unlike religious ones, it is nearly impossible to convert.[11]

Throughout this study, I therefore employ, based on context, the terms "Jewish Israelis," "Zionists," and "Palestinians," distinguishing when necessary

9. On the inextricability of "Arab" and "Jew," see Edward W. Said, *Orientalism* (New York: Vintage, 2003), 286; Shohat, "Sephardim in Israel"; Gil Anidjar, *The Jew, the Arab: A History of the Enemy* (Stanford, Calif.: Stanford University Press, 2003); Gil Z. Hochberg, *In Spite of Partition: Jews, Arabs, and the Limits of Separatist Imagination* (Princeton, N.J.: Princeton University Press, 2010), 4–15.

10. Tamari, *Mountain against the Sea*, 150–66; Menachem Klein, "Arab Jew in Palestine," *Israel Studies* 19, no. 3 (2014): 134–53. For a less favorable view, see Hillel Cohen, *Śon'im: Sipur Ahava* (Tel Aviv: 'Ivrit, 2022), chapters 1–2.

11. Anidjar, *The Jew, the Arab*, 163n1.

between Palestinians "of the outside," or exiled Palestinians, and Palestinians "of the inside," or '48 Palestinians.[12] I use "Arab Jews" when the Arab cultures of (most) Mizrahi Jews are relevant to my argument, but, for the most part, I use "Mizrahi Jews" and "*mizraḥim*" interchangeably. The latter, a common Hebrew term, eliminates the specification "Jews," which is, in certain contexts, precisely the question begged. Unlike the ethnicizing and dehistoricizing terms mentioned earlier, "*mizraḥim*" recalls the historical invention and marginalization of Mizrahi Jews in Israel; largely made in Israel, it is itself part of that racializing history. It also suggests the active self-rewriting of Mizrahi history, evoking the 1980s adoption of the noun *mizraḥim* (as opposed to the then common use of the adjective *mizraḥiyyim*) by Mizrahi activists aiming to form linguistic parity with *ashkenazim*. Conjuring the many histories of Mizrahi cultures throughout the "Eastern" world and their transregional interactions, the term also, as Ella Shohat argues, "affirms a pan-oriental identity that diverse communities developed in Israel" and, at least within certain critical circles, it "at times, invokes a desire for a future of revived cohabitation with the Arab-Muslim East."[13]

Given these various complications, the use of the expression "Palestine-Israel" in the title of this book is somewhat misleading, since it collapses a plethora of identities and cultures into a dichotomous opposition. Indeed, the book itself exceeds "Palestine-Israel" as it engages Arabic and Hebrew literary works beyond the categories "Palestinian" or "Israeli": it examines, for instance, Hebrew prose by Haim Hazaz that predates the State of Israel, and it addresses the Arabic novel *Bab al-Shams* (Gate of the Sun, 1998) by the Lebanese author Elias Khoury. Additionally, while the expression "Palestine-Israel" serves as an expedient reminder of the historical and geographical entanglement of today's Israel with both historic Palestine and the contemporary Occupied Palestinian Territories (henceforth, OPT), it reinforces the problematic dyadic structure discussed earlier. In the absence of a perfect solution—a notion that this study rejects—I kept "Palestine-Israel," in the title and throughout, as a marker of those entanglements and of the false dichotomy that the term "conflict" suggests. When possible, however, I shift the emphasis to the literatures involved and speak of "Arabic" and "Hebrew." By focusing on languages as signifiers of cultural production, I bracket nationalism as the privileged framework for discussing communities. The phonic proximity between the names of the two languages, near cognates with shared meanings—*ʿaravit and ʿivrit*

12. I use these terms, although they are far from perfect. On the intricacies of naming Palestinians in Israel, see Chapter 3, especially note 25 and the sources therein.

13. Shohat, "Rupture and Return," 68.

(in Hebrew), *ʿarabiyya and ʿibriyya* (in Arabic)—evokes the Semitic source of both. Unlike the dichotomy between "Palestinian" and "Israeli," or "Arab" and "Jew," Arabic and Hebrew sustain zones of indeterminacy and do not draw up sharp communal borders in advance, even while their relationship, too, is not always simple.

This Conflict Is Not Separate from Literature

Although it is tempting to think of literature as a sphere of compassionate relations that is somehow exogenous to the realm of violence, it is by no means separate from war and conflict. This is particularly obvious in the case of the Hebrew literary canon, where names of literary generations are often indexed to different Israeli wars or stages of colonization.[14] By contrast, by focusing mainly on colonial influences on the Arab world—and particularly on Palestine—American scholars of Arabic literature tend to engage Arabic literary texts merely as sociological records and thus, as Tarek El-Ariss observes, ignore their aesthetic qualities.[15] While it is true that the poetic complexity of recent Arabic literature has been understudied, the easy division between the aesthetic, on the one hand, and the sociological or the political, on the other, seems to me a bit too facile. In fact, the two aspects are often deeply intertwined in both Arabic and Hebrew literature. In Palestine-Israel, literature does not simply reflect different facets of life; it is also conditioned by them and, in turn, is a vehicle for their constitution, preservation, or reconsideration. As Chapter 1 demonstrates, for instance, the Palestinian author Ghassan Kanafani was able to figure his political positions only through his literature. Conversely, the ingenuity of Kanafani's politics lies in his innovative and fragmentary poetics—in revolutionizing political language itself.

Recently, in response to the separation paradigm prescribed by the notion of conflict, scholars have increasingly sought to challenge it by establishing and examining relations between Jews and Arabs. A number of historians have dedicated works to unearthing Arab-Jewish relations prior to the petrification of the divide between the two groups, often focusing on Ottoman and Mandate-era Palestine.[16] Similarly, in critical theory and cultural studies, works such as

14. For more on the implication of Hebrew literature in war and security, see Uri S. Cohen, *ha-Nusaḥ ha-Biṭḥoni ve-Tarbut ha-Milḥama ha-ʿIvrit* (Jerusalem: Mosad Bialik, 2017).

15. Tarek El-Ariss, *Trials of Arab Modernity: Literary Affects and the New Political* (New York: Fordham University Press, 2013), 9–10.

16. See, for instance, Moshe Behar and Zvi Ben-Dor Benite, eds., *Modern Middle Eastern Jewish Thought: Writings on Identity, Politics, and Culture, 1893–1958* (Waltham, Mass.:

Ammiel Alcalay's *After Jews and Arabs* (1992), Anidjar's *The Jew, the Arab* (2003) and *Semites* (2007), and Ariella Azoulay's *From Palestine to Israel* (2011) have explored cultural expressions of interactions between "Jews" and "Arabs," thus complicating these categories and undermining their contemporary incongruity. In the field of comparative literature, too, scholars have begun to take note of literary representations of the so-called Israeli-Palestinian conflict. Both Gil Z. Hochberg's *In Spite of Partition* (2010) and Lital Levy's *Poetic Trespass* (2014) have undertaken the weighty task of revealing relations between Arabic and Hebrew literary works—relations that precede and defy the processes dictating their separation. Assuming that the meaning of conflict in Palestine-Israel is self-evident and accepting its dyadic form, both aim to bridge the dichotomy and "bring together" the two literatures by detecting moments of contact between the two cultures and expressing them in a rhetoric of "passage" and "migration." Hochberg articulates such relations as repressed and forgotten libidinal ties that expose the limits of partition, while Levy, focusing on linguistic exchanges, presents them as instances of trespass that generate a bilingual no-man's-land of language as "a contested site of history, memory and identity."[17] Both turn to literature for its capacity to expose and record current and past relations, as well as for its ability to reimagine—either historical and political realities or the bounds of language.

While building on these scholarly landmarks, this book significantly departs from them. It aims, first and foremost, to complicate the common notion of conflict, rethinking both its definition and the method that yielded it. Second, in arguing that poetics is entangled with politics, this study foregrounds and explores the complicity of literature in violence. It is thus not satisfied with demonstrating the antecedence of relations between Hebrew and Arabic, Jews and Arabs, or West and East. Such demonstrations risk ontologizing relations, rendering them given, symmetrical, and primordial, thereby occluding the

---

Brandeis University Press, 2013); Michelle Campos, *Ottoman Brothers: Muslims, Christians, and Jews in Early Twentieth-Century Palestine* (Stanford, Calif.: Stanford University Press, 2010); Abigail Jacobson, *From Empire to Empire: Jerusalem between Ottoman and British Rule* (Syracuse, N.Y.: Syracuse University Press, 2011); Abigail Jacobson and Moshe Naor, *Oriental Neighbors: Middle Eastern Jews and Arabs in Mandatory Palestine* (Waltham, Mass.: Brandeis University Press, 2016); Mark LeVine, *Overthrowing Geography: Jaffa, Tel Aviv, and the Struggle for Palestine, 1880–1948* (Berkeley: University of California Press, 2005); Zachary Lockman, *Comrades and Enemies: Arab and Jewish Workers in Palestine, 1906–1948* (Berkeley: University of California Press, 1996); Gershon Shafir, *Land, Labor and the Origins of the Israeli-Palestinian Conflict, 1882–1914* (Berkeley: University of California Press, 1996).

17. Hochberg, *In Spite of Partition*, 16–17; Lital Levy, *Poetic Trespass: Writing between Hebrew and Arabic in Israel/Palestine* (Princeton, N.J.: Princeton University Press, 2014), 4.

history of their production and its violence. Claiming that the mere existence of relations is not necessarily transformative and that their nature is not necessarily harmonious, *Conflicts* articulates instead their specific modes of operation and the ways in which they are fashioned in and through conflicts. Finally, this study does not approach literature as a record, either of realities or of latent utopian imaginations; instead, it moves beyond the referential qualities of literature to consider poetics as a kind of diagnostic, capable of reconceptualizing politics.

To break down "conflict" and to better express the fine detail of the Palestinian-Israeli context, the book turns to local conceptual figures—more loosely structured concepts, whose figuration is derived from the poetics of the works. When speaking of such conceptual metaphors or figurative concepts, I employ the broadest possible definition of metaphor to showcase the theoretical force of poetic language, which marks out structural patterns without universalizing them.[18] While conceptual metaphors are explored at length in Chapter 1, it is worth noting already here that their dual modality—their production of meaning both synchronically and diachronically—renders them both structural and historical, allowing them to maintain the advantages of these two conflicting modes. As historical, such figures were influenced by other cultural, social, and political contexts in the past. By claiming that these figurative concepts are local or indigenous, I therefore do not suggest that they have somehow sprouted out of the soil in complete isolation. Such a fetishization of authenticity would be both absurd and Orientalist. What I propose, rather, is that these Hebrew and Arabic conceptual figures are in fact embedded in traditions that contain points of contact, influence, coercion, and clashes with others—including colonial and imperial cultures—yet their meaning is far from exhausted by existing concepts in those cultures. As structural, such figures move beyond epistemological critique, beyond the interventions of deconstruction and postcolonialism, to offer new, concrete reconceptualizations of the world. Their power is thus not limited to their breeding ground, for they open the door to a rethinking of "conflict" in innumerable other sites and contexts. Resisting the usual consignment of indigenous epistemes to the

18. I use "metaphors" in the Aristotelian sense, which includes not only "metaphor proper" but also its various subspecies, such as metonymy, synecdoche, and analogy, as well as tropes more broadly. The scope of these figures is very similar to the scope of *majāz* in classical Arabic rhetoric, at least until al-Sakkaki. See Aristotle, *Poetics*, trans. S. H. Butcher (New York: Hill and Wang, 1961), XXI.99; B. Reinert, J. T. P. de Bruijn, and J. Stewart Robinson, "Madjāz," in *Encyclopaedia of Islam*, 2nd ed., ed. P. Bearman, Th. Bianquis, C.E. Bosworth, E. van Donzel, W. P. Heinrichs (Brill, 2012), accessed online: http://dx.doi.org/10.1163/1573-3912_islam_COM_0605.

particularized realm of ethnic knowledge—regarded as merely supplemental to the universality of hegemonic knowledge—these figures forge a conceptual armor, an anti-colonial humanism, that is useful beyond the context of Palestine, yet remains embedded in its history. When their poetic qualities, historical specificity, and conceptual contributions are taken together, these figurative concepts might also pave the way to perceiving the context of Palestine-Israel in a historico-aesthetic light, outside the order of the political.

This Conflict Is Not One

Because "the Israeli-Palestinian conflict" is deeply asymmetrical and involves multiple parties, I argue that it is not, in fact, a conflict—that is, it cannot be adequately represented by the term "conflict" as it is conventionally understood and deployed. But what *is* this conventional concept of conflict? What are its sources, and what broader functions might it serve?

In May 2021, in the Palestinian neighborhood of Sheikh Jarrah in Jerusalem, Palestinian residents were opposing the ongoing Israeli attempts to evict them from their homes—attempts that emblematize the continuous process of Zionist ethnic cleansing in Palestine-Israel, which Palestinians have long dubbed *al-nakba al-mustamirra* (the ongoing *nakba*). It was the month of Ramadan, so protesters held outdoor nightly iftar meals, breaking their fast communally to protest their displacement and to show support for the Palestinian uprising crystalizing around the al-Aqsa Mosque. When a far-right Jewish Israeli party, *Otsma Yehudit* (Jewish Power), set up shop across the street, clashes soon began. The Israeli police rushed to arrest Palestinian protestors and used hyperbolic force to subdue the neighborhood. Amidst these events, the Israel Ministry of Foreign Affairs released a statement:

> Regrettably, the PA and Palestinian terror groups are presenting a real-estate dispute between private parties, as a nationalistic cause, in order to incite violence in Jerusalem. The PA and Palestinian terror groups will bear full responsibility for the violence emanating from their actions. The Israel police will ensure public order is maintained.[19]

This framing of the events, I argue, is paradigmatic of the Israeli construal of violence and antagonism in Palestine-Israel and of the normative meaning of

19. Israel Foreign Ministry, "Regrettably, the PA and Palestinian Terror Groups Are Presenting a Real-Estate Dispute between Private Parties, as a Nationalistic Cause," *Twitter*, May 7, 2021, https://twitter.com/IsraelMFA/status/1390632182398529536.

"conflict" more broadly. This statement translates the clashes, with their various facets—systemic colonialism, police violence, national struggle, local resistance—into a legal dispute between two parties vying over real estate in a zero-sum game. Since all the main building blocks of the normative juridico-political concept of conflict are here—(two) parties, (legal) dispute, real estate, and violence—this paradigmatic statement is useful for elucidating its meanings and implications.

A "dispute" convenes the parties in a tribunal, a *legal* rather than a social arena, where a decision is expected. The rhetoric of litigation is suggestive of two parties with equal legal claims and responsibilities, thus generating the dyadic logic and false symmetry critiqued earlier. (In trying fully to pass responsibility to Palestinians, however, the ministry's statement inadvertently discloses the stark disparity between state-sanctioned police violence, which is aimed at maintaining colonial order, and Palestinian violence, inspired by an anti-colonial national cause.) The notion of legal dispute is also eschatological. It mortgages the present for the sake of a future decision, a final judgment, that may or may not materialize. In this sense, "conflict resolution" is itself a mode of "conflict management": by depicting present conditions as a neutral starting point for negotiations and as merely temporary—and thus as legally acceptable, at least for now—it whitewashes and facilitates the ongoing colonization, its asymmetry, and its violence.

As the previous statement implies, moreover, this juridical concept of conflict fixes the dispute on "real estate," thus framing the zero-sum antagonism as a clashing, specifically, over the right to possess, exploit, and occupy a territory. The land—which prior to colonization was thought of as communal and shared, as a gathering and grazing ground for general use—is repackaged as property and considered, within this spatial imagination, as a delimited and enclosed space, whose habitation and use are necessarily exclusive.

By centering on property and its law, "conflict" suggests an antagonism not only between two parties but also between two—and only two—models of conflictuality. This dualistic perception is the legacy of a very long philosophical tradition in which conflict has typically been portrayed in one of two interrelated ways. On the one hand, owing to such thinkers as Thomas Hobbes and Jean-Jacques Rousseau, conflict is perceived as a *pre-political* war of all against all. This "state of nature" is envisioned as inspiring chaotic, universal violence precisely because property is not yet safeguarded and everyone has "a right to all things."[20] Lawless conflict over property serves as the ultimate

20. Thomas Hobbes, *Leviathan*, ed. Richard Tuck (Cambridge and New York: Cambridge University Press, 1996), 91–92.

justification for the juridical binding of the community in the universal of the State and its laws. On the other hand, the State, thus contracted to protect property ownership, is tied to *political* conflict—that is, to war as a legal competition over territories and its habitual sublimation as a zero-sum juridical dispute between opposed camps. This logic, developed by Hobbes, Rousseau, and Kant, culminates in the decisionist thought of Carl Schmitt, which also invokes the possibility that the enemy become internal and that violence become "law preserving" in the form of the police.[21] As Chapter 1 shows, Western political philosophy has regularly used the threat of the first, pre-political model of conflict, with its aimless violence, to justify the second, legal conflict as the *only* acceptable model for political conflict. (And while Hegel's dialectics seems to offer a third approach—the historical movement of contradictions, for which war is a central trope—one might argue, with Foucault, that it is simply a merger of the two aforementioned forms, whereby, crudely put, a conflict between two antithetic camps is eventually sublated in—or, as Foucault has it, colonized by—the universal of the state.)[22]

The juridico-political concept of conflict therefore constructs the clashes in Palestine-Israel as an opposition not only between two parties but also between pre-political, illegal, "private" violence and authorized state violence that

21. Carl Schmitt, *The Concept of the Political*, expanded ed., trans. George Schwab (Chicago: University of Chicago Press, 2007). The notion of law-preserving violence is, of course, Walter Benjamin's, whose reading of European politics as doubly imbricating the law with violence—violence being both its origin and telos—resonates closely with my argument. In his "Critique of Violence," Benjamin famously distinguishes between an originary lawmaking violence, operating before the law or outside politics—in a future anterior that characterizes both the mythic time of the "state of nature" and the exogenous revolutionary moment vanishing between two legal regimes—and a law-preserving violence, operating legally at the service of the state. This distinction, however, quickly collapses as Benjamin suggests that law-preserving violence always carries within it seeds of lawmaking violence. The two functions of violence are thus part of a single narrative, just as the correlating Benjaminian juxtaposition between natural law (with its justified natural violence) and positive law (with its justified legal violence) exposes their shared philosophical tradition (with its linear discourse of ends and means, whereby natural violence/law is the means for justifying positive law and its state violence). In this tradition, war—typically considered "primordial and paradigmatic of all violence," a violence "used for natural ends"—is in fact the founding of positive law, which in turn bars individuals from the (natural) right to violence. Benjamin, "Critique of Violence," *in Walter Benjamin: Selected Writings*, ed. Michael William Jennings and Marcus Paul Bullock, trans. Edmund Jephcott (Cambridge, Mass.: Belknap, 2004), 1:236–52. See also Jacques Derrida, "Force of Law: The 'Mystical Foundation of Authority,'" in *Deconstruction and the Possibility of Justice*, ed. Drucilla Cornell, David G. Carlson, and Michael Rosenfield, trans. Mary Quaintance (New York: Routledge, 1992), 3–67.

22. Foucault, *"Society Must Be Defended,"* 58.

enforces juridical order. Because state violence supposedly serves a public good, it no longer appears as violence at all. Indeed, in the Ministry's statement, the violence that "the PA and Palestinian terror groups" supposedly inspire is presented as a threat to public order, which Israeli law enforcement—whose disavowed violence is simply omitted—merely aims to restore and maintain. In this schema, the Palestinian Authority (PA), the representative body of Palestinians in the West Bank, is equated with "terrorist groups," transforming all Palestinian actors into "terrorists"—that is, those whose violence is necessarily illegal, lying beyond the bounds of politics. This concept of conflict thus blames Palestinians for all violence, presents all Palestinian violence as necessarily unlawful ("terrorism"), and masks state violence by sanctioning it as law (or as law enforcement).

By regarding pre-political conflict as a threat that the state subdues and regulates and political conflict as the field through which sovereign states decide to wage war against external or internal enemies, Western philosophy has established the notion that conflict is the basic condition of politics. As the case of Palestine-Israel demonstrates, however, conflict is not at all primary; rather, it is manufactured by politics—and, specifically, by the State—as its origin and justification. State-based politics is thus not merely the management of preexisting conflict but rather its retroactive and continuous production. The Israeli Ministry's statement reveals this mechanism through the language of "terrorism" and "incitement." By depicting unlawful violence as always lurking underneath the surface, waiting to be ignited by any mention of the Palestinian national cause, this statement necessitates the state, its legal institutions, and its law enforcement. By constructing (unlawful, violent) conflict as the underlying security threat and itself as the (legal, political) dam, the state has positioned itself as the only effective form of collective existence and attained a monopoly on violence.[23]

Finally, the language of legal dispute, sustaining the colonial status quo with its forever deferred decision, also criminalizes political opposition. It outlaws actions that challenge the current state of affairs, painting them as a refusal to accept the allegedly objective rules of the juridical game by attempting to force a decision through extra-juridical means. What the case of Sheikh Jarrah makes abundantly clear, however, is the fact that the law is not an impartial universal common sense; rather, it is always written in the idiom of those in

23. Finding legal authority insufficient for securing the monopoly on violence, Max Weber, who famously popularized this phrase, supplemented the law with the powers of charisma and tradition. See Weber, *Rationalism and Modern Society*, trans. Tony Waters and Dagmar Waters (New York: Palgrave Macmillan, 2015), 137–38.

power. Despite repeated appeals to the law, in different courts and from different legal angles, Palestinian residents of Sheikh Jarrah were unable to secure the right to live in their own homes. This failure is structural rather than incidental. The history of the relevant legislation is long and complex, yet suffice it to mention that Israeli law permits Jews to reclaim homes and lands owned prior to 1948, while depriving Palestinians of the same right. A few dozen Jewish settlers are thus entitled to a "right of return" to Sheikh Jarrah that is denied to hundreds of thousands of Palestinians. As a legal dispute, this antagonism became a case of what Jean-François Lyotard called a differand (*différend*): "a conflict, between (at least) two parties, that cannot be equitably resolved for lack of a rule of judgment applicable to both arguments." In this zero-sum game, "applying a single rule of judgment to both in order to settle their differend as though it were merely a litigation would wrong (at least) one of them."[24]

This impasse, however, with its false choice between stalemate and injustice, between leaving the "dispute" forever unresolved or wronging one side by conducting the litigation on and in the other's terms, stems from the juridico-political logic of "conflict." It is within this logic, which even Lyotard adopts in critiquing it, that legal judgment becomes the sole framework for understanding the operation of "conflict." Because it has become so dominant, so all-pervasive, the calcified perception of conflict as judgment—as a scene of legal dispute, which always carries along its threatening shadow, lawless violence—obscures all other possible frameworks for understanding Palestine-Israel, as well as conflicts more broadly. Yet, if we shift our perspective and consider conflict outside the juridico-political realm, viewing it instead as an aesthetic social form, we might notice other models of conflictuality. Indeed, the conflictual apparatuses involved in the Israeli occupation are a tangled hodgepodge of forms. One might argue that this combinatory mode is in fact intentional: first, because it fractures Palestinian society along the differentiation lines drawn by different mechanisms of control, and second, because it guarantees its own endurance and open-endedness (if articulating the problem is impossible, then confronting, halting, or redefining it is out of the question).[25]

The "Israeli-Palestinian conflict" is therefore not a conflict. This is not only because it does not conform to the common definition of conflict but also

24. Jean-François Lyotard, *The Differend*, trans. Georges Van Den Abbeele (Minneapolis: University of Minnesota, 1989), xi.

25. On the heterogeneity of conflictual Zionist apparatuses, see, for instance, Yael Berda, *Living Emergency: Israel's Permit Regime in the Occupied West Bank* (Stanford, Calif.: Stanford University Press, 2017); Ariella Azoulay and Adi Ophir, *The One-State Condition: Occupation and Democracy in Israel/Palestine* (Stanford, Calif.: Stanford University Press, 2012).

because it is not a single conflict. Instead, this context is made up of multiple conflictual mechanisms and conditions that the singular label "conflict" obscures. Such conflictual technologies, mediations, and settings, as expressed and produced by literature, are what this book sets out to find and articulate. Certainly, there is some tension between my rejection of the banal concept of "conflict" and my efforts to think conflictuality otherwise, to supposedly imbue it with new meanings. Since this concept comes with heavy baggage, I considered replacing it with a different overarching term. I quickly found, however, that the differences between "conflict" and its cognates—agonism, antagonism, contradiction, strife—are slight, as they all sprouted from the same tradition. I therefore kept this term while attempting to unhinge and redeploy it, starting by speaking of conflictual modes or conflictual mechanisms instead of conflict per se and continuing by rearticulating the terms of their contradictions and giving these proper names.

To speak of conflictual modes is to speak of conflicts in a broader sense. It is to speak not only about the conflictual relations between people or groups but also about the conflictual conditions that structure these relations. Conflict understood as judgment, for instance, results not simply from an antagonism between two legal adversaries but rather from the conflictual relations between the pre-political and the juridico-political. Conflict as judgment thus names not simply the relationship between two parties but rather the conflictual terms through which their relations are structured and understood—the realm of law versus "terroristic" transgression, state politics and police violence versus pre-political violence.

Refusing the gravitational pull of "conflict," I attempt to think of these conflictual modes less as juridico-political structures and more as literary-historical forms that recenter aesthetics, sociality, and everyday life. Following a critical investigation of conflict as judgment, this study offers a series of figurative conceptions of conflictual modes that operate along various fracture lines and on intersecting plateaus to precondition relations, violent or otherwise, in Palestine-Israel. Taken together, these conflictual modes set the stage for a more conceptually capacious and historically nuanced understanding of Palestine-Israel and propose their own epistemologies of conflict that often exceed the political and constitute portable diagnostic prisms.

Chapter 1, "Conflict (Judgment/*Ishtibāk*)," examines the normative conception of conflict as judgment. To excavate its historical origins and current form, the chapter interlaces readings of canonical political philosophers—particularly, Hobbes, Locke, and Kant—with the writing of the Palestinian author Ghassan Kanafani (1936–72). It demonstrates that contemporary conceptions of conflict, stranded between a zero-sum decisionist logic and the chaos of the state of nature, are based in and limited by the Enlightenment notion of judgment, conceived in opposition to the polysemy of literary language and as a sublated violent conflict. To tease out the implications of this notion, the chapter turns to Kanafani's novella "'A'id ila Ḥayfa" (Returning to Haifa, 1969), which considers the 1948 colonization of Palestine from a 1967 perspective and metaphorizes it as the forced adoption of a Palestinian child by Jewish Israeli parents. Staging a scene of judgment, whereby the son is called upon to decide on his true parents, the novella turns out to be a careful study of judgment and its coloniality. Showing that the parameters for judgment are always materially set by the colonizers, Kanafani contests its impartiality. He further reveals the moral imperialism of judgment's analogies, which allow his Israeli characters to equate the predicaments of both parties and demand a "civilized" conversation in search of solutions. While Kanafani thus insists that dialogue under colonial conditions is ultimately nothing but "a conversation between the sword and the neck," his writing also suggests that, in the intimacy of violence, something nonetheless passes, even if it is not communicative or representational—a struggle or a "clashing engagement" (*ishtibāk*), a different mode of conflict reducible neither to legal war nor to the state of nature. This passing is inextricable from Kanafani's creative metaphors (catachreses), which break open narrative time and link ongoing processes with irruptive events, structure with history. Proliferating worldviews and lodging them together, such metaphors render perceptible the not yet seen or expressible, generating not only new modes of thinking, speaking, and acting but also the conditions of possibility for what Kanafani calls *ishtibāk*. The metaphorization of the occupied land as an adopted child, for instance, produces an arena in which the two historical disasters associated with Israel's establishment—*sho'a* and *nakba*—could be discussed together. Far from being a dead metaphor, catachresis emerges as a revolutionary reconceptualization of the political sphere, a historical-aesthetic mode based in the nuances of the everyday. Following Kanafani's cue, the main structuring device of this book is creative metaphors as localized theoretical concepts.

In analyzing pre-State Hebrew prose, Chapter 2, "*Levaṭim* (Disorienting Dilemmas)," introduces early Zionist ideology and its relationship to the Orient. It focuses on the short stories of Haim Hazaz (1898–1973) to detect a crucial Zionist poetic schema: the recurrent narration of ceaseless dilemmas (*levaṭim* in Hebrew). By displacing political contradictions to the psychological realm, Hazaz—like other Hebrew authors of the 1930s and 1940s—tries to simultaneously participate in and morally distance himself from the Zionist colonial project. The melancholia of endless reflexive *levaṭim* rhetorically removes both narrator and author from the realm of action, freeing them of political responsibility and thus easing the path of colonization. In Hazaz's writing, such inner dilemmas also dis-Orient his protagonist, pitting him against the Orient within and without him, thus registering the dis-Orienting colonial relationship of Zionism to its various Easts—Eastern European exile, Oriental Jews, and Palestine. Much like judgment, *levaṭim* set up clear oppositions and vest their trust in the agency of an intending subject who theoretically chooses between them; unlike judgment, however, they frustrate the moment of solution, leading to endless oscillation. Paradoxically, it is precisely through this failure that Hazaz, like Zionism, achieves a certain resolution, producing an ideal superiority over nature—an ability to "see beyond" it and gauge its true potential—that is then applied to the East and the Eastern. *Levaṭim* is thus a metaphorical name for the productive inner conflict of the phenomenological subject and its violent separation from, and domination of, the East.

Chapter 3, "*Ikhtifāʾ* (Anti/colonial Disappearance)" explores the trope of disappearance (*ikhtifāʾ* in Arabic), which is remarkably prevalent across Palestinian literature and cinema. Zeroing in on the case of Palestinians of Israel, whose histories, towns, and homes were erased or appropriated in the years of the Military Rule (1948–66), it suggests that "disappearance" offers a local metaphorical conception of Palestinian dispossession that is more accurate than the (largely imported) dominant paradigms in the field. In the films of Elia Suleiman and the writing of Ibtisam Azem, Emile Habiby, or Sayed Kashua, disappearances embody the systemic Israeli erasure of, and blindness to, Palestinians—a mode of colonial displacement, racialization, and segregation that enables greater value extraction from land, people, and culture. *Ikhtifāʾ* names, moreover, not only the material legacies of settler appropriation but also a mode of anti-colonial indigenous resistance. Through disappearances, both thematic and formal, authors extensively record historical, cultural, and social life in Palestine. In their poetics of disappearance, by adopting a humorist tone that downplays authorial agency, they evade censorship while showcasing the absurd consequences of Israeli colonial disappearance. As against the Zionist "seeing beyond" discussed in Chapter 2, these authors refuse the confessional mode, with its deep psychology, in favor of a disappeared poetics whose decryption—the key for deciphering the Palestinian histories and subjectivities that they produce—depends on intimacy with local cultures and social codes. Referring to the onto-epistemic conflict between presence and absence, visibility and invisibility, *ikhtifāʾ* also foregrounds clashes of power and different narrative modes.

Chapter 4, "*Ḥoḳ* (Mediating Law)," examines whether a self-critical stance—one that does not replicate the internal conflict of *levaṭim* and its justification of colonization—is possible for Israeli society and writers. Exploring the law (*ḥoḳ* in Hebrew) in its self-critical role, this chapter studies a 1988 legal case of Israeli soldiers' fatal brutality against Palestinians and analyzes its portrayal by the Jewish Israeli poet Dahlia Ravikovitch (1936–2005). Ravikovitch reveals the unfolding of the logic of judgment in this court case and exposes the law as a mechanism for normalizing generalized colonial violence by making individual exceptions. Her critical poetic system is devised to undermine the separatism of judgment and the universalizing blindness of the law. By alluding to, yet carving out, her own tradition she actively decenters the self, and by utilizing direct quotations from the trial records and inventories of proper place names she futilely attempts to circumvent mediation, to convey the singularity and corporeal materiality of the case, stressing their irreducibility to the language of positive law. By focusing on the singular case at hand and the type it forms, Ravikovitch suggests an immanent mode of evaluation—a casuistry (*pilpul*) that is in every way opposed to judgment. Through the philology of the Hebrew word *ḥoḳ*, the chapter demonstrates its fitness for metaphorically naming both Ravikovitch's anti-mediative poetics and the conflict between signification and the real, the deliberative space of appearance and the shadowy realm of the body, underlying democratic perceptions of the law and of the public sphere. Finally, a coda explores the historical novel *Tafṣil Thanawi* (Minor Detail, 2017), by the contemporary Palestinian author Adania Shibli (b. 1974), to foreground her critique of historiography as a mediation mode afflicted with the same forensic limitations as legal procedures when attempting to account for colonial violence.

Chapter 5, "*Inqisām* (Hostile Severance)," investigates Israeli use of severance as a control mechanism that produces the very hostilities it purports to manage. The chapter demonstrates that the internal societal splintering of both Palestinians and Mizrahi Jews keeps the two groups alienated from one another and is key to their co-constitutive adversarial racialization. Instead of "post-Oslo," the present moment is considered here as distinguished rather by the 2007 forced split (*al-inqisām* in Arabic) between Gaza and the West Bank. By analyzing Adania Shibli's writing, the chapter examines a sense of surging hostility within Palestinian society, fueled by severing technologies of border control and security insourcing—namely, the checkpoint and collaboration—that destabilize the most foundational coordinates of reality: time, space, self, and community. This post-*inqisām* moment is also marked by intensifying Mizrahi hostility toward Palestinians, which is shaped by Mizrahi Jews' growing role in operating these very same technologies. Exploring the Israeli TV series *Fauda* (dir. Avi Issacharoff and Lior Raz, 2015–22), the chapter shows how the expanding function of *mizraḥim* as the executors of Israeli state violence contributes to their imagining of Palestinians as equal rivals in an ahistorical cycle of revenge rooted in quasi-familial alliances. To historically contextualize this hostility, the chapter discusses early Zionist importation of *mizraḥim* to replace Palestinian labor and the 1950s affair of the disappeared Yemenite, Mizrahi, and Balkan children as these are represented by Khoury's *Bab al-Shams* and by the contemporary Mizrahi poet Shlomi Hatuka (b. 1978). The chapter reveals the paradoxical racializing process that both folded Mizrahi Jews into the family of the Jewish nation (through de-Arabization) and constructed them as relatively expendable bodies (through Arabization). The severance of Mizrahi children is thus regarded here as not at all tangential but fundamental to the so-called Israeli-Palestinian conflict, for it both radically assimilates Mizrahi Jews and feeds the manufactured hostility between Palestinians and *mizraḥim*. Although *inqisām* might appear as opposed to conflict and thus as the most defamiliarized concept in this book, it in fact names the processes of internal severance that generated racialization and "tribalization" in Palestine-Israel and led to the hostile stalemate of the present, where nothing seems to stir but isolated hatred.

Finally, a brief postscript contends with the tension between this book's focus on conflict and the disavowal of conflict by societies of *nihul* (management, administration) and specifically by the "conflict management" practices so central to Israeli politics. It also explains why existing political terms and paradigms are insufficient for fully comprehending Palestine-Israel, reflecting on the book's methodology of drawing new, figurative concepts out of local literatures and considering both the possible limitations and the constructive formats of conceptual comparisons.

Before delving in, a few brief methodological remarks are in order. First, although most chapters follow each other in rough chronological order, my approach is genealogical rather than historical. What I aim to foreground are particular figures or mechanisms that I find to be paradigmatic in this context. The order in which they are presented is not sequential—it does not aim to suggest teleological progress or evolution, whereby history replaces defective models with better ones. While I focus on different moments in the history of Palestine-Israel, I believe that the different conflictual forms I detect in them are largely co-extensive, intersecting with one another in various situations and texts. In this sense, their separation into chapters is artificial—dictated by the generic demands of academic writing.

Second, with a few exceptions, the literary repertoire presented here privileges works that are either familiar to readers of Hebrew and Arabic or available in English translation. This choice of texts was intended to increase the relevance and accessibility of this study both within and beyond its immediate contexts. Seeking to trouble the very notion of national canons, *Conflicts* also does not aim to encompass Israeli or Palestinian literatures in their entirety. Because of its genealogical method, it focuses rather on an exemplary set of fecund literary figures that allow a taxonomic articulation of conflictual mechanisms. In elaborating these mechanisms, this book is quite eclectic in its choice of theoretical, historical, anthropological, and literary sources.

Third, studies that emphasize either poetics or antagonism risk raising the expectation that they follow in the footsteps of deconstruction, which deemed all language to be conflictual, all rhetorical conflict to lead to an impasse, and all this impasse to be productive. Alternatively, such studies might be regarded as trailing another, more political branch of post-structuralism in which scholars either universalize conflict as a necessary ontological impasse (Lyotard, Agamben) or view it as a spontaneous aesthetico-political event, which, despite its radical appearance, seems to generate nothing but liberal progress (Rancière). While this book engages with these branches of scholarship, it sharply diverges from their methods and tenets. It refuses not only to accept a singular, universal definition of conflict but also to regard any of the conflictual forms presented here as either a stalemate, an ontological condition, or a mode of democratic deliberation and protest. Instead, some of the conflicts discussed are proven to be politically productive but only for some, their colonial and racializing effects varying across positions (such as *levaṭim*). Other conflicts (such as *ishtibāk*) produce movement that is neither dialectical nor progressive, a movement whose impact is to problematize the normative categories of the political without necessarily setting it on a new course of action or offering a clear solution.

Finally, bracketing debates over the nature of world literature and its alternatives while simultaneously rejecting the ghettoization of "Middle Eastern literatures" in area studies, the book takes on a comparative approach despite the liberal command to speak only for oneself. Since literature is always cross-cultural—since links and trespasses are to be expected—what matters, I argue, is the specific ways in which shared nodes are brought to light.[26]

26. In recent years, both Jewish literature and Arabic literature have become paradigmatic for the potentially cross-cultural nature of a single literary canon. Each has been explored as itself constituting "world literature." See, for instance, Gil Anidjar, *Semites: Race, Religion, Literature* (Stanford, Calif.: Stanford University Press, 2007), 84–102; Lital Levy and Allison Schachter, "Jewish Literature/World Literature: Between the Local and the Transnational," *PMLA* 130, no. 1 (2015): 92–109; Michael Allan, "How Adab Became Literary: Formalism, Orientalism and the Institutions of World Literature," *Journal of Arabic Literature* 43, no. 2/3 (2012): 172–96. For a study of Palestinian literature as transnational, see Maurice Ebileeni, *Being There, Being Here: Palestinian Writings in the World* (Syracuse, N.Y.: Syracuse University Press, 2022).

Instead of relying on off-the-rack categories for the discussion of literary relations—the postcolonial, world literature, south-south relation—the book examines Hebrew and Arabic literary texts to gauge the specific terms of comparison that they themselves offer. The method of comparison that *Conflicts* thus reveals is, perhaps unsurprisingly, that of conflict. Instead of comparison per se—those comparative methods that draw connections or bring together, thus forming a mirage of symmetry that equalizes at best and subordinates at worst—this study focuses on problem spaces, exploring the different ways in which these are diagnosed, articulated, and challenged by different literary works and traditions. The relationship between these various literary interpretations is, more specifically, that of *ishtibāk*, or clashing engagement—namely, conflictual relations that are neither harmonious nor symmetrical nor consensual, which exist beyond communication and do not offer a standard that might ground their judgment.

1
Conflict
(Judgment/Ishtibāk)

*My political position springs from my being a novelist. Insofar as I am concerned, politics and the novel are an indivisible case [*qaḍiyya—*also, issue and cause] and I can categorically state that I became politically committed because I am a novelist, not the opposite. I started writing the story of my Palestinian life before I found a clear political position or joined any organization.*

—GHASSAN KANAFANI, IN AN INTERVIEW WITH *AL-SIYASA*

To open this book with the writing of Ghassan Kanafani is to open with *the* figure of revolutionary literature. It was, after all, Kanafani who coined the phrase "resistance literature" (*adab al-muqāwama*) to investigate what Palestinian literature is and could be. In this chapter, I return to Kanafani's novella "'A'id ila Ḥayfa" (Returning to Haifa, 1969), studied by many before me, to argue that it constitutes a reconceptualizing novella—a novella dedicated to revolutionary explosion and redefinition of key political terms. The concepts that Kanafani diagnoses, starting with the juridico-political notion of conflict, are fundamental; they structure normative perceptions of Palestine-Israel and of politics more broadly. In a rather Socratic manner, Kanafani's protagonists wonder, for instance, "what is a homeland," "what is fatherhood," and "what is a man," interrogating and dismantling these categories, which are the ideological building blocks of such political institutions as the nation, patriarchy, and the subject. For Kanafani's protagonists, raising each of these "wild spinning" questions is like "throwing a window wide open to an unexpected cyclone."[1] In a truly realist fashion, such questions disturb and dismantle given assumptions, demanding answers that are simply impossible to conceive without a radical aesthetic refiguration.[2] Throughout the story, those categories acquire new meanings. This reconceptualization, however, is largely attained not through explicit narration, stable thematization, or direct speech, but metaphorically, by innovatively placing one context next to another to make them reverberate.[3]

Indeed, to open this book with Kanafani is to open with the figure of the revolutionary. Born in Acre in 1936 and raised in Jaffa, Kanafani was expelled from Palestine in the 1948 War. In refugee camps in Lebanon, Syria, and Kuwait, Kanafani completed his secondary education, received an UNRWA teaching certificate, and taught art to uprooted Palestinian children. He studied literature at the University of Damascus, conducting research toward his books *Fi al-Adab al-Ṣihyuni* (On Zionist Literature, 1967) and *Adab al-Muqawama fi Filasṭin al-Muḥtalla* (Resistance Literature in Occupied Palestine, 1968). Kanafani eventually settled in Beirut, where he edited several newspapers and published a constant stream of essays and short stories. In 1967, he joined the Popular Front for the Liberation of Palestine (PFLP) and, for the rest of his tragically short life, served as its official spokesperson and the editor of its organ, *al-Hadaf* (The Goal). As a leader in the PFLP, Kanafani was instrumental in pushing the movement to officially adopt Marxism-Leninism, transitioning from a Nasserist pan-Arabism to a Palestinian revolutionary struggle, linked with broader Third World anti-imperialism. In 1972, the Israeli Mossad booby-trapped his car, assassinating both Kanafani and his young

1. Ghassan Kanafani, "Returning to Haifa," in *Palestine's Children: Returning to Haifa and Other Stories*, trans. Barbara Harlow and Karen E. Riley, Arab Authors (Boulder, Colo.: Lynne Rienner, 2000), 171. In Arabic: Kanafani, "'A'id ila Hayfa," in *al-Athar al-Kamila* (Beirut: Mu'assasat Ghassan Kanafani al-Thaqafiyya: Dar al-Ṭali'a, 1980), 1:337–409.

2. Fredrick Jameson argues not only that "genuine realism is a discovery process," but also that "its emphasis on the new and the hitherto unreported, unrepresented, and unseen, and its notorious subversion of inherited ideas and genres" render it in fact a kind of modernism; Jameson, "Antinomies of the Realism-Modernism Debate," *Modern Language Quarterly* 73, no. 3 (2012): 476. It is no surprise, then, that Kanafani combines modernist episodism and stream of consciousness not only with social realism—his recurrent focus on camp life—but also with realism in this deeper sense. Indeed, Kanafani was familiar with conversations on the realist genre and its aesthetic and political implications (as an editor, for instance, he published a positive review of Lukacs's writing on realism in 1971).

3. I use the term "metaphor" throughout this chapter in the broadest possible sense. See note 18 in the Introduction.

niece.[4] In one decade of political engagement, however, Kanafani had furnished the Palestinian revolution with some of its key myths, commitments, and rallying cries.

Kanafani is also widely regarded as a central figure of Palestinian literature. He was a leading novelist and essayist; his English obituary described him as a commando whose "weapon was a ballpoint pen and his arena the newspaper pages."[5] Scholars too often regard Kanafani's writing, and especially his later work, as didactic—that is, as voicing a clear and simple propagandist call to join the armed struggle.[6] Other scholars, by contrast, endeavor to "save" Kanafani from his active support of violent resistance by reading him against the grain. They effortfully recast "'A'id ila Ḥayfa" as undermining its own explicit call to arms by reducing the novella to either unresolved trauma or a meta-discussion of national narrative that exposes its universal shortcoming (insofar as all national narratives require the "erasure of the other").[7] Kanafani's statement in the epigraph, however, interferes with perceiving his work as merely didactic. And yet, I argue, the complex and multivalent interpretative possibilities underneath the novella's didactic level in no way annul its call for violence. As this chapter demonstrates, Kanafani's conflictual mode of engagement or struggle, here termed *ishtibāk* (Arabic for "clashing engagement"), is distinct from both a didactic perception of revolution (as reduced to mere violence or the logic of ends, ushering in a new set of laws) and those "against the grain" liberal recuperations. Kanafani also explicitly insists, as the epigraph suggests, that literature, far from being a vehicle for broadcasting preformed political ideas and positions, is in fact the medium within which they are figured. Truly experimental—at once realist and modernist yet exceeding both—Kanafani's literature aims to break apart existing

4. For recent accounts of Kanafani's biography, see Bashir Abu-Manneh, *The Palestinian Novel: From 1948 to the Present* (Cambridge and New York: Cambridge University Press, 2016), 71–72; Elizabeth M. Holt, "Resistance Literature and Occupied Palestine in Cold War Beirut," *Journal of Palestine Studies* 50, no. 197 (2021): 3–18.

5. Barbara Harlow, "Return to Haifa: 'Opening the Borders' in Palestinian Literature," *Social Text*, no. 13/14 (1986): 9.

6. 'Abbas Iḥsan, Fadi al-Naqib, and Elias Khoury, eds., *Ghassan Kanafani: Insanan wa-Adiban wa-Munaḍilan* (Beirut: al-Ittiḥad al-'Amm li-l-Kuttab wa-l-Ṣuḥufiyyin al-Filasṭiniyyin, 1974); Muhammad Siddiq, *Man Is a Cause: Political Consciousness and the Fiction of Ghassan Kanafani* (Seattle and London: University of Washington Press, 1984); Yochai Oppenheimer, *Me'ever la-Gader: Yitsug ha-'Aravim ba-Sifrut ha-'Ivrit veha-Yiśra'elit, 1906–2005* (Tel Aviv: 'Am 'Oved, 2008).

7. Ian Campbell, "Blindness to Blindness: Trauma, Vision and Political Consciousness in Ghassan Kanafani's 'Returning to Haifa,'" *Journal of Arabic Literature* 32, no. 1 (2001): 53–73; Gil Z. Hochberg, *In Spite of Partition: Jews, Arabs, and the Limits of Separatist Imagination* (Princeton, N.J.: Princeton University Press, 2010), 164n13.

philosophical and political paradigms. It breaks open normative concepts, so that they might begin to express the post-*nakba* crisis and pierce through the screen of hegemonic political language to figure new modes of thinking and doing. *The* figure of revolutionary literature, then.

Kanafani's reconceptualizing poetics affects not only concepts but also narrative and temporality. In fact, one of the reasons for my focus on "'A'id ila Ḥayfa" is its episodic form, which artfully adjoins—places side by side on the page—not only different contexts but also different times, creating a resonance, a clashing engagement, between them, without determining the terms of their relation. More specifically, I am interested in the temporality of this novella because of the key role it accords the notion of return. "'A'id ila Ḥayfa" introduces the 1948 Palestinian catastrophe (*al-nakba*) through the lens of 1967: it delineates the story of a Palestinian couple who travels—immediately after the 1967 occupation of the West Bank and the opening of the border—from Ramallah to their home in Haifa, from which they were expelled during the 1948 War. Upon arrival, Said and Safiyya S. learn that the Jewish immigrants who have come to occupy their house have also adopted their son, Khaldun, who had been left behind as an infant in the turmoil of the battles. Only through the protagonists' 1967 revisiting of the home and of the 1948 events is the *nakba* grasped and figured. Thus, the novella's narrative of return already sets up a metaphorical epistemic structure: by bringing one context to interpenetrate with another for the first time, something hitherto inexpressible is brought to light and thought. The narrative return also reveals the temporality of the *nakba* as both the radical, irruptive event of 1948 *and* a whole history that is still unfolding, of which the 1967 occupation is but one, if central, iteration. This dual modality—both event and history—is mirrored in the novella's temporal structure (reminiscence) and its mode of metaphorization (catachresis).

More crucially, perhaps, "'A'id ila Ḥayfa" suggests two principal models for understanding conflict: the normative model of judgment and the clashing engagement (*ishtibāk*) model of catachresis. (In between, it also limns the morally imperial model of analogy.) By endowing concepts with new, defamiliarized meanings, the novella prods the reader to interpret, or judge, more actively and experimentally, and thus to practice what it preaches. If the text is didactic, it is largely in this sense, for it might indeed teach readers something about judgment by making them experience it in its various modalities.

To showcase Kanafani's exploration of the normative concept of conflict and the regime of judgment that subtends it, the chapter focuses on the main encounter in the novella, between the Jewish and Palestinian protagonists in the Haifa home. Moving on to explore the metaphoric structure of this encounter, it reveals how creative metaphors undermine conflict-as-judgment, producing and upholding instead a specific form of conflict—struggle, or *ishtibāk*—that takes place in the realm of aesthetics and everyday life rather than the juridico-political sphere. The clashing engagement formed by creative metaphors multiplies worlds and worldviews, setting them in refractory relations of struggle that no one has the authority to resolve. In reorienting what could be perceived, thought, and said, Kanafani's metaphors also reconfigure what could be done. Through the "return"—in their reuse of existing words, phrases, and discourses—such metaphors also break apart narrative time, linking structure with rupture, historical processes with disruptive events, and serving as the very hinge by which these estranged orders intersect.

Beyond the juridico-political concept of conflict, then, the theoretical problems guiding this chapter invoke the long-standing question of dead and new metaphors, of conceptual and poetic language, which conjures the specter of deconstruction. Both Paul de Man and Jacques Derrida have underscored the figurative origin of all philosophical language and both privileged catachresis—the use of an existing term to designate a phenomenon yet without a name—as the main site of metaphoricity and of its sublation in concepts.[8] In Derrida and de Man's readings of Western philosophy, catachresis is regarded as dead metaphor and comes to universally designate a violent abuse of language—the monstrous and ghastly imposition of signs.[9] All difference between dead, trite, or innovative metaphors is lost, along with historicity, cultural specificity, and the racio-colonial implications of the philosophical distinction between the two categories or of choosing one trope over another.

Still considering catachresis a violent abuse, Gayatri Spivak, by contrast, aims to take account of its colonial effects. Translating Derrida and de Man's generalization of catachreses into postcolonial theory, she uses "catachresis" to signify "master concepts," either those alleging to represent a group (e.g.,

8. Paul de Man, "The Epistemology of Metaphor," *Critical Inquiry* 5, no. 1 (Autumn 1978): 30, 21; Jacques Derrida, "White Mythology: Metaphor in the Text of Philosophy," in *Margins of Philosophy*, trans. Alan Bass (Chicago: University of Chicago Press, 1986), 219, 255.

9. Both de Man and Derrida seem to privilege the tradition inaugurated by Cicero, who considers catachresis an abuse because it denotes, for him, the inexact use of a kindred word in place of a precise and proper one. But there was always another tradition, that of Quintilian, who understood catachresis as a creative, legitimate borrowing act that brings into being an object that had been nameless (even if he declared the Latin translation of catachresis as *abusio* to be correct). See Marcus Tullius Cicero, *Rhetorica ad Herennium*, ed. Harry Caplan, Loeb Classical Library (Cambridge, Mass.: Harvard University Press, 1954), IV.xxxiii.45, 343; Quintilian, *The Orator's Education*, ed. D. A. Russell, vol. III, IV, Loeb Classical Library 124–27, 494 (Cambridge, Mass.: Harvard University Press, 2002), 8.6.34; 445.

"women") or those key Western "regulative political concepts" ("democracy," "nationhood," "citizenship") imposed on other cultures without adequately corresponding to any historical referent in them.[10] The political problem that Spivak justly detects, however, seems to be one of translation, predominantly pertaining not to metaphors but to concepts and their misapplication (her imposing catachreses seem to resonate rather with the Platonic Idea). She also overlooks the possibility that metaphorical terms might change in their encounter with "subaltern" cultures or that "subalterns" might have different accounts for, and anti-colonial practices of, metaphoricity, utilized in defiance of colonial powers or even in complete disregard of them.[11]

Departing from these seminal works, this chapter is concerned with the possibility of reviving catachresis, of examining the transformative possibilities inherent in new, creative—dare I say—revolutionary metaphors, given historical change and geographic rootedness. After all, metaphors work. And they work differently than concepts, with their universalizing vocation. Beyond the distinction between dead and living metaphors, the specific manners in which different metaphors work in specific sites are significant. The investment here is less in what a metaphor *is* than in *how* metaphors work and to what effects. In viewing catachresis as a model of conflict, the chapter also reexamines its implications for politics and for thinking conflict beyond the juridico-political. What is at stake here is the possibility of severing signs from intention while maintaining the potential for transformative collective actions.

Judgment (Medina/Madīna)

A judgment by law assumes a sovereign arbitrator who must pick a side, make a decision in favor of one party or the other, for in each case only one of them could be in the right. The absurd severity of this logic is beautifully illustrated by the biblical story of the Judgment of King Solomon, in which the king must rule in a dispute between two women, each claiming to be the legal mother of a newborn infant. Precisely because the juridical logic of conflict assumes that a living child cannot possibly be shared, the king cunningly proposes to cut the

10. Gayatri Chakravorty Spivak, *Outside in the Teaching Machine* (New York: Routledge, 1993), 127, 60.

11. In dialectical reaction to centuries of imperial over-intervention, ontologies of insurmountable difference and zero-communication calcified in certain postcolonial academic corners. Certainly, one should be careful transferring metaphors from one culture to another, yet the assumption that any catachrestic act is universally violent is too facile. Instead, its operations and their stakes should be examined within specific contexts.

baby in two and grant each half to each of the mothers. By raising the specter of random, brute violence, the king moves the biological mother to withdraw her claim so as to spare the child's life. This verdict is traditionally viewed as a stratagem for exposing truth and deemed the ultimate testament to the king's infinite wisdom. In its absurdity, however, it may also be read as the biblical narrator's clever remark on the ludicrous nature of juridical conflict as such—for the two women, the Bible tells us, lived in one and the same house and could, at least potentially, raise the child together (1 Kgs 3). (Note that this theoretical alternative is not a resolution of conflict; instead, it simply displaces conflict from the juridico-political realm to that of everyday life, transforming it into a mundane experience whose nature is not yet clearly formulated.)

This either/or logic of judgment has come to dominate contemporary perceptions of conflicts, both in general and in the Palestinian-Israeli context in particular. Such "us or them" logic is evident, for instance, in recent Israeli acts of legislation aiming to cement Jewish political domination, police the lines between the two collectives, limit possible comparisons between them, and even criminalize the publication of Palestinian grievances. Examples include the Nakba Law (2011), which financially penalizes institutions for commemorating the Palestinian catastrophe of 1948; the Anti-Boycott Law (2011), which renders individuals and organizations that support Boycott, Divestment, and Sanctions (BDS) against Israel open to civil suits; Amendment No. 28 to the Entry into Israel Law (2017), which prohibits foreign BDS supporters from entering Israel; and bills banning the use of vocabulary and imagery associated with the Jewish holocaust to speak of any other calamity (1995, 2001, 2007, 2012, 2014). A current Israeli "Judicial Reform" (still ongoing, as of 2023) aims to introduce fundamental changes into the legal and political system, further entrenching the Jewish character of the state, removing anti-discriminatory protections for Palestinians, and accelerating the erosion of their citizenship rights. In addition to their legal force, such initiatives have a palpable discursive "chilling effect." The very fact that they form the subject of discussion in both Parliament and media renders them a performative apparatus for shaping public opinion and constraining debate, reinforcing and weaponizing the cord separating "us" and "them."

A similar "us" or "them" political framework seems to be at play in Kanafani's "'A'id ila Ḥayfa." After their long journey from Ramallah, teeming with flashbacks to the early days of the war in April 1948, Said and Safiyya finally arrive at their lost Haifa home, which they were forced to flee during that war.[12]

12. Since names are often dead metaphors, their dormant meanings are useful. Like the names of many of Kanafani's protagonists, *Sa'id* is derived from the root *s-'-d*, which belongs to the semantic field of "success," "happiness," and "luck," as well as "help" and "support." The

There, they quickly discover that their home is now occupied by Miriam, a Jewish holocaust survivor who arrived in Palestine in 1948, and that Miriam, together with her late husband, Iphrat, had also adopted their son, Khaldun, who is now a young Israeli soldier named Dov.[13]

Before Khaldun-Dov arrives and a confrontation ensues, Said and Safiyya conduct a short conversation with Miriam, who clarifies her expectations for the coming encounter:

> Listen, Mr. Said. I wanted you to wait for Dov—or Khaldun, if you like—so you could talk to each other and the matter could end as it naturally should end (*kamā turīd lahu al-ṭabīʿa an yantahī*). Do you think this hasn't been as much a problem for me as it has been for you? For the past twenty years I've been confused, but now the time has come for us to finish the matter. I know who his father is. And I also know that he is our son. But let's call on him to decide (*li-nadaʿhu yuqarrir bi-nafsihi*). Let's call on him to choose. He's of age and we must recognize that he's the only one who has the right to choose (*al-ḥaq fī ʾan yakhtār*). Do you agree? (*a-tuwāfiq?*)[14]

The basic premise of the novella—a conflict over a child between two sets of parents, of which only one could be "natural," "real," and hence justified—thus alludes to the Judgment of Solomon and to the decisionist logic of

---

name *Ṣafiyya* means "pure," "clear," and "serene" and relates to happiness and fortune. Both names thus appear rather ironic in the context of the novella. The Hebrew names, fully transliterated, are *Miryam* and—probably—*Efrat*. The Arabic vowel system, as well as the use of the letter "fāʾ" for "V" when rendering words from foreign languages, allow for different readings of the name as *Efrat*, *Ifrat*, *Evrat*, and *Ivrat*. Determining exactly what name Kanafani intended for the Jewish father is difficult, especially since, of these options, *Efrat* is the only conventional Hebrew name yet is exclusively feminine. (The Hebrew version of "ʿAʾid ila Ḥayfa" simply glossed over this mystery by translating the name as Efrayyim, an easily recognizable male Hebrew name.) In the Bible, Efrat is the geographic area of the tribe of Efrayyim in today's West Bank and it is specifically identified with the city of Bethlehem (Gen 48:7). Efrat is also, according to Rabbinic exegesis, another name for the Prophet Miryam herself (*Bavli* [Babylonian Talmud], Sota 11b–12a). Dov, a Hebrew name meaning "bear," is yet another odd choice, perhaps stressing strength. On Miriam's name, see further in note 47 in this chapter.

13. Kanafani, "Returning to Haifa," 163–65. I refer to the son interchangeably as Khaldun-Dov or Dov-Khaldun, since the priority of one identity over the other is precisely what is at stake. The name *Khaldūn*, meaning "the eternal one," is as ironic as his Palestinian parents' names, since Khaldun does not, in fact, eternally remain Khaldun.

14. Ibid., 172/383–84.

judgment as such.[15] By staging the characters' encounter not only as a confrontation but also as a scene of judgment, where the son is called on to decide on his true parents, Kanafani reveals the formal resonance between what is known as "the Israeli-Palestinian conflict" and judgment. He thus constructs a studio, a poetic laboratory, for diagnosing the logic of judgment and its conflict—for investigating not only what they are and how they work but also *why* they operate the way they do.[16]

Indeed, the language of Miriam's expectations—her insistence that Dov-Khaldun is of age, that he must choose, that he has the right to choose—reveals the common perception of the Palestinian-Israeli context as a zero-sum legal dispute, with its various connotations explicated in the Introduction. The territories occupied, personified by the son, are perceived here precisely as that infant in King Solomon's trial, whose sharing is outright inconceivable. Palestinians and Israeli Jews are thus presented as two opposed parties in symmetrical conflict, whose incommensurable claims must be juridically settled, or else the dispute would inevitably lead to (unlawful) war. The novella seems to conform to this Hobbesian logic, concluding with Said's realization that his second son, Khalid, who intended to join the armed struggle much against his father's wishes, was in fact right all along.[17] On its surface, then, "'A'id ila Ḥayfa" contrasts juridico-political conflict, conflict as a scene of judgment, with armed conflict, or war, where the antagonism is reduced to violence alone. This violence is thus commonly viewed, from one side, as bound to a political end—the formation of a national Palestinian state—and from the other, as lawless and irrational.

This political ontology could be traced back to the Enlightenment's conception of conflict as judgment. It was shaped in the seventeenth and eighteenth centuries, mostly by proto-liberal philosophers, in opposition to and as a sublation of the chaotic, pre-political, and violent conflict of the "state of nature." If in Medieval Europe monarchic sovereigns ruled in the name of divine right, then the modern state came to derive its right to sovereignty from nothing other than conflict, so that conflict came to replace God. For instance, Jean-Jacques Rousseau's various mythical accounts of the origins of society all

15. The mothers' trust that the "natural" bond will determine the son's decision is, according to Mohammad Siddiq, yet another reference to the Judgment of King Solomon; Siddiq, *Man Is a Cause*, 56.

16. As Nasser Abourahme observes, Palestinian revolutionary novels, such as Kanafani's, "are not saying 'this is the way things are,' they are saying 'this is the *why* things are the way they are and this is what you need to do about it'"; Abourahme, "'Nothing to Lose but Our Tents': The Camp, the Revolution, the Novel," *Journal of Palestine Studies* 48, no. 1 (2018): 41.

17. Kanafani, "Returning to Haifa," 186–87.

begin with the introduction of difference into the hypothetical state of nature—be it through the unequal accumulation of property (judging what belongs to whom) or as a result of the rise of linguistic representation (judging what something means).[18] The indifferent state of nature, egalitarian and free, is thus quickly replaced by an almost equally primordial world of difference, bringing about conflict with all its avatars: war, vice, poverty, dependency. Rousseau famously proposed a twofold juridical solution to this conflictual condition: the social contract, which gives birth to the body politic, and the laws that both obtain their authority from it and sustain it.[19] The state, seemingly a contractual self-curtailment of liberty, is thus constructed as a protective dam against the surge of antediluvian violent conflict. Paradoxically, this ancient conflict is also ever-present, for what underwrites the body politic and its laws, the general will, is nothing other than a sublation of the many particular—indeed, conflicting—wills and judgments of the citizens (and only of the citizens).

That this notion of conflict was both conditioned and limited by the Enlightenment's notion of judgment becomes more explicit in Thomas Hobbes's writing. Although Hobbes, unlike Rousseau, regarded social differences as essential and thus perceived the state of nature as already conflictual—the infamous war of all against all—his theory of sovereignty was intended to solve the same problem: that hypothetical primordial violent conflict. The solution, per Hobbes, is the absolutist state, or the commonwealth, whose birth is premised on setting up a sovereign juridical arbitrator to whom all citizens must transfer their right of judgment, or else they will immediately find themselves amidst anarchic war.[20] In both Hobbes's and Rousseau's writing, then, political collectivity is reduced to two extremes: the chaotic, utterly heterogeneous conflicting wills of the multitudes, retrospectively projected onto the prehistory of society, and the unified will of "the people," bound together by contract and law that serve as a talisman against the return of repressed violence—a unity that is geared from the start toward conflict with another, similarly constituted, polity.

As it is conceptualized in direct relation to judgment, this dual mode of conflict maps rather perfectly onto Hobbes's distinction between private and

18. Jean-Jacques Rousseau, *Discourse on the Origin of Inequality*, ed. Patrick Coleman, trans. Franklin Philip (Oxford and New York: Oxford University Press, 2009); Jean-Jacques Rousseau, *Essay on the Origin of Language* (Chicago: University of Chicago Press, 1986).

19. Jean-Jacques Rousseau, *The Social Contract, Or Principles of Political Right*, trans. Maurice Cranston (Harmondsworth: Penguin Classics, 1968), 80–87.

20. Thomas Hobbes, *Leviathan*, ed. Richard Tuck (Cambridge and New York: Cambridge University Press, 1996), 86–91, 32–33.

public judgment. It is judgment all the way down. Judgment is the problem: its private use, considered a universal right in the state of nature, is, in Hobbes's view, a deadly poison to the body politic, leading to war and chaos.[21] Private judgment thus becomes nearly synonymous with that pre-political unlawful violence—a chaotic conflict between a throng of different "final sentences" that culminates in general war. Judgment is also the solution: to counter this violence, Hobbes introduces a "public" use of judgment, the judgment of the sovereign, to whom all citizens alienate their right of judgment—whether by "institution" (consensually) or by "acquisition" (coercively, by conquer and enslavement)—in a contract that purportedly binds and protects society. Insisting that this contract is consensual even when "acquired" under threat of death, Hobbes is nonetheless pushed to concede that it does in fact require constant safeguarding by the sovereign's sword. The imagined "natural" pre-political conflict is thus sublated in the political judging sovereign, whose violence—a negation of the negative—is considered a public good and therefore no longer appears as violence. Not merely problem and solution, judgment is also the means mediating between them, the very name of the sublation: it is by an act of judgment, by an irreversible legal decision, that the private judgment of citizens is translated into public judgment.

Conflicts waged by sovereigns, then, are envisioned as taking place between one cohesive, legal polity and another (and, later, possibly against an internal enemy as well)—a zero-sum game of violence that itself gives the body politic its unity. Political conflict thus takes the form of judgment, of a juridico-political choice or competition in which only one party satisfies its claim, for any other configuration will necessarily suspend politics and lead to the omnipresent violence of the "state of nature" with its "poisonous" private judgments.[22] By projecting violent conflict onto a pre-state (egalitarian) past—but also onto thieves to be disciplined and Native Americans to be conquered[23]—these theories warrant the state and its laws, veiling its formative violence behind the construct of the sovereign as judge (such comments also expose the violence of enslavement, colonialization, and enclosure that precondition the rise of the judging, self-possessed subject and its domination). Conflict in the form of judgment is regarded as a panacea against unlawful conflict, so that interstate legal war and juridical deliberation now appear as the solution for violence and never as its cause.

21. Ibid., 223, 91–92.
22. Ibid., 93–94, 120–21.
23. Ibid., 89.

Serving together as a useful diagnostic metaphor, the Hebrew word for "state" (*medina*) and the Arabic for "city" (*madīna*) reveal the close bond between state, judgment, and conflict. In a sense, both are translations of Western terms. In the Middle Ages, Arab writers translated the Greek philosophical notion of *polis* as *madīna*. The modern Hebrew cognate, *medina*, was chosen as the translation of "state," drawing on biblical Hebrew and later Aramaic uses of *medina* for "province." The reason for the shared semantic field—state, province, city—is the etymological relation of all three to *din*, whose most immediate Hebraeo-Aramaic sense is "judgment," "law," "jurisprudence." Combining the root *d-i-n* with the nominal pattern of place names (or, in Hebrew, of instruments), one meaning of *medina* and *madīna* is the place of judgment and law, a region or instrument of shared jurisprudence. Since this choice of translation was not inevitable, *medina/madīna* expose Arabic and Hebrew speakers' sense that the foundational Western concepts of *polis* and state are defined by judgment and law. In Hebrew, moreover, the root *d-i-n* is also related to *diyyun*—"discussion," upon which judgment depends—and *madon*, "strife," thus framing the state as a tool for managing conflict, a conflict sublated in deliberation and judgment. Finally, in Arabic, *din* also famously means "religion"—in the broadest, hard to translate sense, related to what is given and owed—so that *madīna* evokes the possibility of collectivizing based on other principles. It also attests to the disavowed theological origins of the state and to the substitution of the threat of unlawful conflict for God as its source of authority. With *madīna/medina*, the *polis*—the state, the political—emerges as deeply rooted in judgment, in a secularized religious justification, and in imagining conflict as its raison d'être.

Certainly, this philosophical tradition is not monolithic. Yet conflict as judgment runs through it like a red thread. In protesting too much against social conflict, Hobbes's *Leviathan*, as Michel Foucault shows, in fact reveals a competing contemporaneous discourse that regarded politics as an ongoing war between races and interest groups. Yet, this other discourse, too, centers politics on conflict and valorizes judgment as the key political tool—whether in the English and French revolutionary moments explored by Foucault, in Arendtian republican deliberation, or in agonistic democracy. The juridico-political discourse not only survives alongside others to this day; it has—again, per Foucault—cannibalized that revolutionary discourse of "politics as war," taking the form of either nineteenth-century dialectics or twentieth-century biopolitics, where the race war (Marx's original term for class struggle) has morphed into the state's power to decide on forsaking one race, abandoning it to its death, to ensure the life, purity, and prosperity of the other. (As I claim in the Postscript, when death is managed rather than waged, politics as administration is still underwritten by the same juridico-political conflict, which is simply concealed.)[24]

Returning to Kanafani's novella, I claim that Miriam's approach clearly embodies the logic of *medina/madīna*. She not only regards the matter as a zero-sum legal dispute between two parties, but also constructs a judgment scene in hope that deliberation toward decision, with its sublated violence, will solve her prolonged "problem" and confusion, seemingly caused by the war. Said, by contrast, rejects the juridical setting and argues, twice, that the matter will only be settled by war—one that is necessary precisely because the *medina/madīna* framework obfuscates the violence done to him and structurally excludes his claims. It is not that the 1948 War led to juridico-political conflict and thus mandates judgment; it is this conflict that constructs war as its cause, as always lurking and bubbling underneath, like Miriam's twenty-year-"problem," which requires and justifies judgment.

A key mechanism through which conflict is reduced to the "either/or" of judgment is highlighted by Miriam's insistence on conclusively ending the matter, on jettisoning any confusion by forcing a decision born out of reflection (*yuqarrir bi-nafsihi*). This reduction passes through the Enlightenment definition of judgment as the cognitive faculty responsible for distinguishing and deciding between objects and distributing them under categories. Judgment is, as in the Kantian first *Critique*, "the ability to subsume under rules"—to discern whether a case does or does not fall under a given category, whether it is or is not the case.[25] It is imagined and spatialized as a tribunal within the subject, where "I that am but one man, sustain three persons; mine own person, the person of my adversary, and the person of the judge."[26] A rather remarkable fictive abstraction, judgment is framed through such imagery as a process by which, in order to know or experience the world, a self must first divide itself. By generating the fiction of a transcendental self that is separate from its own material nature and can master it, judgment grants this Cartesian subject the right to make universal ontological and political claims about whatever is considered "nature." In its "mastery" over nature, the position of the sovereign judging self, a prerogative of certain Western subjects, also

24. Michel Foucault, *"Society Must Be Defended": Lectures at the Collège de France, 1975–1976*, trans. David Macey (New York: Picador, 2003).

25. Immanuel Kant, *Critique of Pure Reason*, trans. Werner S. Pluhar (Indianapolis: Hackett, 1996), 206.

26. Hobbes, quoting Cicero in his Answer to John Bramhall's "The Catching of the Leviathan," in Quentin Skinner, "Hobbes and the Purely Artificial Person of the State," *Journal of Political Philosophy* 7, no. 1 (1999): 13.

bolsters a colonial racial regime of domination (these processes are examined further in Chapter 2).[27]

With the image of the judging subject as tribunal, it is philosophical deliberation—"dialogue"—that becomes the only acceptable model for addressing conflict, other than lawful war. Creating a false equivalency between Said and Safiyya's predicament and her own, Miriam is very eager to solve her problem and demands Said's agreement to the terms of their deliberation ("do you agree?"). Her words reveal hope for an amicable, collaborative, and voluntary conversation between equals, one that will resolve the matter once and for all. Gilles Deleuze's name for this philosophy, "the judgment of God," seems particularly apt. It refers precisely to the Kantian tribunal, to determinative judgments that subsume particulars under universals by judging "this is x," producing both signification and the subject. Deleuze critically characterizes this philosophical approach as a collaborative, voluntary dialogue between friends ("Listen, Mr. Said"), guided by the logos and the search for knowledge ("I know . . . I also know . . ."), based on conventional and universal agreement ("he is of age," "we must recognize"), and bolstered by its self-naturalization ("the matter could end as it naturally should end").[28] This mode of conversation teleologically aims for a solution while disavowing the very conflict, the very violence, that it is meant to solve yet in fact creates.

The centrality of judgment to Western epistemology has shaped not only the concept of political conflict but also a much larger political framework—call it liberalism—that, through the juridical, tied subjectivity and sovereignty to nation and property. Playing the role of the sovereign in this Judgment of Solomon scene, Dov-Khaldun is also still cast as the child and therefore cannot be cut in half. He must be either Khaldun, Said and Safiyya's Palestinian son by nature, or Dov, Miriam and Iphrat's Jewish son by nurture, a proud soldier in the Israeli army. The stakes of this zero-sum enframing are intensified by Said's recurrent association of Khaldun-Dov with both home and homeland (or, more

27. As Denise Ferreira da Silva argues, "The mind (the rational thing) retains self-determination, alone occupying the seat of decision (judgment) in knowledge and political existence. That is, the mind alone *determines* (resolves, judges, adjudges) the rules and motives through which universal reason governs, respectively, the motions of things and actions of human beings." At the same time, "formalisation (a tool and effect of scientific universality), the referent of the notion of difference refigured in the arsenal of raciality (in signifiers of racial and cultural difference), produces the racial subaltern subject as a mind that cannot occupy the seat of decision"; da Silva, "No-Bodies," *Griffith Law Review* 18, no. 2 (2009): 214, 219.

28. Gilles Deleuze, *Nietzsche and Philosophy*, trans. Hugh Tomlinson (London and New York: Continuum, 2002), 20; Deleuze, *Proust and Signs*, trans. Richard Howard (Minneapolis: University of Minnesota Press, 2000), 94–95.

accurately, hometown, the city, *al-madīna*), tying conflict to territory and to the exclusive relation of private property. On the car ride to Haifa, for instance, Said reports that, in his mind, his hometown refuses to acknowledge him and that he has a similar feeling about both the house and Khaldun. "We shouldn't have left anything. Not Khaldun, not the house, not Haifa!" he later tells Safiyya, strengthening this tripartite link.[29] Within the Solomonian metaphysics of spatial indivisibility, home, homeland, and son can accommodate only one family. In positing the impossibility of a shared state, this judgment scene necessitates a relation of subjugation, whereby only one party may own the land while the other must relinquish all claims.

"The conflict" is thus constructed as a zero-sum struggle for exclusive property rights. In the history of philosophy, judgment—as juridical arbitration and the source of political sovereignty—was largely an answer to imagined threats to property posed by the conflictual "state of nature." For Hobbes, property cannot exist as such, cannot be protected and individuated, without the alienation of judgment to the sovereign. This rationale was perfected by John Locke, who considered private property the precondition for commerce and personhood, liberty and political participation, and therefore dedicated his writing to its safeguarding.[30] To this end Locke formulated not only his notion of the social contract but also a labor theory of property that fully hinges on clear borders—physical fences secure one's property, while laws as metaphorical hedges stabilize the political system. What secures borders in the cognitive and discursive realm, for Locke, is none other than judgment, which "separate[s] carefully, one from another, *Ideas*, wherein can be found the least difference."[31] This paradigm, as Wendy Brown observes, paves the way for Locke's argument that, given "the lack of clear and settled dominion over land . . . 'Indians in America' cannot be said to enjoy political sovereignty and thereby remain in a state of political savagery."[32] In this "possessive individualism," enclosure becomes a prerequisite for freedom and politics. Thus, an alleged indigenous failure of appropriation, of judgment as a system of boundaries and distinctions, serves as pretext for colonization (even while colonization—the dispossession integral to settlement—was itself the historical breeding ground for

29. Kanafani, "Returning to Haifa," 173.

30. John Locke, *Two Treatises of Government*, ed. Peter Laslett (Cambridge: Cambridge University Press, 2003), 286–88.

31. John Locke, *An Essay Concerning Human Understanding*, ed. Peter H. Nidditch (Oxford and New York: Oxford University Press, 1979), 156.

32. Wendy Brown, *Walled States, Waning Sovereignty* (New York and Cambridge, Mass.: Zone, 2010), 44.

the idea of exclusive property).[33] As the power to nicely separate things, judgment subtends the entire edifice of colonial liberalism—private property, free market, the state, and the distinction between legal persons and racialized non-subjects, whose lands are construed as *terra nullius*.

As Said expected, when Khaldun-Dov eventually enters the room with his IDF uniform, his very first response is a refusal to acknowledge his Palestinian parents. After Miriam introduces them, the young man states, addressing her, "I don't know any mother but you. As for my father, he was killed in the Sinai [War] eleven years ago."[34] As the conversation develops, the antagonism grows rapidly. Said asks:

> "You're in the Army? Who are you fighting? Why?"
> The young man jumped to his feet.
> "You have no right to ask those questions. You're on the other side."
> "I? I'm on the other side?"
> Said laughed heartily. And with that explosive laughter he felt as if he was pushing out all the pain and tension and fear and anguish in his chest. He wanted to keep on laughing and laughing *until the entire world was turned upside down* (*ḥattā yanqalib al-ʿālam kulluhu*) or until he fell asleep or died or raced out to his car. But the young man cut him off sharply.
> "I see no reason to laugh."
> "I do."
> He laughed a little longer then stopped and became silent as suddenly as he had burst out laughing.[35]

Soon after, Said "rips" Dov-Khaldun's army cap from the table. Bothered by this gesture and by Said's non-communicative laughter, Khaldun-Dov tries to reestablish a collaborative conversation by demanding to "talk like civilized people" (*ka-unās mutaḥaḍḍirīn*). Said's reaction, however, is precisely to laugh again. Associating the request for the conversation to be "civilized" with negotiation, Said states, "You don't want to negotiate (*tafāwuḍ*), isn't that right? You said you and I are on opposite sides. What happened? Do you want to negotiate or what?"[36]

33. Onur Ulas Ince, *Colonial Capitalism and the Dilemmas of Liberalism* (New York: Oxford University Press, 2018), 28–29. See also Brenna Bhandar, *Colonial Lives of Property: Law, Land, and Racial Regimes of Ownership* (Durham, N.C.: Duke University Press, 2018); Hagar Kotef, *Movement and the Ordering of Freedom: On Liberal Governances of Modernity* (Durham, N.C.: Duke University Press, 2015), 76–78.

34. Kanafani, "Returning to Haifa," 179.

35. Ibid., 180/399, emphasis mine.

36. Ibid., 181/400.

Said's non-communicative laughter thus communicates a great deal. Expressing Kanafani's critique of judgment and of the dialogue it presupposes and demands, Said's repeated laughter signals a rejection of negotiation, of "civilized conversation" with its collaborative deliberation in search of solutions. In a famous interview, conducted by the Australian journalist Richard Carleton in Beirut in 1970, Kanafani was asked why the PFLP refuses to "enter into peace talks with the Israelis." In response, he first reconceptualized the question—"you mean, surrender talks"—then proceeded to explain that any such negotiation is, in fact, "a kind of conversation between the sword and the neck." This statement exposes the disavowed violence behind deliberative "civilized conversations"—in such dialogues, a decision has already been made ("surrender talks"), and therefore they merely demand the victims' assent to their own subjugation.

Kanafani's statement also reveals the inflection of such dialogue by colonial material conditions, concealed by the pretense of an objective, universal philosophical method. This critique of dialogue is sharpened in yet another key instance of Said's laughter. When Miriam first proposes her judgment plan, Safiyya, desperate to reunite with her son, accepts its terms, exclaiming, "I'm certain Khaldun will choose his real parents. It's impossible to deny the call of flesh and blood." Said bursts out laughing, a laughter "filled with a profound bitterness that bespoke defeat," then tells Safiyya, "What Khaldun? What flesh and blood are you talking about? . . . They've taught him how to be for twenty years, day by day, hour by hour, with his food, his drink, his sleep. . . . The matter is finished. They stole him."[37] Before Dov-Khaldun even makes a decision, Said's laughter already humorously laments (or bitterly ridicules) the conditioning of any judgment by parameters set up in advance by the colonizers, which guarantee his defeat. In the absence of a rule of judgment applicable and acceptable to both parties, the regulation, in Jean-François Lyotard's terms, always takes place in the idiom of the sovereign.[38] Stressing the power imbalance between sword and neck and their radically incommensurable positions, Kanafani contests the impartiality of judgment. While Lyotard's critique reassesses and condemns the procedure of judgment on its own terms, Said's laughter critically attacks the juridico-political as such. Suggesting that judgment is always determined by material, everyday practices, by both the aesthetic and the social, Said rejects its impartiality and universality. Even kinship, Said intimates, is determined by mundane, repetitive praxis, which constitutes it as natural and almost biological—as "flesh and blood."

37. Ibid., 172.

38. Jean-François Lyotard, *The Differend*, trans. Georges Van Den Abbeele (Minneapolis: University of Minnesota, 1989), 9.

Ishtibāk (Clashing Engagement)

This short antagonistic exchange clarifies that the encounter is not in fact a dispute, with an obvious endpoint and a designated judge, such as the conversation for which Miriam had been hoping. Instead of a voluntary and collaborative dialogue, it is an involuntary struggle, a bitter strife. This exchange establishes Said and Khaldun-Dov's mutual recognition of each other as belonging to different "camps" and spells out their rejection of negotiation. They are clearly not trying to convince one another of their rationales, conduct an investigation for an objective truth, or negotiate a compromise. Instead, the two express notions that are non-communicable, utterly incomprehensible when subjected to the other's epistemic prism. And yet those notions are nonetheless voiced. Additionally, this exchange is imposed on both. Dov-Khaldun has clearly not chosen to partake in it, and Said's desire to meet his lost son has long subsided, having realized before the young man even entered the room that "the matter is finished."

This forced clash is not without violence, yet it is not exhausted by it. In any case, it is not simply a state of war. War, an armed conflict aimed at vanquishing the other party, is *not yet* part of this story. Khaldun-Dov has not yet been to battle. Nor has Khalid, Said's second son, who is planning to join the resistance. As Dov-Khaldun believes that by participating in war he will be able to prove his belonging to his Jewish family and collective, war in the novella is associated with demarcated concepts and identity categories, with clearly defined ends, and thus with the juridico-political.[39]

In his *'An al-Rijal wa-l-Banadiq* (Of Men and Rifles, 1968), a collection of stories of struggle against the Zionist colonization, Kanafani distinguishes, as Samera Esmeir shows, between war and struggle—*ishtibāk*, or "clashing engagement," in Esmeir's attentive translation. Kanafani writes, "This was the time of war. War? No. But clashing engagement itself. Constant fighting with the enemy." If during war there might be a ceasefire, then during the time of clashing engagement "the fighter is always about to be shot, he is moving between two bullets."[40] Because this perpetual, existential struggle has no fixed ends or external regulating ideals, it challenges the teleological logic by which

39. "I haven't been in direct combat yet so I can't describe my feelings . . . but perhaps in the future I'll be able to confirm to you what I am about to say now: I belong here, and this woman is my mother"; Kanafani, "Returning to Haifa," 182.

40. Ghassan Kanafani, *'An al-Rijal wa-l-Banadiq* (Beirut: Mu'assasat al-Abḥath al-'Arabiyya, 1968), 73, quoted and translated by Samera Esmeir, in "The Time of Engagement, Zaman al-Ishtibak," *Law, Culture and the Humanities* 10, no. 3 (2014): 10.

the juridico-political order either subsumes struggles under the language of legal disputes or criminalizes them as unlawful conflicts. Esmeir further insists that, in *ishtibāk*, action seizes on the time between the two bullets and arises from an ongoing potentiality, which inheres in a collective's life and is thus always embedded in the past (as opposed to Arendt's definition of action as natality, as the initiation of a new beginning).[41] Reducible neither to judgment nor to violence alone, clashing engagement emerges as a different mode of conflict—a revolutionary, ongoing struggle that is not completely open-ended but based in historical potentialities.

In no way a dialogue, this struggle is nonetheless a form of engagement and even of transformation. Said's laughter—like other nonverbal instances in "'A'id ila Ḥayfa," most notably silences—in fact communicates *something* to Dov-Khaldun while explicitly refusing conversation. Uncommunicative as it is, it serves as an outlet for pain, frustration, and "profound bitterness"—an outlet that speech fails to provide. Adding no new words, no information or descriptions, this moment involves ongoing silent reevaluation rather than a judgment pursuant to deliberation. With this laughter, the judge is dethroned. In the presence of this laughter Khaldun-Dov also realizes, uncomfortably, that Said in fact refuses the rules of his juridico-political game, that something else entirely might potentially happen, a realization that leads him to vocally insist on speaking "like civilized people." This moment is also transformative for Said: while laughing, he learns that things are "upside down" and discovers the power of his laughter to turn the world on its head, to revolutionize and reinvent both being and knowledge. It is this "explosive laughter" that melts away the conceptions to which Said has been clinging for nearly twenty years, inaugurating a change in his very conceptualization of the world and in that world itself.

This reconceptualization, this mode of clashing engagement that somehow reinvents the world, is born in "'A'id ila Ḥayfa" out of catachrestic moments—moments that creatively thrust together two contexts, as in the forced clash between Said and Dov-Khaldun. Like Said's laughter, creative metaphors set up encounters between two worldviews, whose relations defy "the judgment of God." As against the clear conceptual margins of judgment, creative metaphors are murky; they do not depend on the goodwill of thought or on voluntary decision. They are based, instead, on what forces one to think, on chance encounters with signs. Instead of universal assent and common sense, they involve struggle and incommensurability. Equating this mode of thinking with

41. Esmeir, "Time of Engagement," 8–9.

style, Deleuze also describes it as nothing other than metaphor, but only insofar as metaphors are themselves metamorphosis.[42] In their clashing engagement, Kanafani's creative metaphors effect change—reconceptualizing perception, thought, and possibly action. Perhaps these are the effects of figurative language that led Hobbes and Locke to regard it as such a threat to the edifice of judgment?

Catastrophes of Analogy: Holocaust *and* Nakba

Enlightenment thinkers articulated judgment, as a political concept, in analogy to its roles in both cognition and language. More specifically, Western philosophers often defined the faculty of judgment in opposition to wit and fancy and to their product: the polysemy of figurative language. For Hobbes as for Locke, judgment is propositional and discursive; it happens in and through language. Their conceptions of judgment, like their perceptions of society and the physical world, are not merely dependent on language but shaped in its very image. Locke defines judgment as the capacity for separating ideas from one another and, since his epistemology analogizes ideas and words (and things), declares judgment to be "a way of proceeding quite contrary to Metaphor and Allusion."[43] Hobbes, too, regards judgment as the cognitive capacity to distinguish things—to "observe their differences and dissimilitudes" and to judge what they are—as well as its discursive product, the "final sentence of him that discourseth." Contrasting the use of judgment with that of metaphors, Hobbes claims that reasoning must proceed by way of judgment for reasoning through metaphors and other "ambiguous words" leads to "contention and sedition"—that is, to conflict.[44] While excluding metaphors from reasoning, however, Hobbes does entertain the use of some "apt similitudes" for opening up the understanding.[45] Although Hobbes never defines "apt similitude," a meaning might be derived from his own usage of figures and based on his recurrent exaltation of perspicuous words. Indeed, in Hobbes's master metaphors—leviathan, artificial man, the path to knowledge—the correlation is always overtly explicated, and no term is ever missing. The extended metaphor of the body politic is a case in point: the commonwealth is an artificial man, whose elements are compared at every point to those of natural man (e.g., sovereignty is its soul, laws its will, colonies its reproduction, and

42. Deleuze, *Proust and Signs*, 48.
43. Locke, *Essay*, 156.
44. Hobbes, *Leviathan*, 47, 36.
45. Ibid., 52.

sedition its sickness). What makes such similitudes "apt," it appears, is their analogical form, where meanings are clearly coded and neatly divided into two controlled, symmetrical, and hierarchical sets.[46]

I find that anything Hobbes vehemently advocates should inspire suspicion and require further investigation. Before turning to creative metaphors, I therefore propose a short detour through Kanafani's critical treatment of analogies, which clarifies that, in the case of Palestine-Israel as in others, collapsing figuration or comparison into the form of analogy, with its equivalences and interpretative hierarchy, tends to result in narcissistic prisms and moral imperialism that preclude conceptual transformation.

Soon after Said and Saifiyya first meet Miriam, the story of their visit in the present of 1967 is paused and a subplot outlining Miriam and Iphrat's history is introduced. Having survived the holocaust, the couple arrived in Palestine in 1948. Despite their common journey, their views on the 1948 War and its effects vary greatly. Though Iphrat had observed the battles in Haifa firsthand and thus knows that Palestine is not a "land with no people for a people with no land," Palestinians are completely transparent to him. He regards the war between Jewish Zionists and Palestinians as "taking place between men and ghosts, nothing more." Owing to this blindness, Iphrat is able to unproblematically celebrate the results of the war—the expulsion of most Palestinians from Haifa—and to marvel, without any qualms, in his first "true Jewish Sabbath." Miriam's response, by contrast, vocally laments the loss of "true Sabbaths" on Fridays and Sundays, for, with the depletion of the Muslim and Christian Palestinian population, their weekly holy days will no longer be observed in the city.[47] Recognizing the fundamental injustice at the core of Israel's establishment, she does so by reference to her own tradition.

The text posits Miriam's broader critique of Zionism as based in her own experience of violent state racism. For Miriam, we are told, everything changed dramatically the day she witnessed two *Hagana* men hoisting a dead Arab child

46. Ibid., 9. Hobbes's metaphor of the artificially made man is particularly revealing, as it subordinates both nature and God's power of creation to the imagery of a mechanical automaton with its scientific order. Both sets, and their analogous order, are vital here: the organic set ("natural man") justifies the state as both natural and divinely ordained, while the mechanical set dominates, allowing the state to utilize and subjugate "nature" and "men" in the name of scientific analysis and regulation.

47. Kanafani, "Returning to Haifa," 167–68. It is worth mentioning that the name "Miriam" is related to the Hebrew word *meri* and the Arabic cognate *mirā'*, both meaning "rebellion," "dispute," "opposition," and "resistance." The name thus reflects not only Miriam's rebellion against hegemonic Zionist ideas and practices but also her desire for a clear oppositional structure, such as that of judgment.

into a truck in *Hadar* (a mostly working-class Jewish neighborhood in Haifa). Horrified, she points out the incident to Iphrat, who wonders how she knows that the child is Arab. A Jewish child, Miriam replies, would have never been tossed like refuse into a truck. We are told that Iphrat wanted to probe further, but "when he saw her face, he became silent." Miriam's expression, which triggers Iphrat's silence, is never portrayed. Nor is its cause provided. Instead, Kanafani begins a new paragraph, whose first sentence simply states, "Miriam had lost her father at Auschwitz eight years before." Immediately after the death of her father, the paragraph further recounts, Miriam had witnessed the murder of her ten-year-old brother by Nazi German soldiers. The transition from Miriam's outrage at the soldiers abusing a Palestinian child's body to her personal holocaust trauma is subtle, and the relationship between the two scenes is not explicitly drawn. They are merely set one next to the other on the page. This physical proximity, however, is already suggestive of some form of relation between Miriam's compassion for the Palestinian boy and her own unfathomable loss. A metaphorical structure—a side-by-sidedness—is thus set up between the two events and between the two catastrophes they represent: the holocaust and the *nakba*.[48]

At first, the side-by-side figure allows Miriam a point of identification through which to recognize both the suffering caused by colonial violence and her own complicity in it. Indeed, Miriam is so overtaken with indignation that she wishes to go back to Italy, the last stop in the couple's journey to Palestine.[49] Yet, she never leaves. First, because Iphrat resists her persuasions; and later, because the Jewish Agency offers the couple not only an expropriated Palestinian house but also the child who was found in it.[50] Earlier, Miriam related to Palestinians' suffering by seeing the deceased Palestinian child alongside the loss of her brother, without necessarily hierarchizing the two

48. On this side-by-side, non-comparing comparison, see my interview with Elias Khoury in Liron Mor, "At Af Pa'am lo Ḥozeret, at Holekhet: Re'ayon 'im Elias Khoury," *Erets ha-Emori* (blog), July 25, 2013, https://haemori.wordpress.com/2013/07/25/khoury/.

49. Kanafani, "Returning to Haifa," 169. Scholars often treat Miriam as the first fully developed figure of an Israeli, or even of a Jew, in Arabic literature. The celebration is somewhat disproportional and condescending, since Kanafani had extensively researched Zionist literature and culture. See Ghassan Kanafani, *Fi al-Adab al-Ṣihyuni* (Beirut: Munaẓẓamat al-Taḥrir al-Filasṭiniyya, Markaz al-Abḥath, 1967). For accounts of Kanafani's empathetic treatment of Miriam, see Kamal Abdel-Malek, *The Rhetoric of Violence: Arab-Jewish Encounters in Contemporary Palestinian Literature and Film* (New York: Palgrave Macmillan, 2005), 67; Elias Khoury, "Rethinking the Nakba," *Critical Inquiry* 38, no. 2 (2012): 255; Siddiq, *Man Is a Cause*, 54–55. For a critique of this laudatory claim, see Sasson Somekh, "Falestina'i she-Hetsits ṿe-lo Nifga'," *Ofek* 2 (1972): 151.

50. Kanafani, "Returning to Haifa," 169–70.

experiences or taking ownership of both; now, she takes over the suffering Palestinian child by literally making him her own, perhaps as a substitute for the lost brother. Unlike the Prophet Miriam, who watched over her brother while hiding in the reeds and then, for his own protection, handed him over to Pharaoh's daughter to raise, this Miriam watches her brother's murder from her hiding place and then adopts another's child, allegedly for his own protection, too. Replicating Zionist mythology, Miriam sees herself as saving an abandoned child, who stands in for an abandoned home and land. Her historic tragedy becomes the implicit pretext for this very appropriation. Miriam's figure thus demonstrates that, by seeing the Palestinian catastrophe only through the perspective of their own, even "benevolent" colonizers tend to subject the *nakba* to the holocaust. Using the latter as justification for the former, they resolve the tension between recognizing the colonial injustice and being implicated in its perpetuation given their very presence in the land. Thanks to the adoption, moreover, Miriam may perceive herself as making amends, as somehow righting the historical wrong—an ideologeme that alleviates remorse and thus smooths the path toward colonization.

The figurative comparison between the two catastrophes, the story seems to suggest, fails to induce any change. Regarding Miriam as working through her trauma and complicity by adopting the child—finding in him both compensation and atonement—is one possible explanation for this failure. Another, which underlies the first, is Miriam's retreat into her established ideological bounds by thinking in analogical terms—Fridays and Sundays are for Muslims and Christians as Saturdays are for Jews, the *Hagana* murder of the Palestinian boy is like the Nazi murder of her brother. As analogies subsume one set of terms under the other, Miriam ultimately subordinates the *nakba* to the holocaust. By adopting the narcissistic lens of liberal identification, which universalizes one's standards (and moral predicaments), she fails to grasp the Palestinian catastrophe on its own terms.[51] A mere pretense of understanding, then, such analogies as Miriam's are, in Saidiya Hartman's terms, "double-edged, for in making the other's suffering one's own, this suffering is occluded by the other's obliteration."[52] Indeed, when an analogical comparison subjects others to the colonizers' own idiom, it is nothing but, to paraphrase Clausewitz, the continuation of colonialism by other means. In "'A'id ila Ḥayfa," through the adoption trope, the tendency of such analogies to appropriate Palestinian suffering as one's own is literalized.

51. Michael Rothberg, "From Gaza to Warsaw: Mapping Multidirectional Memory," *Criticism* 53, no. 4 (2011): 535–36.

52. Saidiya Hartman, *Scenes of Subjection: Terror, Slavery, and Self-Making in Nineteenth-Century America* (New York: Oxford University Press, 1997), 19.

Along with this interpretative hierarchy, analogies also create the impression of equivalence. Privileged by Aristotle as the most ordered and elegant metaphor, analogy implies similarity between its sets. When the two contexts brought together in analogy are ones whose relations are colonial, the implied equivalence effaces the power imbalance. As Lital Levy argues with regard to holocaust and *nakba* comparisons, "Equivalence does not undergird this comparison; to the contrary, equivalence is an effect of the comparison."[53] Because of the false symmetry and the centering of empathy on the self, the analogizing of holocaust and *nakba* presents Jews and Palestinians as equal victims vying for recognition and fails to understand the colonial injustice or to assume collective responsibility for it. Suggesting not only symmetry between their sets of terms but also known and equivalent relations within those sets, analogies risk presenting asymmetrical parties as equally culpable toward one another. This representation is particularly skewed in the Palestinian-Israeli context, where Zionism is directly responsible for the Palestinian catastrophe, but the reverse cannot seriously be claimed.

The black hole of the holocaust, both as an incomparable meta-physical event and as a constitutive ineffable trauma, indeed tends to swallow everything whole. A series of recent works have undertaken to reconsider the possibility of comparing the holocaust and the *nakba*. They demonstrate that the holocaust not only takes precedence as the underlying cause of and justification for the *nakba* and its perpetuation, but also ignites a competition with and appropriation of the other's victimhood, relegating the Palestinian catastrophe to a secondary position.[54] Building on these vital works, I argue that these effects are produced, more specifically, by the analogical form of the comparison. Hierarchical and clearly ordered, analogy is a rather catastrophic metaphor. It resolves the ambiguities integral to other tropes, exacts too tight a control over interpretation and comparison, and centers the judging self. By subsuming the unfamiliar under the familiar, it forecloses the space of reevaluation and bolsters liberal moral imperialism that fails to see beyond self-injury. Creating a false equivalency between two positions of victimhood and adopting Palestinian suffering as her own, Miriam's analogies elide the colonizers' responsibility for its perpetuation. By raising the specter of the road not

53. Lital Levy, "'You Just Can't Compare': Holocaust Comparisons and Discourses of Israel-Palestine," in *Israel-Palestine: Lands and Peoples*, ed. Omer Bartov (Berghahn, 2021), 71.

54. Rosemary Sayigh, "On the Exclusion of the Palestinian Nakba from the 'Trauma Genre,'" *Journal of Palestine Studies* 43, no. 1 (2013): 51–60; Bashir Bashir and Amos Goldberg, eds., *The Holocaust and the Nakba: A New Grammar of Trauma and History* (New York: Columbia University Press, 2018); Levy, "You Just Can't Compare."

taken—of going back to Italy, of refusing the house and the child—the novella is critical of Miriam's analogical reasoning. Associated with the logic of judgment and its "civilized conversation," Miriam's analogy is framed as a metaphorical modality to avoid.

"But How Differently Each Sees It!"

Critical of analogies, Kanafani offers his readers a different figurative mode—creative metaphor and its clashing engagement. At the height of the narrative, Dov-Khaldun can no longer be contained in a neat analogy for the home and the homeland, and his complexity irrupts. Departing from his well-prepared speech, he accuses his biological parents of abandoning him, of being too weak, frightened, and "backwards" to return and fight for him.[55] Remarkably, this charge is extremely similar to accusations voiced by the "Second Generation"—the sons and daughters of holocaust survivors—toward their parents: the implicit, yet prevalent, accusation of being too weak and passive, of "walking like sheep to the slaughter."[56] The ideology behind this accusation is reflected, for instance, in the name chosen for the holocaust memorial day in Israel—*Yom ha-zikaron la-sho'a ve̜la-gevura* (Holocaust and Heroism Memorial Day)—which conditions the commemoration of immeasurable loss and suffering on the simultaneous centering and glorification of the few heroic resistance attempts.

The sense that Khaldun-Dov is blaming all his parents is heightened when he passionately cries out, "You're all weak! Weak! (*'ājizūn! 'ājizūn!*) You're bound by heavy chains of backwardness and paralysis (*al-takhalluf wa-l-shalal*)! Don't tell me you spent twenty years crying!"[57] The paralysis and weakness attributed to holocaust survivors is thus combined with the internalized anti-Semitic accusation of backwardness leveled by Zionists against diasporic Jews (see Chapter 2). Attributed here to the Palestinian parents, however, this alleged backwardness reinforces the metaphoric link between the two families and between their historical contexts. While the plural form employed by Dov-Khaldun, "You're all weak!," seems addressed to his biological parents and perhaps to the Palestinian people more broadly, it might also refer to all the parents in the room, including Miriam, the "weak," "paralyzed," and "backward" holocaust survivor. Precisely when his anger erupts, when a clashing engagement explodes, Dov-Khaldun becomes a metaphorical vehicle that

55. Kanafani, "Returning to Haifa," 185.

56. See, for example, Tom Segev, *The Seventh Million: The Israelis and the Holocaust* (New York: Hill and Wang, 1994), particularly 153–86, 421–45.

57. Kanafani, "Returning to Haifa," 185/409, emphases added.

cuts through both contexts, both catastrophes, bringing them together in one and the same body. He is no longer the son who must be given to one mother or the other in an act of judgment lest he be murdered in an absurd partition. Instead, he is shared, even if *this sharing is not harmonious or consensual, nor discussed or agreed upon*. Through this metaphoric overlaying—the reuse of post-holocaust vocabulary to express a post-*nakba* reality—the son defies the zero-sum game of judgment and paves the way for a clashing engagement, as conflictual as it may be.

The metaphorical relation created by this encounter takes on the form of catachresis. It is in no way analogous. Nothing is directly compared or subordinated. Instead, the same accusation is hurled at both sets of parents; the same angry son is lashing out at both, inventively adjoining two families, two catastrophes, two worlds and worldviews, without trying to unify, resolve, or equate them, nor explicate the terms of their relation.

As a catachresis, this metaphorical encounter multiplies worlds and worldviews and lodges them into one another. This aesthetic revolution is evident from the very beginning, when Said and Safiyya first enter the house and begin looking around in silence and bewilderment, seeing their old belongings—"intimate and personal"—redeployed in strange, uncanny ways. The life that Said and Safiyya had known in this home is still present. Material possessions have remained in place—the bell, the copper lock, the peacock feathers, the Syrian carpet. At the very sight of the Haifa home, their old lives reawaken before their eyes—Said envisions the young Safiyya leaning from the balcony and recalls the neighbors' children filling the stairway with their voices.[58] Simultaneously, this world is overlaid with Miriam's world, with her additions to the home—like those new chairs that now complete Said and Safiyya's set, "out of harmony with the rest," per Said. Miriam had also made alterations to their old possessions—for instance, rearranging the familiar peacock feathers in a new vase. Objects that have disappeared are also showcased: Safiyya's eyes pierce the corners of the room "as though counting up the things that are missing."[59] Even Miriam's belongings are seen by Said through his missing ones: her new curtains conjure the ones Safiyya once made, which have now disappeared *(ikhtafat)*. With their present absence, Safiyya's disappeared curtains recall the past while still attesting to Miriam's life-world (more on this disappearance in Chapter 3). In this catachrestic scopic practice, as in metaphors more broadly, it *is* and

58. Ibid., 161–62/362.
59. Ibid., 162–63/365.

is not at the same time—it is and is not the curtain; it is and is not their home.[60]

Said and Safiyya's observation transforms in turn Miriam's way of seeing her own home and life, for she, too, now looks at things in the room "as though she were seeing them for the first time." Without Said and Safiyya communicating a word to her, their metaphorical reading of their lives through hers defamiliarizes the most intimate things, which are suddenly seen in a new, problematizing light. As Miriam sees her home anew, Said and Safiyya involuntarily follow her gaze (*baṣar*, sight), through which they now see things differently. This metaphorical encounter thus palimpsestically overlays the different lives lived in this home at different times and the different ways of perceiving them. Various memories of the space and its objects are held together and meet the defamiliarized perspective of others' sight. As Said thinks to himself upon this frantic proliferation of views, "How strange! Three pairs of eyes looking at one thing . . . but how differently each sees it!"[61]

The defamiliarizing force of creative metaphors is at the core of Nietzsche's well-known discussion contrasting new metaphors with the worn-out abstractions of dead ones. Per Nietzsche, what we forget when we submit ourselves to the social contract of moral truth—truth as concepts, as those familiar dead metaphors, conventional lies that help ward off the war of all against all—is the possibility of creating new metaphors or creatively reinterpreting existing ones (even if the innovation is temporary). The path to destabilizing the liberal social contract, to "violating the order of castes and class rank" dictated by concepts, passes through catachreses—the fabrication of "forbidden metaphors" and "unheard of combinations of concepts," which problematize given categories, trouble the coherence of the world, and render it eternally new.[62] Kanafani's novella first achieves this defamiliarization through the metaphorical overlaying of gazes and perceptions, while its key metaphorical figure—the son—performs this creative function not only formally but also thematically, in his narrative role as an orphan child. "The orphan," as a figure, quite literally de-familiarizes, pushing against the neat ordering of the family nucleus, possibly cutting through classes and violating established hierarchies.

60. "The metaphorical 'is' at once signifies both 'is not' and 'is like.' If this is really so, we are allowed to speak of metaphorical truth, but in an equally 'tensive' sense of the word 'truth'"; Paul Ricoeur, *The Rule of Metaphor: Multi-Disciplinary Studies of the Creation of Meaning in Language*, trans. Robert Czerny (Toronto and Buffalo: University of Toronto Press, 1977), 6.

61. Kanafani, "Returning to Haifa," 164.

62. Friedrich Wilhelm Nietzsche, "On Truth and Lies in a Nonmoral Sense," in *Philosophy and Truth: Selections from Nietzsche's Notebooks of the Early 1870s*, trans. Daniel Breazeale (Atlantic Highlands, N.J.: Humanities, 1999), 84–85, 96.

Crucially, however, the multiplication of worlds and worldviews by the metaphorical encounter does not remain at the level of "tolerant multiculturalism." Instead, these are put into conflict—a forced chance encounter that sustains a clash between multiple contexts, as in the case of Said and Khaldun-Dov's vehement clashing over the very terms of their discussion. By no means an invitation for amicable conversation, this clash is described with all the bitterness of enmity. It is a conflict, but one where no one is vested with the authority to force a universal rule of judgment. In such metaphors, this conflict relates—*is the only thing that relates*—the two contexts to one another, so that their relationship emerges as that of parts, never fused into a unitary whole. Dwelling outside the realm of the juridico-political, this clash refuses decisionism or compromise, negotiation or solution, and produces engagement despite the absence of communication per se.

Although such metaphors communicate nothing new—perhaps even nothing at all—they effect changes in worldviews, a revolutionary transformation of consciousness that comes from others without being dictated by them. This reevaluation is realized, first and foremost, through an axiomatic change in what is perceptible. As a clash—as, one might say, a dissensus—the metaphorical encounter brings about that "partitioning of the sensible," consisting, according to Jacques Rancière, in "making what was unseen visible; in getting what was only audible as noise to be heard as speech; in demonstrating to be a feeling of shared 'good' or 'evil' what had appeared merely as an expression of pleasure or pain."[63] In the novella, too, metaphors induce such reconfigurations of perception. They allow Said and Safiyya, for instance, to grasp something that was so far merely felt—the tumultuous underlying pain they had been carrying for twenty years, utterly inexpressible yet fully present, accompanying their every activity.[64] Even on their way to Haifa, Said and Safiyya talk about everything *but* the events of 1948 or the child who is the single motivation for their journey. The protagonists' loss, whose incommunicability the novella recurrently stages and stresses, becomes expressible and political only through the creative metaphorical structure of the return and the encounter.

63. Jacques Rancière, *Dissensus: On Politics and Aesthetics*, trans. Steven Corcoran (London and New York: Bloomsbury Academic, 2010), 38.

64. For instance, Said "was amazed that he had never thought about what that suffering must have meant to [Safiyya], and about the extent to which it was buried in the wrinkles of her face and in her eyes and in her mind. It was with her in every bite of food she took and in every hut where she had lived and in every look she cast at her children and at him and at herself"; Kanafani, "Returning to Haifa," 152.

Indeed, following the encounter, Said changes his entire political worldview, including his perception of what the homeland is. If before meeting Miriam and Dov-Khaldun he believed Palestine to be his past and memories—a lost paradise to be regained some day—he eventually realizes that the "true Palestine" is in fact the fight for the future.[65] In the encounter, moreover, the anger and pain are transformed into a political program—supporting his second son, Khalid, the "new Palestinian," who joins the resistance. As for Dov-Khaldun, despite having known about his biological parents well before meeting them, he similarly lacked the means for talking or thinking through this information. Only the conflictual encounter pushes him beyond his rehearsed speech, forcing him to reevaluate his perception of the world and his place in it. Commenting that Dov-Khaldun has surely "lost himself after all this," Said prophesizes that the young man will "never be the same as he was an hour ago."[66] Khaldun-Dov's words, intended to criticize and reject his biological parents, also render the Palestinian *nakba* visible, even inescapable, for both him and the readers. Coming up against another worldview for the first time, it is Khaldun-Dov's own words that trouble his worldview.

This change is brought about only through the bitter clash between Said and Khaldun-Dov. It is precisely at the height of their passionate clashing engagement, in a moment of heated aggression, that Dov-Khaldun produces the creative metaphor by which a hitherto inexpressible phenomenon is delineated and brought to the protagonists' attention. As Kanafani's catachresis alters the protagonists'—and possibly the readers'—audio-visual regime, it unlocks new paths for action and relation. His creative metaphor, however, simply sketches out the existence of a phenomenon, without yet fixing it in a proper name. While it is deictic—a way of pointing out and saying "this," "here," "look at this!"—this metaphor does slightly more than simply point. It selects. It limns the contours of a phenomenon, separating it from the rest, thus involving a minimal interpretative act, which already says *something* about this "this."

In classical Arabic literary theory, tropes (*majāz, tashbīh, kināya, isti ʿāra*) are part of *ʿilm al-bayān*, commonly translated as "the science of figures." The word *bayān* is derived from a root related to looking and knowing, to making visible and evident, as well as to differentiating, opposing, and conflicting with. The clarity associated with *bayān* is thus related to distinguishing something

65. Ibid., 186–87.
66. Ibid., 183.

from its surroundings, so that one might be able to see it as an entity.[67] Alternatively, *bayān* might be understood as signs that change one's way of seeing. As Grunebaum argues, the earliest quasi-definitions of *bayān* are descriptive figurative aphorisms, such as, "Reason is the guide of the soul, knowledge, the guide of reason, and *bayān*, the interpreter of knowledge" (Sahl ibn Harun, d. 215/830–31). Ibn al-Muʿtazz (d. 295/908) similarly defines *bayān* as "the interpreter of the heart, the polisher (*ṣayqal*) of the mind, the dispeller of doubt."[68] The clarity associated with *bayān* is thus tied to selection as interpretation, with "polishing" an evocative metaphor for this procedure. In this sense, creative metaphors are conducive to "seeing as." Defined as "the sensible aspect of poetic language," "seeing as," Ricoeur contends by quoting Hester, is an intuitive experience-act that works essentially through selection, by choosing the relevant aspects out of "*the quasi-sensory mass of imagery one has on reading metaphor.*"[69] Indeed, this redescriptive power of metaphors, their ability to "bring before the eyes" and revolutionize modes of seeing, pleasuring by rendering their audience active in trying to solve their riddles, was already lauded by Aristotle.[70] While Derrida's insistence on sight as the essential figure for Western conceptualization of metaphors is therefore not surprising, his heliotropic reading reduces their effects to seeing, while *bayān* stress instead the "as" in "seeing as," underscoring the creative interpretation invoked and demanded by metaphors.

"Man Is a Ca(u)se"

The sole instance of agreement in the conversation between Said and Khaldun-Dov is the enigmatic phrase "man is a cause" (*al-insān huwa qaḍiyya*).[71] It is first mentioned by Dov-Khaldun during his rehearsed speech:

67. Hans Wehr and J. Milton Cowan, *Arabic-English Dictionary: The Hans Wehr Dictionary of Modern Written Arabic*, 4th ed. (Ithaca, N.Y.: Spoken Language Services, 1993), 105–6; Stanley Lane, *Arabic-English Lexicon* (New York: F. Ungar, 1874), 288.

68. Both quoted in G. E. von Grunebaum, "Bayān," in *Encyclopaedia of Islam*, 2nd ed., ed. P. Bearman et al. (Leiden: Brill, 2012), accessed online: http://dx.doi.org/10.1163/1573-3912_islam_SIM_1298..

69. Ricoeur, *Rule of Metaphor*, 252.

70. Aristotle, *Poetics*, trans. S. H. Butcher (New York: Hill and Wang, 1961), XXII; Aristotle, *On Rhetoric: A Theory of Civic Discourse*, 2nd ed., trans. George A. Kennedy (New York: Oxford University Press, 2006), 113.

71. I use "man" in this formula despite myself, to keep with the existing translation and scholarship; however, the original term, *insān*, while grammatically gendered masculine, is more capacious and could easily be translated as "person" or "human."

> From the time I was small I was a Jew. . . . When they told me I wasn't their own child, it didn't change anything. Even when they told me—later on—that my original parents were Arabs, it didn't change anything. No, nothing changed, that's certain. After all, in the final analysis, man is a cause.

Struck by this metaphor, Said asks Dov-Khaldun for the source of his quotation. The young man admits he does not recall and asks Said about the reasons for his interest. Said explains: "That's exactly what was going through my mind at this moment."[72] The "agreement," or resonance, between the two is therefore not based on dialogue; it did not result from an exchange of ideas. Instead, both men come to formulate this realization separately.

There is no guarantee that the two in fact understand this metaphoric formula in the same way. Khaldun-Dov invokes it as a final judgment, claiming that one's identity is a matter of ideological choice. Indeed, *qaḍiyya*, the Arabic word translated here as "cause," belongs to the juridical realm (it means a "legal affair," "legal action," even "ruling"), and thus seems to be reiterating the logic of judgment. By contrast, Said argues soon after:

> Man, in the final analysis, is a cause. That's what you said. And it's true. But what cause? That's the question! Think carefully, Khalid is also a cause. . . . When we talk about man [*naqif maʿ al-insān*, stand with a man] it has nothing to do with flesh and blood and identity cards and passports. . . . The guilt isn't yours alone. . . . Isn't a human being made up of what's injected into him hour after hour, day after day, year after year? If I regret anything it's that I believed the opposite for twenty years![73]

If it is indeed a quotation, the formula might be borrowed from Ralph Waldo Emerson, the American writer who proclaimed that "every true man is a cause, a country, and an age" (the quotation seems plausible, considering that English is the presumed language of this conversation).[74] In subscribing to this formula, Said gives greater weight to the part of Emerson's quotation that the novella omits: it is not only the political cause for which people fight, but also their everyday life, their place and time—their "country" and "age"—that shape

72. Kanafani, "Returning to Haifa," 181.

73. Ibid., 183/404.

74. On the presumption that the conversation is conducted in English, see Siddiq, *Man Is a Cause*, 62.

them, so that a cause is less a decision than an interpellation (hence even Dov-Khaldun is somewhat absolved).

The semantic field of *qaḍiyya* also includes such meanings as "problem," "case," "issue," "matter," and "question."[75] In fact, the word is associated with the very code phrase for the colonization of Palestine and the struggle against it—"the Palestinian issue" (*al-qaḍiyya al-filasṭīniyya*). This metaphoric formula may therefore suggest that a person is not only a legal case to judge, nor merely the cause or principle for which she is fighting, but also a unique problem, the specific case, that she *is*. When trying to evaluate this case, proper names, identity cards, and biology are of little use. What must be considered is precisely that which escapes categories and even words—the lifelong accumulation of detail, of what is injected into us "hour after hour, day after day, year after year," with our food, drink, and sleep.[76] If a person is a singular, lived case and not merely an identity or even a political cause, then interpretation should likewise aspire to evaluating based on the case at hand, considering it as a problem not to be resolved, rather than judging it according to set categories.

As suggested by Said's speech, some form of transformational transmission, of engagement, does transpire between the worlds of Khaldun-Dov and his biological parents. This transformation occurs, however, without communication in its habitual sense, for—even if inspired by the external encounter—it seems to pass within each protagonist solipsistically and differently. How are these worlds, which are illegible to one another, nonetheless engaged? The metaphor formed by the encounter seems to produce the very site in which this engagement is even possible. It convenes the two incommensurable discourses: the one laying claim to the land on the basis of an unfathomable suffering in Europe and the other based on "biological" ties and national determination. Not only a place of conflict and suspended judgment, Kanafani's metaphors could also be seen as *the very mechanism by which a place for conflict itself is carved out, by which judgment itself operates*.

If in examining judgment and its conflict we had started with Kant's first *Critique*, then perhaps the judgment found here is more akin to aesthetic judgment in the third *Critique*.[77] When Lyotard turns to explore Kant's faculty of

75. Wehr and Cowan, *Arabic-English Dictionary*, 803–4.

76. Kanafani, "Returning to Haifa," 183.

77. Kant's aesthetic judgment is indeed an obvious place to start. The Kantian sublime is an instance of dissension between the faculties. And, while Hobbes, Locke, and Edmund Burke all view judgment as the faculty that nicely separates things, Kant regards it *also* as "a way of bringing given cognitions to the objective unity of apperception." Judgment, for Kant,

judgment, he discovers it everywhere in the form of the "as if," mediating between different faculties in the aesthetic realm.[78] For Kant, he argues, judgment not only divides the faculties but also mediates between them. Kantian judgment thus seemingly operates *solely* through a metaphorical procedure that borrows from one realm to engage a term in another, which either has no name or, more dramatically still, has no prior sense. Adopting a Wittgensteinian vocabulary to metaphorize the Kantian faculties as "phrase families," Lyotard expands judgment's mediating role from faculties to discourses. It is no longer (cognitive) judgment understood as "the judgment of God"—the presiding judge, who must decide between the two sides, declaring "this is X"—but rather (aesthetic) judgment as the precondition for interpretation. Judgment itself now appears as a catachresis: the bringing together of (at least) two worlds, two discourses, in a productive conflict, which allows a passage—literally, a metaphor, a carrying over (*meta-pherein*)—between them.[79]

Lyotard claims, however, that critical judgment today no longer allows such mediation and instead emphasizes disputes, leading to fundamental incommensurability between different discourses.[80] He thus equates conflict with standstill, the impossibility of communication in the absence of a shared language where the parties' claims might become legible to one another. Many contemporary agonists either follow Lyotard in considering conflict an indecisive free play of difference, never to be resolved, or join Rancière in reducing conflict to the single issue of inclusion, be it a progressivist march toward greater inclusion or a perpetually shifting demarcation line that randomly reconfigures the part included in politics. Other agonists, like Chantal Mouffe, advance a "pragmatic" construction of conflict as political decision-making and as an outlet for social grievances, thus ultimately reproducing conflict as

---

is therefore *the* central cognitive faculty that integrates and coordinates between the different functions of intuition, imagination, understanding, and reason to produce a single cognitive product: *a* judgment. Not only an associating faculty, Kantian judgment is also "the indirect cognition of an object, viz., the presentation of a presentation of it," and its procedure is the figurative procedure of the "as if" (*als ob*). Indeed, in Kant's third *Critique*, judgments of taste act *as if* they were universal, the work of artistic genius is analogous to the working of nature and, by assuming an analogous concept, beauty is a symbol for morality; Kant, *Critique of Pure Reason*, 206, 184, 122; Immanuel Kant, *Critique of Judgment*, trans. Werner S. Pluhar (Indianapolis: Hackett, 1987), 159–62, 173–78, 225–30.

78. Jean-Francois Lyotard, *Enthusiasm: The Kantian Critique of History*, trans. Georges Van Den Abbeele (Stanford, Calif.: Stanford University Press, 2009), 6, 13, 16, 37.

79. Jean-Francois Lyotard, "The Sign of History," in *The Lyotard Reader*, ed. Andrew Benjamin (Oxford and Cambridge, Mass.: Wiley-Blackwell, 1991), 410.

80. Ibid., 409–10.

public deliberation, notwithstanding their overt critique of the rationalist optimism behind deliberative democracy.[81]

Kanafani's writing offers, as we have seen, a different epistemology of conflict in which, without a shared language and despite the impossibility of communication, something nonetheless passes. This non-comminating communication is by no means a mode of deliberation. Nor is it reducible to the single question of inclusion. It is, rather, that "conversation between the sword and the neck." And its medium, that through which anything might pass, is silence.

It is possible to gloss this non-communicating communication another way, skipping over Lyotard and his heavy-handed translation of Kant. From the perspective of the present, the notion of communicating through non-communication calls to mind the Palestinian BDS campaign. A boycott is, fundamentally, a refusal of conversation. Neither armed struggle nor a symbolic act in the political realm of representation, BDS is a clash—it exerts real force, meant to negatively affect lives. This clash nonetheless exhibits a pedagogical role and is directed at *some* audience. Its audience is not friendly—neither the convinced choir nor a partner for "civilized conversation"—but rather the enemy (and the enabling and spectating international community). It is by avoidance, through severing communication, through silence, that BDS aims to engage, to make something pass, to introduce change. Building on the history of anti-Apartheid, Palestine once again offers an innovative model of anti-colonialism that bypasses the representational order of the political, exerting force, a certain degree and form of violence, without it becoming war. A clashing engagement through avoidance and silence. An *ishtibāk* whose ends are given only minimally, in the negative (decolonization, the dissolution of a settler colonial state), without prescribing a clear solution. Successful or not, this mode of transformational non-communication does not yet have a proper name in philosophy.

The Empty Case

Silences. Absences. Those are the spaces in which Kanafani's clashing engagement resides. In them, his mode of exchange and change, his conflict, emerges as distinct from others. Paradigmatic of Kanafani's innovative use of silence and its non-communicating communication is his earlier novella, "Ma Tabaqqa Lakum" (All That's Left to You, 1966). As the protagonist, Hamid,

81. Chantal Mouffe, "Deliberative Democracy or Agonistic Pluralism?," *Social Research* 66, no. 3 (1999): 745–58.

attempts to make his way from Gaza to Jordan, an Israeli soldier stumbles upon him in the desert. Held by Hamid's blade, the soldier awaits rescue, unaware of Hamid's plan to kill him as soon as rescue approaches. They sit together, "two ghosts separated by a blade," knowing that, at best, only one of them will live, waiting "for the single moment of truth to come, an event that seemed as distant as their shoulders were close." Their encounter is so dramatic that, as Hamid tells the soldier, their inability to communicate—for lack of a shared language—appears absurd.[82] Yet quite a lot passes between them in this overnight encounter. Hamid announces his fatal plan by pressing his blade to the soldier's body at the first sign of help. In the soldier's eyes and helpless behavior, Hamid reads the man's realization of his coming death. The two communicate extensively through gazes. Some exchanges concern practical matters (the soldier requests water; Hamid refuses); others are more significant. Interested in his opponent's "name and purpose," Hamid leafs through the soldier's papers, despite the language barrier. While the latter refuses Hamid's gestural request to read aloud his name off his Hebrew identity card, his "cause"—the colonization of Jaffa—is exposed when, in the faint light of dawn, Hamid detects on the card, in Latin script, the word "Jaffa." He then tells the solider, in Arabic, about being expelled from Jaffa and is convinced, based on motions and stares, that the man fully understands him.[83] The foreclosure of verbal communication is thus intensely transformative for both characters, as something nonetheless transpires between them (and this transformative quality is not annulled by the imminent death both face).

In "'A'id ila Ḥayfa," too, the constant invocation of silence produces a unique mode of engagement. Time and again Kanafani's words push toward the outside of language—depicting moments in which there is nothing to say, moments that no words could ever express. Through gazes and gesticulations or by her palpable presence, Safiyya often silently influences the events, and her silence is thus never a simple muteness. For instance, after she first broaches the idea of returning to Haifa, Safiyya falls silent. She never answers Said's questions about what she hopes to find there. For the entire week that follows, although she did not mention the idea again, it "remained hanging over them, day, and night. . . . They ate it with their food and slept with it, but they did not speak a word about it." Following this silent reevaluation, it is now Said who suggests

82. Ghassan Kanafani, *All That's Left to You: A Novella and Other Stories*, trans. May Jayyusi and Jeremy Reed (Northampton, Mass.: Interlink, 2005), 34–35. In Arabic: Kanafani, "Ma Tabaqqa Lakum," in *al-Athar al-Kamila* (Beirut: Mu'assasat Ghassan Kanafani al-Thaqafiyya: Dar al-Ṭali'a, 1980), 1:153–234.

83. Kanafani, *All That's Left to You*, 45–47.

that they visit Haifa, despite his earlier reluctance. At different moments, Said's silences, too, deeply affect the narrative, marking inexpressible feelings or thoughts and often framing his most radical realizations.[84]

Engagement and change thus occur in blank spaces in the novella. A particularly powerful absence is that of the two peacock feathers, for it is Said's realization of their disappearance that conjures the past and exposes Dov-Khaldun's present existence. The missing feathers also mark time passed, the time of Khaldun-Dov's childhood without his biological parents: as Miriam tells Said when he inquires, the feathers were probably lost when Dov played with them as a child.[85] This absence thus ignites a certain engagement between Miriam's world and Said's and facilitates a transition between the present and the past—between Said and Safiyya's life in this home twenty years ago and Dov-Khaldun's childhood with Miriam, and between both these times and the present. By invoking Khaldun-Dov, this absence also denotes that which could not have been mentioned or expressed before; through it, however, Dov-Khaldun now emerges as the "truth" of these disparate moments and worlds, their common element.

Like the missing feathers, silences and absences in the novella are often the place of metaphors. Not simply metaphorical, however, these are the medium through which creative metaphors and their engaged clashes work. Catachreses keep silent about the new sensation or phenomenon to be illuminated. They operate solely through a re-use that adds no new words or information, and instead leaves some empty space to inspire movement.

This idea is nearly literalized by a key absence in the novella: the empty rectangle on the wall of Faris al-Lubda's home. In a subplot, Said takes advantage of a moment when Miriam is absent to tell Safiyya about the parallel experience of their neighbor, Faris. Like the couple returning to Haifa, Faris had recently returned to his old home in Jaffa, from which he was expelled in 1948. Unlike them, however, Faris finds there a Palestinian man who was himself displaced. As soon as he enters the house, Faris discovers the portrait of

84. Moments of silence in the novella, according to Mohamed Radi, are not a form of nonbeing or negativity. Instead, they offer a different kind of presence and fullness, forming "an integral part of the composition, which means much more than words themselves." They operate, in fact, in various, essential ways: as frames that emphasize crucial moment, as figures of passing time, as a fragmenting device, as means for redirecting attention to the difficulty of communication while nonetheless aiming to express the inexpressible and serving as the only possible expression of ineffable pain; Radi, "Les échos du silence dans 'Retour à Haïfa' de Ghassan Kanafani," *Thélème: Revista Complutense de Estudios Franceses* 26 (2011): 276–77, translation mine.

85. Kanafani, "Returning to Haifa," 165.

his martyred brother Badr, still decorated with a black mourning ribbon, on the living room wall. The unnamed current occupant of the house tells Faris that Badr's portrait had become an integral part of his and his family's life. The portrait, the man recalls, was the first thing he noticed when he first entered the house. Recently released from a prison camp after fighting in the 1948 War, the man felt isolated in Jaffa, whose Palestinian population was depleted during the war. Badr's photograph was the reason he decided to rent this home. A source of comradery and comfort, the portrait helped him "not just to resist (*al-rafḍ*) but to remain (*al-baqā'*)." When Faris prepares to head back home to Ramallah, he asks for the portrait, and the man happily obliges. Only when Faris arrives back in Ramallah does he realize that the photograph belongs in the old home with its new family. He drives all the way back to Jaffa to return it. Following this encounter, Said whispers to Safiyya, Faris al-Lubda had decided to join the armed resistance.[86]

When the man removes the photograph from the wall to hand it to Faris, it leaves behind "a pale, meaningless rectangle. A disturbing void." Conversely, upon Faris's return of the portrait, the man is ecstatic to reunite with it, explaining that in its absence, "I felt a terrible emptiness when I looked at the rectangle left behind on the wall. My wife cried and my children got very upset. I regretted letting you take the picture. In the end, this man is one of us."[87] The empty case, that rectangle of slightly fresher coat of paint, manifests the time lapsed between the brother's death in the battles of 1948 and Faris's visit nearly twenty years later. As Ian Campbell poetically describes it (and with only a hint of Orientalism), the "square testifies to twenty years of wear and tear on the paint of the wall—twenty years of sunlight, of tobacco smoke, of the aroma of tasty Palestinian food—twenty years of life for the man's family." The photograph, Campbell claims, had served as a psychological talisman that facilitated repression, and its removal exposed an insufficiently addressed trauma.[88]

The relation of the rectangle to the wall, however, could also be read as a metaphorical marker of time—both the eruption of the past in the present *and* its continuous subsistence throughout. Not so much a symptom of the ineffable Real, the empty rectangle is rather the hinge between the past event and its present unfolding. The removal of Badr's portrait reveals the past all at once, allowing 1948 to burst into the present. But Badr also survives as an ongoing history, especially in little Badr, the man's son who is named after Faris's

86. Ibid., 177–78/391–92.
87. Ibid., 177/393.
88. Campbell, "Blindness to Blindness," 62–63, 71–72.

brother. Like Dov-Khaldun, who is himself metaphorized at the beginning of the novella as a photograph, the portrait is a creative metaphor that straddles two times and two temporalities.

The creative metaphor of Badr's portrait also spans two worlds. Like the dead brother himself, it stands in for a generation of fighters, for a lost brotherhood or community, but also for resistance and steadfastness (*ṣumūd*). Rather than a mechanism for avoiding confrontation with a traumatic past, the photograph may be seen as a mode of expressing—or addressing—inexpressible loss. It allows the family that stayed in Jaffa to relate to its past, as well as to those expelled. When Badr's portrait was gone, the man tells Faris, "I said to my wife that if you all wanted to reclaim him, you all would have to reclaim the house, Jaffa, us. . . . The picture doesn't solve your problem, but with respect to us, it's your bridge to us and our bridge to you all."[89] The picture thus becomes a mobile object, a conduit, between the worlds of Palestinians "of the inside" and Palestinians in the West Bank, allowing some communication between them. It does so, however, without cohering these two severed parts into an organic whole that glosses over historical differences or colonial borders.

Because their clashes engage whole contexts, Kanafani's creative metaphors are discursive rather than merely semiotic or semantic. Through Khaldun-Dov as metaphor, the context of Said and Safiyya's lives and loss—the *nakba* and its unfolding, the broader experiences of Palestinians during and following the *nakba*, and the vision of the "new Palestinian"—is brought into contact with the series of Miriam and Iphrat's lives and loss, the holocaust, the Jewish experience of this catastrophe and its aftermath, including the establishment of the State of Israel and the creation of the "new Jew." A third series unfolds between Khaldun-Dov, Palestine as memories, and Palestine as future and struggle. Badr's portrait (like Badr himself) also brings into contact whole contexts—the series of abu-Lubda's life, his loss, and the experience of Palestinians in exile; and the series of the man's life, his fighting and loss, and the experience of '48 Palestinians. A third series operates between the portrait, the wall as time, and the dead brother as loss. It is thus that the portrait serves as a bridge—a connecting metaphor that is also a metamorphosis.

What facilitates movement between these contexts is the empty case and that which is missing from it—the empty rectangle and the portrait, the missing feathers and Khaldun-Dov. Deleuze's notion of the empty case (*la case vide*) is similarly accompanied by the "object=x"—a correlated mobile object,

89. Kanafani, "Returning to Haifa," 177/393, translation modified.

always missing from its place. Both elements are points of convergence of contexts, displacing and redistributing terms, making them reverberate.[90] Empty cases—silences, absences—and all those objects missing from their places, are inexpressible phenomena around which everything in the novella turns. Kanafani's metaphors do not aim to cover over these absences by naming or explicating, by introducing new concepts that will clearly represent and define them. Instead, only by refusing conceptual speech, by never fully covering over the empty case, creative metaphors give it expression. They manifest it precisely as empty and missing, as a silence that cannot be fully delivered into speech and yet must be foregrounded. Revolutionary metaphors are therefore of the order of silence, which is required for their unique movement between different contexts, times, and temporalities.

Coda: Metaphors and The Time of Return

The exploration of time is essential to Kanafani's writing. In "Ma Tabaqqa Lakum," Kanafani made time into one of the characters, along with the human protagonists and the desert. In an earlier novella, "Rijal fi al-Shams" (Men in the Sun, 1963), time is the key antagonist: as the protagonists attempt to cross the border into Kuwait smuggled inside a sweltering water tank, it is time that they must beat in order to survive.

In "'A'id ila Ḥayfa," too, time plays a crucial role, as is suggested by the centrality of the return to the novella. But what kind of time is it? The novella is composed of fragmented moments told from different points of view, most of which take place either in 1948 or in 1967. The transitions between them are never fluent or clearly marked. The narrative proceeds in fits and breaks, leaping back and forth in time through cinematic flashbacks. It forms a disjointed net of events, where the past never neatly follows an introduction in the present. In his formative essay on post-1948 Arab prose, Edward Said linked Kanafani's episodism, that "rhythmic succession of scenes" attempting to substitute for "quasi-organic unity," with the temporality of the post-*nakba* Palestinian and Arab existence. Between the defeats of the Arab armies in 1948 and 1967 and the ongoing threat of Israeli colonialism and U.S. imperialism, between a haunting past disaster and the "specter of national fragmentation and extinction" looming over the future, the present, claims Said, becomes a paradox, an

90. As such, the empty case is a special instance of metaphor: "*its own* metaphor, and *its own* metonymy"; see Gilles Deleuze, "How Do We Recognize Structuralism?," in *The Two-Fold Thought of Deleuze and Guattari: Intersections and Animations*, trans. Charles J. Stivale and Melissa McMahon (New York: Guilford, 1998), 184.

impossibility. Kanafani's insistence on the scene is thus not merely a poetic reflection of a present crisis but also an attempt to make the present, to produce a wanting contemporaneity.[91]

In the episodic narrative of "'A'id ila Ḥayfa," the past often emerges as a local, condensed explosion in the present, a sort of disruptive event that reveals some deeper truth to be reworked. It erupts, violently and involuntarily, so that "things suddenly return, an incredible return, behind the back (*warāʿ ẓahr*) of reason and logic."[92] Similarly, when Said and Safiyya arrive in Haifa, we are told that "the memory didn't return to [Said] little by little. Instead, it rained down inside his head the way a stone wall collapses, the stones piling up, one upon another. The incidents and the events came to him suddenly and began to pile up and fill his entire being." While Said and Safiyya have been avoiding speaking of the past for twenty years, it now erupts "as though forced out by a volcano" (*kamā yandafiʿ al-burkān*) and, soon after, "sharp as a knife."[93] In these metaphorical expressions, the past is treated as a trauma or an extraordinary event and, crucially, as a moment that is complete and done, as powerful as it may be. This moment haunts the present, detaches itself from the linear march of present moments called history, and insinuates itself into the current moment, uncontrollably disruptive, like the return of the repressed.

In other moments in the novella, however, the past coincides or is entangled with the present, a coexistence that Deleuze terms "reminiscence" and regards as a metaphor in the temporal realm.[94] Such infusion of the past in the present is evident when Said drives his car in 1967 Haifa according to the topography and street names of 1948 and feels "as though he hadn't been away for twenty years." Or when, at the sight of Haifa and under the influence of his flashbacks, Said felt that "the events were mixed up, the past and present running together (*al-māḍī yatadākhal maʿ al-ḥāḍir*), both in turn jumbled up with the thoughts and illusions and imaginings and feelings of twenty successive years." Most tellingly, the omnipresent narrator recounts that Said "made the whole thing appear, to himself and to his wife, perfectly natural, as though the past twenty years had been put between two huge presses and crushed until they became a thin piece of transparent paper."[95] Expressed in figurative language, the past in these instances is not merely one moment in the

91. Edward W. Said, *Reflections on Exile and Other Essays* (Cambridge, Mass.: Harvard University Press, 2000), 47–51.

92. Kanafani, "Returning to Haifa," 158/357, translation modified.

93. Ibid., 149, 151–52/344, 346.

94. Deleuze, *Proust and Signs*, 55.

95. Kanafani, "Returning to Haifa," respectively, 152, 154, 161/345, 351, 362.

chain of events now erupting in the present. Instead, the past and the present are coextensive, the two sides of the same piece of paper. The shift between them is instantaneous, a crossing through the looking glass. While forming parts of the same sheet, they are not necessarily harmonious, coherent, or unified; they are brought together only by their clashing. Seeing 1967 Haifa through a 1948 lens, Said feels like he is not seeing Haifa as much as the Israelis are showing it to him in what constitutes nothing other than a continuation of war by other means.[96] The clash between the protagonists' memories of Haifa and the present urban scene is thus in itself part and parcel of the war.

These two configurations of narrative time reveal a key characteristic of the *nakba* and its temporality. As Elias Khoury observes, starting with Constantin Zurayk's book, *Maʿna al-Nakba* (The Meaning of the *Nakba*), published while the 1948 War was still raging, the *nakba* has been commonly perceived as a momentary event in time, delimited and completed, "a historical event that happened in the past and once for all."[97] It might be haunting the present but only in the form of a repressed memory, of a traumatic event that has nonetheless ended. For most Palestinians, however, the *nakba* is an ongoing affair, systemically manifested in the dispossession of present absentees, the refugee camps and the refusal of return, the direct occupation of Palestinian territories, the siege and attacks on Gaza, the Israeli apartheid system, and so on. Treating the *nakba* as a memory or as past history, Khoury insists, "is a way to cover up the struggle between presence and interpretation that has not stopped since 1948."[98]

The two temporal modes—the evental and the structural—are integral to Kanafani's *ishtibāk*. In his perception of clashing engagement, as Esmeir argues, "struggles are at once a part of time as potentialities," which are ongoing and embedded in a collective's history, "and also interruptive of time, carving out an opening in the present," as if new.[99] Kanafani's metaphors share this dual temporality. Badr's portrait brings together not only different worlds but also different temporal modalities. Like other creative metaphors in the novella, it is the pivot between event and structure—in this case, between the *nakba* as a historical event and the systemic ongoing *nakba*. Creative metaphors thus generate and sustain the transition not only between event and history but also between historical contingency and structure. Figures, as even one of their greatest haters had to concede, perform a unique role in structures:

96. Ibid., 151.
97. Khoury, "Rethinking the Nakba," 259.
98. Ibid., 263.
99. Esmeir, "Time of Engagement," 8–9.

metaphor and metonymy are "*the* two structural factors." Being multi-serial, they express the two available degrees of displacement, across series and within a series.[100] As the animating element of the structure, metaphors keep it from stagnating, taking the structure *post* structuralism.

The function of metaphors as the hinge between contingency and structure is the seat of their power. Metaphors, as Ricœur explains, "stand at the crossroads of two orders of consideration," combining both systematic and historical aspects. While polysemy is, strictly speaking, synchronistic, he writes, metaphors' capacity for accumulating meanings over time renders their polysemy a diachronistic fact.[101] Instead of dichotomizing their structural and historical facets—as deconstruction has done by focusing on the forever unstable difference between concepts and figures, dead systematized metaphors and living historical ones, which condition one another—metaphors should be perceived in their dual function, for they exist in time as historical constellations, both structured and contingent. Such an understanding of metaphors might allow, by contrast, for a certain intervention in their uses, specifically within and against juridico-political language. This is beautifully demonstrated by Kanafani's novella, whose narrative offers *qaḍiyya* as a new conceptual metaphor and revolutionizes the figurative conceptual meaning of "Palestine" (and "homeland"), "man" and, more implicitly, both "conflict" and "1948," giving all new life and stressing their circumscribed, contemporary, structural senses.

This chapter began by presenting the common perception of conflict as judgment, which is foundational to the current political order—the *din*, judgment, that conditions the state, *medina*—a framework that the rest of this book aims to displace and replace. Following a consideration of the pitfalls of analogies, the chapter also demonstrated how certain metaphors can be seen to affect metamorphosis, to *be* a metamorphosis. The question is no minor one: by what means might language bring about change, and how to render such transformative events ongoing without immediately absorbing them under the representational political order? The means proposed here is catachresis—a selective repetition that adds nothing new, that works through silences rather than accurate naming, and that puts contexts into productive clashes, from which a new perceptual mode, both aesthetic and epistemic, might arise. This clash is a form of engagement—it admits impact and exchange without representative (or ends-based) communication. Instead of subordinating a different discourse to one's own, it triggers change in both. While this clash might

100. Deleuze, "How Do We Recognize Structuralism?," 182, 184.
101. Ricoeur, *Rule of Metaphor*, 142.

fizzle one day, become a dead or dormant metaphor, it may still be awakened, just like Khaldun-Dov is disturbed from his dogmatic sleep. The ability to detect and create new metaphors that engage worlds in struggle in order to force a perceptual change is never—could never be—limited.

In the subsequent chapters, I present several metaphors of this kind, highlighting their structural nature without eliding their historical and geographical contingency. Lodging worlds and worldviews into one another, these conceptual metaphors entertain a clashing engagement between the contrasting conditions of possibility of various plateaus in Palestine-Israel. My hope is that these metaphorical concepts break open some hardened conceptual and perceptual molds to reconceptualize this context, however modestly, by selecting and combining existing literary works and their contexts. Claiming that *all* the upcoming figures take on the conflictual form of *ishtibāk* would be too simplistic. Yet, something of the side-by-sideness, of the noncommunicating communication, of the unresolved yet agile conflictuality of *ishtibāk*, recurs throughout. It is perhaps most pronounced when an anti-colonial humanism, such as Kanafani's neck and sword, defines the stakes. Or when the terms of the juridico-political do not press too closely on the neck. This conflictual mode is not exhausted by any of the theoretical models currently available in literary or political theory. Its exploration and nuancing are a recurrent thread running through the following pages.

2 Levaṭim

(Disorienting Dilemmas)

Hebrew literature sought, so it seems, to avoid a repetition of the biblical affair of the twelve spies[1] *. . . , so reluctant was it to mention an Arab in the Land of Israel! Instead, it restrained itself—at first, consciously, and later, out of habit—from engaging matters that violate Zionist ideology. As a result, many contradictions in the souls of the characters, observing their surroundings and the circumstances of their time, concealed themselves from view.*

—AVOTH YESHURUN ON THE RADIO, JULY 16, 1969, MY TRANSLATION

The moral dilemma introduced in Chapter 1 and faced by Miriam, one of the protagonists of Kanafani's "'A'id ila Ḥayfa," became in some ways archetypal in Israeli culture. Miriam, a holocaust survivor critical of Zionism, is so haunted by the sight of a dead Palestinian child tossed in a truck in 1948 that she wishes to extricate herself from the colonial violence of the nascent state by returning to Europe. Yet, when she is offered a Palestinian house and a Palestinian boy, both courtesy of the Jewish Agency, she remains in Palestine despite her misgivings. How might one reconcile the stark cognitive and

1. During the biblical exodus of the Israelites from Egypt, ten of the twelve spies dispatched by Moses to scout the promised land reported back that "it does flow with milk and honey" but "the people who live there are powerful, and the cities are fortified and very large. We even saw descendants of Anak there. The Amalekites live in the Negev; the Hittites, Jebusites and Amorites live in the hill country; and the Canaanites live near the sea and along the Jordan" (Nos. 13:27–29, NIV). Persuaded thus that conquering the land is impossible, the Israelites were punished with forty years of wandering through the desert.

affective dissonance between Miriam's moral objections to the Zionist project and her decision, ultimately, to participate in it?

This type of dilemma came to be known in Israel as "shooting and crying" (*yorim u-vokhim*). First gaining journalistic currency after the Six Day War as a term of abuse for repentant soldiers, it soon evolved into a discursive and literary technique that allows individuals to revel in their impeccable morals by critiquing colonial violence while partaking in it.[2] It refers specifically to the elegant moral alchemy by which combatants' lamentation of violence or expressions of empathy for their victims turn complicity into indignation and indignation into victimhood.

While its name is a product of the 1960s, this practice is as old as Zionism itself. And its use by Zionist authors has far greater implications for readers and writers alike. A paradigmatic example is the historical fiction of S. Yizhar (Yizhar Smilansky, 1916–2006)—an army officer during the 1948 War and, later, a Member of Knesset, the Israeli Parliament. His famous novellas "*Ḥirbet Ḥiz'a*" (Khirbet Khizah, 1949) and "*ha-Shavuy*" (The Prisoner, 1948) parade the inner dilemmas and tortured soul of a soldier witnessing—but never intervening in—the grotesque colonial brutalities of the 1948 War. Although Yizhar's narrators question Zionism's morality, their objections always take the form of a poetics of indecision, fashioned as an internal monologue of endless dilemmas (*levaṭim*) that never leads to action. In displacing political conflict to the psychological realm and sustaining indecision, Yizhar's torn (*mitlabeṭ*) narrator morally distances himself from the colonial project in which he participates, a project nonetheless exposed through the formal elements of the works.[3] As Hannan Hever observes, by forging a rhetorical continuum between his own voice as a public figure and that of his indecisive narrators,

2. The phrase first appeared in 1967 in response to the publication of *Śi'aḥ Loḥamim* (Combatants' Discourse)—a collection of critical testimonies of Israeli combatants who participated in the 1967 War. "Shooting and crying" was thus a pejorative term, intended to ridicule critics of a war generally regarded by the Israeli public as a swift and glorious victory.

3. Amongst these formal elements—landscape descriptions, metaphors, intertextual references—the biblical references most forcefully elucidate the unjust nature of the expulsion. The finale of *Ḥirbet Ḥiz'a* alludes to the destruction of Sodom and Gomorrah and explicitly compares the uprooting of Palestinians to the Israelites' exodus. As Elias Khoury notes, however, the biblical imagery tends to "mute" the expelled Palestinians and merge them with the landscape. By casting Palestinians as "the Jews of the Jews," moreover, Yizhar projects onto them internalized anti-Semitic assumptions, presenting them as dirty and vile, too weak to resist, and complicit in their own expulsion. See Shaul Setter, "S. Yizhar, Sipur she-lo Nigmar: 'Al Ḳol Tse'aḳa shel Ḳahal Yehudi-Falesṭini be-'Sipur Ḥirbat Ḥiz'a,'" *Ot* (Fall 2016): 191–213; Elias Khoury, "The Mirror: Imagining Justice in Palestine," *Boston Review*, July 1, 2008; Elias Khoury, "Rethinking the Nakba," *Critical Inquiry* 38, no. 2 (2012): 250–66.

Yizhar arrogated their reflexive dilemmas to himself, thereby whitewashing his decisions and actions as a Zionist politician.[4] Subversive as these melancholic quandaries may appear, then, they in fact facilitate colonization by rhetorically removing author, narrator, and reader from the realm of action.

Both as discursive practice and as literary genre, "shooting and crying" is still prevalent in Israel today.[5] More crucially, these incessant dilemmas and pestering contradictions are not limited to the moral sphere. Rather, they constitute a central structure of Zionist ideology and a systemic motor of its practice. In ways explored in this chapter, Zionism is defined by its contradictions. It is made of nothing but contradictions, looping over themselves and spinning out of control. Nothing about this self-contradictory structure should work. It appears as though it must be dialectically resolved or else risk imploding, canceling itself out.[6] Despite it all, this unsustainable contradiction is inexplicably sustained. In fact, the ideological structure of the Zionist

4. For instance, as a Knesset member, Yizhar did not support ending the martial rule to which Israel subjected '48 Palestinians until 1966. See further in Hannan Hever, "The Crisis of Responsibility in S. Yizhar's 'The Prisoner,'" in *Hebrew Literature and the 1948 War: Essays on Philology and Responsibility* (Leiden: Brill, 2019), 78–104; Hannan Hever, "Sug ha-Omets she-Ḥaser le-Samekh Yizhar," *Haaretz*, April 7, 2020, https://www.haaretz.co.il/literature/study/.premium-1.8748400. Another early literary iteration of "shooting and crying" is the poetry of Nathan Alterman (1910–70), whose tendency to "shoot and cry (and write)" Uri S. Cohen terms "empathic sadism" and describes as a dual enjoyment of violence—enjoying both an empathy for the other's suffering and a moral pity for the aggressor; Cohen, *ha-Nusaḥ ha-Biṭḥoni ve-Tarbut ha-Milḥama ha-'Ivrit* (Jerusalem: Mosad Bialiḳ, 2017), 173–212. In fact, Alterman's enjoyment of violence could be depicted as tripartite, as it also enjoys the spoils of this violence.

5. A significant example in contemporary Israeli discourse is *Shovrim Shtiḳa* (Breaking the Silence), an NGO dedicated to collecting testimonies of serving, reserve, and discharged Israeli army personnel about crimes and injustices committed by the IDF. "Shooting and crying" is also still dominant as a literary genre, such as in the novels of Amos Oz and David Grossman and in films like *Waltz with Bashir* (2008) and *Lebanon* (2007). See Gil Z. Hochberg, "From 'Shooting and Crying' to 'Shooting and Singing': Notes on the 2019 Eurovision in Israel," *Contending Modernities* (blog), May 17, 2019, https://contendingmodernities.nd.edu/global-currents/shooting-and-singing/.

6. Compare with Mahmoud Mamdani's claim that ambiguities and contradictions are the foundation of the State of Israel: "Israel is a sovereign state with no defined borders. It claims to be guided by universalistic legal principles and the rule of law, but it has no constitution, and its laws are explicitly discriminatory. It is neither a secular state nor a theocracy. It is a home to all Jews, yet its Jews are arranged hierarchically." This last contradiction—"welcoming [Mizrahi] Jews while loathing them, protecting [Mizrahi] Jews while eliminating their culture—turned out to be productive in that Mizrahim were perfectly placed to lead the Israeli settler incursion into the West Bank" (a complementary variation on this argument is presented in Chapter 5). See Mamdani's *Neither Settler nor Native: The Making and Unmaking of Permanent Minorities* (Cambridge, Mass.: Belknap, 2020), 256, 271.

project is sustained *only* through and by its contradictions. Since these paradoxes are generative for Zionism, it has no interest in resolution; it aims precisely to keep them unsettled. Such contradictions take various forms: on the liberal left, "shooting and crying" or the current protest movement (2023) defending democracy and minority rights but for Jews only; on the right, the settlement project, which accelerated illegal land grab and expanded territorial acquisition by ostensibly opposing the state's directives, thus protecting the latter's juridical integrity and democratic façade.[7] The productive failure generated by these contradictions establishes state sovereignty and guarantees the endlessness of the Zionist project.

In literature, such irreconcilable yet productive contradictions take the form of endless psychological dilemmas between opposing terms—or in Hebrew, *levaṭim*. The word is what Translation Studies scholars often term an "untranslatable," having no exact equivalent in English. The plural form of the noun *leveṭ* (never used in the singular), *levaṭim* refers to incessant dilemmas, a constant shifting back and forth between two, or several, options. The related verbal noun, *hitlabṭut*—the act of having such dilemmas, of being forever torn between opposing poles—combines the same root (*l-v-ṭ*) with a reflexive pattern, thus implying an action that is either reciprocal or performed on or for oneself. Unlike the English term "indecision," which suggests a static result, *hitlabṭut* refers to an ongoing inner process, a continuous back-and-forth movement, whose dramatic arena is the split psyche of the torn self. Paradoxically, and unlike "indecision" or "undecidability," *hitlabṭut* and *levaṭim* also imply that this endless indecision is nonetheless committed to an eventual judgment, that it is forever on its way to settling the paradox.

Early Zionist prose is saturated with such incessant psychological dilemmas. While *levaṭim* were common amongst Hebrew writers of Yizhar's generation, known as *Dor Tashaḥ* (the 1948 Generation), they were even more widespread amongst those of a previous generation, *Dor ha-Teḥiya* (the Revival Generation, 1881–1947), which featured such monumental figures as Haim Nahman Bialik (Israel's national poet, 1873–1934), Micha Yosef Berdichevsky (1865–1921), Yosef Haim Brenner (1881–1921), Uri Nissan Gnessin (1879–1913), Shaul Tchernichovsky (1875–1943), and Haim Hazaz (1898–1973), one of the youngest figures of this generation, already on the cusp of the next. Writing both in Palestine and in Eastern Europe, the authors and political thinkers of

7. For detailed discussions of the productive tensions between the Israeli state and the settlement movement, see Idith Zertal and Akiva Eldar, *Lords of the Land: The War Over Israel's Settlements in the Occupied Territories, 1967–2007* (New York: Nation, 2009); Eilat Maoz, *Ḥoḳ Ḥay: Shiṭur ve-Ribonut taḥat Kibush* (Bene Beraḳ: *ha-Ḳibuts ha-Me'uḥad*, Van Leer, 2020).

the Revival Generation laid the foundations for a modern Hebrew canon and established the coordinates of Zionist ideology. Their works were full of tensions—between the old world and modernity, religion and secularism, exile and Zionism, the collective and the individual, East and West—and often centered on the psychological torments and inner conflicts that these contradictions cultivate in the soul of a young man.[8]

Haim Hazaz, whose works will be the focus of this chapter, claimed that the Zionist readership was enthralled with the literature of his predecessors, Brenner and Berdichevsky, because "in their dilemma-ridden, soul-tormented" writing (*be-levaṭim she-lavṭu, be-ʿinuye-nefesh shelahem*) the two perfectly resonated with the tortured melancholy of the pioneering Zionist youth. According to Hazaz, Berdichevsky's style was masterful: few other writers had his genius for and unique style of indecision (*meʿaṭim lavṭu ka-mohu*) or his talent for seeing into psychological depths, for finding there the opposite of what lies on the surface. But, for Hazaz, it was Brenner who truly epitomized the ideal Hebrew author: "Tormenting himself into intricate knots of dilemmas (*nitlabeṭ ve-lavaṭ livṭe-levaṭim*)," Brenner in his extreme agonies "became a paragon of the spiritual biography of the people of Israel."[9]

Why was this poetics of indecision so prevalent in Hebrew literature and so attractive to its Zionist readership? Why would Hazaz view Brenner's literary *levaṭim* as exemplary of the "spiritual biography" of Israel, no less? This chapter suggests that *levaṭim* are in fact the particular contradictory form that animates Zionist ideology and its self-representation, especially during its early decades. I reject the notion that, by expressing a writer's personal failure to meet the Zionist ideal, such melancholic dilemmas offer a counternarrative to Zionism's success story.[10] Instead, I contend that *levaṭim*, precisely

8. These inner conflicts were often related to the theme of the rootless young fellow, common in Hebrew literature of the late nineteenth and early twentieth centuries. Literature of "the rootless" (*ha-talush*) foregrounded the crisis, loneliness, and melancholic dilemmas created by the protagonist's separation from the old world and exacerbated by his alienation from the modern one, which he nonetheless desires.

9. Haim Hazaz, *Mishpaṭ ha-Geʾula*, ed. Aviva Hazaz (Tel Aviv: ʿAm ʿOved, 1977), 22, 62–63. Brenner is so archetypical of the indecisive poetics of early Hebrew prose that his last—and, arguably, most famous—novel, *Shekhol ve-Khishalon* (Breakdown and Bereavement, 1920), was subtitled *Sefer ha-Hitlabṭut* (The Book of Indecision). On the dilemma-ridden writing of Brenner and Berdichevsky, see Hannan Hever, *Producing the Modern Hebrew Canon: Nation Building and Minority Discourse* (New York: NYU Press, 2001), 40–43. On dilemmas and ironic distance in the works of their contemporary Uri Nissan Gnessin, see Dana Olmert, "Ma Hitgala le-Gnessin be-vet Saba?," *Ot* 5 (2015): 93–108.

10. Niztan Lebovic, for instance, argues that such melancholy stems from "the gap between the Zionist language of fulfillment and the failure to realize that ideal" and thus constitutes a

in their paradoxical form and generative failures, are the load-bearing pillars of that story.

In its paradoxes, *levaṭim* is part of a broader Western tradition that struggled to reconcile liberal ideals with the colonial capitalist practices enabling their emergence. Such reconciliation was achieved not by resolving or ignoring the contradictions but through rhetorical maneuvers and literary fictions that recast empire as committed to liberal values without necessarily denying the violence it wielded in the colonies. The liberal strand of British imperialism, for instance, "proved to be rather resourceful and adaptive, to the point of co-opting fragments of anti-imperial critique to use in renewed justifications of expansion and control."[11]

Although continuous with such practices, the concept of *levaṭim* also offers its own singular mode of managing contradictions and putting them to work. The indecision of *levaṭim* aims not only to contend with liability for colonial violence but also to establish a reflexive Zionist subjectivity, one that is heroic and sovereign. While negating exilic Judaism, Zionist ideology also cannibalizes the ironic standpoint of exile, which is paradoxically combined with the logic of judgment and its historicism to generate *levaṭim*—that indecision that nonetheless demands to be resolved. A key effect of this paradox is a disorientation that takes on two forms. First, in insisting on decision, *levaṭim* become endlessly recursive, marking any attempt to overcome this failure and arrive at a clear conclusion as both futile and sublime. Second, in Hazaz's writing, these inner dilemmas *dis-Orient* his protagonist in yet another sense, extracting him from and opposing him to the Orient within and without him, thus expressing the colonial relationship of Zionism to its various Easts—Eastern Europe, Oriental Jews, Palestinians, and Palestine. These two faces of disorientation, I conclude, are in fact intertwined, as it is precisely that restless failure, along with the futile yet idealized attempt to overcome it, that christens the Zionist subject as such, allowing her to separate herself from the East and dominate it.

To clarify the structure and implications of *levaṭim*, I turn to the writing of Haim Hazaz, who made indecision the crux of his poetic system. Hazaz was

---

counternarrative to the hegemonic Zionist story. See Lebovic, *Zionism and Melancholy: The Short Life of Israel Zarchi* (Bloomington: Indiana University Press, 2019), xii.

11. Onur Ulas Ince, *Colonial Capitalism and the Dilemmas of Liberalism* (New York: Oxford University Press, 2018), 29. See also Jeanne Morefield, *Empires without Imperialism: Anglo-American Decline and the Politics of Deflection* (Oxford: Oxford University Press, 2014), on "the deflective impulse" of British and American liberalism, which aims "at drawing critical attention away from the liberal empire's illiberalism by insisting upon its fundamental character," a liberal identity that always stands (2).

born in 1898 in Sidorovichi, a small town in the Jewish Pale of Settlement in Southwestern Russia (today's Ukraine). In Kiev, Kharkiv, and Moscow, he studied informally, exploring both Russian and Hebrew literature.[12] Following the October Revolution, he left Moscow, fleeing from town to town until arriving in Constantinople in 1921. During his eighteen-month stay there he taught Hebrew to Zionists preparing to settle in Palestine and first encountered Jews of the Islamic world. Hazaz then spent a decade in Paris, composing—in Hebrew—his first prose works, which depicted the unraveling of Eastern European Jewish communities during the Russian Revolution.[13] He migrated to Mandate Palestine in 1931 and settled in Jerusalem. Influenced by Russian Romanticism and by symbolist and neo-folkist trends in Yiddish literature, Hazaz developed an interest in the "folk" traditions of various Jewish ethnic communities and in styling the "authentic Jew." He soon took up residence amongst Kurdish Jews and, a year and a half later, feeling the Kurds were not hospitable enough, moved into the Yemenite Quarter. What he presented as the exotic yet authentic lives of Yemenite Jews, based on this ethnography, occupied most of his 1940s writing, including two monumental novels—*Ya'ish* (four volumes, 1947–52) and *ha-Yoshevet ba-Ganim* (Thou That Dwellest in the Gardens, 1944).[14] In Jerusalem, Hazaz was involved in founding the Academy of the Hebrew Language and became a highly acclaimed author: he won the Bialik Prize for Literature twice (in 1942 and 1970) and was the inaugural recipient of the Israel Prize for Literature (in 1953). His prominence, however, waned over the years, and his rival and contemporary, the author Shmuel Yosef Agnon, significantly eclipsed his success.

This chapter focuses on two of Hazaz's short stories that extensively deploy a poetics of *levaṭim*, "Raḥamim ha-Sabal" (Rahamim the Porter, 1933) and "ha-Derasha" (The Sermon, 1942). Though written almost a decade apart, the works are closely related. Bookending the period of the conceptual short story in Hazaz's work, they share thematic and stylistic concerns. Both explore the Zionist migration to Palestine; both showcase fundamental conflicts—at once

12. Although they could take the final examination, Jews were prohibited from matriculating in Russian high schools. Some therefore formed informal groups of "externs" who studied together for the exams. Hazaz was part of one such group. For further details, see Warren Bargad, *Ideas in Fiction: The Works of Hayim Hazaz* (Chico, Calif.: Scholars Press, 1982), 2.

13. On Hazaz's "Revolution Stories," see Dov Sadan, *Ben din le-ḥeshbon: masot 'al sofrim u-sefarim* (Tel Aviv: Devir, 1963), 234–42; Nurit Govrin, "Sipure ha-mahapekha ke-sug sifruti," in *Me'asef: mukdash li-yetsirat Ḥayim Hazaz*, ed. Dov Sadan and Dan Laor (Jerusalem: Agudat ha-sofrim ha-'Ivrim be-Yiśra'el ve-agudat Shalem, 1978), 236–56.

14. For several years, Hazaz published his "Yemenite works" under the Yemenite pseudonym Zekharya Uzali. For Hazaz's biography, see Bargad, *Ideas in Fiction*, 1–14.

internal and external, psychological and social, that this migration has bred—largely by staging a stark affective contrast between characters; both build to an emotional crescendo, culminating in a realization achieved somewhere beyond words; and both conclude with an open, indecisive ending.[15] Taken together, the two stories reveal how Zionism, by both negating exilic Judaism and embracing it as its own irreconcilable, contradictory past, establishes itself as sovereign, discovering within itself an ideal colonial superiority over the East and the Eastern—an ability to "see beyond" it and assess its true potential.

The Zionist Negation of Exile

Hazaz's short story "ha-Derasha" presents a stuttering, frantic diatribe against Eastern European Judaism as a tradition of glorified suffering. This staged tirade demands, then paradoxically rejects, Judaism's replacement by Zionism. It is delivered by the protagonist, Yudka, in front of an unidentified committee, traditionally understood as a kibbutz tribunal of sorts. The story is indeed very much concerned with judgment, in both the redemptive sense (the Last Judgment) and the legalistic, procedural sense, as the sermon is stylized as a juridical proceeding.[16] First published in 1942 in the yearly *Lu'aḥ ha-arets* (The Land's Bulletin), "ha-Derasha" was later re-edited by Hazaz for publication in his monumental twelve-volume collected works, published in 1968.[17] I focus

15. On the similarities between the two stories, see Warren Bargad, "Realism and Myth in the Works of Hayim Hazaz: 1933–1943," in *From Agnon to Oz: Studies in Modern Hebrew Literature* (Atlanta: Scholars Press, 1996), 85–94.

16. This tribunal seems fashioned after the model of the kibbutz's "comrades' trial" (*mishpaṭ ḥaverim*). The story is brimming with juridical rhetoric and judgment metaphors. The chairman, for instance, asks Yudka a question "calmly, like a judge trained to be patient with the public," and orders him to speak as though "putting forward a verdict of sorts (*gazar ke-min gezera*)"; Haim Hazaz, "The Sermon," in *Modern Hebrew Literature*, ed. Robert Alter, trans. Ben Halpern (New York: Behrman House, 1975), 272. In Hebrew: Hazaz, "ha-Derasha," in *Sipurim Nivḥarim* (Tel-Aviv: Devir la-'Am, 1952), 185, 187 (the latter description is omitted from the English translation). On the procedural character of "ha-Derasha," see Michal Wazner, "Ze Ken la-Proṭoḳol: 'ha-Derasha' me'et Ḥayim Hazaz ke-Ṭeksṭ Proṭoḳoli," *Mikan* 9 (2008–9): 42–56.

17. The English translation, which is based on the earlier version of the story considered here, was originally published in the *Partisan Review* in 1956. In the later version, Hazaz introduced some minor linguistic corrections and compressed the story somewhat. Cuts were made almost exclusively to the narrator's text, thus foregrounding Yudka's sermon. The unspecified committee before which Yudka appears was transformed in the later version into "the committee of defense" (*va'adat ha-hagana*), intensifying the atmosphere of persecution and marking the

here on the first, fuller version of the story, with its greater patience for the narrator's voice, whose third-person narration is crucial for producing the story's core conflicts.

Hazaz was not only a forgotten author but also, paradoxically, a polemical one. His writing kindled polarized debates, eliciting "unexplained yet visceral and irritated antagonism" from readers, scholars, and critics alike.[18] The reception of "ha-Derasha" was no exception. Published just as the Jewish settlement in Palestine was first hearing of the Nazi devastation of Jewish communities in Europe, "ha-Derasha"—positing an antipathy between Zionism and Jewish exile and seemingly negating the latter—was truly provocative.[19] Debate centered on whether Yudka's views represented Hazaz's own (and whether these, in turn, should be endorsed). Scholars generally agreed, however, that "ha-Derasha" was a Zionist or proto-Canaanite manifesto fully associating Judaism with exile and demanding the complete severance of Zionism from both.[20] While recognizing Hazaz as an ironist more broadly, scholars tended to deny him any authorial distance from Yudka, thus discounting the story's ironic dimensions.[21]

---

plot as taking place in the pre-state era, when such committees existed. For a comparison of the two versions, see Iris Parush and Brakha Dalmatzky-Fischler, "'Ma Anaḥnu 'Osim Kan?' ('Od Ḳeri'a be-'ha-Derahsa')," *'Iyunim be-Teḳumat Iśra'el* 16 (2006): 4.

18. Dan Miron, *ha-Sifriyya ha-'Iṿeret: Proza Me'orevet* (Tel Aviv: Yedi'ot Aḥaronot and Ḥemed, 2005), 64–65. Translations from Hebrew scholarship, as well as from Hazaz's *Mishpaṭ ha-Ge'ula* and "Ḥavit 'Akhura," are mine. For "ha-Derasha" and "Raḥamim ha-Sabal," I use the existing English translations, with occasional modifications specified.

19. It is unclear whether this provocation was intentional. Some believe that first reports of the internment and massacres of Jews in Europe reached Palestine around the time the story was published, while others claim that Hazaz wrote "ha-Derasha" *after* news had already arrived. See Dan Laor, "me-'ha-Derasha' le-'Ketav el ha-No'ar ha-'Ivri': He'arot le-Muśag 'Shelilat ha-Gola,'" in *ha-Ma'avaḳ 'al ha-Zikaron: Masot 'al Sifrut, Ḥevra ṿe-Tarbut* (Tel Aviv: 'Am 'Oved, 2009), 232; Bargad, "Realism and Myth," 92.

20. *Kena'aniyut* (Canaanism) was a political and cultural movement established in 1939 amongst a small Jewish intellectual group in Palestine. Peaking in the 1940s, its ideology jettisoned Jewish religion, culture, and history for the sake of creating a "renewed" Hebrew people in Palestine. In abandoning both Zionism and Judaism, its members celebrated (and largely intentionally fabricated) a mythical ancient Hebrew-speaking community indigenous to the Middle East. This movement succeeded in rejecting Zionism and in connecting to the region only by displacing the East in time and ignoring its Arab population. On Canaanism and its literature, see Hever, *Producing the Modern Hebrew Canon*, 101–17. On the influence of Hazaz's "ha-Derasha" on Canaanism, see Laor, "me-'ha-Derasha' le-'Ketav el ha-No'ar ha-'Ivri.'"

21. A handful of scholars, however, such as Dan Miron and Baruch Kurzweil, have in fact criticized the simple association of Hazaz with his protagonist. Miron recruited Hazaz's entire oeuvre to demonstrate his complex relationship to Zionism, Judaism, and exile. I agree with

Hazaz was polemical in yet another sense: he tended, particularly in his earlier work, to construct his narratives as polemics, staging contradictions between two diametrically opposed positions.[22] Some see Hazaz as eventually falling on one side of the contradiction, which thus concludes in a definitive value-judgment; others regard him as a dialectician who, in Hegelian fashion, brings conflicts into synthetic resolution.[23] By focusing on his overlooked irony, I propose, by contrast, that Hazaz's poetics of indecision allows neither judgment nor synthesis.

Indeed, the contradictions at the heart of "ha-Derasha"—its *levaṭim*—remain unresolved. Presenting Zionism and Judaism as "two things directly opposite to each other," Yudka argues that Zionism, far from being continuous with exilic Judaism, spells its necessary destruction and end.[24] Zionism, Yudka claims,

> turns away from the people, is opposed to it, goes against its will and spirit, undermines it, subverts it and turns off in a different direction, to a certain distant goal. Zionism, with a small group at its head, is the nucleus of a different people. . . . Please note that: not new or restored, but *different* . . . not at all the same.[25]

But this key contradiction immediately escapes him, for he also maintains that exile is so intimately associated with Zion as to be "nearer and dearer than Jerusalem itself, more *Jewish* than Jerusalem, more ingrained, more spiritual. Far more, there's simply no comparison! Is this a paradox?"[26] It is indeed. It is *the* central paradox of Zionism, comprising as it does both the failed attempt to break with Eastern European Jewish exile and the vexed subjectivity produced by this failure.

Iris Parush and Brakha Dalmatzky-Fischler, however, that this complexity is found in nuce in "ha-Derasha" itself. See Miron, *Ḥayim Hazaz: Asupat Masot* (Merhavia: Sifriyat Po'alim, 1959), 11–26; Parush and Dalmatzky-Fischler, "'Ma Anaḥnu 'Osim Kan?,'" 2–3.

22. For instance, Hazaz's "Revolution Stories" ("Mize u-Mize," 1923; "Pirḳe Mahapekha," 1924; "Shemu'el Franḳfurṭer," 1925) all stage a conflict within the Jewish community between the older religious generation and the younger revolutionary one; "'Ashir ṿa-Rash Nifgeshu" (1927) contrasts a local, wealthy, and languid Sephardi Jew with a poor Ashkenazi Jewish refugee; both "Harat-'Olam" and "Ḥavit 'Akhura" (1937) pose a conflict between the enthusiastically Zionist Eastern European Moroshke and the German-Jewish, indifferent, and petit-bourgeois Hirschfelds.

23. Sadan, *Ben Din le-Ḥeshbon*, 252; Reuven Tsur, "Ḳeri'a be-'Raḥamim,'" in *Me'asef: Muḳdash li-Yetsirat Ḥayim Hazaz*, ed. Dov Sadan and Dan Laor (Jerusalem: Agudat ha-Sofrim ha-'Ivrim be-Yiśra'el ṿe-Agudat Shalem, 1978), 260.

24. Hazaz, "The Sermon," 283–84.

25. Ibid., 285.

26. Ibid., 277/191, translation modified.

How paradoxical. Or ironic? Even as Zionist thinkers emphasize "Judaism" to justify the demand for a Jewish state, they seemingly mean the exact opposite: an entirely new people, a thoroughly non-Jewish state—"no continuity but a break, the opposite of what was before."[27] Yet, Zionism, as Jewish nationalism, has no other pretext: it is a claim for statehood thoroughly conditioned by Judaism as both a (secularized) religion and a (European) history—the religion and history, that is, of the "small group at its head."[28]

The reason Yudka cites for his claim that exilic Judaism must be destroyed and replaced by Zionism is the former's failure of agency: it has "no glory or action, no heroes and conquerors . . . , no rulers and masters of their [own] fate." Jewish history, Yudka asserts, is made up entirely of "oppression, defamation, persecution, and martyrdom and again and again and again, without end."[29] This "Jewish history"—by which he refers in fact only to the past of Europe's Jews, particularly in its Eastern periphery—is not only repetitive and tedious but also utterly passive, imposed by others rather than self-forged. In Yudka's telling, which conjures long-standing anti-Semitic associations of Jews with physical, intellectual, and moral degeneration, Jews are categorically weak and effeminate, having no hand in determining their own fate, only "a special talent for corruption and decay."[30]

In rejecting Jewish history, Yudka parrots the familiar refrain of the Zionist "negation of exile" (*shelilat ha-galut* or *shelilat ha-gola*). This doctrine was foundational to early Zionism and still shapes Israeli historical, political, and cultural consciousness today. It calls for the elimination of all aspects of Judaism allied with diasporic life, such as the Yiddish language and Jewish religion, "intellectualism" and certain professions, and the multilingual, diverse cultures of exile. Out of this erasure, a monolithic new "Hebrew" or "Sabra Jew" was constructed in Palestine, imagined as secular and principled, brawny rather than brainy, engaged in agricultural work and self-defense, speaking Hebrew and only Hebrew—in short, opposed to the "diasporic Jew" in every respect. In this internalized anti-Semitic framework, exile was a pathological condition and its eradication a necessary step toward the normalization and liberation of the Jewish people—an attempt "to set ablaze all that is putrid

27. Ibid., 286.

28. Even if nationalism is always based on secularized theology—for, as Carl Schmitt famously argued, "all significant concepts of the modern theory of the state are secularized theological concepts"—the secularized theology of Zionism has its own nuances, explored here. See Schmitt, *Political Theology: Four Chapters on the Concept of Sovereignty*, trans. George Schwab (Chicago: University of Chicago Press, 2010), 36.

29. Hazaz, "The Sermon," 275.

30. Ibid., 274–75.

and cure all that is anguished."[31] Like Yudka's sermon, this doctrine presented exilic history as a time held in abeyance, an era of nonexistence and passive waiting—during which Palestine, too, was merely waiting—stretching from the ancient sovereign Jewish communities of the Bible to the modern "reestablishment" of a Jewish state.[32]

The confrontation staged in the story appears at first as clear and stable: the Zionist Yudka against the Kibbutz leaders, who are criticized for their presumed attachment to exilic Judaism. Yudka's Zionist rejection of Judaism, however, is immediately complicated and undercut by his stereotypically Jewish character. Already his name—a Yiddish diminutive of the name "Yehudah" and thus of Judaism itself[33]—positions him on the side of Judaism. What he delivers is not a speech (*ne'um*) but a sermon (*derasha*), a traditional religious Jewish genre. The contrasting characterizations of the committee members and Yudka, moreover, perfectly correspond to the Zionist stereotypes of the "new Jew" and the "exilic Jew" respectively: they are "all clean-cut and positive, like captains and heroes in council," masculine and healthy, while Yudka is restless and terrified, "parting his lips in an injured smile, faint and sickly," delivering his sermon in a state of mental and physical deterioration. His words are met with derision, in the midst of which we learn that one of the committee members has cuckolded him.[34] And, on top of it all, Yudka is also an intellectual—quoting from the Bible and Rabbinic literature, raising doubts and questions like a skeptic, and conducting long theoretical inquiries in public.[35] This "intellectualism" elicits contempt from

31. "Le-laheṭ et kol ha-raḳuv ule-rape et kol ha-daṿuy"; Yonatan Ratosh, as quoted in Laor, "me-'ha-Derasha' le-'Ketav el ha-No'ar ha-'Ivri,'" 241.

32. For an elaborate critical engagement with the "negation of exile" paradigm, see Amnon Raz-Krakotzkin's seminal essay "Exile within Sovereignty: A Critique of 'The Negation of Exile' in Israeli Culture," in *The Scaffolding of Sovereignty: Global and Aesthetic Perspectives on the History of a Concept*, ed. Zvi Ben-Dor Benite, Stefanos Geroulanos, and Nicole Jerr (New York: Columbia University Press, 2017), 393–420.

33. "Yehudah" is the Hebrew name of both Judah—the son of Jacob and the tribe he fathered—and Judea, the geographic region and the kingdom of that tribe, considered the "origin" of the Jews. At a minimum, "Yehudah" (Judah/Judea) is the etymological origin of *yehudim* (Hebrew for "Jews") and of *Jews* and its various European cognates.

34. Hazaz, "The Sermon," 271–73.

35. In constructing a supposedly muscular and healthy Jewish body, Zionism erased a long history of learning and erudition and reclaimed Jewish honor only by "understanding the Jewish past just as Europeans did, as deformed and oriental. In this discourse, becoming European depended on leaving Europe and the history of penury, supposed effeminacy, intellectualism, and all else that was linked with exile." See Sherene Seikaly and Max Ajl, "Of Europe: Zionism and the Jewish Other," in *Europe after Derrida: Crisis and Potentiality*, ed. Agnes Czajka and

the committee members, who ridicule him for "philosophizing," telling him he belongs in the university with the intellectuals of *Brit Shalom*.[36] Because this manufactured dichotomy between "old" and "new" Jews reproduces European notions, it bears the impress of the traditional anti-Semitic opposition between Jews and Gentiles. In fact, Yudka uses the same words (*pur'anut, yisurim*) to convey both his humiliation at the hands of the committee and Jewish suffering in exile.[37]

Yudka's anti-Jewish, prosecuting, Zionist statements and his depiction as a persecuted Jew are thus so tightly interwoven as to form a paradoxical knot rather than a simple contradiction. The entire sermon is staged as an attempt to untangle this knot—to comprehend what Zionism is and thereby sever it from Judaism. Yet the attempt is beset throughout by layers of paradoxical contradictions. The ambiguities of the opening is a case in point:

> Yudka was no speaker. He didn't make public addresses. . . . So he was considered a man whose strength was not in self-expression. And even though he was not just as he was considered to be, his reputation had its effect. It became second nature to him [*signon ya-ṭeva'*, style and nature], so that he quite forgot how to open his mouth in public and say something in proper form.[38]

The narrator distinguishes between perceptions of Yudka and his true nature, only to blur that distinction as the former steals over and transforms the latter. On the occasion of the sermon, however, Yudka sheds this second nature and acquired reticence to deliver a long, rambling, polemical speech in public. "I should have remained completely silent," says Yudka at the outset. "Do you comprehend what it means to speak up when one is supposed to be silent?"

Bora Isyar (Edinburgh: Edinburgh University Press, 2014), 128. Importantly, both anti-Semitic representations of Jewish difference and Jewish responses that countered them (such as Zionism and *Wissenschaft des Judentums*), "were, in essence, arguing over norms of manliness" even while they "disagreed—and profoundly—as to whether or not Jews fulfilled these norms." Later Zionist developments, such as the idealized "muscle Jew," suggest an overturning, and thus an implicit acceptance of the same logic. See Daniel Boyarin, Daniel Itzkovitz, and Ann Pellegrini, eds., *Queer Theory and the Jewish Question* (New York: Columbia University Press, 2003), 2–3.

36. Hazaz, "The Sermon," 284. By mentioning *Brit Shalom*—a failed movement of binational cultural Zionism led by such luminaries as Hugo Bergmann, Martin Buber, Gershom Scholem, and later, Hannah Arendt—the text discloses the existence of other political possibilities at the time, even within Zionism and on its margins.

37. Hazaz, "ha-Derasha," 186–87, 195.

38. Hazaz, "The Sermon," 271/184.

he asks the committee, soliciting acknowledgment of his internal conflict. "But I must speak!"[39]

Levaṭim, as encapsulated in Yudka's statement, construct an irresolvable contradiction that nonetheless demands to be settled. They postulate a stable subject, with a knowable intention that lurks "behind" her words and ideas, thus allowing her to debate between them, as well as a stable link between signifier and signified, whose differences do not hinder decryption. *Derasha*, the Hebrew term for "sermon" and the title of this story, is related to *derash* and *midrash*—to the act and tradition of interpretation, respectively. Since the Jewish exile of the first century, *derasha* has been a pillar of Jewish liturgy. It is a public retelling and reexplanation of the weekly Torah portion—or of Prophetic stories or Midrashic conundrums—whose intertextual interpretative techniques range from direct translation and exposition to tangential parables and moral exhortations. This genre is associated with exile, religious practice, and a long Jewish tradition of cyclical intertextuality. Classifying Yudka's rant against Jewish history as a *derasha* is thus richly ironic. It frames Yudka's rhetoric squarely within the very tradition it indicts, even suggesting, by the implied affiliation with exegesis, that its quarry is as elusive, as dappled with doubts and mysteries, as sacred texts, however slapstick the pursuit. "I don't understand anything at all," Yudka declares. "It's been years since I've understood. . . . I just want to know: what are we doing here?" The whole sermon is thus posited as an attempt to understand, to know, to interpret—an attempt foiled on all sides by stammering qualifications.

Finally, after much hesitation, Yudka begins. He opens not by making a statement, but rather by declaring *what he wishes or intends* to say:

> I want to state . . . that I'm opposed to Jewish history. . . . I have no respect for Jewish history! . . . "Respect" is really not the right word, but rather what I said before, I'm opposed to it! . . . I'm opposed to it, I don't recognize it. It doesn't exist for me! What's more, I don't respect it, although "respect" is not the right word still I don't respect it. . . . I don't respect it at all! But the main thing is, I'm opposed to it. What I mean is, I don't accept it![40]

The more unequivocal the stance he strives for, the more clarity and eloquence elude him, and the more the committee laughs. Through hyperbolic,

39. Ibid., 272/185, translation modified.

40. Yudka continues further: "Not a single point, not a line, not a dot. Nothing, nothing . . . nothing at all! Will you believe me? Will you believe me? You can't even imagine how I'm opposed to it, how I reject it, and how . . . how . . . I don't respect it!'"; Ibid., 272–74/185–86, translation modified.

intensifying expressions of objection Yudka's rhetoric strives to stabilize and refine itself in an endless asymptotic ascent toward some grounding principle. His attempts to emphasize just how absolute his negation is, to be as loyal as possible to what he *really* means, only serve to undermine his claim, betraying his own suspicion that this negation cannot ever be fully realized. The goal of conclusively negating exilic Judaism is as doomed as his quest for comprehension. In losing control of his words, Yudka appears as a failed subject, not quite up to the task he undertook. His exaggerated conviction quickly turns into indecision as he begins to entertain the opposite position, like a boxer swinging so hard he does an about-face.

Yet, the failure proves highly generative. Yudka's *levaṭim*, his conflicted musings about the meaning and implications of Zionism for Judaism, are in fact the lip service paid by Hazaz and his literary milieu in exchange for continuing the Zionist project. Having delegated the psychological confrontation with these issues to their protagonists, they are free to carry on with colonization.

Moreover, it is precisely this gap between Yudka's intention and his words that constitutes him as a (modern, Western, Zionist) literary subject, complete with psychological depth. By separating a speaker from her words, intention from expressions, the indecision of *levaṭim* spatializes the text, staging it as a specular scene in which an authoring subject stands behind her expressions or, alternatively, hovers above them. As such, *levaṭim* stress agency, the willful act of an author, the intentionality that allows a subject to differ from her language and thus produces her control over it. It is only once such differences appear within the self and it may start making comparative judgments, hesitating between one option and another, that it becomes possible to speak of a transcendental self that "stands above any of its particular experiences and toward which any particular self is always underway." This topological construction of the self is, according to Paul de Man, the very structure of irony.[41] But Yudka refuses to leave it at that, to accept the "free play" of indecision that the ironic speaker enjoys. He adamantly seeks a conclusive judgment, a final word, on the nature of Zionism. It is this resolve—to fathom

41. Paul de Man, "The Concept of Irony," in *Aesthetic Ideology*, ed. Andrzej Warminski (Minneapolis: University of Minnesota Press, 1996), 175. The strong link between irony and subjectivity has long been noted. A common definition of irony—irony as a figure of speech—explains it precisely as the gap between intention and words, which divides the self and generates those specular structures within it. Søren Kierkegaard, for instance, sees Socratic irony as producing interiority itself—a self that transcends any of its specific expressions—and therefore as the very first appearance of subjectivity in world history; Kierkegaard, *The Concept of Irony/Schelling Lecture Notes: Kierkegaard's Writings*, trans. Howard V. Hong and Edna H. Hong, repr. ed. (Princeton, N.J.: Princeton University Press, 1992), 2:264.

what he truly means, to aim for a decision within the indecision—that separates the Zionist subjectivity of *levaṭim* from the (imagined) exilic position of pure irony.

Returning to History

Hebrew prose of Hazaz's period is often seen as fashioning a universal subject through "well-rounded," deep characters with plausible, universal traits.[42] By welding ironic indecision to a commitment to judgment, however, this Zionist literary subject has far more dramatic qualities and consequences. It constructs Jewish exile as pure indecision (or pure irony), rejecting it only to reintroduce it as Zionism's constitutive failure. In *levaṭim*, the efforts to overcome the failure of decision builds up this subject as heroic and as dominant over the East. Importantly, the bid to bring the destabilizing power of Jewish exile into the juridico-political realm of decisive judgment commits Zionism to a "return to history"—a particular form of historicism that posits Zionism as secularized redemption: both the end of time and its origin.

While Yudka's indecision, his *levaṭim*, is committed to a conclusive truth, he portrays exilic Judaism as pure indecision, completely indifferent to it. Lamenting the absence of agency in Jewish history, he depicts Jews as not only accepting and enduring suffering but longing for it. This longing is based on "the myth of the Messiah," he says, which is at once a wild fantasy (*hazaya*, "hallucination"; later: *agada*, "myth" or "fiction") and a necessary one, an absolutely calculated vision, with a practical purpose. Binding themselves to this ideal, he argues, Jewish people are freed from the obligation to actively better their situation: since redemption will come "not by their own will or their own act, but from Heaven," they "have nothing to do but sit and wait for his coming. In fact, it is forbidden to get involved in the whole matter, to force the end. Forbidden!"[43] Ironic indecision thus produces not only the passivity of diasporic Jews but also their innocence; nothing happens by their own hands.[44]

42. Hever, *Producing the Modern Hebrew Canon*, 40–43.

43. Hazaz, "The Sermon," 279.

44. This irony has its early resonances in Jewish scripture. The biblical narrator makes extensive use of ironic omissions and silences, as Menahem Perry and Meir Sternberg demonstrate by reading the biblical story of King David's murder of Uriah. By concealing their motivating intentions, deeds that appear valiant at first are later revealed as unjust ("praise to blame") and vice versa. Like the modern practice of "shooting and crying," irony serves the biblical narrator to manufacture innocence: hinting at two opposed interpretative possibilities, the narrator outsources the work of judgment to the reader. While this practice is quite understandable as a preemptive mode of self-defense when accusing a mythological king of murder, its meaning

Considering "true" history as composed of "bold deeds, heroes," and "great fighters," Yudka finds their passivity to render Jews completely outside history.[45] But the myth of the Messiah turns out to be more complex: skeptical and practical to a fault, diasporic Jews, Yudka claims, even as they believe in the Messiah fantasy with "the mad and burning faith of all the heart and all the soul," somewhere "in the secrecy of their hearts . . . deep down in some hidden fold . . . somewhat they don't believe." In Yudka's telling this stance is less one of non-commitment than of purposeful ambiguity: a "deliberate intent [*kayana*] . . . not to be saved, not ever to go back to the land of their fathers."[46] This commitment to avoiding redemption while believing in it takes the form of pure indecision, with its irresolvable contradictions.

By insisting that Jews both believe and do not believe in the Messiah, by painting exilic Judaism as ironic, its indecision both pure and intentional, Yudka reinvests it in fact with the very subjectivity and agency he declared it to lack. The Jewish people thus become a nation like any other, with true agents and intentional deeds, and Yudka's claim that it has no real history is undermined. And yet—as Yudka suggests when he stresses its radical refusal to settle—not *quite* like any other. Jewish attachment to the paradoxical Messianic myth has motivations beyond the desire for innocence. Why wish for redemption when "power has its limits but there is no limit or end to our suffering (*sevel*, also "endurance")? By willing to endure, Eastern European Jews gain the ability to negate and scorn all actual power, because power must materialize in limited forms whereas their passivity is limitless. Thanks to this love of suffering, Yudka claims, the Jewish people can say, "You shall not conquer us, nor break us, nor destroy us! . . . The more we are oppressed, the greater we grow."[47]

Nihilistic as this passivity might seem, it also constitutes, for Yudka, the "eternal creation" of the Jewish people, without which "they would finally have to go right back to Palestine or somehow or other pass on out of the world."[48] The kernel of disbelief within perfect faith allows for the perpetuation of exile and keeps it from stagnating (in the form of a nation-state) or dissipating—the two options that Yudka, as a Zionist, is capable of imagining. This stance

changes drastically when performed by a sovereign hegemon. See Perry and Sternberg, "The King through Ironic Eyes: Biblical Narrative and the Literary Reading Process," *Poetics Today* 7, no. 2 (1986): 275–322.

45. Hazaz, "The Sermon," 274–75.

46. Ibid., 280, 282.

47. Ibid., 277.

48. Ibid., 279.

is negative in its repudiation of anything constructive, of taking political action; infinite in its negation not of this or that aspect of actuality but its entirety; and absolute in that the Messianic redemption, the ideal guiding its negation, does not (yet) exist. This passive waiting for a Messiah who shall not come perpetuates Jewish externality to history understood as the realm of political action. By linking an ideal with an indifference to its attainment, exilic indecision becomes the pure virtual: elevated above actuality, it defies all present limitations and enjoys boundless possibilities. Aligning with Søren Kierkegaard's definition of "pure irony" as "infinite absolute negativity," it combines a commitment to the absolute with its limitless negation—with an awareness of its untenability—becoming a nihilistic force far superior to any actual power in the world.[49] Exile in "ha-Derasha" partakes of this force in its total and vigorous perpetual motion, which permeates Hazaz's oeuvre. This thematic and narrative principle is, according to Dan Miron, a major innovation of Hazaz's work and the fulcrum of his literary system. It is a constant movement in time and space that only exile allows and even necessitates and that only the thresholds of destruction and redemption justify. A people that settles in a land produces a stationary poetics and loses the capacity for thinking of others or elsewheres.[50]

The infinite ironic deferral of exile in Hazaz's work and the preoccupation with paradoxes in *levaṭim* call to mind all that ink spilt in twentieth-century literary theory on ambiguity, aporia, and indecision. Opposing an earlier ideal of univocal signification, deconstruction celebrated undecidability, generalizing it to characterize the conditions of possibility of language, presenting it as either inevitable and ontological or productive, even liberating: that crack in everything through which the light gets in. This productive, liberatory power was then conferred upon the reader facing the polysemy of the text.

In *levaṭim*, by contrast, the Romantic free play of language is yoked to that older ideal of univocal signification, and it is this dialectic relation that produces their imperial power. In other words, Zionist *levaṭim* appropriate the pure indecision of exile—with its critical innocence, nihilistic passivity, and ironic possibilities—and welds it to an insistence on judgment, a commitment to history as the progression of heroic deeds and intentional decisions. While deconstruction centers on the text's production of aporias for the reader (and thus on irony), *levaṭim* shift the focus to the protagonist's indecision, thematized as

49. Socratic irony, according to Kierkegaard, lies in the constant search for a transcendental Idea—a search whose end point is forever deferred and only given negatively; *Concept of Irony*, 26.

50. Miron, *ha-Sifriyya ha-ʿIẓeret*, 53, 64.

elicited by the real-life demands of judgment. The resulting power accrues not to the reader but to the author and his milieu. That power, moreover, however subversive when vested in a persecuted, peripatetic minority, becomes oppressive once this collective is settled as sovereign on others' lands.

Yudka raises his own questions about the effects of ending perpetual exilic indecision with the final judgment, the fiat, of state founding:

> But what if [diaspora Jews] really have something to fear? What if it's true that Judaism can manage to survive in Exile, but here, in the Land of Israel, it's doubtful? . . . What if this country is fated to take the place of religion, if it's a grave danger to the survival of the people, if it replaces an enduring center with a transient one, a solid foundation with a vain and empty foundation? And what if the Land of Israel is a stumbling block and a catastrophe, if it's the end and finish of everything?[51]

The danger of being "redeemed" from exile by Zionism, Yudka is painfully aware, is, in Miron's words, a "fall from the sublimity of time to the lowliness of place."[52] Yudka describes exilic temporality as "a chronicle of a congregation" (*pinḳas shel ḳehila*)—a form of petty record-keeping, accumulating on the page almost statically, with little differentiation between periods and generations—which he explicitly contrasts with history proper.[53] This temporality is time unto itself, condensed in a single moment. What the pure indecision of Jewish exile refuses is, in Walter Benjamin's famous terms, the homogeneous, linear, and empty time of historicism, which produces an "eternal image" of the past while causally linking events to one another, running them in sequence through the historian's fingers "like the beads of a rosary." Instead, it adopts an immanent conception of "the time of the now," laced with shards of "messianic time"—"messianic" not because eschatological but because it constitutes a redemptive, "revolutionary chance in the fight for the oppressed past."[54]

If ironic exilic indecision is the pure virtual of infinite possibilities, then Zionism, as a conclusive judgment, is their realization, the establishment of a new set of rules that halts negative freedom by tying it to historicism. Yudka

51. Hazaz, "The Sermon," 282.

52. Miron, *ha-Sifriyya ha-'Iṿeret*, 64.

53. Hazaz, "The Sermon," 286/201.

54. Walter Benjamin, "Theses on the Philosophy of History," in *Illuminations: Essays and Reflections*, ed. Hannah Arendt, trans. Harry Zohn (New York: Harcourt, Brace & World, 1968), 262–63.

recognizes the invidiousness of this transaction, sacrificing the infinite for the sake of a transient polity built on an "empty foundation." But his rant against it also smuggles in the Zionist solution for this downfall, a clever compensatory offset. As secularized redemption—equating "to be saved" with "to go back to the land of their fathers"—Zionism positions itself as that once asymptotic absolute toward which exilic irony had always aspired, only in a negated, detheologized form. Realized as a specific actuality, it not only terminates the motion of infinite possibilities but comes to comprise them. This secularized redemption thus arrogates to itself both the status of an ideal and the curve ascending toward its realization. Exilic indecision becomes Zionism's conquered past, a disavowed past that brings Zionism back into the realm of history by furnishing the materials for its historical narrative.

The indecisive decisionism of Zionism, here termed *levaṭim*, divides the self hierarchically into a material, past self that is failed, indecisive, and unaware of its inauthentic existence and a transcendental self that is fully aware of the paradox (even if unable to escape it).[55] By denigrating exile and positing it as Zionism's mystified, failed, past self, the practice of *levaṭim* not only inserts Zionism into history but also positions it as history's very summation. Indeed, Zionist *levaṭim* are haunted by an unreachable finality, for only the retrospective viewpoint of the "end of time" allows true demystification and conclusive judgment. Their insistence on solving ironic indecision demands judgment from an impossible locus—standing at the end of history or soaring high above it. Their viewpoint is thus not simply historicist: the linear progression of homogeneous time. It is the viewpoint of the totality of history. In this proleptic view, the past is not only perceived as a mystified time and therefore negated; it is also sublated in a present that considers itself a finality, an ideal that had always already guided the past and thus necessitates and justifies its own continuity.

Because Zionism, like Yudka, perceived exile as outside history, it adopted this proleptic historicism. It figured Jewish "normalization"—transforming the Jewish people into a sovereign nation through a "return" to the Land—as both a "return to history" and history's consummation. Ironically, the price of this "return to history" was the negation of Jewish history, for Zionism returned to a Christian concept of history as a teleological advancement toward redemption.[56]

55. Cf. Paul de Man, "The Rhetoric of Temporality," in *Blindness and Insight: Essays in the Rhetoric of Contemporary Criticism*, 2nd ed., rev. (Minneapolis: University of Minnesota Press, 1983), 222.

56. As Raz-Krakotzkin contends, in negating its exilic past, Zionism became "the ultimate conclusion of history." It thus also obscured the diverse histories of Jews across the globe, as well as the history of Palestine; Raz-Krakotzkin, "Exile, History and the Nationalization of

This Christian historicism, as Amnon Raz-Krakotzkin shows, considered Jews' exile an exit from history, resulting from their rejection of the Gospel. Their perception as being external to history persisted in secularized form through the Enlightenment and served, together with their alleged Oriental nature, to justify their integration. The Zionist embrace of this concept of history therefore has substantial and ironic implications. It meant accepting the very dogma whose rejection had previously defined Jewish identity; it meant a modern Jewish identity that largely secularized Christianity rather than Judaism; it meant adopting the historical logic that, in Europe, served to exclude Jews as the Orient; and it meant Zionism succeeding in defining itself as European only by migrating to the Orient and serving as a bastion against it, thus rendering itself forever alien and hostile to its surroundings.[57] Thanks to the Zionist acceptance of a Western idea of history, Eastern European Jews have been *dis-Oriented*: transformed into Occidentals but only by leaving the West to become its frontline in the East.

Zionism as a mode of assimilation into European culture—and the Jewish dis-Orientation that results—is the subject of one of Yudka's many digressions:

> It's well known that we're all ashamed to speak Yiddish, as though it were some sort of disgrace. . . . But Hebrew, and none other than Sephardic Hebrew, strange and foreign as it is, we speak boldly, with a kind of pride and vanity, even though it is not as easy and natural as Yiddish, and even though it hasn't the vitality, the sharp edge and healthy vigor of our folk language. . . . In the same way, we are ashamed to be called by the ordinary, customary Jewish names, but we are proud to name ourselves, say, Arzieli or Avnieli. . . . We had the same kind of thing before, it's the way of assimilationists. There it is understandable, we were living among strangers, people who were different and hostile, and we had to hide, to dissimulate, to be lost to sight, to appear different from what we really were. But here? Aren't we among our own, all to ourselves, with no need for shame, or for hiding, or anyone to hide from?[58]

In the new habit of Hebraizing "too Jewish" names, Yudka hears the echo of diasporic assimilationist practices, likening Zionism to European cultures that have previously rejected (unassimilated) Jews. Yudka's refusal to acknowledge

Jewish Memory: Some Reflections on the Zionist Notion of History and Return," *Journal of Levantine Studies* 3, no. 2 (Winter 2013): 48, 58–59.

57. Ibid., 38–39.

58. Hazaz, "The Sermon," 285–86, translation modified.

the existence of other people living in the land ("Aren't we among our own, all to ourselves . . . ?") melds with his scorn for Sephardi pronunciation to reveal the three-point dis-Orientation through which Zionist assimilation was achieved: self-denial of anything Eastern European, externalized in scornful rejection of local Sephardi Jews and in the disappearance of indigenous Palestinians.[59]

Zionism adopted the Christian concept of the "end of history" as a Jewish return—to the church but also to the "shared source" of Judaism and Christianity, to Palestine.[60] In negating exile, Zionism sought to discard the entirety of Jewish history *except* the biblical myth, used in its secularized and nationalist form to justify the colonialization of Palestine. In taking this myth out of history and making it trans-historical or über-historical, Zionism effectively eternalized it. More specifically, it projected the unreachable anteriority of an imagined origin onto the (now incarnated) "end of time," so that the ideal actualized by Zionism is imagined as its very foundation. Zionism is thus both the beginning and the end, the alpha and the omega, the first and second coming that frame Christian eschatology. This Jewish return to history turns out to be not only Christian but a thoroughly ahistorical endeavor: precisely because Zionism negates exile—presenting it as an inauthentic, indecisive time—its own history becomes an empty frame, historiographic bookending. In their commitment to judgment, Zionist *levaṭim* emerge as an ironic search for an eternal, absolute Ideal, conducted however without the recognition of and exilic indifference toward the structural impossibility of its attainment. This impossibility nonetheless haunts Zionism as its own tragic irony. Since the "negation of exile" is never achieved in full, since some indecision always remains, Zionism is compelled eternally and hyperbolically to repeat this negation, with its disorienting vertigo ("I don't respect it!").

59. Hazaz explicitly saw Zionism as the conclusion of both Christianity and Europe: Christianity, "the storm that came out of Jerusalem two thousand years ago" and passed all throughout Europe, is now, through Zionism, finally "returning to its origin, to Jerusalem." In his story "Harat-'Olam" (The World's Conception), the protagonist Moroshke voices similar ideas, claiming that Jews are not only its origin but also Europe in its totality and universality, while the nations of Europe are merely pseudo-European. Moroshke asserts, "We here are remnants of Europe, its relics, a small sect of Europe in the Land of Israel, in the world's abode, in the laboratory for the world's creation and amendment. . . . Here, something is coming into being, erupting . . . a passing of the baton . . . the world's conception (*harat-'olam*)." That slight disbelief in the Messiah's arrival and the attendant "love of suffering" in "ha-Derasha" now appear as a Christian attitude, whose secularization in Zionist redemption might indeed be considered "the height of Christianity"; Hazaz, *Mishpaṭ ha-Ge'ula*, 37, 169; Hazaz, "Harat-'Olam," in *Avanim Rotḥot* (Tel-Aviv: 'Am 'Oved, 1965), 149–51.

60. Raz-Krakotzkin, "Exile," 48.

Disorientation and Overcoming

Fusing exilic ironic undecidability with the demands of judgment, *levaṭim* escape neither and transfigure both. If Zionism associates exile with pure indecision, then its own *levaṭim* become tied to the romanticist "form of the paradox" and its tragic melancholy. And while judgment (per Chapter 1) may be understood as demanding a decision between opposing sides in line with Kant's determinative judgment, then perhaps *levaṭim* might be conceived in reference to the aesthetic judgment of the sublime. Combining an opening position of failure—exilic undecidability perceived through neo-Romantic tropes of decadence—with an aspiration toward conclusive judgment and decisive historical actions, Zionist *levaṭim* become disoriented. Despite and through this disorientation, in the sublime combination of failure and calling, Zionism finds a "supersensible" power that elevates it over and allows it to conquer the natural world—and, specifically, the East—by seeing beyond its manifest façade and into its latent possibilities.

First, then, the indecision of Zionist *levaṭim* has failure as its precondition. While the "pure irony" of exile enjoys the impossibility of judgment,[61] the disjunctive structure of *levaṭim* exacts a judgment. The procedure of *levaṭim* differs from that of judgment, however, in its structural frustration of the moment of decision. Demanding judgment while rendering it impossible, *levaṭim* become endless and dizzying. In Romantic thought, the infinite back-and-forth motion between undecidable interpretations leads to a vertigo (*Schwindel*, according to Schlegel) or, to an "unrelieved *vertige*, dizziness to the point of madness."[62]

In "ha-Derasha," this vertiginous structure makes Yudka lose his senses, particularly his sense of direction. Discussing the Jewish refusal of redemption, he "really looked lost. He seemed for a moment to have forgotten himself completely, and not know where he was." Later, he is "half-paralyzed," looking "from one to another in a sort of driven frenzy." Realizing the return to the land means the end of the Jewish people, Yudka is completely bewildered: "All at once his words ran together and his voice broke and sputtered with

61. Quintilian distinguished between irony as a figure of speech, understood as the opposition between intention and words, and irony as a trope, which substitutes one word for another to which it is opposed. For Friedrich Schlegel, irony as a trope is "the form of the paradox"—an exclusive disjunction, an either/or relation between terms linked only by the ironic statement itself. See Quintilian, *The Orator's Education*, ed. D. A. Russell, vols. III, IV, Loeb Classical Library 124–27, 494 (Cambridge, Mass.: Harvard University Press, 2002), 58–61; Schlegel, *Philosophical Fragments*, trans. Peter Firchow (Minneapolis: University of Minnesota Press, 1991), 6.

62. Schlegel, *Philosophical Fragments*, 15; de Man, "Rhetoric of Temporality," 215.

feeling, his eyes flickered to and fro like one who doesn't know which way to go."[63] By the end, even the committee members are disoriented: "As if uprooted and displaced, they seemed still hanging in the air in mid-passage."[64] What is this vertigo, this disorientation, that befalls Yudka? In his attempts to understand, to posit Zionism as somehow above the paradox, Yudka struggles to find a higher principle or universal law that would orient his judgment. This repetitive search for a meta-discursive point from which to judge, positioned *above* discourse, is frequent in discussions of irony. Failing ever to establish a stable Archimedean point for judgment, this effort becomes endlessly recursive.[65]

While this failure sounds tragic, it is in fact key to the productive force of *levaṭim* and to its engineering of power relations. It is, in this way, perhaps *all too tragic*. After all, is the tragic hero ever constituted other than through failure and incomprehension? Could Oedipus ever become Oedipus without striving and failing to escape his destiny? It is indeed this inability to escape fate that cultivates his interiority, allowing his subjective intentions to appear as such. His tragic yet heroic afterlife follows his self-inflicted physical blindness but is made possible by his metaphorical blindness, his unawareness. It is his heroic overcoming of this fundamental epistemic failure that makes him more than human. Tragic death, as Benjamin writes, is "ironic immortality."[66]

The alchemy by which a failure of judgment is converted into heroism is essentially Romantic. One example was that pure indecision of exile, whereby the ironic failure of decision constituted a form of negative freedom. Taking this a step further, the Romantics found in undecidability a means for aesthetic creativity and for overcoming the negative. Reading their works, de Man identified this failure with the notion of a fallen self. In the very act of falling, the

63. Hazaz, "The Sermon," 281–82, 286.

64. Ibid., 284/201, translation modified.

65. For instance, for Kierkegaard, the ironic figure of speech exhibits "a certain superiority, deriving from its not wanting to be understood immediately, even though it wants to be understood." Schlegel regards irony as "the mood that surveys everything and rises infinitely above all limitations, even above its own art, virtue, or genius," an "infinite parabasis." For Schlegel, as De Man claims, "irony engenders a temporal sequence of acts of consciousness which is endless" and is thus "repetitive, the recurrence of a self-escalating act of consciousness"; Kierkegaard, *Concept of Irony*, 248; Schlegel, *Philosophical Fragments*, 6; de Man, "Rhetoric of Temporality," 220.

66. Benjamin, "Trauerspiel and Tragedy," in *Walter Benjamin: Selected Writings*, ed. Michael William Jennings and Marcus Paul Bullock, trans. Harry Zohn (Cambridge, Mass.: Belknap, 2004). According to Benjamin, the tragic hero dies of immortality: since no one can live in fulfilled time, the hero must die in tragedy (1:56). However, this could also be read in reverse order: it is precisely because a hero dies that he becomes immortal.

failed, ironic self produces both an imagined "unfallen" original past (paradise lost) and a future in which this failure is overcome by aspiring to a higher ideal (paradise regained). It thus attempts to overcome its predicament and resolve the tension between itself and the world speculatively, by envisioning an external point of view of future unity.[67] Binding failure to a higher ideal, such indecision converts human limitations into a power beyond nature, which is always necessarily superior to nature itself.

In celebrating this failure of decision as productive, these thinkers rarely if ever considered its potential exploitation for colonial aims. Yet, this productive failure is not constitutive of and generative for every self; it is used to produce certain hegemonic selves, yielding not only their subjectivity but also their superiority and domination. While the colonial and racializing effects of this structure—its conditioning of hierarchies within and across societies—were occluded, they are rather explicit in post-Romantic Kierkegaard's contrasting of Greek ironic "refraction" with the Oriental wish "for the vegetative still life of the plant," which thus associates "Orientals" with the static world of nature.[68]

Transforming failure into superiority is the very definition of the sublime turn. In both forms of the Kantian sublime, through a reflexive, inner conflict, deficiency or inferiority is transfigured into a superiority, specifically a superiority over nature. In the mathematically sublime, the imagination's failure to grasp nature's infinitude contrasts with reason's vocation to try, thus arousing "the feeling that we have within us a supersensible power" capable of reflecting on the idea of totality, so that what is "absolutely large" is no longer the natural object itself but the power of reason.[69] In the dynamically sublime, an encounter with a great natural power that exposes "our" physical limitations also "reveals in us a superiority over nature that is the basis of a self-preservation quite different in kind from the one that can be assailed and endangered by nature outside us." Thus, through an inner conflict, by overcoming the part of the self that constitutes nature "within us" and is indeed

67. De Man, "Rhetoric of Temporality," 214, 219–20.

68. Kierkegaard juxtaposes Socratic irony with Oriental mysticism, regarded as a form of "dying away," a desire "to become more bound" rather than freer, a "wishing for the foggy, drowsy wallowing that an opiate can procure rather than for the sky of thought, wishing for an illusory repose in a consummation connected with a *dolce far niente* [sweet idleness] rather than for the energy of action. But the Grecian sky is high and arched, not flat and burdensome; it rises ever higher, does not anxiously sink down; its air is light and transparent, not hazy and close. . . . Thus the Oriental wants to go back behind consciousness, the Greek to go over and beyond the sequence of consciousness"; Kierkegaard, *Concept of Irony*, 65–66.

69. Immanuel Kant, *Critique of Judgment*, trans. Werner S. Pluhar (Indianapolis: Hackett, 1987), 106.

inferior to the might or magnitude of nature, "we"—or, rather, certain "we"s—become superior to nature "outside us," acquiring a "supersensible" power to which nature's "simple" might could never compare.[70]

The sublime turn thus requires both a starting position of failure, which is the prerogative of the reflexive, fallen subject, and an ideal toward which one strives (absolute totality and freedom as ideas of reason). The constructed, Cartesian conflict between an empirical, finite self and a transcendental self is projected onto the relation between "nature" and the subject, so that a clear order of domination is established. Since nature is imagined as inert, neither conflicted nor reflexive, whatever or whoever is associated with its passivity is denied any supersensible power and is perceived as inferior and subjected. Association with nature in turn is deeply racialized. "Kant's transcendental subject purges himself of the senses," Susan Buck-Morse explains, because "they make him passive ('languid' [*schmelzend*] is Kant's word) . . . , susceptible, like 'Oriental voluptuaries.'"[71] In Kant's aesthetic writing, Oriental and African subjects lack self-reflection and are associated with the passivity of nature, thus having no "talent" for the sublime.[72]

The racializing effects of the sublime turn throw light on Yudka's *levaṭim* and their disorientation. Through his vertiginous indecision, his failure to abide by his own ideal and commit to a verdict on what Zionism means for Judaism, Yudka elevates himself above his "empirical" self. Exilic Judaism is the constitutive failure, the empirical, mystified self that Zionism overcomes and subdues on its path to heroic redemption. This mechanism of sublime reversal pervades Hazaz's speeches and essays as well, as he often presents exile as the fundamental failure that enables Zionist overcoming. "Exile itself existed solely for the sake of redemption," he writes, and "Hebrew was removed from the mouths of the people [in exile] solely for the sake of Zionism."[73] Absence from the land, like the failure to speak Hebrew, thus appears as absolutely necessary for Zionist redemption, for only by overcoming such deficiencies can Zionism come into being and appear heroic—sovereign, historical, dominant. Exile, with its "lachrymose history," is not simply negated by Zionism; it is also maintained as a necessary past failure, dialectically utilized for its reversal into

70. Ibid., 120–23.

71. Susan Buck-Morss, "Aesthetics and Anaesthetics: Walter Benjamin's Artwork Essay Reconsidered," *October* 62 (1992): 9; Kant, *Critique of Judgment*, 133–34.

72. This perception is even more evident, as Emmanuel Chukwudi Eze argues, when Kant's aesthetic work is read alongside his *Anthropology from a Pragmatic Point of View* (1798); Eze, "The Color of Reason: The Idea of 'Race' in Kant's Anthropology," in *Postcolonial African Philosophy: A Critical Reader* (Lewisburg, Pa.: Blackwell, 1997), 106.

73. Hazaz, *Mishpaṭ ha-Ge'ula*, 143.

"supersensible" superiority. If, prior to colonization, the only relation colonizers have to the land is one of distance, then Zionism makes masterful use of its initial absence, its exile: more than a "coming," or even a "coming over," Zionist colonization becomes an "overcoming," with attendant notes of tragic heroism and ironic immortality.[74]

The decisive indecision of Zionist *levaṭim* is speculative in nature but produces real colonial effects. In its specular, paradoxical figure, judgment mandates "seeing beyond" the given, looking either into the depth of souls or to the height of ideals, which become a weapon against indigenous presence.[75] "All the transformative projects for Palestine, including Zionism," Edward Said argues, "have rationalized the denial of present in Palestine with some argument about a 'higher' . . . interest, cause, or mission."[76] Indeed, as Said shows, Zionists justified their colonial settlement by contrasting their intentionality and visionary idealism—their plans to improve the land by seeing beyond what meets the eyes—to the "mere" presence of the indigenous population. *The Question of Palestine* gives myriad examples of this Zionist rhetoric of "vision"—invoking everywhere a "capacity for seeing not only what was there, but what *could* be there"—to bolster claims for appropriation.[77] While presenting Palestinians as "merely" subsisting on their land, Zionists saw themselves as gazing into its future, overlooking the sensible world to speculate over its prospects and hidden meaning (often by utilizing their exile, their failure to be there and thus see).[78] The deep, buried potential of the land is the mirror image of the deep subject, who is its condition of possibility. Precisely because subjects can reflect and speculate about various plans for the land—weighing them against each other and engaging in *levaṭim*—these subjects become, in their own mind, its rightful conquerors and true owners.

Thus, by the disorientation that stems from the impossible demand for decision, by hierarchically splitting the self and seeing beyond the sensible

74. I elaborate on Zionist "overcoming," its sublimity, and its dependence on speculation in Liron Mor, "Zionist Speculation: Colonial Vision and Its Sublime Turn," *Theory & Event* 26, no. 1 (2023): 154–85.

75. On irony as a mode of seeing beyond sensible knowledge—a kind of paranoid vision—see Claire Colebrook, *Irony in the Work of Philosophy* (Lincoln: University of Nebraska Press, 2002), xi–xiv.

76. Edward W. Said, *The Question of Palestine* (New York: Vintage, 1980), 15.

77. Ibid., 92–94.

78. This Lockean "ideology of improvement," as Brenna Bhandar observes, was central to Zionist appropriation of Palestinian lands and to its constitution of the indigenous population as itself in need of improvement; Bhandar, *Colonial Lives of Property: Law, Land, and Racial Regimes of Ownership* (Durham, N.C.: Duke University Press, 2018), 48.

world, Zionism establishes its domination over whatever it considers nature within it (exile) and nature outside of it (Palestine and the Orient). Zionism's various "natures" thus coincide with its various Easts—Eastern European Jewish exile, Palestine and Palestinians, and "Oriental" Jews. It is in this sense, too, that *levaṭim* disorient: the sublime vertigo of their indecision cuts Zionism off from its various Easts and pits it against them. An internal conflict within a European subject is projected onto the social field in the form of domination and colonization, thus ultimately becoming a conflict with others.

Disorientation and Overcoming: "Raḥamim ha-Sabal"

To clarify the colonial operation of *levaṭim* and its racializing effects, I turn to an earlier short story by Hazaz, "Raḥamim ha-Sabal" (Rahamim the Porter)—originally published in the literary supplement of *Davar* in 1933.[79] The story, which takes place in Mandate-era Jerusalem, sets up a dramatic encounter between the Kurdish porter Rahamim, who migrated to Palestine from Iraq during World War I, and Menashke Bezprozvani, who arrived in Palestine around the same time from—it appears, based on his Slavic surname—what once was the Russian Empire.[80] Menashke is a Yiddish diminutive of Menashe—a common Jewish name. While, unlike Rahamim, he is repeatedly mentioned by his full name, his surname, ironically enough, simply means "nameless" in Russian.[81] The eponymous porter's Hebrew name, Rahamim,

79. Haim Hazaz, "Rahamim," in *Modern Hebrew Literature*, ed. Robert Alter, trans. I. M. Lask (New York: Behrman House, 1975), 257–64. This English translation is based on an early version of the story: Haim Hazaz, "Raḥamim ha-Sabal," in *Reḥayim Shevurim: Sipurim* (Tel Aviv: ʿAm ʿOved, 1941), 215–22. References to the Hebrew original refer to this version, unless otherwise noted.

80. Because Menashke's Hebrew is far more fluent, the reader is tempted to believe that he has resided in Palestine far longer than Rahamim, but references to historical events suggest that they both migrated around the same time. Robert Alter pinpoints Menashke's arrival in Palestine to the Third *Aliyah* (1919–23); Alter, "Introduction (to 'Rahamim')," in *Modern Hebrew Literature*, ed. Robert Alter (New York: Behrman House, 1975), 252.

81. In the Bible, Menashe (Manasseh or Manasses) is one of Joseph's two sons and thus also one of the twelve tribes of Israel. The biblical name sheds light on several aspects of Menashke's character. "It is because God has made me forget (*nashani*) all my trouble and all my father's household," says Joseph, explaining his choice of the name for his newborn son (Gen 41:51). Its root is etymologically related to forgetfulness (and womanhood), thus stressing Menashke forgetting of his "father's household" (even if forgetting his troubles is beyond him). The biblical Menashe is, moreover, a forefather of the people of *Gilʿad* (Gilead), so that the name closely ties Hazaz's Menashe to kibbutz Kfar Gileadi (*Kefar Gilʿadi*), where he once lived, and to the Zionist settlement movement more broadly. Finally, Menashe is one of a series of biblical

prevalent only among Mizrahi Jews, means "mercy" or "compassion." It evokes, as Robert Alter remarks, the idea of *midat ha-raḥamim* (the measure of mercy), which Rabbinic thought contrasts with *midat ha-din* (the measure of justice or law, in all its severity), considering both together the qualities on which the world is founded.[82] Rahamim and Menashke are thus aligned with mercy and judgment respectively, and the opposition set up between them is dialectical in two senses: first, in the Platonic sense, staging a *hitlabṭut* of sorts—a back-and-forth dialogue between the two positions; and second, in the Hegelian sense, for the title of the story appears to promise resolution in and through *raḥamim*, the measure of mercy.

Indeed, the contrast between the two, representing the prototypes of the Sephardi Jew and the Ashkenazi Jew, is staged in perfectly diametric terms. Hazaz presents the "Oriental" Rahamim as simple and content, the very epitome of health and masculinity: a "short fellow with thick black eyebrows, a beard like a thicket, his face bright as a copper pot and his chest uncommonly virile and broad." Rahamim is all body and abundance. His life is imagined as so plentiful that he has not one but two wives and is himself "a sort of doubled-over and redoubled-over man," his face broadening till "it beamed like two copper pans."[83] Depicted as primitive, both in his religiosity and in his life lessons and beliefs ("no belly without belly button, no man get on without a missus!"),[84] his speech is rendered in pidgin Hebrew peppered, for good folkist measure, with Aramaic. Hazaz's choice of Aramaic is realist, for a dialect of modern Aramaic was indeed spoken by several communities of Kurdish Jews in Iraq. But it is also evocative, for it utilizes the history of Aramaic as a biblical and Rabbinic language to portray Rahamim as the authentic, primordial Jew—as native to Palestine as Jesus himself. Free and trusting in his speech, Rahamim delivers whole stories directly, with little mediation by the narrator.

The reader is introduced to Rahamim's home life only indirectly, through Menashke's fantastic imagining. This yields an Orientalist vision of Rahamim surrounded by his large family and flanked by his wives, "heavy as two ready beds and as many garden plots made for sowing," whose skirmishes are kept at bay by Rahamim's glance, which "falls like five rains upon the soil." Rahamim's

---

figures whose birthright is stolen by their younger brothers in a scandalous reversal of the law of primogeniture. To be the true favorite of God, the book of Genesis suggests, one must not have a right to power by birth, so that this initial inferiority might be dramatically overcome and overturned later, transformed into a superior power.

82. Alter, "Introduction (to 'Rahamim')," 254.

83. Hazaz, "Rahamim," 261, 259.

84. Ibid., 258, 260.

journey to Palestine follows the Jewish-Iraqi trade route into India and is replete with exotic images of Eastern abundance: from Zakho in northern Iraq he travels to Baghdad and then Basra, where he works for a "rich man, plenty blessing he has, His Name be blessed." Because the way to Damascus is obstructed by war, Rahamim travels to Bombay, where for "two months, and every day, every day [he] walked in the garden of Señor Sassoon, eating and drinking and walking . . . until at last he went to the land of Israel."[85] The text itself, however, betrays the symbolic nature of this Orientalist plentitude, attesting to Rahamim's great poverty (he is "dressed in rags and tatters") and to his lower social class (he regularly refers to Menashke as *adon*, "Sir").[86]

The Ashkenazi Menashke, by contrast, is presented as a secular bourgeois intellectual, introspective, lonely, and bitter. His characterization as an unemployed wanderer, restless, poor, and ill, replicates and transposes anti-Semitic stereotypes, internalized by the Zionist "negation of exile" discourse. Beyond his gauntness and sickly pallor, we learn little of Menashke's physique; his figure remains almost an abstraction. While Rahamim is verbose, Menashke is reserved. When he does speak, however, his language is eloquent and proper. A subjective third-person narration reveals to the reader the thoughts and sentiments behind Menashke's silences, furnishing him with psychological, reflexive depth. (No free indirect speech is ever accorded to Rahamim, whose words are merely reported.)

Menashke is introduced by way of a landscape sketch, at once real and imagined:

> The heat was like that of an oven stoked with glowing coals, and the white light dazzled to blindness and distraction. The street quivered uncertainly in the light as though in a dream; it *might have been* so much barren soil or else a field left fallow because of drought; or it might have been anything you like in the world. The sun was interweaving clashes amongst (*sikhsekha*) the stones and the windows. . . . Through the barrenness and dryness yellowed the mountain slopes on the horizon and the skies in their purity of pale blue called eternity and worlds-without-end to mind.[87]

Out of place, Menashke struggles to acclimate to the Middle East, depicted as inhospitable and associated with conflict. In the heat haze of the vista, even the great city of Jerusalem is, for him, a dried-out field—a barren canvas

85. Ibid, 262/220, translation modified.
86. Ibid., 258.
87. Ibid, 258/216, emphasis mine; translation slightly modified.

shimmering with potential, with that "might have been." Menashke's gaze is at once exhausted and speculative.

Thence, his inner conflict, his *levaṭim* over "the domination of Zionist Imperialism," is introduced. Entertaining despite himself a great love for the land, "his complaints were no more than half-hearted," so "he complained all the more, denying everything and destroying everything in thought." Like Kanafani's Miriam or Yizhar's narrators, Menashke "colonizes and cries," indecisively and melancholically criticizing the imperialism of Zionism as lip service that eases its continuation. His *levaṭim*, like Yudka's, render him a reflexive, specular subject, whose failure of decision is matched only by his commitment to a future judgment, to overcoming his tormented nature and gaining mastery of his surroundings. Menashke's forlorn *levaṭim* distill a lifetime of "fever and hunger, of unsettled wandering from one agricultural commune to another, of vexations and suffering and troubles enough to drive a man out of his mind and make him lose his strength."[88] Explicitly tied to the absence of true home, health, and sustenance, they are the bittersweet fruit of exile.

Elsewhere, in his essayistic writing, Hazaz explicitly names these two opposed sets of stereotypes the "Sephardi style" and the "Ashkenazi style," respectively. In his simple plentitude, Rahamim exemplifies what Hazaz describes as the "Sephardi style" in Hebrew literature: "a complete and abundant world (*'olam male*), open to the light, open to love and happiness, to feast and wine, to friendship and alliance, to desiring, play, and laughter. . . . It is whole and does not lack a thing."[89] In his constant inner oscillations (*ṭalṭelot*) and intricate dilemmas (*livṭe levaṭim*), Menashke represents, of course, the "Ashkenazi style." Replete with introspective conflicts, this style, according to Hazaz, is rooted in the memory of pogroms and exhibits "no light or happiness, no fun and games, just Torah, law, interpretations, atonements and lamentations written in the blood of brevity." For Hazaz, this style—Ashkenazi reflexive complexity born out of its "lachrymose history"—is epitomized, of course, by the writing of Brenner and Berdichevsky, whose dilemmas and soul-torments captivated the young Zionist readership.[90] The torn, indecisive protagonist, whose neo-Romantic figure plagues Hazaz's oeuvre, thus seems to exhibit the pure irony of exile, aiming at "denying everything and destroying everything in thought." Settling in Palestine, however, the protagonist terminates the

88. Ibid., 257–58.

89. To be fair to Hazaz, he further described this world as open to "critique, research and philosophy, to astronomy and Kabbalah"; Hazaz, *Mishpaṭ ha-Ge'ula*, 63.

90. Ibid., 62–63.

endlessness of absolute negativity, displacing it from thought to world, thus using indecision as a technique of domination.

Unlike Rahamim's simple corporeal presence, Menashke's involves foresight and overcoming. While Rahamim is portrayed as incapable of representing his own home life, resorting to platitudes when pressed on it,[91] Menashke is endowed with a deep and mysterious interiority. Specifically, his inner dilemmas are described as a bitterness whose mystery is greater than its interpreted or explicit meaning (*she-setuma gadol mi-perusha*).[92] When imagining Rahamim in his home, by contrast, the formula is flawlessly inverted: Menashke extracts an explicit meaning, an imaginative interpretation, out of the mysterious and veiled (*meforash min ha-satum*), drawing on both his bitter, reflexive dilemmas and his absence from the cozy familial scene to do so, thus turning failure into a source of mastery.[93] Surmounting the inaccessibility of Rahamim's home to his gaze, Menashke not only overcomes his epistemic failure and physical absence but also employs these as springboards for speculating beyond the empirical world, appearing to know more about Rahamim than he himself does. The story thus establishes not only the fact of Menashke's superiority to the Oriental Rahamim but also the method by which this superiority is produced.

A particular scene in "Raḥamim ha-Sabal" may elucidate the speculative method that renders Menashke's inner conflicts and failings productive, generating hierarchy between him and Rahamim and preparing the ground for his heroic overcoming. Following a brief initial conversation, Rahamim offers Menashke some fresh eggs. (These, the reader soon discovers, he had denied his family, intending to sell them to support a hospitalized daughter.) Menashke, although unemployed and quite feeble, refuses the eggs for no apparent reason. At this moment, he notices two copper rings on Rahamim's fingers. When Rahamim learns that Menashke wears no rings, he tells him a Babylonian fable about a man in love:

> "Once it happened he had to go a long journey. He said to her, to that beauty: Lady! because that I love you much, you give me your ring,

91. When asked about his two wives, for instance, Rahamim responds, "Eh! Mountain looks at mountain and valley between them," "If a young one in house, old one always brrr, brrr"; Hazaz, "Rahamim," 260.

92. Ibid., 257/215, my translation.

93. Ibid., 262/220, my translation. As Reuven Tsur argues, this reversal also takes place at the level of narration. So identified with Menashke and so reluctant to allow Rahamim interiority, the narrator is hindered from conveying anything about Rahamim beyond his actions in the present. Hazaz turns this weakness, however, into a superior power by putting the description of Rahamim's home in the mind of Menashke. See Tsur, "Ḳeri'a be-'Raḥamim,'" 270–71.

> and as long as I see it on my finger I remember you and long for you. And that beauty who was sharp, never wish to give him her ring but said to him: Not so, only every time you look at your finger and see my ring not there, you remember me because I never give you ring, and you long for me. . . ."
>
> Ending his tale, he burst into a peal of laughter. "Ha-ha-ha!" He threw his head back and filled the whole road with his powerful, noisy laughter. "And so you also, ha-ha-ha!" His laughter and the yarn he had spun turned Menashke Bezprozvani's mind in a different direction. Despite himself, he began to think of his own girl—her merits, her queernesses and the whole of that chapter.[94]

Rahamim suggests a similar if less literal lack in Menashke's life—an absence of relationships, of belonging, of reliance on others (as in refusing the eggs). And Menashke, sure enough, turns inward to brood on just that.

The rings on Rahamim's fingers so potently represent his wives that he need never miss them. He lacks for nothing, sexually and semiotically, and the contrast with Menashke's abortive affairs and prismatic inwardness is stark. Yet, the popular wisdom of the fable also offers an important lesson about the power of Menashke's "Ashkenazi style," suggesting that absence can be even more semiotically potent than presence. In recording a failure, absence also conjures a potential, that which could have been or might be eventually. Whether past or future, this unrealized potential requires reflectiveness and longing, the power to see beyond the immediate and sensible world. The woman in the fable sarcastically reveals the hierarchy between the two positions: simply having rings that directly correspond to loved ones—uncomplicatedly standing in for them in a "Sephardi style" of mere presence—is not as powerful or romantic as the lack of rings, as using absence as a marker of what *could* be, choosing to utilize and overcome lack by speculatively envisioning potentials.

This wisdom exposes the structure of *levaṭim* described thus far. The disorienting operation of *levaṭim*, like that of the sublime, leverages subjective failure in order to see beyond the sensible and conjure the endless possibilities of negative freedom. In the settler colonial context, such phenomenological speculation yields the power to establish ascendancy and dominion. By

94. Hazaz, "Rahamim," 261. In a later version of the story, Rahamim opens the fable with the words "Itwa, litwa"—the Aramaic for "there was or there was not," a common opening phrase in fables and stories of the Arab and Muslim worlds; Hazaz, "Raḥamim," in *Sipurim Nivḥarim* (Tel-Aviv: Devir la-'Am, 1970), 128. Hazaz's care with the Aramaic he puts in Rahamim's mouth might be the result of the literary ethnography he undertook when he settled in the Kurdish Jewish neighborhood of Jerusalem.

highlighting intentional vision, *levaṭim*, the internal conflicts of a colonizing subject, give his presence a power surpassing the mere, simple presence—however ample and vigorous—of he who has no dilemmas and is thus considered mere nature. Indeed, it is through his speculative *levaṭim* and by exploiting Rahamim's "good" and "simple" nature that Menashke overcomes his melancholic dilemmas and failures, turning his foreignness and initial distance from Palestine into an advantage. (Note that, porter though he is, Rahamim is portrayed as enjoying a life of simple abundance rather than as overcoming hardships and penury. Similarly, the lack and inferiority that Menashke overcomes are fictional and do not represent real economic conditions.)

Despite Menashke's estrangement and misgivings, he remains in Palestine and is eventually cured of his melancholic dilemmas by the happy-go-lucky Rahamim. Importantly, Rahamim appears in the story—and heals Menashke—while riding a donkey. He even boasts about owning eight donkeys, humorously declaring himself "an experienced and well-versed donkey-doctor!" thus intensifying his construction as wealthy or at least as content with his material conditions.[95] The recurrent motif of the donkey (*ḥamor*) in Hazaz's work relates to the dialectics of exile and redemption—for the Messiah is expected to arrive by donkey—so that Rahamim is presented as Menashke's redeemer. But the donkey is also related to the animal world and to matter (*ḥomer*) itself, a link that also draws, according to Miron, on Kabbalistic literature.[96] The "authentic" Oriental Jew settled in Palestine thus embodies both secularized redemption for Ashkenazi Zionism and the bodily world of nature, matter, and labor.

Indeed, the overcoming of melancholic *levaṭim* and lack in "Raḥamim ha-Sabal" occurs only through the Oriental man. While Rahamim's shining copper face integrates him with the sunny surroundings, he is also depicted through tropes of water. His glance is like "five rains," his home is built on a cistern, and he is thus the balm for Menashke's dejected and arid nature. "It is precisely the blatant, physical attributes of Rahamim," Warren Bargad tellingly writes, "which calm Menashke and distract him from his feelings of frustration and melancholy. The concrete, physical, Aliya to Erets Yisrael is traumatic, but in spite of it all, and, in great measure, due to Rahamim's solicitude, Menashke will overcome the trauma."[97] It is thus Rahamim's corporeality that redeems Menashke and helps ease his way to colonization.

This perception of "Oriental" Jews was in fact common amongst Zionists at the time, who speculated not only about the hidden prospects of Palestine

95. Hazaz, "Rahamim," 260.
96. Miron, *Ḥayim Hazaz*, 149.
97. Bargad, "Realism and Myth," 88–89.

but also about the healing potentials of Mizrahi Jews. Shabtai Keshev, for instance, wrote in *Davar* in 1950 that Ashkenazi Zionists "suffer from an overabundance of intelligence, from too much cerebral work and too many cerebral workers." Zionists were thus

> in desperate need of respectable amounts of "injections" of naturalness, simplicity, commonness, of being in the body. These naïve childish Jews [from Arab countries], with their simplicity and with their intelligence—which is . . . "not like Einstein's"—they are the life potion, an antidote for our cerebral over-probing, which is the source of most of our troubles.[98]

And Dr. Nahum Goldmann, a Zionist leader who was the president of the World Zionist Organization (1956–68), said at a meeting of the Jewish Agency directors:

> We integrated (*kalaṭnu*) two hundred thousand Jews from North Africa. They were for us like matter (*ḥomer*, also "clay") in the hands of the creator (*yotser*, also "potter"). We took them from the boat and sent them directly to settlement. We didn't ask them what they wanted, and this practice worked out nicely.[99]

Rahamim represents the East so generally that he comes to stand in for Palestinians as well. First, his encounter with Menashke takes place immediately after their sole appearance in the story. The plot begins *in medias res*, when Menashke, completely engrossed in his vexed thoughts, is startled by a "dozen or so Arabs dash[ing] excitedly among the crowd in the street, yelling at the top of their voices as though attacked by robbers: '*Barud! Barud!!*'" Local to Jerusalem, *barud* is a customary exclamation intended to alert bystanders to an impending planned explosion, undertaken for the purpose of development (e.g., for extracting resources or leveling off the ground for rebuilding). The "Arabs" in the story are hysterical—too afraid of, or too enthused by, the coming explosion—thus presented as mindlessly excitable bystanders to progress and to the development of Palestine. Menashke, by contrast, calmly waits for the explosion to pass. When resuming his stroll, he suddenly finds Rahamim riding a donkey beside him.[100] Rahamim's explosive appearance thus associates him with both the "Arabs" and the improvement of the land. Second, although he, too, is a recent immigrant, Rahamim is consistently imagined as belonging to

98. Shabtai Keshev (Klugman), "Ele sh-En Tiḳva le-Yaldehem," *Davar*, March 3, 1950.

99. Protocol of Jewish Agency directors' meeting, March 7, 1957, quoted in *The Ancestral Sin* [Hebrew: *Salah, Po Ze Erets Iśra'el*], dir. David Deri, Reshet 2017, documentary series, episode 2.

100. Hazaz, "Rahamim," 258.

the East, even as local. His "copper face," mentioned three times, is seemingly of a piece with the coppery, sun-lit surroundings, the very climate that makes Menashke's mind so torn and fevered.[101] Finally, Rahamim's expertise with donkeys echoes Hazaz's short story "ha-Tayar ha-Gadol" (The Great Wanderer, 1933), published in the same collection. In "ha-Tayar ha-Gadol," which explores early relations between Jews and Muslims in Palestine, the donkey, ridiculous and bestial, becomes an ironic symbol of competing religious claims for the land.[102] Through this intertextual motif, Hazaz transfigures Zionism's inner conflict into a conflict with Palestinians over (no longer sacred) land.

After the two men part ways, Rahamim returns—to the animal score of his donkey's hoof-taps—and practically begs Menashke to stop being so sad. Utilizing Rahamim's simple and corporeal nature, Menashke's healing must nonetheless take place introspectively. Only *after* Rahamim truly departs, when "the guilty and soothing smile of that porter and his face which had been bright with love and humility" is conjured *in the imagination*, can Menashke overcome his bitterness.[103]

The story concludes in a moment of silent reflection. After Menashke's soul has been elevated above his hardships, a melancholic tune still haunts him: "His spirits rising within him" and bringing tears to his eyes, Menashke begins "to hum to himself the words of the song which the children had been accustomed to sing at Kfar Gileadi in those days of hardship and hunger: In Kfar Gileadi, in the upper court,/Next to the runnel, within the big butt/There's never a drop of water." Precisely when Menashke finally prevails over his "arid" nature, when his dilemmas are being quenched by Rahamim, he chooses to repeat a tune that revels in the dearth of water.[104] The children's hymn reflects a central myth of the Kibbutz movement and of Zionism more

101. Several decades after the publication of "Raḥamim ha-Sabal," Palestinian workers began to replace Kurdish Jewish workers as cheap laborers at the bottom of the Israeli workforce pyramid. See Salim Tamari, "What the Uprising Means," *Middle East Report*, no. 152 (1988): 24. In this sense, Hazaz's Kurdish porter is quite literally (even if anachronistically, only in teleological retrospect) a precursor of the Palestinian worker.

102. In Hazaz's "ha-Tayar ha-Gadol," when Reb Meshel Yeshel's donkey dies, he buries him lovingly under a mound of stones. The Safed Grandsire comes across the burial ground and announces it the grave of an important saint, Rav Hamnuna. It becomes the site of the saint's annual festivity, to which those seeking miracles undertake pilgrimage, until "Arabs" take it over and pronounce it the grave of one of their saints, Alsheikh Nunu. Meshel Yeshel passing by their festival sees them worshiping the tomb and stops by to explain that it is in fact the grave of his donkey—an explanation for which he is killed.

103. Hazaz, "Rahamim," 263–64.

104. Ibid., 264. On water and desert as contrasting motifs in "Raḥamim ha-Sabal" and on the tears as engendering a classic tragic turn in this scene, see Tsur, "Ḳeri'a be-'Raḥamim,'" 264–66.

generally—that of overcoming thirst and hunger, of "making the desert bloom," of envisioning and realizing the potential in an "empty" land. Specifically, the hymn celebrates the overcoming of physical limitations and the defeating of nature—thirst, the absence of water—which leads Menashke to discover a kind of transcendental quenching power, a sort of "supersensible" water, as his reflexive *levaṭim* make him trickle with tears (*meḥalḥel be-dema'ot*). Invigorated by Rahamim's simple "Sephardi style," drawing on his "Oriental" bodily nature yet reflexively "seeing beyond" it, Menashke prevails over his own bitter "Ashkenazi style"—a microcosm of Zionism prevailing over its exilic roots by exploiting "Oriental" lands and workers while "seeing beyond" them.

Incidentally, "Menashke" was the name Hazaz initially intended for Yudka's character in "ha-Derasha."[105] The two stories are indeed interwoven. The conflict between Menashke and Rahamim is, to some degree, internalized in Yudka, transubstantiated into a conflict between Zionism and Judaism. Unlike "ha-Derasha," however, "Raḥamim ha-Sabal" ends with a landscape sketch suggestive of possible synthesis and reconciliation: sitting on a rock, Menashke gazes at "the Mountains of Moab—desolate in their pale blue, indistinct in outline—as though they had been swallowed by the sky or, perhaps, as though the sky had been swallowed by them."[106] Echoed in the landscape, Menashke's overcoming appears dialectical—valorizing melancholy, driven by "the negative" as manifested in inner conflict and achieving positivity only through this negative.[107] The blue stillness of this picture resonates, moreover, with the opening scene, when "the skies in their purity of pale blue called eternity and worlds-without-end to mind." This interpenetration of sky and desert, beginning and end, not only resolves opposites but also eternalizes the scene, imbuing it with the spiritual sanctity of the twin temporalities of redemption—the origin and the brink—suggested by Zionist proleptic historicism.[108]

105. After Hazaz's death, his widow, Aviva, revealed that, from the proof sheets of "ha-Derasha," she discovered the protagonist's original name. See Hazaz and Hazaz, "'u-Ven 'Av le-Ḥavero Ma'afilim ha-Shamayim, Sheḥore-Sheḥorim,'" *Haaretz*, April 16, 2014, https://www.haaretz.co.il/literature/prose/.premium-1.2295687.

106. Hazaz, "Rahamim," 264.

107. "Three ideas define the dialectic: the idea of a power of the negative as a theoretical principle manifested in opposition and contradiction; the idea that suffering and sadness have value, the valorization of the 'sad passions,' as a practical principle manifested in splitting and tearing apart; the idea of positivity as a theoretical and practical product of negation itself"; Gilles Deleuze, *Nietzsche and Philosophy*, trans. Hugh Tomlinson (London and New York: Continuum, 2002), 195.

108. As Miron argues, this sketch of the Palestinian landscape is recurrent in Hazaz's writing: merging earth and sky, Hazaz produces a sense of holy time, a time that is both before and

In "Raḥamim ha-Sabal," then, Zionist *levaṭim* constitute a disorienting indecision that both demands and frustrates its own resolution. This combination of melancholic failure and higher calling allows Menashke to speculate and overcome "nature within" him and thus gain, in his own eyes, dominance over what he considers "nature without." In contrast to Menashke's reflexivity, Hazaz's depictions of the "Oriental" Rahamim regularly associate him with the material world, which is exploited for the supersensible overcoming that enables the continuation of Zionism. Though the conflictual model of *levaṭim* is fundamentally solipsistic, its claim to the universality of an ideal has real repercussions for others. Zionism is, as Chapter 3 demonstrates, the unilateral projection of this internal conflict outward, "seeing beyond" the indigenous Palestinians or making them disappear. Its adversarial racialization of Palestinians and Mizrahi Jews, as explored in Chapter 5, fully hinges on their widespread perception as bodies in space.

To Do without Philosophy

When settled and decided, Zionism stops the exilic perpetual motion between antithetical extremes. Since the indecision of *levaṭim* can never be fully decided, however, those who believe they are able to judge still always suspect the joke is on them. *Levaṭim* therefore require endless repetition for their stabilization. That is precisely what Yudka attempts by the spiraling hyperbole and reiterations of his sermon, as he pathetically tries to get at what he truly means. And yet, even as "ha-Derasha" nears its end, Yudka is unable to solve the paradox of Zionism: "I'm not the one to say what Zionism is. . . . In a word, no one has yet said the right . . . the . . . the hidden, the deepest . . . no one has revealed, or explained, fully . . . just talk, elementary things, banalities, you know, empty, meaningless phrases. . . ."[109] Though Zionism might have been meant as the end of Eastern European Judaism, it is nonetheless constantly haunted by Judaism and the East as its contradictory, ironic doubles. Indeed, while *levaṭim* give off the impression of a contradiction belonging to a liberal past—and in a certain sense, they are—the contradiction presently playing out in Israel (2023) reveals the return of these haunting Easts in the rise of both religious Zionism (a certain Ashkenazi interpretation of Judaism) and the rhetorical weaponization of the underrepresented Mizrahi populace, waged by one Ashkenazi elite against another.

---

beyond history, both prehistorical and eschatological, thus presenting the landscape as exclusively Jewish; *Ḥayim Hazaz*, 176–77.

109. Hazaz, "The Sermon," 284. Save for the first, all ellipses in the original.

Throughout "ha-Derasha," the committee members recurrently ridicule Yudka, laughing at his expense. By the end, however, all laughter is gone. Their confidence in Yudka's ignorance and their own epistemic grounding is shaken, and for a moment at least they are silent, sitting upright in their chairs, waiting anxiously to hear what else he might have to say. They begin to suspect that the joke here is in fact at their expense, that they do not truly know how to judge. This transformation happens in a moment of silence—the kind of silence that falls "after a quarrel" or conflict (*she-le'aḥar keṭaṭa ve-din u-devarim*). Yudka, by contrast, seems to conclude his sermon with great certainty and finality: "With this I had said a great deal, the whole thing . . . everything I had on my mind . . . and now I don't want to say anything more. I have nothing more to add. . . . Enough!"

After a short pause, however, when the chairman asks if he is done, Yudka "[jerks] to his feet" and begins anew, with fresh panic:

> I've said much too much. . . . That's not how I meant it, not the way I thought it. It came out by itself. The devil knows how. . . . Such nonsense! Trifles, side issues. . . . It was ridiculous, quite unnecessary. . . . What I mean, I really just wanted to explain. . . . I no longer know how to tell you . . . the main thing, what I'm after. . . . It's not just . . . yes! Well, now. Now to the main thing. I beg you a few more minutes of patience.[110]

At the end of it all, we learn that the sermon we read was not in fact the one we were meant to read, that the main thing still lies ahead, outside the text. When the tape runs out, so to speak, Yudka is still talking. He appears flustered. This is not what he meant; his words are too much and too little all at once; and what he truly wants to say still eludes him. Yudka's attempt *li-drosh*—to deliver a sermon but also to interpret, to demand an interpretation—has failed, and Zionism as a concept is still beyond his grasp. The reader now suspects, even without access to the rest of the sermon, that it will forever escape him. "ha-Derasha" in its entirety is a grand failure, flawlessly executed: performing the impossibility of interpretation, it denies the reader a stable footing for judgment, thus producing its own authority.

It ends with yet another twist: "Say what you want," the chairman tells Yudka, "and try, as much as you can, to do without the philosophy."[111] But the contradiction or indecision presented here—the colonial form of disorienting dilemmas, or *levaṭim*—depends on the judging, detached, reflexive self of

110. Ibid., 286–87/201. Most ellipses in the original.
111. Ibid., 287/202, translation modified.

speculative philosophy. Deeply internal and reflexive, "to do without the philosophy" is precisely its impossible, failed calling. Shifting perspectives, Chapter 3 turns to examine how this indecision is experienced from the outside, as it were, by Palestinians, for whom the correlate of the Zionist "seeing beyond" is their own colonial disappearance. It thus examines Palestinian poetics of disappearance (*ikhtifāʾ*) as both an indigenous literary theory of colonialism in Palestine and a poetic form of anti-colonial resistance to the Zionist claim for speculative vision and interpretative closure. While the decisive indecision of *levaṭim* binds us to the ideal, to what we must mean, the humorous model of anticolonial disappearance says that which could not be meant.

3
Ikhtifāʾ
(Anti/colonial Disappearance)

"From al-Birwa?" the military governor yelled.

She made no response but continued to stare at him.

He then pointed his gun straight at her child's head and screamed, "Reply, or I'll empty this into him!" . . .

"Yes, from al-Birwa."

"Are you returning there?" he demanded.

"Yes, returning."

"Didn't we warn you," he yelled, "that anyone returning there will be killed? . . . Go back anywhere you like to the east. And if I ever see you again on this road I'll show you no mercy."

The woman stood up and, gripping her child by the hand, set off toward the east, not once looking back. Her child walked beside her, and he too never looked back.

At this point I observed the first example of that amazing phenomenon that was to occur again and again. . . . For the further the woman and child went . . . the taller they grew. By the time they merged with their own shadows in the sinking sun they had become bigger than the plain of Acre itself. The governor still stood there awaiting their final disappearance (ikhtifāʾahumā)*. . . . Finally he asked in amazement, "Will they never vanish?"*

—EMILE HABIBY, *AL-MUTASHAʾIL* (TRANSLATION MODIFIED)

What if all Palestinians simply disappeared one fine day? Adopting a magical realist tone, Ibtisam Azem's novel *Sifr al-Ikhtifaʾ* (The Book of Disappearance,

2014) explores what might have happened if this disavowed fantasy of Zionism came true.[1] The extreme, exceptional case—the complete elimination of a native population—thus emerges as the implicit telos of Zionism, and disappearance is presented no longer as a mere side-effect of Zionist state-building or of its colonial wars but rather as its organizing core principle.

The plot of Azem's novel unfolds mainly through the voices of two narrators: Ariel, a Jewish Israeli journalist attempting to single-handedly solve the mystery of the Palestinian disappearance—and, particularly, of his friend and neighbor Alaa—and Alaa himself, a Palestinian cameraman whose voice emerges only through his journal, which Ariel finds in his vacated apartment and reads in the narrative present. The journal also features Alaa's grandmother's memories, which depict Jaffa before, during, and after its 1948 colonization.

Sifr al-Ikhtifa' thus reveals multiple levels of Palestinian disappearance, which form the subject of this chapter. First, the fantastic disappearance resonates with the very real 1948 mass expulsion of Palestinians and with other modes of ethnic cleansing before and after. Azem often layers the fictive, contemporary disappearance with familiar tropes from accounts of 1948—empty chairs next to meals abandoned in haste, the smell of coffee still hanging in the air.[2] By framing the fictional Palestinian disappearance as an echo or repetition of the *nakba*, she presents this colonial disappearance as ongoing, unfolding within a long history of massacres, displacement, juridical exclusion, appropriation, ghettoization, and so much more. Second, in her insistence on the Palestinian cartography of greater Jaffa, which Israel has attempted to efface, Azem documents not only this epistemological erasure but also traces of resistance and the generational continuities they sustain. "I was certain that your city, the one you kept talking about, has nothing to do with my city," Alaa writes, addressing his grandmother. "The names, orange groves, scents, al-Hamra Cinema, Apollo, weddings, Prophet Rubin's feast, Iskandar Awad Street, al-Nuzha Street, al-Sa'a Square . . . etc. Where do all these names come from? . . . Names not written on signs."[3] Third, the novel reveals the status of Palestinians as a captive and often invisible market and workforce. It

1. Ibtisam Azem, *Sifr al-Ikhtifa'* (Beirut: al-Jamal, 2014). An English translation by the author Sinan Antoon was published as *The Book of Disappearance: A Novel* (Syracuse, N.Y.: Syracuse University Press, 2019). The novel resonates with African American works of speculative fiction, such as William Melvin Kelley's novel *A Different Drummer* (1962) or Douglas Turner Ward's play *Day of Absence* (1965), in which an entire black population disappears.

2. Azem, *Book of Disappearance*, 197; 76.

3. Ibid., 15–16.

invokes, for instance, the history of Tel Aviv, "the White City," which devoured and depleted Jaffa, exploiting its labor power and resources. This kind of appropriation, systemic and inconspicuous and far less dramatic than seizure of land, may indeed be Azem's main theme. At its most camouflaged it infects the narrative and emotional logic of *Sifr al-Ikhtifaʾ* itself. Ariel occupies not only Alaa's apartment but also his seat as the author: resting his feet on Alaa's coffee table and sipping Alaa's "Arabic coffee," Ariel picks the fruit of his intellectual labor. He appropriates Alaa's and his grandmother's memories, stories, and views, copying and translating segments from the journal for a future book, which he titles *Chronicle of Pre-Disappearance*.[4] This "book" is nested within Azem's and echoes its title; yet what Ariel sees only as an event, Azam understands as a perpetual condition.

Indeed, Palestinian literature is absolutely rife with disappearances.[5] The very word—*ikhtifāʾ* in Arabic—appears in the titles of many notable Palestinian works, from Emile Habiby's formative novel *al-Waqaʾiʿ al-Ghariba fi Ikhtifaʾ Saʿid abi al-Naḥs al-Mutashaʾil* (The Strange Circumstances of the Disappearance of Saeed the Ill-Fated Pessoptimist, 1974),[6] to Elia Suleiman's film *Sijill Ikhtifaʾ* (Chronicle of a Disappearance, 1996), to Sayed Kashua's short story "Hertsel Neʿelam be-Ḥatsot" (Herzl Disappears at Midnight, 2005, Hebrew), to Azem's aforementioned *Sifr al-Ikhtifaʾ*. Beyond titles, disappearances are also all-pervasive in the narrative machinery, often constituting the very motor of the work. Spinning a black hole around which both narrative and action are plotted, disappearances serve as the condition of possibility for both. Azem's novel joins a long line of works—beginning with Habiby's *al-Mutashaʾil* and continuing with Jabra Ibrahim Jabra's *al-Baḥth ʿan Walid Masʿud* (In Search of Walid Masoud, 1978), Ibrahim Nasrallah's *Barari al-Ḥumma* (Prairies of Fever, 1985), Anton Shammas's *ʿArabeskot* (Arabesques, 1986, Hebrew), and Ahmed Masoud's *Vanished: The Mysterious Disappearance of Mustafa Ouda* (2015)—in which the disappearance of a central character sets in motion both the main action (an investigation into the circumstances of this disappearance) and its subsequent retelling.

4. Ibid., 225.

5. The word "literature" here and throughout is used as shorthand that also refers to the films discussed, especially given their poetic qualities.

6. Emile Habiby, *al-Waqaʾiʿ al-Ghariba fi Ikhtifaʾ Saʿid abi al-Naḥs al-Mutashaʾil* (Beirut: Dar Ibn Khaldun), 1974. The English translation, by Salma Khadra Jayyusi and Trevor LeGassick, bears the title *The Secret Life of Saeed: The Pessoptimist* (New York: Interlink, 2002), thus somewhat eliding the centrality of disappearance to the novel.

Palestinian poetry, too, is punctuated with disappearances. A key example is Mahmoud Darwish's *Fi Ḥaḍrat al-Ghiyab* (In the Presence of Absence, 2006), describing his family's struggle to return to their village, al-Birwa, only to find it nearly erased. Given the scale and explicitness of such historical erasure, it is no wonder that disappearance figures prominently in literary reckonings with 1948. What *is* surprising is its persistence, pervasiveness, and elasticity as a trope in depicting contemporary colonial conditions. Sorting the many meanings of disappearance in Palestinian literature, teasing out their formal possibilities and political implications, and reading these against the conceptual limitations of recent theoretical frameworks—specifically, the ecumenical analytics for approaching settler colonialism developed by Patrick Wolfe and other Anglophone scholars—will be the main purpose of this chapter.

The literal erasure setting Azem's novel in motion perfectly aligns with a key principle of settler colonial states, known in contemporary settler colonial theory (SCT) as "the logic of elimination." In its metaphorical reverberations, however, Azam's literary disappearance pushes its bounds. Indeed, the metaphorical concept of disappearance presented here attempts to answer the question "What kind of elimination?"—"What form of negation *exactly* does Zionism enact?"—to further hone the prism through which colonialism in Palestine is viewed and to better account for its seemingly contradictory objectives of elimination, segregation, and exploitation. Representations of economic exploitation in the novel, for instance, sit uncomfortably with SCT's distinction between "old" colonial empires, which "destroy to exploit," and settler colonial states, which "destroy to replace," forever uninterested in the labor power of the indigenous population.[7] Centering land over labor, SCT obscures the extractive—both exploitative and appropriative—mode of Zionism and its attendant principle of separation. Simultaneously, Israeli segregation exceeds apartheid, for Israel, unlike apartheid South Africa, attempts to erase the national difference of the "minority." Neither "settler colonialism" nor "apartheid," then, manages to encompass this context in all its contradictions. Tying Israel's goals to political commitments or solutions, these terms fail to grapple with its basic desire to "disappear" the Palestinians. As *Sifr al-Ikhtifaʾ* demonstrates, however, disappearance—as thematized and formalized in Palestinian literature—might propose a more supple and precise theory of Israeli segregation, extraction, and racialization through erasure.

As an indigenous literary theory, disappearance expresses not only the material legacy of colonial eradication and extraction but also, crucially, indigenous

7. Patrick Wolfe, "Settler Colonialism and the Elimination of the Native," *Journal of Genocide Research* 8, no. 4 (2006): 388.

strategies of anticolonial resistance. The authors surveyed here often reclaim their invisibility as agential, using it to document, criticize, and defy Zionist invisibilization. In *Sifr al-Ikhtifaʾ*, this may take the form of narrative withholding, as when the grandmother refuses fully to deliver her story. Or it may take the form of a dramatic vanishing act, as when all Palestinian prisoners evaporate from the suggestively named "Prison 48," leaving the guards themselves trapped.[8] The image of 1948 as a prison exposes Israel as founded on the ongoing isolation and invisibilization of Palestinians. Its designation as a *secret* prison, moreover, clarifies that it conceals not only its prisoners but the very circumstances of their incarceration. Comprehending the operation of this prison and conceiving of means for escaping it are thus vital tasks. The poetic concept of disappearance is central to both.

In a sense, "disappearance" is the poetic name given by Palestinian writers to the processes of Zionist overlooking surveyed in Chapter 2. With disappearance, however, the focus veers from phenomenological distinctions (reality and appearances, intentions and manifestations) to ontological and epistemological ones (presence and absence, visibility and invisibility), from refusal or failure to see what is there to its active erasure or enduring concealment. The Arabic word *ikhtifāʾ* bears this dual meaning, conveying vanishings both real and apparent, thus bridging the gap between Zionism's settler colonial drive to eliminate and its apartheid tendencies to separate and exploit. Its root, *kh-f-y*, moreover, proposes the semantic field of "covering," "secrecy," and "concealment," thus stressing the continuous existence of that which is hidden and the protection that covering might afford.[9] As a literary concept, *ikhtifāʾ* suggests a colonialism that operates not solely or necessarily though indigenous elimination, but rather through segregation, concealment, and exploitation, while also stressing the agency, endurance, and covert modes of resistance of the colonized.

There is, moreover, Palestinian precedent for the use of disappearance as an analytic. While Palestinian scholars and writers such as Fayez A. Sayegh, Jamil Hilal, and Edward Said had used the framework of settler colonialism

8. Azem, *Book of Disappearance*, 40. Is Waleed, the first prisoner reported missing, named for the titular hero of Jabra Ibrahim Jabra's 1978 novel? Have we finally found Waleed Masoud, just as he disappears again? The close-knit referential network of Palestinian literature seems at times to be performing a collective secrecy, a power afforded by literary disappearance.

9. In a book published just as work on this one has wrapped up, Saree Makdisi similarly conceptualizes erasure through the verb "to occlude," observing that it "also encourages us to think of the ways in which something might be carefully placed in the way of something else, 'to exclude or render obscure, as if by a blockage; to overshadow,'" as the Oxford English Dictionary has it; Makdisi, *Tolerance Is a Wasteland: Palestine and the Culture of Denial* (Oakland: University of California Press, 2022), 10–11.

to highlight Zionist land appropriation and territorial expansion (well before the so-called settler colonial turn in Palestine Studies),[10] they also employed the term "disappearance" to conceptualize 1948 and its aftermath. In 1980, Said claimed that, after 1948, "every Palestinian disappeared nationally and legally."[11] Soon after, Elias Sanbar—a Palestinian author and the cofounder of the *Revue d'études Palestiniennes*—elaborated:

> In 1948 our country was not merely occupied but was somehow "disappeared." That's certainly the way that the Jewish settlers, who at that moment became "Israelis," had to live the thing. . . . in order for this disappearance to succeed, it had to function from the start as if it had already taken place, which is to say by never "seeing" the existence of the other who was indisputably present all the same. In order to succeed, the emptiness of the terrain must be based in an evacuation of the "other" from the settlers' own heads.[12]

The destruction of Palestine and the disavowal of Palestinians, Sanbar suggests, were necessary not only for building a Zionist state and identity but also for concealing this constitutive violence. While Israeli scholars have recently begun to question the centrality of erasure and concealment to Zionism—claiming that its spatial history is irreducible to erasure alone and that its oppression is in fact known and exposed, even constituting part of the colonizing self itself[13]—contemporary Palestinian scholars such as Honaida Ghanim and Saree Makdisi echo Sanbar as they insist that Palestinian oppression rests on the fundamental colonial dialectics of destruction and affirmation, both material and psychological, and that erasure, even if not always successful, is *the* organizing principle of

10. Omar Jabary Salamanca et al., "Past Is Present: Settler Colonialism in Palestine," *Settler Colonial Studies* 2, no. 1 (2012): 2, referring to Fayez Abdullah Sayegh, *Zionist Colonialism in Palestine* (Beirut: Research Center, Palestine Liberation Organization, 1965); Jamil Hilal, "Imperialism and Settler Colonialism in West Asia: Israel and the Arab Palestinian Struggle," *UTAFITI: Journal of the Arts and Social Sciences* 1, no. 1 (1976): 51–70; Edward W. Said, "Zionism from the Standpoint of Its Victims," *Social Text*, no. 1 (1979).

11. Edward W. Said, *The Question of Palestine* (New York: Vintage, 1980), 111.

12. Elias Sanbar and Gilles Deleuze, "The Indians of Palestine" [1982], trans. Timothy S. Murphy, *Discourse: Journal for Theoretical Studies in Media and Culture* 20, no. 3 (2013): 28.

13. While these scholars and their shared socioeconomic milieu might be familiar with the history and facts of Israeli colonialism, most Jewish Israelis are not—a cultivated ignorance achieved through both silence and verbosity; respectively, Noam Leshem, *Life after Ruin: The Struggles over Israel's Depopulated Arab Spaces* (Cambridge and New York: Cambridge University Press, 2016); Gil Z. Hochberg, *Becoming Palestine: Toward an Archival Imagination of the Future* (Durham, N.C.: Duke University Press, 2021); Hagar Kotef, *The Colonizing Self: Or, Home and Homelessness in Israel/Palestine* (Durham, N.C.: Duke University Press, 2020).

the Zionist colonial project.[14] Perhaps more vocally still, the literary works surveyed here similarly stress the centrality of disappearance to the Palestinian experience of space, history, and culture. They also suggest that, although *ikhtifāʾ* refers to a largely twentieth-century phenomenon, its thematic recurrence in contemporary novels and films betrays continuities in the present.

While Palestinian academic and journalistic writing on these topics abounds, there are decisive reasons for turning to literature, too, for their theorization. First, literature was vital to Palestinian national cohesion and political discourse. In Israel, specifically, state censorship led to greater reliance on cultural modes of expression for preserving Palestinians' histories, expressing political views, and nurturing a national identity, at least until the 1970s.[15] Second, literature is often better able to convey the texture, absurdity, detail, and diversity of Palestinian experiences than academic writing.[16] Because Palestinian literature has long engaged with traditional Arabic genres and experimented with writing modes that depart from—while also building on, playing with, or satirizing—Western writing and thinking styles, it conforms to these less than scholarship does.[17] The poetic concept *ikhtifāʾ*, or "colonial disappearance," as articulated by Palestinian authors, thus offers a more locally grounded theoretical prism for understating coloniality and resistance in Palestine.

This proposed concept of *ikhtifāʾ* requires stepping back from "settler colonialism" toward the greater generality afforded by "coloniality." In forsaking the "settler," we do not necessarily lose the comparative and transnational force of SCT but rather expand it to include cases that, while not strictly "settler colonial," share important characteristics with the colonization of Palestine—characteristics often viewed as "merely" colonial (such as labor exploitation, involvement of European powers, and the imposition of Western values and culture). Distinctions between colonial and settler colonial frameworks are, at any rate, themselves unstable and often blurred. When Lorenzo Veracini,

14. Honaida Ghanim, "'Hekhan Kulam!': Diʾaleḳṭiḳa shel Meḥiḳa u-Veniya ba-Proyeḳṭ ha-Ḳolonyali, ha-Tsiyoni," *Zmanim*, no. 138 (2017): 102–15; Makdisi, *Tolerance Is a Wasteland*.

15. Nadim N. Rouhana and Areej Sabbagh-Khoury, "Settler-Colonial Citizenship: Conceptualizing the Relationship between Israel and Its Palestinian Citizens," *Settler Colonial Studies* 5, no. 3 (2015): 210.

16. As Said argues in *The Question of Palestine*, literary works, such as Kanafani's and Habiby's, sketch "the complete picture of Palestinian identity as no purely political tract can. Both writers record the Kafkaesque alternation between being and not-being there for Palestinians, whether inside Israel or in the Arab world" (153).

17. I discuss Habiby's complex interactions with Western literature in Liron Mor, "Humor and the Law of Rights: Voltaire's Cosmopolitan Optimism and Emile Habiby's Dissensual Pessoptimism," *Comparative Literature* 71, no. 2 (2019): 171–93.

for example, sets out to demarcate them, he finds himself repeatedly qualifying his assertions, conceding that characteristics of the two frameworks are "routinely concomitant."[18] Moreover, if we use the term "coloniality" in a broader sense, as a principle of the distribution of power, resources, and movement along racialized or national lines, then we may address colonialism in Israel as it applies not only to Palestinians but also to Mizrahi Jews (as well as African refugees and migrant workers).[19]

Simultaneously, this concept also involves a step "forward" toward greater specificity, centering on the concrete uses of disappearance in the Palestinian literary archive. By amassing a gallery of these uses, a structure or a concept emerges. Indeed, without a structural framework, as Omar Jabary Salamanca et al. argue, analytics tend "to target or accommodate settler colonial outcomes rather than aiming to decolonise the structure itself."[20] Allowing for a literary practice of decolonization, which might chime with other colonial contexts, this structural concept is also malleable. Based in a body of literature, it remains receptive to new works or interpretations that add to and modify its meaning. First, then, *ikhtifāʾ*, or colonial disappearance, is thus a poetic structural-historical indigenous concept of coloniality.

Disappearance as Colonial Elimination and Concealment

Above all, disappearance in Palestinian literature expresses the violent Zionist removal of Palestinians from Palestine and the invisibilization of those who remained in what became the State of Israel. In the late nineteenth century and the first half of the twentieth, Zionist efforts took the dual form of piecemeal acquisition of private lands and of negotiating with imperial powers—over the indigenous population's head—for the right to establish a Jewish state in Palestine. From the early days of Zionism, Palestinians recognized that the very "intention to create the Jewish National Home is to cause the disappearance or subordination of the Arabic population, culture and language," as the Arab delegations asserted in 1922 in response to Winston Churchill's White Paper.[21] A number of Zionists have also acknowledged this. Speaking at a Zionist convention in Basel in 1905, the Hebrew teacher Yitzhak Epstein clarified

18. Lorenzo Veracini, "Introducing Settler Colonial Studies," *Settler Colonial Studies* 1, no. 1 (2011): 2.

19. Anibal Quijano, "Coloniality of Power, Eurocentrism, and Latin America," *Nepantla: Views from South* 1, no. 3 (2000): 533–80.

20. Salamanca et al., "Past Is Present," 4–5.

21. Said, *Question of Palestine*, 83.

that Palestine was neither empty nor uncultivated. Fallow lands were in fact so scarce, he explained, that every Zionist land purchase, usually from absentee landlords, spelled the eviction of the Palestinian peasants who had cultivated it, sometimes for centuries. Recognizing that this crucial question—how Zionism should face the indigenous Palestinians—was "not merely forgotten" from consideration but rather constitutive, Epstein named it *the* "disappeared question" at the heart of Zionism.[22]

The gradual displacement and dispossession that began with land purchases intensified in the 1948 War. Zionist forces expelled about 750,000 Palestinians, destroying hundreds of villages and towns and depleting cities of their Palestinian population. Following the war, Israel sought to "Judaize the territory" (*yihud ha-merḥav*) by effacing traces of Palestinian towns and villages, both physically and symbolically, transferring land ownership to Jewish hands and, subsequently, erecting Jewish settlements in their stead.[23] Despite the vast expulsion, about 160,000 Palestinians remained within the 1949 Armistice Line (the "Green Line"), forming a minority in the new state, amounting to about a fifth of its population.[24] These Palestinians and their descendants are known today as "Palestinian citizens of Israel," "'48 Palestinians," or "Palestinians of the inside" (*fī al-dākhil*).[25] Remarkably, many of the writers of disappearance

22. Yitzhak Epstein and Alan Dowty, "'A Question That Outweighs All Others': Yitzhak Epstein and Zionist Recognition of the Arab Issue," *Israel Studies* 6, no. 1 (2001): 39. Epstein's words were printed two years later in *ha-Shiloʿaḥ*, a major Zionist journal, under the title "A Disappeared Question" (*sheʾela neʿelama*).

23. Nur Masalha, *Expulsion of the Palestinians: The Concept of "Transfer" in Zionist Political Thought, 1882–1948* (Washington, D.C.: Institute for Palestine Studies, 1992); Ilan Pappé, *The Ethnic Cleansing of Palestine* (Oxford: Oneworld, 2007); Nadim N. Rouhana and Areej Sabbagh-Khoury, "Memory and the Return of History in a Settler-Colonial Context: The Case of the Palestinians in Israel," *Interventions* 21, no. 4 (2019): 527–50. Other places, such as Ein Ḥoud or Yafa (Jaffa), which were not physically demolished, were emptied out of all or most of their Palestinian population and transformed into Jewish towns, complete with new, homonymic Hebrew names (Yaffo, Ein Hod). On this practice of erasure, see Rouhana and Sabbagh-Khoury, "Settler-Colonial Citizenship," 208.

24. Maha Nassar, *Brothers Apart: Palestinian Citizens of Israel and the Arab World* (Stanford, Calif.: Stanford University Press, 2017), 4; Rouhana and Sabbagh-Khoury, "Settler-Colonial Citizenship," 206.

25. For decades, Israeli state institutions and scholars referred to this group as "Arabs of Israel," reflecting both the official Israeli view of this population as an integrated ethnic minority and the pan-Arab inclination of some members of the community. Palestinians in Israel have increasingly rejected this label. Viewing this term as "one that denies their Palestinian national affiliation and functions as a form of settler colonial erasure," some prefer "Palestinian citizens of Israel," "Palestinians in Israel," Palestinians "of the inside," and "'48 Palestinians." These designations manifest not only a concrete Palestinian experience and consciousness—as op-

mentioned earlier—Azem, Habiby, Kashua, Shammas, Suleiman—belong to this group. Indeed, this chapter tends to focus on '48 Palestinians, whose perspective, I suggest, is not only essential to any analysis of Palestine-Israel but might also better illuminate the broader picture, stressing colonial continuities across the "Green Line." Is it significant that *ikhtifāʾ* is more prevalent in '48 Palestinians' works? And why and how is this concept significant to them?

One possible explanation is the status of about one-third of Palestinians in Israel as "present absentees" (*nokheḥim nifḳadim*), a juridical designation that has become a synecdoche for the living conditions of '48 Palestinians more broadly. The term refers to Palestinians internally displaced during the 1948 War—"present" within the borders of the state but driven out, and therefore "absent," from their towns and villages. Israel soon appropriated their lands and property by enacting the Absentees' Property Law (1950). Marking Palestinians as subjects who abandoned their homes and collaborated with the enemy, the rhetoric of the law aims to justify expropriation and to deny Palestinians refugee status, thereby barring them from returning or seeking reparations.[26] The law thus not only erased Palestinians from sight but also made the very processes of their erasure disappear. As the Palestinian scholar Abdul-Rahim al-Shaikh puts it, "As if the denial of justice [were] not enough, [our] disappearance was itself vanquished."[27]

Another explanation is the isolation that accompanied this legal erasure. Citing the Palestinian writer and literary scholar Anton Shammas, Maha Nassar claims that the Palestinian experience in Israel during its first decades was dominated by isolation, physical and cultural, both within the new state and in relation to the Arab world. Subject to martial law in Israel until 1966, '48 Palestinians were politically isolated from each other—surveilled and monitored, their work opportunities limited and their freedoms of movement and expression curtailed. The state and its institutions also culturally isolated Palestinians from their heritage, aiming to become the sole source of their cultural nourishment.[28] Over the years, the invisibility of Palestinians within the

---

posed to an implied generic Arabness—but also the distinct history of this particular Palestinian branch; see Nassar, *Brothers Apart*, 13–14.

26. Sabri Jiryis, "Domination by the Law," *Journal of Palestine Studies* 11, no. 1 (1981): 84.

27. Al-Shaikh, *Qalb al-Ḥimar*, 47, as quoted and translated by Rana Barakat, in "Writing/Righting Palestine Studies: Settler Colonialism, Indigenous Sovereignty and Resisting the Ghost(s) of History," *Settler Colonial Studies* 8, no. 3 (2018): 360. Edward Said similarly argues that "Zionism has hidden, or caused to disappear, the literal historical ground of its growth, its political cost to the native inhabitants of Palestine, and its militantly oppressive discriminations between Jews and non-Jews" (*Question of Palestine*, 57).

28. Nassar, *Brothers Apart*, 4.

state took on many forms, such as a separate education system, underfunding and underdevelopment, over- and under-policing, and discriminatory laws. Invisibilization continues today in such acts of legislation as the 2018 Nation State Law, which revoked the status of Arabic as an official state language and declared the right to exercise self-determination in Israel "unique to the Jewish people," and the 2011 Nakba Law, which empowers the finance minister to withhold state funds from institutions, municipalities, or organizations that partake in activities commemorating the Palestinian catastrophe.

Regionally, Israel restricted its citizens from traveling to or trafficking in textual materials from Arab countries, while the Arab League in turn boycotted Israeli citizens and goods. Palestinians in Israel were thus all but cut off from pan-Arab political and cultural discourse and became invisible to their neighbors. Even after 1967, when the figure of the Palestinian poet-resister was celebrated by the Arab world, Palestinians in Israel still had a tense relationship with their Arab counterparts.[29] This sense of being invisible to the Arab world animates Ghassan Kanafani's depiction of Iraqi smugglers exploiting Palestinian refugees in his 1963 novella "Rijal fi al-Shams" (mentioned in Chapter 1). When the refugees, desperate to cross the border in search for employment, finally find a Palestinian driver willing to smuggle them inside an empty water tank on his lorry, they suffocate to death on the Iraq-Kuwait border under the August sun, unseen and unheard by everyone, including the readers.[30] Written by an exiled Palestinian, the novella suggests that this invisibility beset Palestinians on both sides of the infamous "Green Line," itself a product of colonial erasure.

Palestinians were also isolated internationally. As Elias Khoury notes, "The Western world found that washing its hands of Jewish blood with Palestinian blood was the easiest way to break with the atrocities of the Second World War. The Palestinians were alone. Nobody was ready to hear the story of their

29. Ibid., 5–7.

30. Kanafani formally underscores the Palestinian characters' invisibility by abandoning free indirect discourse and "muting" them once they enter the water tank: the reader is no longer privy to their thoughts and feelings. The driver later wonders why the suffocating men kept silent and did not knock on the sides of the tank for help. As Elias Khoury observes, however, the driver has no way of knowing whether they knocked, since he was not present. Indeed, in the film adaptation of the novella *al-Makhduʿun* (The Dupes, dir. Tawfiq Saleh, 1972), the men do beat on the walls of the tank and go unheard. The driver's rhetorical question thus reflects a wishful blindness, a certain Arab insistence that Palestinians' suffering is merely the result of their reluctance to resist; see Kanafani, "Men in the Sun," in *Men in the Sun, and Other Palestinian Stories*, trans. Hilary Kilpatrick (Boulder, Colo.: Lynne Rienner, 1999), 74; Elias Khoury, "Rethinking the Nakba," *Critical Inquiry* 38, no. 2 (2012): 260–61.

pain."[31] In recent decades, however, Western attention to their cause has grown. Activists and movements on the ground are shifting public opinion, especially amongst younger generations, who increasingly view Palestine as comparable to other, less contentious settler-colonial cases. By focusing on that which is easily translatable, however, this form of attention risks concealing the particularities of the Palestinian case. In the refugee camps, for instance, a growing appeal to the international community since the 1980s has led, as the anthropologist Diana Allan shows, to an NGOization of the camp—replacing struggle with an economy of commemoration that emphasizes Palestinian cultural heritage and steadfast attachment to pre-1948 Palestine. Influenced by Western notions of testimony, this commemorative culture reduces the complexity of Palestinian realities to a single narrative. While the story of the Palestinian *nakba* as a past trauma is politically vital and economically crucial—drawing political and financial support from international networks—it occludes everyday forms of suffering, current economic and social realities, and narratives and subjectivities that do not align with the national cause. For Palestinians to appear on the international stage, their refusal to disappear was foregrounded through an emphasis on steadfastness and the right of return. Other aspects of their lives had to fade into the background.[32]

"Disappearance" thus expresses the Zionist displacement, dispossession, and isolation of Palestinians. Yet, ethnic cleansing is perhaps its chief characteristic. An obvious case is the 1948 War, with its premeditated mass expulsion and overt massacres (famous cases include Deir Yassin and now, Tantura).[33] These practices—along with their related, ongoing forms, such as the refugee camps or the Israeli refusal of the right of return—demonstrate that the Zionist disappearance of Palestinians entailed, and still entails, the elimination of Palestinians from Palestine. In framing this elimination as the telos of Zionism, *ikhtifāʾ* aligns with SCT. That said, this disappearance differs from native elimination in other contexts: in Israel a sizable part of the indigenous population remained. While eager to "transfer" the remaining Palestinian population, Zionist leaders understood that international opinion would not tolerate another expulsion.[34] The new state therefore turned instead to entrenching the line between the expelled Palestinians, prohibited from returning, and the

31. Khoury, "Rethinking the Nakba," 261.

32. Diana Allan, *Refugees of the Revolution: Experiences of Palestinian Exile* (Stanford, Calif.: Stanford University Press, 2013), 5–8.

33. Nur Masalha, "On Recent Hebrew and Israeli Sources for the Palestinian Exodus, 1947–49," *Journal of Palestine Studies* 18, no. 1 (1988): 121–37.

34. Nassar, *Brothers Apart*, 4.

Palestinians within its borders, offering the latter the carrot of citizenship and the stick of isolation and erasure.

What happens, then, if we reject the divide between 1948 and 1967, expanding our view to consider instead the colonization of Palestine as continuous? From the perspective of the present, Israel's "elimination of the native," in its literal sense, appears to have failed, for Palestinians presently make up about half of the population between the river and the sea. Attempting to reconcile this contradiction, Veracini argues that Israeli rule is settler colonial within 1948 Israel, yet simply colonial in the OPT.[35] This solution not only rehearses the colonizers' division of Palestine, as Rana Barakat observes,[36] but also misses the fact that both parts are subject to a shared colonial logic of disappearance, one not exhausted by "elimination."

Azem's novel, too, appears to exceed a simple framework of elimination. She refuses to solve the mystery of the collective disappearance of Palestinians, which takes place on both sides of the 1949 armistice line and in defiance of it. Spoiler alert: the reader never learns what truly happened or how the Israeli government eventually reacted. But the responses and hypothetical explanations of Jewish characters, rendered with no small amount of irony, are revealing. Some regard the disappearance as a clean, surgical solution to their problem—nothing short of a political miracle. Others, like Ariel's mother, see it as an opportunity to seize "abandoned" real estate, highlighting Zionists' material gains from Palestinian expulsion.[37] Liberal characters like Ariel recoil from the idea that Israeli security forces might be implicated. Perhaps protesting too much, he repeatedly insists that the disappearance took place "without a drop of blood" spilled. He utterly rejects the possibility of IDF involvement and speculates that "other Arabs" are responsible. Another character truly captures Israeli *hasbara*, describing the disappearance as "the 'cleanest' campaign of ethnic cleansing witnessed by humanity."[38]

These responses, while diverse (especially across class), converge to reveal a liberal Israeli obsession with ethical culpability, both past and present: a desire to conceal colonial violence itself. They evoke a long-standing Zionist rhetoric according to which the 1948 expulsion "was a miraculous cleaning of the land; the miraculous simplification of Israel's task."[39] As Ariel explains, liberal Zionists

35. Lorenzo Veracini, "The Other Shift: Settler Colonialism, Israel, and the Occupation," *Journal of Palestine Studies* 42, no. 2 (2013): 27–29.

36. Barakat, "Writing/Righting Palestine Studies," 350.

37. Azem, *Book of Disappearance*, 63–65, 139, 217–18.

38. Ibid., 106–7, 127, 197, 205, 212.

39. Chaim Weizmann, as quoted in Said, *Question of Palestine*, 21.

crave security, which they associate with the elimination of Palestinians; yet they also wish to see themselves as moral, to retain their self-image as "the only democracy in the Middle East."[40] Because of the history of Israel's establishment—the holocaust, the elimination of Jews from Europe—Israelis often struggle to sustain the cognitive dissonance between humanism and an eliminatory drive. Because of the time of Israel's establishment—a period of shifts in international law and moral norms—the desires for utter elimination had to be repressed. Azem's characters express the collective moral stakes of this dissonance and the inability to resolve it by physically eliminating the native population—or by rendering it a numerically insignificant minority—as other settler states did (though some Zionist groups explicitly advanced "transfer," and such calls are increasingly becoming more vocal, especially amongst the religious right). The characters' responses reflect the historical Zionist reluctance to carry the project to its genocidal end. The wish for a miraculous disappearance thus expresses distaste for the actions necessary for making Palestinians disappear—a liberal mode of disregard or disavowal. As the former Israeli prime minister Golda Meir put it in 1969, "We can forgive the Arabs for killing our children, but we cannot forgive them for forcing us to kill their children."[41]

Israel had to find a different solution, a colonial method that would reconcile maintaining control over a substantial Palestinian minority with repressing its ethical implications. This method is disappearance. In place of utter elimination, *ikhtifāʾ* aims to sustain yet contain and subjugate the Palestinian population by way of concealment, allowing Jewish Israelis to ignore colonial violence and to dissolve their moral qualms. Its displacement, segregation, and epistemological erasure are executed by a motley and complex set of apparatuses—bureaucratic, military, juridical, economic, and cultural. Various as they are, these share the same goal: appropriating the resources of Palestine, including both labor-power and cultural capital, without assimilating Palestinians into the Jewish collective or allowing them to appear as nationally distinct—that is, as Palestinians. The ethical dissonance that motivates disappearance might also explain seemingly inexplicable Israeli practices such as systemically maiming Palestinians instead of killing them or keeping the Gaza Strip population on the verge of a humanitarian disaster without quite letting this disaster detonate.[42]

40. Azem, *Book of Disappearance*, 107.

41. The origin of Meir's quotation is difficult to establish, yet it is widely quoted and forms part of Zionism's historical vocabulary; see Yonatan Mendel, "Forced To . . . ," *LRB* (Blog), July 25, 2014, https://www.lrb.co.uk/blog/2014/july/forced-to.

42. Jasbir K. Puar, "Spatial Debilities: Slow Life and Carceral Capitalism in Palestine," *South Atlantic Quarterly* 120, no. 2 (2021): 393–414; Eyal Weizman, *The Least of All Possible*

Disappearance as Colonial Segregation

Israel categorically resists assimilating Palestinians and instead perpetuates sharp racial and national divides. It is ardently opposed to the demographic, political, or cultural integration of Palestinians from the OPT, which would defeat its very raison d'être as a Jewish state. While '48 Palestinians, by contrast, eventually gained formal citizenship, their assimilation all but stopped there. They were, at best, accommodated or tolerated by the state, but only through racialized segregation—for instance, by forming separate "Arab divisions" within Israeli institutions, such as the Education Ministry and the *Histadrut* (Israel's national trade union).[43] This segregationist tendency distinguishes Israel from other settler colonial states, where native elimination is perpetrated not only by physical eradication but also by assimilation into the colonizing society, through such processes as education and miscegenation. Unlike the U.S. or Australia, Israel did not undertake grand projects for "acculturating" the indigenous population. If assimilation exists, it is merely in the labor market—what Ahmad Sa'di calls "incorporation without integration."[44]

A fantasy of assimilation nonetheless haunts the literary archive. In "ʿA'id ila Ḥayfa" (see Chapter 1), the exiled Kanafani was able to imagine the Palestinian who remained in Haifa only as one adopted by Jews and fully assimilated. Kanafani's novel ostensibly resembles the novel *be-Or Ḥadash* (In a New Light, 1966, Hebrew), by the '48-Palestinian author Athallah Mansour, in which

---

Evils: Humanitarian Violence from Arendt to Gaza (London and New York: Verso, 2011). As Puar writes, the right to maim, like the slow death of disaster capitalism, points to "the economic and ideological productivity of maintaining a population in a state of perpetual injuring" or risk. Economically, "justified as moral because it doesn't kill, [it] is a mode of producing value from disposable bodies while all but ensuring a slow death." Ideologically, maiming is "a tactical refusal of producing a victim-subject, an abnegation of access to the version of the 'human' manifested by human rights discourses" (296).

43. As'ad Ghanem, *The Palestinian-Arab Minority in Israel, 1948–2000: A Political Study* (Albany: State University of New York Press, 2001); Rouhana and Sabbagh-Khoury, "Settler-Colonial Citizenship." Oded Erez and Arnon Yehuda Degani term the voided citizenship of Palestinians in Israel "subordinate integration." Yet, the continual segregation of Palestinians from Jews (for instance, by including Palestinians in the *Histadrut* only in a separate Arab department) complicates naming this process "integration," even while modifying it as "subordinate"; see Erez and Degani, "Songs of Subordinate Integration: Music Education and the Palestinian Arab Citizens of Israel during the Mapai Era," *Ethnic and Racial Studies* 44, no. 6 (2021): 1008–29.

44. Ahmad H. Sa'di, "Incorporation without Integration: Palestinian Citizens in Israel's Labour Market," *Sociology* 29, no. 3 (1995): 429–51.

an orphaned Palestinian is adopted by an Israeli Jewish family and into the kibbutz society—a highly implausible scenario.[45] Other scholars have framed the two as comparable narratives of assimilation and lost identity.[46] I suggest instead that comparing them exposes assimilation as a fantasy of the outsider. Unlike Kanafani, who conjures a fully assimilated Palestinian, Mansour presents us with a protagonist who, even in the most extraordinary conditions—adopted into the collectivist heaven of the kibbutz—fails to assimilate. Israeli society severs the protagonist's links to his culture without ever embracing him. For Palestinians in Israel, Mansour suggests, assimilation is an outlier. Indeed, if such literary figures are "figures of loss" (or "lost figures"), as Gil Hochberg argues, their loss is not, pace Hochberg, the price of assimilation. Rather, they have been culturally and historically "disappeared" precisely without that compensation.

Beyond elimination and concealment, then, a denationalizing segregation in lieu of assimilation is a crucial dimension of colonial disappearance brought to light by Palestinian literature. Habiby, another '48 Palestinian author, explores this dimension humorously in *al-Mutashaʾil*, with its protagonist's perpetually ill-fated attempts to adapt himself to the colonizers' European culture and its languages. Greeted by an English-speaking Zionist soldier with the Hebrew "shalom," the protagonist Saeed responds in English, "peace"—thus "showing how civilized [he] was"—but the soldier laughingly one-ups him by translating Saeed's response "back" to Arabic, exclaiming, "Salaam! Salaam!"[47] In a later scene, no matter how close Saeed's familiarity with Shakespeare is, nor how accurately he quotes from his plays, Saeed's jailers always outdo him—if not by their knowledge of Shakespeare, then by sheer violence.[48] Saeed's Jewish interlocutors thus always frustrate his attempt to "Westernize" and find a way to remind him of his "rightful place," forever excluded from their culture. Many of the novel's jokes turn precisely on Saeed's incomplete

45. A Palestinian son adopted into a Jewish family is also featured in a novel by another "outside" Palestinian—see Susan Abulhawa's *Mornings in Jenin* (New York: Bloomsbury, 2010). Note that in all these cases, the assimilation is into Ashkenazi families. However, in most documented cases of Palestinians who "passed" (not adopted) as Jews, it was as *mizraḥim*; see Hillel Cohen, *Śonʾim: Sipur Ahava* (Tel Aviv: ʿIvrit, 2022), 227, 262–64. On the trope of passing in Palestinian literature, see Maurice Ebileeni, *Being There, Being Here: Palestinian Writings in the World* (Syracuse, N.Y.: Syracuse University Press, 2022), Chapter 3.

46. Gil Z. Hochberg, "To Be or Not to Be an Israeli Arab: Sayed Kashua and the Prospect of Minority Speech-Acts," *Comparative Literature* 62, no. 1 (2010): 73.

47. Habiby, *Pessoptimist*, 41.

48. Ibid., 123/169.

familiarity with Hebrew, on his inability to ever get it quite right despite his every effort.[49]

Sayed Kashua's more recent novel, *'Aravim Rokdim* (Dancing Arabs, 2002, Hebrew), experiments wittily with the possibility of a '48 Palestinian "passing" as an Israeli. These passings are never fully successful. Even Hochberg, who regards Kashua's novel as yet another assimilation narrative and likens it to boarding-school novels in other colonial contexts—where the colonizer's education system is the arena for of the culture clash of assimilation—concedes that it is through failed passings that "Kashua dramatizes the impossibility of being an Israeli Arab."[50] Not at all representative, Kashua's example is, in more ways than one, the exception that proves the rule. The very humor of the writing turns on the exceptionality of his case, as the only Palestinian in a Jewish neighborhood, the only one in a Jewish classroom, or the only one in the Israeli television industry.

Israel had never established boarding schools for the purpose of assimilating Palestinians. Education in Israel in fact reproduces and reinforces segregation and hierarchization. The Israeli education system has separate institutions, as well as separate curricula, for Jewish and Palestinian students, both controlled by the state. The curriculum for "Arab schools" was formulated under the assumption that Palestinians are a security risk: as Majid al-Haj notes, its goal was to empty Palestinian education of any Arab or Palestinian national content, seeking instead "to reinforce the religious-cultural component and the Israeli-citizenship component."[51] Criticizing the colonial pilfering of the curriculum,

49. On the role of untranslatability in the novel and on its humor, see Lital Levy, *Poetic Trespass: Writing between Hebrew and Arabic in Israel/Palestine* (Princeton, N.J.: Princeton University Press, 2014), 113–25; Mor, "Humor and the Law of Rights." In one scene, for instance, Saeed, who does not yet speak Hebrew fluently, manages to come up with the Hebrew words needed to ask a passerby for the time, only to completely misunderstand the response. The Jewish worker replies *aḥat*, meaning "one" in Hebrew, yet Saeed hears *acht*, German for eight. This misunderstanding is not entirely Saeed's fault, for it relies on a difference in pronunciation introduced by Jews of European descent into Modern Hebrew—substituting for the pronunciation of the letter *Ḥet* (*ḥ*) the Ashkenazi-inflected pronunciation *kh*, thus in effect saying *akhat*; Habiby, *Pessoptimist*, 48.

50. Hochberg, "To Be or Not to Be an Israeli Arab," 74–75. Both Kashua's writing and his biography clarify that his integration into Jewish society has ultimately failed, despite having the best opening conditions. He decided to leave Israel in 2014 and soon after stopped writing for his Hebrew audience; see Kashua, "Why Sayed Kashua Is Leaving Jerusalem and Never Coming Back," *Haaretz*, July 4, 2014, https://www.haaretz.com/.premium-for-sayed-kashua-co-existence-has-failed-1.5254338.

51. Majid Al-Haj, *Education, Empowerment, and Control: The Case of the Arabs in Israel* (Albany: State University of New York Press, 1995), 122. A new history curriculum for Palestin-

Alaa, the Palestinian narrator of Azem's *Sifr al-Ikhtifaʾ*, laments spending his school days studying the colonizers' "white dreams about this place" rather than his own history.[52] And while this curriculum limited Palestinians' exposure to their own heritage, it did not serve as a conduit for socialization into Jewish society. The content excised from the Palestinian curriculum was not replaced with content taught in Jewish schools. In teaching history, for instance, Jewish schools emphasized their national history and the contributions of (European) Jews to the culture of humankind; Palestinian schools, prohibited from teaching their national history, instead impressed the joint contributions of Jews and Arabs to world culture, emphasizing values of Arab-Jewish coexistence (albeit with Jewish superiority)—none of which featured in the Jewish curriculum.[53] Palestinian students were thus denied both their own history and a shared curriculum with their Jewish counterparts.

Elia Suleiman presents this mode of educational segregation in his film *al-Zaman al-Baqi* (The Time that Remains, 2009) by depicting an "Arab school" choir performing the song "ʿId Istiqlal Israʾil" (Israel's Independence Holiday). This scene rehearses a common humiliating ritual in 1960s Israel, whereby this propaganda song was regularly performed in Palestinian schools on Israel's Independence Day. Written solely for the use of Palestinians, it was intended to replace and bar Palestinian "national content," its lyrics providing the liturgical script for compelling Palestinian schoolchildren in effect to celebrate their own *nakba*.[54] "ʿId Istiqlal Israʾil" is not a translation of a Hebrew song, nor does it set Arabic lyrics to the music of an Israeli tune. It exists to disappear Palestinian history, to forestall the commemorative practices of Palestinians without assimilating them, and to generate racial rather than national difference.

If assimilation usually presents itself as an economic exchange whereby the loss of cultural identity is simply the price for social admission, then Palestinians in Israel seem to have lost on both ends of the transaction (which, admittedly, is never fair). Azem's novel, too, clarifies that Israeli education is not a

---

ian high schools introduced in 2007 slightly shifted this policy, encouraging greater familiarity with Arab culture and "values" in addition to loyalty to the state; Hatim Mahamid, "History Education for Arab Palestinian Schools in Israel," *Journal of Education and Development* 1, no. 1 (2017): 37–47.

52. Azem, *Book of Disappearance*, 88.

53. Al-Haj, *Education, Empowerment, and Control*, 129–30.

54. Erez and Degani, "Songs of Subordinate Integration," 1,019–20. As the authors argue, however, by being forced on a whole generation of '48 Palestinians, the song "became a symbol of oppression in ways that at once hindered a sense of civic inclusion and, paradoxically, contributed to the solidification of a distinct Arab-Israeli identity" (1024).

door to the Jewish collective and that assimilation is, in fact, impossible. In Alaa's dream, a street prophet announces that the only solution left for all Palestinians is converting to Judaism (*al-ḥal al-waḥīd huwa an nadkhul jamīʿan bi-l-diyāna al-yahūdiyya*). Addressing his grandmother, Alaa muses, "You would've laughed at my dream and told me, 'It wouldn't make any difference, dear.'"[55] Conversion is futile because "Jew" in Israel is not merely a religious or cultural category, no more than "Arab" is merely a cultural category and "Palestinian" a national one. Rather, all are also markers of racial difference. While conversion in Israel is necessarily religious, the theological operates here as "a racial amnesty."[56] Defining itself as a Jewish state, Israel offers no national category that is divorced from racialized "Jewishness" (for "Israeli" is a civic category). Yet conversion into Judaism is foreclosed for Palestinians and with it the path to full assimilation.[57] This racial divide is one of the specificities of Israeli colonialism: if other settler-colonial states endeavored to erase the natives' heritage for the sake of assimilation, Israel sought to make Palestinian history and culture disappear in order to separate Palestinians from their past and from the Jewish collective, insisting on their racial difference. In this process of denationalization, it is the Palestinianness of Palestinians that is pushed to disappear, while their separation and marginality are actively maintained.

Disappearance as Exploitation and Appropriation

Israeli settler colonialism benefits from Palestinian disappearance in various ways that appear inexplicable when land ownership is regarded as its sole motive. Zionism often prioritizes economic gains—as well as political control and global support—over indigenous elimination and territorial expansion. To resolve this apparent contradiction, Sobhi Samour argues that, even if its economic advantages are not essential to Israeli settler-colonialism, the exploitation of Palestinian labor is a political advantage, "key to managing the Palestinian

55. Azem, *Book of Disappearance*, 117/124.

56. Ronit Lentin, *Traces of Racial Exception: Racializing Israeli Settler Colonialism* (London and New York: Bloomsbury Academic, 2018), 106.

57. The racialized impossibility of conversion into Judaism is explored by Nadeem Karkabi through the exceptional case of Nasreen Qadri, a contemporary Palestinian pop singer wholeheartedly embraced by the Israeli mainstream. Despite her superstar status, despite committed romantic relationships with Israeli Jews, and despite her unwavering support for the state and the IDF, Qadri was unable to convert to Judaism in a manner recognized by the state. Her failure to surmount colonial segregation exposes the line crossed by conversion as racialized rather than religious; see Karkabi, "The Impossible Quest of Nasreen Qadri to Claim Colonial Privilege in Israel," *Ethnic and Racial Studies* 44, no. 6 (2021): 966–86.

population."[58] But what if we consider these economic gains as in fact integral to the Zionist project, while indeed entwined with political gains? The limit case of Gaza may illustrate my point. Since 2005, Israel has formally relinquished all territorial claims for the Strip while maintaining a firm grip on nearly every aspect of life there. Some view this "disengagement" process as "the amount of formaldehyde" necessary to ossify the political status quo, while others see it as "warehousing"—the incarceration of a "surplus population," kept impoverished yet alive, to avoid thorny legal and humanitarian issues or diplomatic blowback.[59] Gaza as open-air prison is not only politically strategic but also economically lucrative: while Israel no longer directly extracts labor or natural resources from Gaza, as it does in the West Bank, it profits indirectly by using it as testing grounds for war and surveillance technologies. Like both traditional colonialism and apartheid, Zionism has always had an exploitative dimension, one better served by containment and separation than by simple elimination. Unlike South African apartheid, however, Zionism strives to render this separation itself invisible, setting apart Palestinians without granting them their national difference.

Disappearance is thus profitable both ideologically and economically, allowing for more effective extraction of Palestinian labor value. Indeed, Jewish employers have continuously relied on cheaper Palestinian labor to increase profits despite the Zionist ideologemes of *kibush ha-'avoda* (the conquest of labor) and *'avoda 'Ivrit* (Hebrew labor), formed as early as the Second *Aliyah* (1904–14). While Gershon Shafir's 1996 definition of Israel as a model "pure settler state"—one that avoids indigenous labor and imports its workers instead—has become a truism of SCT, many Palestinians were and are employed in low-wage jobs in agriculture, construction, industry, and service, from the early days of Zionism to this day.[60]

58. Sobhi Samour, "Covid-19 and the Necroeconomy of Palestinian Labor in Israel," *Journal of Palestine Studies* 49, no. 4 (2020): 54.

59. Dov Weisglass, a senior adviser to the then prime minister Ariel Sharon, advanced the formaldehyde explanation. According to him, by using the disengagement plan, Israel managed to freeze the peace process, to "prevent the establishment of a Palestinian state, . . . [as well as any] discussion on the refugees, the borders and Jerusalem. . . . And all this with authority and permission"; see Ari Shavit, "Top PM Aide: Gaza Plan Aims to Freeze the Peace Process," *Haaretz*, October 6, 2004, https://www.haaretz.com/1.4710372. On warehousing, see Jeff Halper, "The Palestinians: Warehousing a 'Surplus People,'" *ICAHD*, May 23, 2019, https://icahd.org/2019/05/23/the-palestinians-warehousing-a-surplus-people/.

60. On the historical role of Palestinians in the Israeli construction industry, see Andrew Ross, *Stone Men: The Palestinians Who Built Israel* (London and Brooklyn: Verso, 2019).

The disappearance wrought on Palestinians in Israel by colonial labor relations is exposed in a digressive chapter on "the many virtues of the Oriental imaginations" in *al-Mutashaʾil*. Saeed reflects drolly on Palestinian workers adopting Hebrew names for themselves (and, by implication, hiding their Palestinian identity): "Don't forget Shlomo, in one of Tel Aviv's very best hotels. Isn't he really Sulaiman, son of Munirah, from our own quarter? And 'Dudi,' isn't he really Mahmud? 'Moshe,' too; isn't his proper name Musa, son of Abdel Massih? How could they earn a living in a hotel, restaurant, or filling station without help from their Oriental imagination?"[61] Israeli employers and customers are generally quite happy to rely on underpaid and disempowered Palestinian labor in the service sector, as long as staff do not insist on appearing as Palestinians in public. While this trend may be shifting, with '48 Palestinians (especially women) becoming more visible in service work, shedding "Palestinian features" is still essential. The continuity of Palestinian self-invisibilization could be gleaned from Sayed Kashua's more recent novel, *Guf Sheni Yaḥid* (Second Person Singular, 2010), which echoes Habiby's in depicting Palestinian kitchen staff assuming Hebrew names. Kashua's protagonist begins to hide his identity and attempts to "pass" as Jewish once he realizes that, in Jerusalem restaurants, only Jews work as waiters; Palestinians are consigned to the kitchen, where the work is harder and the pay lower.[62] Despite complications during "tense" periods, many of Jerusalem's restaurants still rely on Palestinian chefs and cooks from the West Bank and Jerusalem who are tucked away in kitchens while the front of the house is staffed mostly by Jewish women.[63]

Saeed's own employment reflects several disappearance techniques that allow colonizers to exploit Palestinian workers without having to see them or interact with them. He works in the "Arab Unit" of the Israeli *Histadrut*, which institutionally segregates the Palestinian labor union. His employment also illustrates the Israeli use of middlemen and contractors to avoid direct contact with Palestinian workers. Saeed's immediate supervisor is a Mizrahi man, Jacob, who releases the Ashkenazi "big boss" from seeing or interacting with Saeed. In turn, Saeed himself is a middleman of sorts, whose job consists in spying on other Palestinian workers to thwart "communist activity," ensure political compliance, and smooth the path of economic production.

61. Habiby, *Pessoptimist*, 101.

62. Sayed Kashua, *Guf Sheni Yaḥid* (Jerusalem: Keter, 2010), 190–91.

63. The racial division of labor is difficult to quantify but Ahmad Asmar and Marik Shtern's report provides a sense of its prevalence: mi-Baʿad le-Tiḳrat ha-Zekhukhit: Falasṭinim ṿe- Yiśraʾelim be-Shuḳ ha-Taʿasuḳa bi-Yrushalayim" (Jerusalem: Mekhon Yerushalayim le-Meḥḳare Mediniyut, 2017).

Saeed opens his story by stressing the great extent of his disappearance at his workplace, claiming that he was always so invisible that he drew absolutely no attention. As a spy and a collaborator, Saeed's life requires so much secrecy and self-effacement that he ends up raising a son whose cries are stifled in his crib, who—only ever hearing whispers at home—barely learns to talk. Disappearance at work, Habiby's novel thus suggests, tends to spill over into one's home life and reproductive labor, affecting family and community members and replicating itself across generations. In being invisible at work, Saeed claims, he is just like "the rest," thus expressing a collective rather than individual condition.[64] The fact that Saeed is a worker in the workers union adds a meta dimension to the generalization and suggests that colonial and capitalist modes of exploitation intersect in disappearance.

From 1967 until the First Intifada, Israel has also exploited the labor and consumption powers of Palestinians from the West Bank and Gaza. Employing Palestinians at low wages, Israeli employers decreased labor costs, expanded production, and enjoyed economic growth. Because their wages in Israel were higher than in the OPT (although lower than those earned by Jewish Israelis), Palestinians' quality of life initially increased. In the long run, however, this process created a captive labor market, led to the neglect and loss of Palestinian farming land, and interfered with industrial development in Palestine, forming a self-perpetuating cycle.[65] Likewise, Israel created a captive Palestinian commodity market by limiting imports and preventing Palestinians from producing such commodities themselves. The Palestinian economy was rendered heavily reliant on Israel and was severely hit when large numbers of Palestinian workers were replaced by migrant workers in the 1990s. Even so, at the end of that decade, just before the Second Intifada, about 110,000 Palestinians—roughly one-third of the Palestinian labor force—were employed within Israel.[66]

The number of work permits issued by Israel soon plummeted—from 100,000 in the year 2000 to about 30,000 in 2011. Scholars such as Salim Tamari,

64. Habiby, *Pessoptimist*, 7.

65. Leila Farsakh, *Palestinian Labour Migration to Israel: Labour, Land and Occupation* (Abingdon and New York: Routledge, 2005); Shir Hever, "Exploitation of Palestinian Labour in Contemporary Zionist Colonialism," *Settler Colonial Studies* 2, no. 1 (2012): 124–32; Shlomo Swirski, "The Price of Occupation: The Cost of the Occupation to Israeli Society," *Palestine-Israel Journal of Politics, Economics, and Culture* 12, no. 1 (2005), https://pij.org/articles/335/the-price-of-occupation—the-cost-of-the-occupation-to-israeli-society.

66. Eitan Diamond, "Crossing the Line: Violation of the Rights of Palestinians in Israel without a Permit," *B'Tselem*, March 2007, 20, https://www.btselem.org/publications/summaries/200703_crossing_the_line.

Neve Gordon, and Shlomo Swirski therefore argued that Israel had transitioned away from colonial exploitation to a model of separation. However, the Israeli economy still exploits Palestinian labor, even if to a fluctuating degree. Indeed, the number of work permits issued has been steadily increasing since 2012. West Bank Palestinians now make up about 70 percent of the construction labor force in Israel and the majority of workers in industrial zones in the settlements.[67] Factory owners in these industrial zones pay lower rents, receive substantial government subsidies and grants, enjoy reduced taxes and better infrastructure, and have direct access to a vast reserve of exploitable Palestinian labor.[68] Israel's de-development policy in the West Bank—restricting Palestinians from establishing industry and denying them access to natural resources—also led to high unemployment, pushing many to work in Israel illegally. As of 2022, an estimated 50,000 Palestinians work in Israel without permits, endangering their lives and risking arrests whenever they enter Israel.[69] Working without permits—or with them, yet under the constant threat of their revocation—Palestinian workers are especially vulnerable to labor rights violations. During COVID-19, as both unemployment in the West Bank and demand for labor in Israel surged, Palestinians were pushed to subject themselves to both added health risks and increased surveillance through a dedicated phone app.[70] Security and labor exploitation are deeply imbricated in this context, with one often invoked to bolster the other.

With or without permits, the exploitation of West Bank Palestinians working in Israel is sustained through disappearance. It relies on their general

67. Who Profits, "Exploited and Essential: Palestinian Labour under COVID-19 (Flash Report)," *Whoprofits* (blog), June 2020, 4, https://whoprofits.org/wp-content/uploads/2020/06/Exploited-and-Essential-Palestinian-Labour-under-Covid-19-2.pdf. In the first quarter of 2022, 204,000 Palestinians from the West Bank and East Jerusalem worked for Israeli employers, mostly in construction, agriculture, and food plants. Of these, 31,000 were employed in the settlements and about 50,000 worked without authorization. These numbers are based on the Palestinian Central Bureau of Statistics, Labour Force Survey Round (Q1/2022).

68. Hever, "Exploitation of Palestinian Labour," 128; Who Profits, "Industrial Zones in the Occupied Palestinian Territory," *Whoprofits* (blog), June 2019. https://www.whoprofits.org/dynamic-report/industrial-zones.

69. Hagar Shezaf, "Within Two Months, 20 Palestinians Were Shot by Israel While Trying to Cross from West Bank," *Haaretz*, December 23, 2019, https://www.haaretz.com/israel-news/.premium-within-two-months-20-palestinian-were-shot-while-trying-to-cross-from-west-bank-1.8298644; Diamond, "Crossing the Line."

70. Samour, "Covid-19 and the Necroeconomy"; Ihab Maharmeh, "Israel's Violations of Palestinian Workers' Rights: COVID-19 and Systemic Abuse," *Al-Shabaka* (blog), July 15, 2021, https://al-shabaka.org/briefs/israels-violations-of-palestinian-workers-rights-covid-19-and-systemic-abuse/.

invisibility to Jewish eyes and on the aforementioned ambiguities—the shady, exploitative zones of illegality or the threat of authorization revocation. Azem captures this mode of exploitation in a flowery vignette about an Israeli farmer's preference for Palestinian labor:

> Inexpensive foreign labor from China to Romania had flooded the market in recent years. But Shimon preferred Palestinian women from the West Bank. Despite the difficulties of securing work permits for them, they were faster and more efficient. Moreover, he didn't need to worry about finding housing or health care for them, as is done with foreign laborers. A car took them from the edge of Balata refugee camp in the morning and went through the checkpoint to drop them off at the farm. He doesn't know anything about them, or their lives, except for their full names and ID numbers, which he'd recorded. He only dealt with Maryam. Even when he needed to address the other workers, she was his messenger. When he happened to be in a good mood, he joked with them, but that was quite rare. He often chastised them and ordered them to keep plucking flowers whenever he heard chatter, or noticed that their work rhythm had slowed down a bit for whatever reason.[71]

Azem reveals not only the exploitative conditions of Palestinian labor—harder, faster work for lesser pay—but also the form of relations it generates. Shimon expects his Palestinian workers to work in silence and without recognition. He has the privilege of noting nothing about their lives, of engaging them if and when the fancy strikes. And, like many Israeli employers, Shimon relies on a Palestinian "contractor" to minimize contact with them.

Sifr al-Ikhtifa' also dramatizes a form of colonial exploitation that exceeds labor: the extraction of intelligence and the indirect exploitation of Palestinians as test subjects for warfare and control technologies. This happens on several fronts in the story: security officers in Prison 48 view their secret prisoners as sources of information extracted by torture; the vanishing becomes the pretext for a broad intelligence sweep, a data mining of hundreds of thousands of e-mails and messages sent by Palestinians;[72] and Ariel has built a journalistic career on the back of professional connections and language proficiency gained in an intelligence unit. Intelligence-gathering in Israel is not only a military asset but also the grounds upon which civilian careers and private profits

71. Azem, *Book of Disappearance*, 28–29.

72. Ibid., 43, 148. Such platform policing is indeed representative of the mode of surveillance conducted by the Israeli military during the 2015–16 Palestinian uprising.

grow. Like Ariel, many high-tech and start-up developers have jump-started their careers by amassing "military capital" in the IDF, particularly in intelligence.[73] Indeed, warfare, control, and surveillance technologies privately developed in Israel are often dreamed up in militarized colonial spaces. Israeli manufacturers, as Naomi Klein first argued, use the OPT—especially the Gaza enclave—as a laboratory for new weapons and security technologies, whose "tried and tested" status markup their value.[74] Maintaining Palestinians alive but apart, unseen but surveilled, provides Israeli firms with a unique opportunity to capitalize on war and to market arms and security personnel, crowd control and espionage technologies, systems of platform policing and "warehousing" (the art of incarcerating, impoverishing, and controlling "hostile" populations), both domestically and internationally.[75] The Israeli military-industrial complex, a vital and invisible form of colonial extraction, has been steadily growing since the year 2000.[76]

Finally, unlike elimination, disappearance allows for treating Palestinian culture itself as a resource for expropriation, both for profit and as a marker of indigeneity that Zionism claims for itself. In *Sifr al-Ikhtifaʾ*, Ariel pilfers Alaa's journal, absorbing Alaa's and his grandmother's memories, thoughts, and experiences into his own writing. The very title of his book in-progress, *Chronicles of Pre-Disappearance*, attempts to cash in not only on its sensational solution to a national mystery but on the authenticity of its Palestinian voices. A similar logic underlies Israeli appropriation of Palestinian cuisine, which has exploded in popularity in recent years, in Israel as well as in the U.S. and Europe. Chefs have developed international careers by adopting Palestinian dishes, capitalizing on their authenticity while rendering them more accessible to Western audiences. Marketing dishes as "Mediterranean" or regional, these chefs erase their Palestinianness or reduce them to Orientalist tropes, thus

73. Ibid., 80; Erella Grassiani, "Between Security and Military Identities: The Case of Israeli Security Experts," *Security Dialogue* 49, no. 1–2 (2018): 83–95; Ahmad H. Sa'di, "Israel's Settler-Colonialism as a Global Security Paradigm," *Race & Class* 63, no. 2 (2021): 21–37.

74. Naomi Klein, "Gaza: Not Just a Prison, a Laboratory," *Nation*, June 15, 2007, https://www.commondreams.org/views/2007/06/15/gaza-not-just-prison-laboratory. See also Shir Hever, *The Privatisation of Israeli Security* (London: Pluto, 2017); Darryl Li, "The Gaza Strip as Laboratory: Notes in the Wake of Disengagement," *Journal of Palestine Studies* 35, no. 2 (2006): 38–55.

75. Halper, "The Palestinians: Warehousing a 'Surplus People'"; Who Profits, "Proven Effective: Crowd Control Weapons in the Occupied Palestinian Territories," *Whoprofits* (blog), April 2014, https://www.whoprofits.org/wp-content/uploads/2018/06/old/weapons_report-8.pdf.

76. According to official Israeli reports, Israel's defense exports amounted to 12.5 billion dollars in 2022. Its profits were already estimated at over seven billion dollars in 2012. See Yotam Feldman (dir.), *The Lab* (Cinephil, 2013).

aestheticizing them. This mode of extraction is similarly used in Israel's fashion, design, music, and tourism industries, which denationalize what they appropriate even as they fetishize its indigeneity, translating "local" and "authentic" soundbites into easily digestible commodities.[77]

Beyond personal economic gains, the effects are also ideological. Since its inception, Zionism has selectively appropriated elements of Palestinian culture to construct itself as indigenous and thereby distinguish itself from Europe and obfuscate its coloniality.[78] As SCT scholars argue, the ultimate aim of every settler colonial project is to indigenize itself.[79] In the context of Palestine, this process also involves "disappearing" the Palestinian nature of the adopted indigeneity.

This disappearing act is beautifully illustrated by Suleiman's 1996 film *Sijill Ikhtifa'*, dedicated to recording the disappearance of '48 Palestinians. Its first half, "a personal diary," is focused on the paratactic, daily invisibility of Palestinians in Nazareth (a Palestinian city in Israel's northern periphery), while its second half, titled "a political diary," examines the disappearance-by-segregation of Palestinians in Jerusalem. Scenes in Nazareth, draped with the overtones of tourism kitsch, are haunted by the constant creaking sound of a spinning postcard stand outside the "Holyland" souvenir shop. In addition to religious memorabilia, the Palestinian-owned shop offers pilgrims Israeli postcards, which promote a propogandist image of Israel. (That the postcards are sold by a Palestinian shop-owner only serves to stress the structural all-pervasiveness of their message and the complicity that disappearance can produce.)

77. Ortal Ben Dayan, "Kakh Shoded ha-Ma'arav et ha-'Itsuvim ha-Yelidiyim," *Śiḥa Meḳomit* (blog), July 18, 2016, https://www.mekomit.co.il/וקניין-תרבותי-תעשיית-האופנה-/; Oded Erez and Nadeem Karkabi, "Sounding Arabic: Postvernacular Modes of Performing the Arabic Language in Popular Music by Israeli Jews," *Popular Music* 38, no. 2 (2019): 298–319; Mahmoud Hawari, "The Citadel of Jerusalem: A Case Study in the Cultural Appropriation of Archaeology in Palestine," *Present Pasts* 2 (2010): 89–95; Dafna Hirsch, "'Hummus Is Best When It Is Fresh and Made by Arabs': The Gourmetization of Hummus in Israel and the Return of the Repressed Arab," *American Ethnologist* 38, no. 4 (2011): 617–30; Gil Z. Hochberg, "'The Mediterranean Option': On the Politics of Regional Affiliation in Current Israeli Cultural Imagination," *Journal of Levantine Studies* 1, no. 1 (Summer 2011): 41–65; Luma Zayad, "Systematic Cultural Appropriation and the Israeli-Palestinian Conflict," *DePaul Journal of Art, Technology and Intellectual Property Law* 28, no. 2 (2017–18): 81–125.

78. "Zionism aimed to create a society that could never be anything but 'native,'" while it was also "determined not to come to terms with the very natives it was replacing with new (but essentially European) 'natives'"; Said, *Question of Palestine*, 88–89.

79. Veracini, "Other Shift," 28.

Figure 1. "A Postcard Featuring Falafels in a Pita." *Chronicle of a Disappearance*, directed by Elia Suleiman. International Film Circuit, 1996. DVD. Screenshot.

On the forever spinning stand, one postcard of a falafel pita sandwich, planted with a tiny Israeli flag, declares falafel to be "Israel's national snack" (figure 1). Another features a row of kaffiyehs pictured from behind, vacated of Palestinian faces and heads (figure 2), thus becoming, quite literally, an empty signifier of indigeneity. These two examples are paradigmatic. While appropriating the Palestinian kaffiyeh was an early Zionist common practice, now abandoned, the adoption of hummus and falafel as Israel's national dishes endures; it is arguably the most obvious and studied example of Israeli self-indigenization.[80] A third postcard, "Jerusalem," superimposes a camel on the iconic view of the Old City, with the Dome of the Rock at its center (figure 3). The remaining two postcards feature human figures: one of Jewish Israeli pioneering youth; the other of Israeli soldiers against a barbed-wire backdrop, captioned "Patrolling the Border." By contrast, no figures, faces, or national signs of Palestinians are featured on any of these. Only their food, attire, architecture, and religion—all in abstracted form, drained of identity and history—are paraded. Distilled images of "nativeness," these real postcards, sold

80. Ronald Ranta and Yonatan Mendel, "Consuming Palestine: Palestine and Palestinians in Israeli Food Culture," *Ethnicities* 14, no. 3 (2014): 412–35. Pre-state paramilitary organizations, such as the Hagenah and ha-Shomer, adopted Arabic slang and Palestinian clothing, including keffiyeh, as a mode of indigenizing; see Gil Eyal, *The Disenchantment of the Orient: Expertise in Arab Affairs and the Israeli State* (Stanford, Calif.: Stanford University Press, 2006), 1, 43–44.

Figure 2. "A Postcard Featuring *Kaffiyehs*." *Chronicle of a Disappearance*, directed by Elia Suleiman. International Film Circuit, 1996. DVD. Screenshot.

Figure 3. "A Postcard Featuring a Camel." *Chronicle of a Disappearance*, directed by Elia Suleiman. International Film Circuit, 1996. DVD. Screenshot.

throughout the country, promote Israel as integral to the Middle East. As both visual objects and commodities, the postcards epitomize extractive disappearance: they efface the Palestinianness of Palestinian culture and landscape while reifying and marketing their indigeneity for profits economic and ideological. A Jerusalem emptied of people, an Israeli falafel whose origins are elided, and decorative kaffiyehs without Palestinian heads—all for sale.

Figure 4. "A Live Camel." *Chronicle of a Disappearance*, directed by Elia Suleiman. International Film Circuit, 1996. DVD. Screenshot.

In an interlude threading together the two halves of the film, the camera takes the viewers on a winding car ride to Jerusalem that concludes with a living camel in an alley, standing against the backdrop of the city (figure 4). Like the camel, the symbolic disappearance of Palestinians and their culture comes alive in the film's second half, which follows 'Adan, a female Palestinian student, in her failed attempts to rent an apartment in Jerusalem given Jewish Israeli prejudice. Both 'Adan and the film's protagonist, E.S. (played by and named for the director), suffer such level of surveillance that they become reified objects and their inner selves disappear: E.S. is listed in an inventory of objects found in his apartment by soldiers, and 'Adan is replaced by a plastic mannikin without the arresting officers' notice. If settler colonialism is largely defined as concerned only with land and resources and thus as aiming for eliminating the native population, then Suleiman, like other writers of disappearance, presents a colonialism both economically and ideologically dependent on the labor, iconography, and indigeneity of this population. The extraction of the former requires the disappearance of the latter.

Disappearance as Racialization

Absent so far from my account of cultural appropriation is an aspect of Israeli coloniality that all too often goes unnoticed—the role of Mizrahi Jews and of racialization more broadly. The Israeli culinary industry, for instance, appropriates not only Palestinian foods but also Jewish Middle Eastern and North

African foods. It uses these Mizrahi traditions to whitewash the appropriation of Palestinian cuisine, despite considerable differences between the *various* cuisines involved. Some of the Israeli chefs expropriating Palestinian food are themselves Mizrahi Jews. As is the case with Jacob, Saeed's supervisor in Habiby's novel, the fact that *mizraḥim* had themselves suffered colonial disappearance does not preclude their direct participation in visiting the same on Palestinians. While Palestinians for their part do not directly participate in the oppression and exploitation of Mizrahi Jews, they are *indirectly* used by the Ashkenazi hegemony for such purposes. This adversarial exploitation is at the heart of colonial racialization in Palestine.

With great care, Azem incorporates the disappeared colonial history of Mizrahi Jews into her chronicling of Palestinian disappearance. A subplot introduces Habiba, a Jewish Israeli woman originally from Baghdad, who insists on speaking Arabic, adores her Palestinian doctor, and deeply resents the State of Israel. Like other Iraqi Jews, Habiba—perhaps a fictionalized version of the renowned Iraqi-Jewish postcolonial scholar Ella (Habiba) Shohat—did not migrate to Israel out of Zionist commitments. Rather, her migration was initiated, even coerced, by the Zionist leadership, whose vast campaign to import Mizrahi Jews in the early 1950s aimed to establish a Jewish majority in Israel and to replace Palestinian labor.[81] The same colonial project, then, is responsible for both disappearances—of Palestinians from Palestine and of Mizrahi Jews from the Arab and Muslim world. To be sure, Mizrahi Jews are colonizers, complicit in the colonial disappearance of Palestinians; they are also, however, systemically discriminated against. Like so many *mizraḥim*, settled in urban outskirts as ready cheap labor, Habiba found herself living in the "stinky caravans" of ha-Tikvah neighborhood south of Tel Aviv, which she refers to as *Tal al-Khirbe* (the Hill of Ruins) given its "poor and miserable dwellings." Her grandchildren, Habiba laments, are ashamed of their Arab origins, do not speak Arabic, and instead mimic the habits of Ashkenazi Jews.[82] Indeed, as in Palestinian disappearance, Mizrahi histories and traditions, too, were erased by Zionism. The Israeli education system, for instance, subjected *mizraḥim* to forms of acculturation that cut them off from their cultures while funneling them into vocational work.[83] Unlike Palestinians, however, Mizrahi Jews

81. On the Zionist coercion of the migration of Iraqi Jews, see Ella Shohat, "'Sant al-Tasqit': Seventy Years since the Departure of Iraqi Jews," *Jadaliyya* (blog), January 14, 2021, https://www.jadaliyya.com/Details/42239.

82. Azem, *Book of Disappearance*, 44–45.

83. While both populations have seen their pasts "disappear" in Israel, only Mizrahi Jews were assimilated, while Palestinians were separated into their own educational institutions.

gained in return full admission into Israeli society—a counterexample that renders the refusal of Palestinian assimilation all the more glaring.

Both Azem's *Sifr al-Ikhtifaʾ* and Khoury's novel *Bab al-Shams* (Gate of the Sun, 1998) remind their readers of a momentous, yet often forgotten, disappearance in Israeli history: the disappearance of thousands of young Mizrahi children, mostly of Yemenite origin, from hospitals and nurseries between the years 1948 and 1954. Parents were convinced to leave their child there under various pretexts, only to be informed without proof that the child had passed away. Some disappeared children were found years later in Ashkenazi adoptive families, while others were raised in state institutions, and a large number were never found. This case, known as "The Yemenite, Mizrahi and Balkan Children Affair," still haunts Israeli society today. A clear example of elimination-by-assimilation, its resemblance to other colonial supremacist projects stresses the racialized nature of this disappearance.[84]

In the long shadow of both historical events like this one and ongoing, systemic discrimination in resource allocation, Mizrahi faith in and loyalty to Israeli state institutions are not givens. They had to be manipulated into being. In their disappeared and subjugated form, Palestinians are often used to this very end, as an external "other" that keeps the Mizrahi "internal other" in check. Because Zionist ideology associated Arabness with the enemy, Mizrahi Jews had to disavow both Palestinians and their own cultures to demonstrate their worth, loyalty, and belonging. In *Sifr al-Ikhtifaʾ*, Habiba's heart breaks as her grandchildren, ashamed of their own origins, "insult Arabs a lot." Yet, once Palestinians are truly eliminated in the novel, Mizrahi Jews find themselves "mistaken" for Arabs and beaten up in the streets.[85] In these and other details, Azem dramatizes the vested interest *mizraḥim* have in perpetuating the oppression of Palestinians to secure their own racial difference.

Not only cultural ties but also labor conditions, Azem's novel suggests, should make Arab Jews and Palestinians natural allies. Alongside Habiba's, she introduces the story of Yusif and David, a Palestinian and an Arab Jew who befriend each other working in adjacent stalls at the Tel Aviv market and fight

---

The hegemonic education system into which Mizrahi Jews were integrated, however, also disconnected them from their pasts and subjected them to overt discrimination (e.g., their "tracking" into vocational schools). Itamar Taharlev provocatively argues that autonomous Palestinian education has made it easier for Palestinians to access higher education in Israel than for *mizraḥim*; Taharlev, "ha-Brit ha-Ashkenazo-Falesṭinit," *Erets ha-Emori* (blog), May 6, 2013, https://haemori.wordpress.com/2013/05/06/alliance/.

84. For an in-depth discussion of this affair, see Chapter 5 and the sources therein. See also note 22 there for details on other colonial cases of forceful assimilation of children.

85. Azem, *Book of Disappearance*, 45, 221, respectively.

jointly against an overseer's exorbitant fee.[86] The separation between the two populations is thus presented as neither given nor inevitable. As I show in Chapter 5, the animosity of Mizrahi Jews toward Palestinians was largely constructed in Israel—culturally, through (de)Arabization, and economically, through fierce competition. As "Jews in the form of Arabs," *mizraḥim* satisfy the myth of "Hebrew labor" while remaining exploitable. The Zionist attempt to replace one with the other, as Shohat demonstrates, "generated a long-term structural competition" between Palestinian and Mizrahi workers, "now reduced to the status of a subproletariat."[87] While this competition sustained their exploitation, it also pushed many *mizraḥim* to protect any meager advantage in the labor market by adopting what Shafir describes as "casting" and "exclusion"—fighting off the competition by affirming racial and national difference, transforming it into a hard-won privilege, so as to avoid falling to the bottom of the socioeconomic pecking order.[88] In this sense, the settler colonial state incentivizes Mizrahi Jews to adopt and reinforce its consecrated binary between settlers and natives, Jews and Arabs.[89]

For decades, this animosity was generated through social isolation, by reducing direct contact between the two groups and controlling the information they obtain about one another through media and education. In the final scene of Habiby's novel, Saeed finds himself suspended on a stake, a symbol of inaction and isolation, pleading to all other characters for help. The Mizrahi character, Jacob, responds that he has his own stake to worry about, for "we all sit on one!" When Saeed cannot see Jacob's stake and refuses to credit its existence, Jacob explains that no one can see others' stakes: "Each of us is alone, on his own stake. That is our mutual stake."[90] *Ikhtifā'*, in short, also accounts for the disappeared history of *mizraḥim*, for the processes producing the invisibility of Mizrahi Jews and Palestinians to one another, and for the invisibility of these processes themselves. While SCT ontologizes the contrasting categories of natives and settlers, disappearance triangulates the dyad. Without equating the conditions of Mizrahi Jews and Palestinians or ignoring the role of *mizraḥim* as colonizers, it registers the historical effects of colonial erasure on both.

86. Ibid., 32–33.

87. Ella Shohat, "Sephardim in Israel: Zionism from the Standpoint of Its Jewish Victims," *Social Text*, no. 19/20 (1988): 16.

88. Gershon Shafir, *Land, Labor and the Origins of the Israeli-Palestinian Conflict, 1882–1914* (Berkeley: University of California Press, 1996), 20.

89. Lana Tatour, "The Israeli Left: Part of the Problem or the Solution? A Response to Giulia Daniele," *Global Discourse* 6, no. 3 (2016): 487–92.

90. Habiby, *Pessoptimist*, 158.

Finally, *ikhtifāʾ* manifests the ideological and affective economy of racialized national belonging in Palestine-Israel, all too often overlooked. We have already mentioned the author and TV writer Sayed Kashua, whose humor turns on and plays with the racio-national line through instances of failed "passing." Kashua's short story "Hertsel Neʿelam be-Ḥatsot" (Herzl Disappears at Midnight), published in Hebrew in *Haaretz* in 2005, stretches this logic to its absurd conclusion. Every night, between midnight and dawn, Herzl Haliwa, a Jewish Israeli man with a Mizrahi name, is transformed into "an Arab," taking great care to keep it a secret. His affliction stems from his once barren mother's desperate prayer for a child "even if he is half Arab." During his nocturnal transformations Herzl's appearance remains unchanged, yet he speaks only Arabic and dreams of expulsion, war, and exile.

Herzl's condition captures the absurdity of the segregation and (de)Arabization that govern disappearance in Israel. He literalizes the disappearance of Mizrahi Jews, who had to suppress their Arabness to assimilate (even more so until recently). As "the Palestinian" and "the Mizrahi" take turns inhibiting the same body, Kashua reveals their radical segregation—the structural impossibility of their interaction, which stems from their material conditions and, paradoxically, from the intimacy of their shared Arabness. Herzl also manifests the repressed underside of his namesake's vision—the Zionist erasure of Arabness and the displacement, ghettoization, and marginalization of Palestinians, whose disappearance into the night heralds the dawn of the Jewish state. Finally, by effortlessly crossing back and forth between the two identities, Herzl's figure suggests the physical interdependence of Palestinians and (Mizrahi) Jews; it betrays the artificial nature of their separation, which requires endless, nearly compulsive reconstitution through escalating forms of oppression and the constant cultivation of animosity. As the story concludes, Herzl's Jewish girlfriend asks him about the future of "this whole Arab business." "As far as I'm concerned," he replies, "let them all burn."[91]

Disappearance as Anticolonial Resistance

So far, I have considered *ikhtifāʾ* as a poetic analytic framework for understanding the history and present of Zionist colonialism in Palestine. But its value ultimately rests in the transformation it makes conceptually possible; indeed, I share the misgivings of Salamanca et al. regarding any "descriptive category

91. Sayed Kashua, "Hertsel Neʿelam be-Ḥatsot," *Haaretz*, March 10, 2005, https://www.haaretz.co.il/misc/1.1048468 (my translation).

that does not move beyond sentiment and into strategy."[92] Aiming to also delineate anti-colonial practices in and through Palestinian literature, *ikhtifāʾ* resists the rigid structural impulse of SCT, which tends to foreclose and elide the many Palestinians paths of resistance.[93]

Deep into *Sifr al-Ikhtifaʾ*, we finally learn that the Palestinians' disappearance occurs two days after the Israeli parliament ratifies the "Security Belt Law," criminalizing the commemoration of the *nakba*, as well as any objections to the Jewish character of the state. (Azem's fictive law both parodies the Nakba Law of 2011 and anticipates the Nation State Law of 2018.) Transgressors will be "placed in a security zone the government has set up in the south until their fate is decided," held in concentration camps established in the name of preemptive security.[94] This late revelation dissipates some of the enigma, and the Palestinians' disappearance now emerges as an organized act of resistance to this law, an attempt to preempt its preemptive concentration camps. On the eve of being rounded up and made to disappear, then, Palestinians take matters into their own hands. One kind of disappearance upends another. Whereas the one is designed to conceal the history of marginalization, isolation, and disappearance of which it is a part, the other is collective, coordinated, and spectacular—a vanishing *act*. It challenges the juridical attempt to obscure the Palestinian past and present of Palestine by taking it parodically to its absurd conclusion.[95]

Is this form of disappearance merely an escape from one erasure into another, a mere parody? A recurrent hypothesis in the novel is that the disappearance is in fact a general strike. Framed as such, it appears not as escapist fantasy but as active refusal of exploitation and extraction, a weaponized secret that only works collectively. In disrupting "business as usual," the general

92. Salamanca et al., "Past Is Present," 4.

93. The structuralism that allows SCT to establish clear demarcation between native and settler also leads it to delimit Palestinian agency, presenting Palestinians mainly as victims, obscuring past and present Palestinian struggles for decolonization, and erasing them from the repertoire of potential future actions; see Barakat, "Writing/Righting Palestine Studies"; Rachel Busbridge, "Israel-Palestine and the Settler Colonial 'Turn': From Interpretation to Decolonization," *Theory, Culture & Society* 35, no. 1 (2018): 91–115.

94. Azem, *Book of Disappearance*, 148.

95. Crucially, this disappearance mode is radically different from the silencing to which Hebrew literature has consigned Palestinian figures—from the silent mother in Benjamin Tammuz's *ha-Pardes* (The Orchard), to the mute Arab in A. B. Yehoshua's "Mul ha-Yaʿarot" (Facing the Forests), to S. Yizhar's voiceless Palestinians in *Ḥirbet Ḥizʿa* (Khirbet Khizeh). These represent Palestinians as devoid of agency, as "a shadow or a young boy," rendering their story invisible and hindering it from finding an audience; Khoury, "Rethinking the Nakba," 261.

strike calls attention to problems hitherto unnoticed and demands a new order. As a general strike, which has a long history in Palestine and in anticolonial, anti-capitalist struggles more broadly, this disappearance now appears as politically productive rather than simply self-annihilating. The caveats Azem introduces to this theory—e.g., that in a strike, "one still has to *be* somewhere. And Palestinians are neither at home, nor anywhere else"[96]—raise the stakes from the practical to the historical and existential. The strike is made truly general. A divine, law-destroying, revolutionary violence in the Benjaminian sense.[97]

Disappearances in Palestinian literature are often productive in this way: through them, authors write and rewrite the Palestinian collective, its history, geography, and culture, and diagnose the system of its oppression. Apparent concealment and withdrawal are the initiating gestures of a sequence that culminates in extensive and nuanced recording. Throughout Suleiman's cinematic tetralogy, for instance, the resolute silence of his protagonist is the condition of possibility for an epic documentation of Palestinian history and of broad swaths of its culture. The third film in the series, *al-Zaman al-Baqi*, is particularly ambitious, depicting six decades of life in Nazareth in detail of such breadth and granularity as to comprise both the ubiquity of *mujaddara* and the institutional acquiescence of Palestinian schools in the 1960s and 1970s. In *Sifr al-Ikhtifaʾ*, it is Alaa's disappearance that motivates Ariel finally to consider what Palestinians might be experiencing and where they might be, politically. Habiby's *al-Mutashaʾil* was explicitly a response to cultural erasure, motivated, as Habiby explained in an interview, by the Israeli minister Yigal Allon's statement that had a Palestinian nation truly existed it would have developed its own literature.[98] The novel counters an imposed disappearance by documenting Palestinian culture and history, including the Zionist colonization and occupation of Palestine, through the figure of the disappeared Palestinian. A particularly forceful scene takes place in al-Jazzar Mosque in Acre: one by one, each of the "ghostly" refugees seeking temporary shelter in the mosque informs Saeed of the evacuation and destruction of their Galilean community, amassing a spectral archive of place names, thus documenting both the

96. Azem, *Book of Disappearance*, 108.

97. Walter Benjamin, "Critique of Violence," *in Walter Benjamin: Selected Writings*, ed. Michael William Jennings and Marcus Paul Bullock, trans. Edmund Jephcott (Cambridge, Mass.: Belknap, 2004), 1:236–52.

98. Habiby, as quoted in Refqa Abu Remaileh, "Narratives in Conflict: Emile Habibi's *al-Waqa'i al-Ghariba* and Elia Suleiman's *Divine Intervention*," in *Narrating Conflict in the Middle East: Discourse, Image and Communications Practices in Lebanon and Palestine*, ed. Dina Matar and Zahera Harb (London: I. B. Tauris, 2013), 88.

expulsion and these now-erased villages.[99] These works actively resist colonial epistemic and cultural erasure precisely by thematizing disappearance, which then activates a search for knowledge.

Even as Israel disappears Palestinians, it demands to know them inside and out, to make them fully visible to the state. Through torture, surveillance, and elaborate bureaucracy, Israeli security apparatuses persistently require transparency, demanding that Palestinians confess, explain who they "truly" are and what they are "really" doing. Poetic Palestinian disappearances defy this colonial demand for indigenous scopic availability. In the context of Palestinian film and art, Hochberg writes, political transformation and struggle are "dependent on opacity, the ability to disappear, blindness, failed vision, and invisibility at least as much as they are on visibility."[100] Suleiman's film *Sijill Ikhtifaʾ*, she argues, both visualizes the invisible systemic oppression of Palestinians and offers forms of resistance—the subversive power of the Palestinian invisible spectator and the refusal of "proper or restorative representation." Drawing on Eduard Glissant's "right to opacity" in the face of the West's demand for transparency, Hochberg valorizes opacity in and of itself as resistance. A refusal of representational framing is itself subversive, she argues, and the marginalized invisible position of the Palestinian minority in Israel is paradoxically itself empowering.[101]

As Israeli surveillance becomes ever more invasive and as works of Palestinian literature and film increasingly turn to humorist, absurdist, and experimental forms, it is tempting to explain them as an anti-representation, or resistance to interpretation, that is anti-colonial.[102] But anti-colonial disappearance is not anti-representational; as we have seen, it represents and documents plenty. Rather, it might appear opaque for two main reasons: first, because its legibility depends on cultural intimacy, and second, because it eschews the literary conventions of psychological depth and explanatory plots. To escape surveillance and contend with the law, its mode of representation invisibilizes interiority, producing legal deniability while humorously critiquing the absurdity of the law. The inquisitive gaze of the "sympathetic" reader or viewer is

99. Habiby, *Pessoptimist*, 21–22.

100. Gil Z. Hochberg, *Visual Occupations: Violence and Visibility in a Conflict Zone* (Durham, N.C.: Duke University Press, 2015), 7.

101. Édouard Glissant, *Poetics of Relation*, trans. Betsy Wing (Ann Arbor: University of Michigan Press, 1997), 189–92; Hochberg, *Visual Occupations*, 65.

102. Indeed, such arguments currently proliferate; see Shir Alon, "No One to See Here: Genres of Neutralization and the Ongoing Nakba," *Arab Studies Journal* 27, no. 1 (2019): 92–119; Ella Elbaz-Nir, "A-Voiding the Void," *Tel Aviv Review of Books* (blog), April 28, 2021, https://www.tarb.co.il/a-voiding-the-void/.

met with poker-faced denial, with wry eyes that knowingly deflect, that say *the answer is not inside me but all around us, in what enmeshes me and implicates you.* If causal narratives depict violence as a local event within the "normal time" of peace, to be explained away by historical circumstances and to be one day grasped and resolved, then Palestinian authors refuse to diffuse violence with explanatory plots, pointing instead to its structural, invisible, all-pervasiveness. What these works refuse is not representation as such but rather the confessional mode of the deep, conflicted, literary subject encountered in Chapter 2. Depriving their protagonists and narrators of reflexive interiority, Habiby, Suleiman, and Kashua (Azem may be the exception) cling instead to the effects and idiosyncrasies of material conditions, understood through the habitual, the intimate, and the mundane.

Even off the page and screen and in the "purely political" domain, Palestinian practices of anti-colonial disappearance are continuous with this poetic disappearance as deadpan, close-lipped humor. A foundational myth in the history of Palestinian resistance is the substitution of watermelons for the Palestinian flag, purportedly introduced when Israel criminalized display of the latter after 1967. By carrying halved watermelons, which share the four colors of the forbidden flag, or employing these colors in art, Palestinians defied censorship, heightening the visibility of the national cause to allies while hiding it from law enforcement. This practice does not simply render the flag invisible or opaque. Flaunted publicly, watermelon flags are in fact perfectly visible and legible to their intended audience. Unlike an analogy, this metaphor does not offer the key to its interpretation but relies on the audience to hold it. It provides deniability through broad distribution of collective responsibility. Anyone who is part of the community, is familiar with it, or strives to understand its codes, is enlisted. Outsiders are excluded not on a national (or racialized) basis but on the grounds of laziness or inattention, indifference or lack of solidarity. This humorous, surreal practice, in turn, consolidates the community by reiterating its social and cultural codes.[103]

Similarly, the droll daily intimacy of Suleiman's films—aunts gathering in the kitchen and speaking over one another, young men fighting for the honor of taking care of the bill (then somehow leaving without paying)—seem opaque and anti-representational only in the absence of contextual familiarity. Glissant had vaguely hinted at this in asserting that the right to opacity "is not

103. On the creative surreptitious use of the flag colors in Palestinian social media, art, and cinema, including Suleiman's works, see Niall Ó Murchú, "Coloring Palestine: The Flag Device and Cinematic Motivations in Narrative Movies," *Journal of Palestine Studies* 52, no. 1 (2023): 21–42.

enclosure within an impenetrable autarchy but subsistence within an irreducible singularity."[104] *Ikhtifā'*, as trope and tactic in Suleiman, hinges on intimacy with the singular idioms of Palestinian culture in Israel. For instance, 'Adan's announcement in *Sijill Ikhtifa'* that "*Oslo lo ba, Oslo gam lo metsatsel*" (Hebrew, "Oslo is not coming; Oslo is not calling either") is legible only as a reference to a 1985 Israeli pop song, "Meḥakim le-Mashi'aḥ" (Waiting for Messiah), in which a man named Messiah is neither coming nor calling because he had died in a car crash. Recruiting the irreverence of the song to his own purposes, Suleiman frames the Oslo Accords as an eschatological shell game, holding out a forever deferred solution. Suleiman's casting of Menashe Noy as E.S.'s taxi driver in the dark and stormy opening scene of *al-Zaman al-Baqi* manifests a similar stroke of subversive wit. The star of a leftist 1990s Israeli comedy show, Noy stands in for the post-Oslo Israeli liberal left, still in the driver's seat yet mystified, bitterly confessing that "we took a wrong turn" and "lost our way." As Noy, a Mizrahi actor, plays on stereotypes of the over-talkative Mizrahi driver, his first-person plural suggests another lost "we," *mizraḥim* and Palestinians, disoriented and left in the hands of a dispatcher who never responds (*Eli, Eli, eifo ata?*—i.e., Eli [also God], where are you?).[105]

Suleiman's cinematography also mocks and frustrates viewers' expectations of access to the protagonist's interiority. *Sijill Ikhtifa'* is a film about cinematic production and narrative: E.S. is back from exile to make a film "about peace." He visits "the writer," who offers him a story for his film: at various times in his life, "the writer" has asked his grandfather, a former soldier in the Turkish army, to tell him a story about Istanbul. Though he always promises an unforgettable story, the grandfather invariably recounts the one time he ate a well-cooked lamb head in a public garden in Istanbul. With each repetition of the grandfather's story, the film seems to build toward revelation, toward some explanation clarifying the significance of this piece of family history. Anticipation peaks when the grandfather's expulsion from Palestine in 1948 is disclosed, for audiences have been conditioned to expect elderly Palestinians' stories to expose and record past trauma. Yet, the story provides neither explanation nor trauma; it is truly about an unexpectedly beautiful feast as a repose from the routine of disgusting military food. Later, when E.S. is invited to deliver a lecture about the topic of his upcoming film—peace—and about his narrative style, he steps up to the podium and, after an introduction and much anticipation, opens his mouth only to be met with unbearable microphone feedback.

104. Glissant, *Poetics of Relation*, 190.

105. Suleiman, *al-Zaman al-Baqi* (IFC Films, 2012); *Sijill Ikhtifa'* (International Film Circuit, 2005).

The long-awaited confession is aborted. Almost immediately, the audience resumes normal activity—babies cry, people take phone calls, others chat. Thanks to E.S.'s "disappearance," the room itself becomes an answer to the questions posed: this *is* his narrative style. Suleiman's disappearances are thus not at all opaque. Playing with expectations of the confessional mode, they redirect the gaze instead to the details and textures of everyday life, which themselves are the prerequisites for "reading" the film.

In addition to surveillance, Israeli control of Palestinians has always relied on the law. The legal system was central to Israeli efforts to "divide and rule" the Palestinian population and to facilitate its disappearance. Central to this was the martial law to which Palestinian citizens of Israel were subjected until 1966, as was the law that expropriated the property of "present absentees." In 1967, Israel had also established a legal system in the OPT, patched together from pieces of Ottoman, Jordanian, British, and international law. These were supplemented by Israeli "security legislation," a constantly evolving corpus of military decrees and regulations. The law in the OPT is therefore a "flying law." Like the "flying checkpoints" that pop up and disappear throughout the West Bank, it may be constituted and reconstituted in new forms and sites, forever maintaining the element of surprise.[106] Evolving and shifting to fit Israeli interests, this legal system is opaque, nearly impossible fully to comprehend. Palestinians are structurally denied coherent knowledge of the law and thus forever risk transgressing it. Intentionally made into failed subjects of the law, Palestinians are easily incarcerable and presented as incapable of self-government.[107]

From Sigmund Freud to Gilles Deleuze, humor has been theorized as a mechanism for contending with, transgressing, and critiquing the law, particularly of the unknowable kind.[108] In their commitment to intimate familiarity with the Palestinian context and to the nearly mechanical effects of colonial

106. Lisa Hajjar, *Courting Conflict: The Israeli Military Court System in the West Bank and Gaza* (Berkeley: University of California Press, 2005).

107. Hagar Kotef and Merav Amir, "Between Imaginary Lines: Violence and Its Justifications at the Military Checkpoints in Occupied Palestine," *Theory, Culture and Society* 28, no. 1 (2011): 55–80.

108. According to Sigmund Freud, jokes are a mechanism for coping with prohibitions by circumventing societal norms and regulations. Smut jokes, for instance, are a method for expressing and experiencing sexual pleasures that are forbidden and tamed by laws and moral norms. The masochist's humor in Deleuze's writing consists in overly obeying the law in order to expose its absurdity and to release the very movement that the law was intended to prevent; Freud, *Jokes and Their Relation to the Unconscious*, trans. James Strachey (New York: Norton, 1960), 94–102; Gilles Deleuze, "Coldness and Cruelty," in *Masochism*, trans. Jean McNeil (New York: Zone, 1991), 81–90.

reality on life, Suleiman, Kashua, and Habiby share a specific sense of humor. The seeming self-effacement of humor allows them to return to the very law that excluded them, and, by over-zealously repeating it, both transgress it and radically contest its validity. If the indecisive form of Zionist *levaṭim* is dedicated to creating a deep, reflexive, and heroic subjectivity, then the humor in these Palestinian works does the exact opposite: its absurdism eliminates any semblance of plausible interiority not only to reveal the Israeli reduction of Palestinian subjectivities to surveilled objects but also to foreground the structural rather than psychological results of juridico-political actions. Similarly, it forgoes explicit critique of the legal order and its ideals, focusing instead on the surreal cruelty of its consequences to expose its contingency and injustice.[109] By "disappearing" into this logic, repeating its consequences in a literal, nearly mechanical manner, these humorists invisibilize interiority and authority to avoid censure. Their deadpan inscrutability a kind of camouflage, they expose this systemic oppression and its absurdity from within.

Humor is Habiby's main mode of poetic disappearance. One of the funniest and most devastating scenes in *al-Mutashaʾil* takes place immediately after the 1967 occupation. On hearing a radio broadcast commanding all defeated Palestinians to raise a white flag of surrender, the ever-so-loyal Saeed hastens to hang a white sheet from the roof of his house. His supervisor, Jacob, scolds him for his idiocy, explaining that "the big man with the small stature" perceives the flag as an act of treason. The broadcast was intended for the newly occupied Palestinians of the West Bank and Gaza. In raising a white flag in Haifa, Saeed's over-obedience becomes subversive, a rebellious claim that Haifa, too, is part of the occupied Palestinian territories and should therefore be liberated.[110]

If Saeed is constantly surveilled and his loyalty is forever in question, then a logical response is indeed to be exceedingly cautious. On the literal level, Saeed simply wishes to disappear by following a command. Since raising the white flag was already supposed to be a form of punishment and humiliation, however, his eagerness to comply subverts its very purpose. The command meant to separate Palestinians of the newly occupied territories from those living within the old and to mark their defeat as one of a different juridical type: occupation. It thus aimed to differentiate 1948 from 1967, designating the former a legal act of state-building not to be equated with the transgressive audacity of the latter—an explicitly illegal occupation per international law. In his humorous over-obedience, however, Saeed undermines this separation,

109. For this theorization of humor, see Deleuze, "Coldness and Cruelty," 88–89.
110. Habiby, *Pessoptimist*, 120–22.

joining the Palestinians of the newly occupied territories and boldly claiming Haifa to be just as occupied as Ramallah. His compliance ridicules the law as such, mocking its universality by revealing its failure to account for all cases. Presented as illegible and ever morphing, the law is exposed as empty, not intrinsically good or just, but merely serving to perpetuate power.

The wit and efficacy of anti-colonial disappearance in Habiby's novel rely on familiarity with the singular context of '48 Palestinians. During a car ride, Jacob, "with good intentions," tells Saeed a joke:

> The elders of Zikhron Yaakov [a Jewish agricultural colony near Fraydis] disagreed about the following problem: Is it lawful for a man to sleep with his wife on Shabbat, or is the act a kind of work and therefore not lawful on that day? They went to the rabbi for a decision as to whether it was work or pleasure. The rabbi thought long and hard, and then ruled that it was pleasure. When they asked him for his reasoning he replied: "Well, if it were work then you would give it to the Arabs of Fraydis to perform."[111]

The joke exposes the "hidden transcripts" underlying Zionist colonial disappearance.[112] It's funny because it's true. It's true that Palestinian are exploited as cheap laborers in Israel, and it's true that most Jewish Israelis have internalized segregation and cannot imagine Jewish women—or men, for that matter—having sexual relations with Palestinians. (Or, rather, it is a recurring fantasy precisely because the idea is taboo.) By complying with these logics, the joke not only exposes an absurd situation but also disobeys its law. It transgresses the taboo on interracial sexual relations and evokes the possibility of wealthy Ashkenazi Jews engaging in manual labor. At least in our minds.

"My, how we laughed at this story," Saeed reflects afterward, "Jacob because he hates Ashkenazis and I because he laughed." Saeed adds that even "these settlers [from Zikhron Yaakov] laughed good-naturedly when the story about them spread."[113] Thus, the joke elicits laughter from everyone, *even those who are its butt.* Its disappeared humor not only exposes the absurdity of the moral law it transgresses; it also calls into being, however briefly, a community of all those who "get it." Certainly, there are different ways of "getting" the joke, depending on the reader's place, position, and degree of cultural intimacy. Yet

111. Ibid., 80/104–5, translation modified.

112. As Rachel Feldhay Brenner terms them, following James C. Scott in her *Inextricably Bonded: Israeli Arab and Jewish Writers Re-Visioning Culture* (Madison: University of Wisconsin Press, 2010), 94–95.

113. Habiby, *Pessoptimist*, 80.

the joke invites learning, tempting the reader into expanding familiarity and solidarity through a promise of expanded pleasure and of joining the community of laughers.[114] In this momentary affiliative community, familiarity with local cultures replaces the law, as well as national or racial affiliation, as the organizing principle of belonging. The formation of this community requires neither shared values and ideals nor consensus on solutions. Instead of offering some "feel-good" inclusivity, however, it dismantles—for a moment—the segregation and hierarchy imposed by colonial disappearance. It decolonizes without waiting for, or seeking, resolutions or agreements.

The Contemporary Conditions of Disregard

In the eyes of Zionists, as Sanbar argued in 1982, Palestinians' "one and only role consisted in disappearing."[115] Colonial disappearance has meant, first and foremost, the elimination and displacement of Palestinians from Palestine. It also entailed the loss not only of those killed or expelled, severed from their communities and support, but also their potentials and possibilities, achievements and descendants, the totality of their life-worlds. *Ikhtifāʾ*, unlike elimination, aims to capture this cumulative and spectral loss, rarely addressed precisely because it can never find reparation.

Colonial segregation—Israeli attempts to disappear Palestinians and their national identity without fully assimilating them—renders Palestinians, on both sides of the "Green Line," invisible but available for various modes of extraction. Placing Palestinians in the OPT behind walls or in refugee camps and geographically segregating Palestinians throughout most of historic Palestine, Jewish Israeli society has blinded itself to Palestinian existence, oppression, dispossession, anger—and resistance—and to the human cost of their continuation. Since Israeli media and public discourse rarely entertain Palestinians' perspectives or the injustices that Zionism causes, most Jewish Israelis have little occasion to give these any thought. From the state's perspective, this disappearance is expedient, as it aids in consolidating the status quo and safeguarding Jewish domination.[116]

114. While very inclusive, this community does, like any other, exclude some. It excludes precisely those who refuse to take part in the humor, those for whom the logic that the joke transgresses, like the taboo on inter-communal relations, is absolutely sacred.

115. Sanbar and Deleuze, "Indians of Palestine," 27.

116. Following the lead of Palestinian literature, I thus demur from scholars who argue that Zionist violence, oppression, and discrimination are in fact so well known in Israel as to no longer merit critical exposure or archival work; see Hochberg, *Becoming Palestine*; Kotef, *Colonizing Self.*

That said, the epistemic disappearance of Palestinians in Israel is not simply the result of ignorance on the part of Jewish Israelis—as was the assumption of so many 1990s NGOs that made it their mission to document and publicize Israeli crimes, past and present. What disappears is not merely the facts but their political, ethical, social, economic, and cultural meanings. As Sanbar argued, the blindness of the Israeli community to Palestinians, with whom it "physically rubbed shoulders," was "not physical, no one was deceived in the slightest degree." It was based rather "in an evacuation of the 'other' from the settlers' own heads," in a view of Palestinians as beings "on the point of disappearance."[117] Not so much a lie, which would assume knowledge of that which is hidden, it is rather the "ability to excuse oneself from wrought engagement," a refusal to witness, which Ann Laura Stoler calls "the well-tended conditions of disregard."[118] Thus, despite some growing Israeli awareness of the fact of the *nakba,* blindness to its implications persists. For instance, in contemporary brazen right-wing chants that call for a future *nakba*, the relatively new use of this term does not betray increased awareness of its history or meaning and is continuous rather with earlier calls for "transfer." Scholars often distinguish such growing right-wing overt support for violence, viewed as either ignorant or unabashed ("the *flat interiorities* commonly attributed to those with whom we do *not* sympathize"),[119] from liberal self-blindness, seen as combining awareness with deception of self and/or other. Yet the same disappearance underlies both. Both positions "evacuate" Palestinians from mind by ignoring the meaning of their oppression and by (dis)regarding them as about to disappear through either war or political separation (whose current deferral is considered simply their own fault). Both are subtended by the logic of *levaṭim*, which overlooks Palestinians through that reflexive turn inward, ignoring the present in the name of the future and its prospects.

Disappearance persists today even as it transforms. Integration of middle-class '48 Palestinians into Jewish society, for instance, has accelerated since the turn of the twenty-first century. Kashua's two pioneering television series, *ʿAvoda ʿAravit* (Arab Job, 2007–13) and *ha-Tasriṭaʾi* (The Screenwriter, 2015), ushered in a string of Israeli TV shows promising greater representation of and by '48 Palestinians. Palestinians have also increasingly participated in—and won—cooking and music competitions in Israeli reality shows. The

117. Sanbar and Deleuze, "Indians of Palestine," 28.

118. Ann Laura Stoler, *Along the Archival Grain: Epistemic Anxieties and Colonial Common Sense* (Princeton, N.J.: Princeton University Press, 2010), 256.

119. Ibid., 238.

cultural heritage of these Palestinian contestants was enthusiastically celebrated (during "calm" times), yet its aestheticization—like that of the postcards in Suleiman's film—transformed any signs of Palestinian identity into empty, portable, commodified markers of authenticity easily marketable and "shared." When Jewish Israelis encounter Palestinian culture, it is usually in this sampled, decorative, unthreatening form, which is becoming more socially acceptable, even popular.[120]

The ascendence of an urban Palestinian middle class is a result of liberal Israeli economic policies—greater globalization, privatization, entrepreneurship, and readily available debt—that since 2000 aimed actively to expand the Palestinian bourgeoisie to accelerate Israeli economic development more broadly. In some areas, middle-class Palestinian families leave their towns and neighborhoods in favor of traditionally Jewish ones or place their children in Jewish schools to ensure greater social and class mobility. While forming a few de facto mixed towns, thus undermining the Zionist project of "territorial Judaification," this internal "emigration" also attests to and is spurred by the systemic discrimination and neglect of Palestinian municipalities and neighborhoods, where infrastructures and industries are underfunded, where considerably fewer lands are approved for new construction and suffocating overcrowding abounds, and where over- and under-policing have led to a sharp increase in violent and organized crime.[121] Thus, while some upper- and middle-class Palestinians are increasingly able to live and work among Jewish Israelis (as long as they do not flaunt their Palestinian identity), most Palestinians still live in segregated neglected spaces; and these two facts are causally intertwined.

Colonial disappearance in Israel would seem to have succeeded beyond measure. It has greatly contributed to and benefited from economic liberalization, even while negating liberal political values—a contradiction whose affective-ideological modes were explored in the previous chapter and whose juridico-political challenges are taken up in the next. Moreover, the general surprise in the Israeli street at the violent events of 2021 (and 2022) indicates just how—even when more of them live among Jews—Palestinians and their oppression are invisible to Jewish Israeli eyes. As both late capitalism and racialized nationalism intensify, animosity becomes ubiquitous and "blind" through racializing processes that will be taken up in Chapter 5. And yet, these same events—the flare-ups in Sheikh Jarrah, al-Aqsa, and

120. Erez and Karkabi, "Sounding Arabic."

121. Manal Totry Jubran, "ʿArim Meʿoravot be-Hithayut: Ben ha-Peraṭi la-Tsiburi," *Din u-Devarim* 10 (2017): 17–68.

several mixed cities, as well as the general strike that crossed the "Green Line"—also reveal the persistence of Palestinian anti-colonial resistance despite colonial disappearance. After acting violently and resolutely to make Palestinians disappear, Israeli society still wonders, like the military governor in Habiby's novel, when they will *finally* vanish. Their shadows, meanwhile, only grow taller.

4
Ḥoḳ
(Mediating Law)

And the little one rose so early
to go to the pasture.
She doesn't walk with neck outstretched
and wanton glances.
She doesn't paint her eyes with kohl.
She doesn't ask, Whence cometh my help.
. . .
I am not here.
I'm above those savage mountain ranges
in the farthest reaches of the East.
No need to elaborate.
With a single hurling thrust one can hover
and whirl about with the speed of the wind.
Can make a getaway and persuade myself:
I haven't seen a thing.
And the little one, her eyes start from their sockets,
her palate is dry as a potsherd,
when a hard hand grasps her hair, gripping her
*without a shred of pity (*ḥemla*).*

—RAVIKOVITCH, "REḤIFA BE-GOVA NAMUKH"
(HOVERING AT A LOW ALTITUDE)

The 2010s witnessed a relatively new form of violence in Palestine-Israel—unorganized individual attacks, perpetrated by both Jews and Palestinians. Following the 2014 massive Israeli attack on Gaza and in response to Israeli incursions at al-Aqsa Mosque, sporadic Palestinian attacks intensified in fall 2015 and winter 2016, a time now known in Hebrew as the "knives intifada" or the "lone wolf intifada" (*inṭifadat ha-yeḥidim*) and as the "outburst" (*habba*) amongst Palestinians. The Israeli army responded with increased surveillance, brutal suppression of Palestinian protests, and violent raids and arrests. During this period, Israeli soldiers shot and killed about 181 Palestinians suspected of attempted car-ramming or stabbing attacks.[1] Like many others who have shot and brutalized Palestinians over the years, they were never prosecuted. Appointing themselves legislators, judges, and executioners, these soldiers embody what Eilat Maoz termed "living law"—unacknowledged delegates of the state, their very presence and actions form the true meaning of the law (especially in the West Bank) while they themselves are free to break it with impunity.[2]

During the "knives intifada" and in its wake, then, no investigations were opened and no charges were brought against soldiers for attacking or killing Palestinians. With one telling exception, that is: the fatal shooting of 'Abdel Fattah al-Sharif by Elor Azaria in Hebron in March 2016. When al-Sharif, together with Ramzi Aziz al-Tamimi al-Qasrawi, approached a military post and stabbed one of the soldiers in his hand and shoulder, the others immediately opened fire, killing al-Qasrawi and critically wounding al-Sharif. The latter was lying on the ground, badly injured and posing no threat, when Azaria, an IDF medic who was called to the scene, shot him in the head. Because the killing was caught on tape and its details could not be easily denied or distorted, the military uncharacteristically hastened to launch an investigation against Azaria and subsequently charged him with manslaughter (a charge reduced from murder). Although he enjoyed broad support within Jewish Israeli society and the warm embrace of leading politicians, Azaria was eventually convicted. He served nine months in military prison (less than the typical sentence of conscientious objectors).

The law as a mechanism of self-criticism and self-correction is rarely activated in Israel. Only in rare cases, such as Azaria's vengeful and well-documented act, are violent acts perpetrated against Palestinians brought to trial.[3] Even when charges are filed, however, the role of the military legal

1. Ronit Lentin, *Traces of Racial Exception: Racializing Israeli Settler Colonialism* (London and New York: Bloomsbury Academic, 2018), 2.

2. Eilat Maoz, Ḥoḳ Ḥay: Shiṭur ṿe-Ribonut taḥat Kibush (Bene Beraḳ: ha-Ḳibuts ha-Me'uḥad, Van Leer, 2020).

3. In the years 2000–2015, the Israeli human rights organization B'Tselem recorded 739 cases of soldiers' violent attacks on Palestinians and reported these to the military law enforcement system, demanding and facilitating their investigation. Only in 25 of these cases were

system is limited to determining whether soldiers acted in clear violation of orders. It thereby refrains from interrogating the legality and ethics of those orders themselves and of the policies that underwrite them, as well as the responsibility of the officials who devise them. By creating the illusion of dedication to uncovering, investigating, and mending the military's shortcomings and its "excessive" violence, this juridical system serves mainly as a fig leaf that sustains an Israeli self-image of "purity of arms" (*ṭohar ha-neshek̦*) and brands the IDF internationally as "the most moral army in the world."

This chapter continues the study, initiated in previous chapters, of the effects of the juridical on key political concepts and apparatuses. Chapter 1 examined the predication of the concepts of conflict and the state on judgment, whose zero-sum legalistic logic will be further explored here. Chapter 3 stressed the centrality of the law to governing Palestinians and facilitating their colonial disappearance—from the Absentees' Property Law, through the martial law and the motley "flying law" in the OPT, to the 2018 Nation State Law. More specifically, it invoked Emile Habiby's humorous critique of the Israeli use of law to "divide and rule" Palestinians and render them easily surveilled and incarcerable. Ridiculing a forever shifting juridical system that only serves those in power, Habiby's writing challenges the perception of the law as the guarantor of morality and rights. Because Palestinians are *structurally denied knowledge* of this extremely *heterogeneous* law, they are, he shows, always at risk of transgressing it and therefore of *being "disciplined."*

This chapter, by contrast, explores the law in its supposedly *knowable* and *homogeneous* form: the law as it applies to Jewish Israelis, the law as a system of *self-discipline* and *self-critique*. Despite various exceptions and emergency regulations, despite discrimination of Palestinian citizens and uneven enforcement, this legal regime is indeed far more systemic than the patchwork legislation in the OPT. (It is so systemic, in fact, that it applies to Israeli citizens even when they travel to or reside in the West Bank.) As this chapter demonstrates, however, even this homogeneous and coherent law, through its exceptionalizing mechanisms, still amounts to the tautology of "might is right."

To pursue this argument, I turn to the later, more overtly political poetry of the Israeli poet Dahlia Ravikovitch (1936–2005).[4] I focus on her poem "Shir 'Ereś Meturgam mi-Yidish" (A Lullaby Translated from the Yiddish, 1989),

---

charges filed. See B'Tselem, *The Occupation's Fig Leaf: Israel's Military Law Enforcement System as a Whitewash Mechanism (Report)* (Jerusalem: B'Tselem, May 2016).

4. Both Ravikovitch's early and later work were politically engaged, yet in different modalities: her later work confronted political topics directly and urgently, while her early work touched on such issues obliquely and by distancing them to faraway, exotic landscapes. See

written in response to the exoneration of IDF soldiers accused of beating a Palestinian man to death. Ravikovitch's poetics thus interrogates the law (*ḥoḳ* in Hebrew) in its most ideal form—in the exceptional moment when an Israeli court tried soldiers for brutalizing Palestinians and even scrutinized the orders they had received. Reading the poem alongside the related court case reveals Ravikovitch's poetic critique—the exposure of the law as a politico-theological veil that sustains the disappearance of Palestinian suffering by exceptionalizing certain cases. In punishing an individual, an entire system of colonial violence is sanctioned and renormalized.

This chapter also probes the prospect of a Jewish-Israeli ethical self-critique that resists both the attitude of "I haven't seen a thing" (parodied in the epigraph and elaborated in Chapter 3) and the pitfalls of "shooting and crying" and analogizing (discussed in Chapter 2). To this end, it explores Ravikovitch's attempts to push beyond the law and its inherent limitations by employing two distinctive poetic tactics that together form the crux of her critical system. In trying to reckon with Palestinian suffering, Ravikovitch's poetry asymptotically strives to present nothing but the unmediated body in its reality (*ḥaḳḳ* in Arabic).[5] Evaluating this case according to immanent criteria, she is attentive to its singularity while metonymically relating it to other cases. Ravikovitch's poetics also draws on her own cultural tradition yet carves it out or engraves it (*ḥaḳiḳa* in Hebrew), subtracting some of it to make space for something else to appear.

These poetic tactics in turn point at the underside of the law—at those aspects of social, material, everyday life that at once form its tacit foundation and escape it. These aspects are in fact implicit in the Hebrew word for "law," *ḥoḳ*. In European languages, terms for "law" are etymologically derived from verbs for "laying down" or "making stand" (*law, statute, Gesetz, loi, ley, lex, thesmos*), while words for "right"—that is, law in its more general sense—are rooted in the semantic field of "correct" or "straight" (*right, Recht, droit, derecho, directus, nómos*). In Hebrew, by contrast, the root, *ḥ-ḳ-ḳ*, means "to cut in, engrave"—to carve into stone, wood, or metal—thus also "to write, inscribe," and, finally, "to prescribe, fix by decree."[6] *Ḥoḳ* as inscription binds

---

Chana Bloch and Chana Kronfeld, "Dahlia Ravikovitch: An Introduction," *Prooftexts* 28, no. 3 (2008): 267–69.

5. To better visualize the similarity between the Hebrew and Arabic words for "law," I depart here from the IJMES's transliteration system and use *ḳ* instead of *q* for the Arabic letter "Qāf" in "ḥaqq" and related words.

6. For both the Hebrew and Arabic etymologies, see D. B. MacDonald and E. E. Calverley, "Ḥaḳḳ," in *Encyclopaedia of Islam*, 2nd ed., ed. P. Bearman et al. (Leiden: Brill, 2012), accessed online: http://dx.doi.org/10.1163/1573-3912_islam_SIM_2639.

law to signification, to a (mythical) act by which matter is marked, made into a sign, and thereby separated from matter as such.[7] Tied to mediation both juridical and linguistic, *ḥoḳ* names the conflictual relations between the juridical and the ethico-social, representation and reality, the deliberative Arendtian political realm of appearance and the ostensibly apolitical shadowy realm of the body, its singularity, and its needs.

Unlike European words for "law" that spatially metaphorize legislation, *ḥoḳ* embodies the physical practice and material support without which no law can come into being or operate. Derived from the same root, the Arabic cognate *ḥaḳḳ* reinforces this connotation. It means "law" and "right," but also "just," "true," "correct," and, above all, "real." Related words—such as *ḥeḳḳaḳ* (Hebrew: "slit," "engraving"), *ḥuḳḳ*, and *ḥuḳḳa* (Arabic: "hollow," "cavity")[8]—clarify that engraving, for the purpose of either formulating laws or fashioning containers, removes matter, creates relief or space. As inscription, *ḥoḳ* suggests here this mode of meaning-forming through subtraction (and not, as in the poststructuralist infatuation with inscription, a means for treating textuality as itself material).[9] If modern law is Ravikovitch's main object of critique, then her critical tactics rely on what lies in its mythical origin and thus radically differs from it—the singularity of matter and a "carving out" as writing. Ravikovitch's poetic critique suggests that the body is the medium of the law, universality its goal, and historical precedence and exceptionalizing innovation its main methods. To problematize this universal law, she utilizes its underside, showcasing the concrete particularities of corporeal reality and generating counter-memory, a creative reevaluation formed by carving out one's own history. Ravikovitch's sympathetic focus on suffering Palestinians' bodies as evidence, however, risks perpetuating their racialized hyper-embodiment and the consecration of physical pain as the sole motive for solidarity or protest, thus setting a very specific, limited bar for defining wrongs that must be fought.

In a coda, I relate the faults of juridical logic to some of the integral shortcomings of historiography by analyzing the historical novel *Tafṣil Thanawi* (Minor Detail, 2017), written by the Palestinian scholar and author Adania Shibli

7. Andrea Bachner, *The Mark of Theory: Inscriptive Figures, Poststructuralist Prehistories* (New York: Fordham University Press, 2018), 6.

8. Ernest Klein, A *Comprehensive Etymological Dictionary of the Hebrew Language for Readers of English* (Jerusalem: Carta, 1987), 230; Hans Wehr and J. Milton Cowan, *Arabic-English Dictionary: The Hans Wehr Dictionary of Modern Written Arabic*, 4th ed. (Ithaca, N.Y.: Spoken Language Services, 1993), 224.

9. Bachner, *Mark of Theory*, 6.

(b. 1974). Like Ravikovitch's, Shibli's poetics adheres to the corporeal to investigate the erased story of a Palestinian girl, raped and murdered by Israeli soldiers, and to reach beyond the legal affair it ignited. In this case, however, the difficulty exceeds the complacencies of law. It is compounded by the passage of time, which rendered this affair history, and by the inaccessibility of the records, sealed in the Israeli archive. As Samera Esmeir contends, the forensic and evental logic of law and its reliance on state documents as truth—indeed, as the only admissible truth—coincides with a prominent historiographical mode that methodically favors state-sanctioned written documents and state-controlled archives over communal memories and oral testimonies. How might an author push against the epistemic and epistemological limits of juridical historiography to better know and convey a violent past?

"A *Lullaby Translated from the Yiddish*"

Dahlia Ravikovitch was a poet, author, translator, teacher, and political activist. She was born in a suburb of Tel Aviv in 1936 to a petite-bourgeoise family. Her father, an engineer, was originally from Russia. Her mother, a teacher of Jewish Studies, was born to a religious family and, although secular herself, has bequeathed her daughter an attachment to the foundational texts of Jewish tradition. When Ravikovitch was six, her father was killed in a car accident. Seeking support, her mother moved her three young children to Kibbutz Geva. Ravikovitch struggled to adjust to kibbutz life and to the claustrophobic atmosphere of the children's home.[10] She left the kibbutz at the age of thirteen and moved to Haifa, where the pioneer of Israeli literary criticism Baruch Kurzweil became her teacher and personal mentor. Under his patronage and with the encouragement of leading poets at the time, the eighteen-year-old Ravikovitch began to publish her poems. Supported by a scholarship and her work as a teacher, she studied English literature and Hebrew linguistics at the Hebrew University in Jerusalem (a degree she never completed). It was around this time that Ravikovitch published her first poetry collection, *Ahavat Tapuaḥ ha-Zahav* (The Love of an Orange, 1959) to great acclaim. It was followed by ten more collections—seven of poetry and three of short stories—and eight children's books, as well as numerous translations.

10. This collectivist upbringing left its mark on Ravikovitch's writing. See, for instance, her short story, "ha-Ṭribunal shel ha-Ḥofesh ha-Gadol" (The Summer Break Tribunal, 1976), which depicts the potential cruelty of conformism and intense peer pressure by fictionalizing a biographical event—being "court-martialed" by her kibbutz peer group for allegedly "slacking on the job."

Despite her oppositional political stance as a vocal supporter of Palestinians' rights, Ravikovitch was immensely popular in Israel. Many of her poems were set to music and thus reached a wide audience, earning her sweeping admiration and every major Israeli literary award. Ravikovitch's success did not translate into financial prosperity. Despite her reclusive habits, she maintained a vital relationship with her only son, Ido, born in 1978. Ravikovitch was so open about her continuous struggle with depression that when she was found dead in her Tel Aviv apartment in 2005, many speculated that she had committed suicide. The cause of death cited by the pathologist, however, was acute heart failure.[11]

In its attention to political injustice and to the torments Israel inflicts on Palestinians, Ravikovitch's poetry is quite unique in the landscape of Hebrew poetry. Her generation of poets, *Dor ha-Medina* (the Statehood Generation, 1950s–70s), tended to shun overtly political issues in favor of mundane and personal experiences.[12] This tendency is often regarded as a dialectical rebellion against the previous generation, *Dor Tashaḥ* (the 1948 Generation), whose members participated in the war that established the State of Israel and generally prided themselves on the national character of their works.[13] Those few who did write about the Palestinian *nakba* viewed it through the lens of the Jewish holocaust, enslaving the former to the latter, thereby rendering the holocaust the cause and justification for the *nakba* and whitewashing its crimes.[14] Ravikovitch's poetry, by contrast, was highly political, thus differing from the disengaged writing of her own generation; yet it did not merely revert to

11. For Ravikovitch's biography, see Bloch and Kronfeld, "Dahlia Ravikovitch"; Ilana Szobel, A *Poetics of Trauma: The Work of Dahlia Ravikovitch* (Waltham, Mass.: Brandeis University Press, 2013).

12. Among the prominent poets of the so-called Statehood Generation were Yehuda Amichai, David Avidan, Dan Pagis, and Natan Zach. Amichai is an exception, for he did engage political matters in his poems; usually, however, by focusing on their effects on his personal life. Paradigmatic in this regard is his poem "Ani Rotse la-Mut 'al Miṭati" (I Want to Die in My Own Bed). On Amichai's "rhetoric of autobiography" and its politics, see Chana Kronfeld, *The Full Severity of Compassion: The Poetry of Yehuda Amichai* (Stanford, Calif.: Stanford University Press, 2015).

13. This generation of poets, also known as the Palmach Generation, was led by Nathan Alterman and Avraham Shlonsky and included such figures as Haim Hefer and Natan Yonatan. For a discussion of the history of poetic traditions in Israel as an Oedipal generational struggle and on Ravikovitch's place within it, see Michael Gluzman, "ha-Kina ha-'Oletset: 'Al Shene Shirim shel Daliya Raviḳovitch 'al Yona Ṿolakh," in *Kitme Or: Ḥamishim Shenot Biḳoret u-Meḥḳar 'al Yetsirata shel Daliya Raviḳovitch*, ed. Hamutal Tsamir and Tamar Hess (Bene Beraḳ: ha-Ḳibutz ha-Me'uḥad, 2010), 173–74.

14. Hannan Hever, *Al Tagidu be-Gat: ha-Nakba ha-Falasṭinit ba-Shira ha-'Ivrit, 1948–1958: Asupat Shirim* (Tel Aviv: Zokhrot; Parhesyah; Pardes, 2010), 9–55. On such holocaust analogies, see Chapter 1.

the practices of the older generation, which subsumed Palestinian experiences under available Jewish idioms.

Like several of Ravikovitch's poems, "Shir 'Ereś Meturgam mi-Yidish" (A Lullaby Translated from the Yiddish) directly addresses the problematics of law and judgment by constructing a trial of sorts, a specific case to be evaluated.[15] Written in the wake of a military trial known as the Giv'ati Affair, the poem references a concrete violent incident that occurred during the First Intifada, on August 22, 1988, at the Jabalya refugee camp in the Gaza Strip. During the apprehension of a teenager allegedly involved in stone-throwing, four Giv'ati Brigade IDF soldiers brutally beat him, as well as his father. Later that night, while both father and son were detained in a military post, the father, Hani al-Shami, died of his wounds. Following al-Shami's death, the four Giv'ati soldiers were prosecuted for manslaughter in a Military Court, claiming in their defense that they were merely following orders.[16] When medical experts testified that a later beating, committed by other soldiers at the post, was in fact the *more direct* cause of al-Shami's death, the military judges acquitted the defendants of manslaughter and found them guilty of brutality alone. The soldiers involved in the later beating were never found or prosecuted.[17]

"Shir 'Ereś Meturgam mi-Yidish" was originally published in the magazine *Poliṭiḳa* in 1989. A pared-down and more reserved version—simply titled "Shir 'Ereś" (A Lullaby), as though no longer in need to recall its "origin" or be classified as a translation—appeared in Ravikovitch's sixth poetry collection, *Ima 'im Yeled* (Mother with a Child, 1992), which brought her political poetry to an explicit peak. The earlier version, unlike the later, incorporates quotations of testimonies from the trial. Since these quotations constitute one of the two main building blocks of Ravikovitch's critical poetics discussed in this chapter, I focus here on the early version.

The poem's title, which proclaims it to be a translation of a Yiddish lullaby, exemplifies Ravikovitch's regular use of reinterpretative allusions to her own tradition. Indeed, such counter-factual allusions constitute the second building block

15. On trials in Ravikovitch's writing, see Szobel, *Poetics of Trauma*, especially 43–48.

16. These orders—to beat suspects of disturbance of peace to the point of broken limbs during apprehension, whether they resist arrest or not—were indeed, as defense witnesses observed, congruent with the words of the then Israeli minister of defense, Yitzhak Rabin, who famously mandated the IDF "to break their arms and legs." See in the ruling itself in Anis F. Kassim, ed., "The Order to Beat Palestinians: Justice *à la* Israel," *Palestine Yearbook of International Law* 5 (1989): 196.

17. Defendants, investigators, and witnesses, who allegedly saw the beating at the post, all claimed no knowledge or recollection of the identity of those involved in the later beating; ibid., 190–91.

of her critical poetics—an intertextual mode that introduces some space or interruption into Jewish cultural history, thus producing counter-memory. The poem's "translation," however, is not of any particular lullaby but of an intertextual pattern or archetype of this Eastern European Jewish genre, traditionally combined with the lamentation song genre and used largely by women to grieve and protest persecution and devastation.[18] The translation process here thus refers primarily to the importation of the archetypic form of the Yiddish lullaby into the Palestinian-Israeli reality to lament and oppose IDF soldiers' persecution of Palestinians. It is attained by partially removing the Jewish protagonists from the Yiddish lullaby to allow other figures to inhabit it.[19] This carving out is achieved already by the ambiguity concerning the "target language" of the translation. On the surface, the poem seems to translate the language and cultural heritage of Yiddish into those of Modern Hebrew, the language in which it is written. It may also be understood, however, as an intercultural translation—from the history of Yiddish culture to the present "Arab" experience of a Gaza refugee camp—even if it was never written in either of these languages.

The poem consists of three lullaby stanzas, separated by two block quotations from the case. Since Ravikovitch's critique of the law is largely found in the middle stanza of the poem, I will introduce its first parts briefly and circle back to them later:

> Mama and Grandma shall sing,
> shining-white mothers of yours.
> The wing of Mama's shawl
> is touching the covers almost.
> Mama and Grandma shall sing
> an ancient and mournful tune;[20]

18. Chana Kronfeld, "Shira Poliṭit ke-Omanut Lashon be-Yetsirata shel Daliya Raviḳovitch," in *Kitme Or: Ḥamishim Shenot Biḳoret u-Meḥḳar 'al Yetsirata shel Daliya Raviḳovitch*, ed. Hamutal Tsamir and Tamar Hess (Bene Beraḳ: ha-Ḳibutz ha-Me'uḥad, 2010), 527–28. In adopting this dual genre, as Kronfeld argues, Ravikovitch also alludes to the form of the Arabic elegy (*rithā'*), which was likewise the domain of women, thus intensifying both the elegiac quality of the poem and its gendering (524).

19. This gesture, which becomes even more explicit in the final stanza, transgresses a tacit yet tenaciously upheld command in Israel—never to compare any calamity to the holocaust or other anti-Semitic persecutions (a recurrent concern in Yiddish lamentation lullabies). On this command, see Adi Ophir, *'Avodat ha-Hoye: Masot 'al Tarbut Yiśre'elit ba-Zeman ha-Ze* (Tel Aviv: ha-Ḳibuts ha-Me'uḥad, 2001), 12–21.

20. While the translation is mine, it is in dialogue with Bloch and Kronfeld's translation of the later version of the poem "Shir 'Ereś," which appeared in their comprehensive translated collection of Ravikovitch's poems. See Dahlia Ravikovitch, *Hovering at a Low Altitude: The*

These first few verses fashion the classic setting of a lullaby—the physical intimacy of mothers bending over the bed of a child. They situate Ravikovitch's poetic search for justice within this scene as a song addressed to a half-sleeping, largely disinterested, puerile audience. These opening lines also position the reader as the addressee of the poem, as the (male) child who is being put to sleep. In line with the ambiguity of the title, the readers are placed in the position of either a young Jewish Israeli child, about to hear the story of the Giv'ati Affair and hopefully grow to be critical of the realities it discloses, or a Palestinian child, perhaps the very same Palestinian child brutalized by the Giv'ati soldiers. Occupying the seats of both potential victim and potential perpetrator, as well as of a future judge, the readers are invited to evaluate the case by imaginatively experiencing it rather than merely assessing it as a removed object.

Captured by the singing mothers, tucked in like a placid child, the reader is now introduced to a specific scene from the case that repeats three times in the poem:

In the dark cordon in Jabalya
set down, clasped in each other,
a wrecked father, spitting lung-blood,
and his fifteen-year-old son.

This scene, of the shattered father and son being held by each other, portrays a specific moment in the chain of events, when—following the beating at their home, their detention, and their arrival at the military post—soldiers assaulted the two yet again and then left them seated on the ground. Their reported posture recalls the iconography of the *Pietà*—the lamenting Virgin Mary cradling the dead body of Christ—and mirrors that of the singing mothers in the intimate lullaby scene. In its later version, the poem more explicitly puts forward the mournful mother imagery through the biblical trope of "Rachel weeping over her sons"—perhaps a Jewish prefiguration of the *Pietà*.[21]

At that point, Ravikovitch interrupts the lullaby form to introduce the first quotation from the judicial decision—an excerpt of a witness testimony. It repeats the very same scene, yet in the sterilized, supposedly documentary rhetoric of legal discourse:

Collected Poetry of Dahlia Ravikovitch, ed. Chana Bloch and Chana Kronfeld (W. W. Norton, 2009), 219–20; Dahlia Ravikovitch, *Kol ha-Shirim*, ed. Giddo Ticotsky and Uzi Shavit (Tel Aviv: ha-Ḳibuts ha-Me'uḥad, 2010), 241. Henceforth, the two collections are cited as "Ravikovitch," with the page numbers in the original Hebrew following the page numbers in the translation.

21. Ravikovitch, 219/241.

> The first witness who referred to the assault on the deceased at the post was Second-Lieutenant Zaken, Shimon. . . . At the beginning of his testimony the witness notes that he remembers the incident. . . . The deceased was wearing a white galabiya stained with blood. . . . The witness noted that at the time the deceased and his son were leaning against the wall, shoulder to shoulder. . . . Second-Lieutenant Zaken notes that at that time he threatened the deceased and told him to shut his mouth.

Focused on extracting the specific embodied iconography of the mournful mother, Ravikovitch carves out the legal text, discarding whole chunks. The first ellipsis marks the omission of concrete personal details about the witness, such as his identification number and position, while the second excludes the context of the incident, "during which the deceased and his son arrived at the post and were leaning on the western wall of the [soldiers'] rooms." The third ellipsis erases the witness's report of his attempt to converse with al-Shami: "He tried to speak with the deceased, asked his name and address, but only heard him groaning 'I want to die.'"[22] In forgoing the potentially dramatic effect of al-Shami's words, Ravikovitch denies the reader any voyeuristic satisfaction from the pornography of suffering. Repeating al-Shami's refusal to give his formal details to Second Lieutenant Zaken, Ravikovitch avoids putting words in his mouth. Instead, she is laser-focused on the corporal aspects of the scene, now "corroborated" by the quotation: the father and son leaning on each other in a mutual *Pietà* while blood is oozing out of the father's mouth.

"After All, He had His Orders"[23]

Why does Ravikovitch hollow out the quotation from the testimony? Why does she repeat the same scene instead of furnishing new ones? And why does she focus all her efforts on these bodies? The next stanza, which reassumes the lullaby form, clarifies what it is that Ravikovitch is struggling against and by what means.

> Moving in his sleep, the child,
> shaking his innocent head.
> Four angels from the throne of glory
> are flapping their wings above him.

22. For the full testimony, see Kassim, "Order to Beat Palestinians," 198.

23. This is a verse from Ravikovitch's "Tinoḳ lo Horgim Pa'amayim" (You Can't Kill a Baby Twice, 1986), a bitter critique of the Sabra and Shatila massacres (Ravikovitch, 193–94/202–3).

Suddenly trembling seized him
and his mouth dried up like straw.
It is only a nightmare you witnessed,
a dream and not a reality.
Back to sleep, my dear, apple of my eye,
nothing has happened yet.

The child is suddenly awakened by a horrific dream, presented as the most astonishing religious revelation. Echoing a long tradition of lamentation, the stanza forms a complex intertextual prism, combining the throne of glory from the book of Jeremiah (Jer 17:12) with a mystical moment in Ezekiel, where a throne engulfed by four heavenly hybrid creatures is revealed to the prophet (Ez 1:26). Leading the child to be seized by trembling (*ra'ada aḥaza bo*), this revelation also alludes to the book of Isaiah, which depicts sinners seized with fear and trembling in light of God's destructive journey (Is 33:14). Each of these prophets—Jeremiah, Ezekiel, and Isaiah—warned his congregants of the coming destruction of the Jerusalem Temple as a result of their sins. With these allusions in mind, the child's revelation appears as a prophecy of judgment, foretelling the transgressors' punishment.

This revelation thus seems to follow what Gilles Deleuze labels a "classic" conception of the law. For Plato as for Christianity, Deleuze explains, the law reflected the higher principle of the Good, and hence sanctioned the righteous man—he who exhibits the most obedience to the law.[24] Although Deleuze associates this juridical framework with the ancient world, and especially with Paul's overhauling of Christianity, its effects persist in normative perceptions of the law today and in the self-image of the legal system (save for exceptional moments of meta-reflection and of positive legislation; more on that soon). Most people who are not amid a battle with the law tend to speak of it as dictated by the greater good and as correlated to its consequences—that is, they regard legal sentences as a response to an assault on an ideal Good.

The composite allusion to the prophets of destruction, a specter of the classic law, immediately follows the poem's presentation of the brutalized father and son and thus seems at first to simply demand the fulfillment of the prophecy—a punishment for the murderous transgressors. But the allusion could also be seen as critiquing the court's handling of the orders that the Giv'ati soldiers received—to break the limbs of disturbers of peace whether or not they resist arrest. It *ironically* presents the judges' approach as following

24. Gilles Deleuze, "Coldness and Cruelty," in *Masochism*, trans. Jean McNeil (New York: Zone, 1991), 83–84.

the classic juridical framework: as considering the orders acceptable, even good, simply because they were the orders, simply because they came from above. Indeed, because the judges assumed that the law must reflect the Good, they considered the soldiers' obedience to be acceptable, even right, regardless of its brutality, as long as these were indeed the orders given. The judges' obsessive attempts to determine whether these were in fact the orders, so as to determine the soldiers' culpability, thus become a grotesque embodiment of a nightmarish "dated" legal logic.

The nightmare can also be understood, however, as the terror produced precisely by the fact that nothing has happened *yet*, that no punishment has come upon the transgressors, for the court acquitted the soldiers of manslaughter and never prosecuted the other possible murderers. The terror now stems from the mothers' teaching that any hope for adequate punishment is merely "a dream and not a reality." The biblical allusions thus question the authority of the classic law in its purest form—the Godly law, the transcendent, universal law that is one with the infinite wisdom of the Absolute Himself—refuting its correlation to its consequences. At the very least, these allusions assert that any such system of godly judgment, which upholds perfect correlation between the moral good, the law, and its effects, belongs in dreams and is no longer part of this world.

This critical approach is typical of the modern, formal juridical framework. In this Kantian conception, "the law is no longer regarded as dependent on the Good, but on the contrary, the Good itself is made to depend on the law." Having no recourse to a higher principle from which to derive its authority, the law is now self-grounded and valid only by dint of its form, which can take on any content whatsoever. Pure, contingent, and empty, it becomes tautological: "The law is the law." It represents the Good because it determines the Good. It "operates without making itself known. It defines a realm of transgression where one is already guilty and steps the bounds without knowing what they are." And because no one knows, or can ever know, what the law *is*, it can no longer sanction the righteous man.[25] This juridical framework, which Deleuze associates with the Nietzschean "death of God" and the human desire to seize God's place, animates Western legal systems.[26] By positioning judges and legislators in a "godly," external position, this framework allows for positive law, new legislation, and "active" judicial interpretations. In this context, isn't it interesting that the Arabic word for law, *ḥaḳḳ*, is also one of the

25. Ibid., 82–84.

26. Gilles Deleuze, *Nietzsche and Philosophy*, trans. Hugh Tomlinson (London and New York: Continuum, 2002), 152–56.

names of God? Or that, according to Rabbinic exegesis, the Bible reserves the word *ḥoḳ* for those laws that are unknowable, even seeming irrational, yet must be followed nonetheless simply because they are the law?[27]

Through her tableau of biblical allusions, then, Ravikovitch puts forward both a historical and a philosophical claim. Because they are biblical, these references imply that both perceptions of law, classic and formal, in fact existed in antiquity. (Hegel's reading of Antigone suggests the coexistence of a similar pair in the ancient Greek world.)[28] Their concomitance, moreover, is to be expected, for the two juridical frameworks imply and reinforce one another. It is precisely because the formal law dialectically maintains the empty space of the dead, secularized God that legislators and judges can take on a sovereign utopian role. If biblical allusions in Modern Hebrew poetry can undo the sacred-profane dichotomy and elevate everyday language and existence, as Chana Kronfeld argues,[29] then in Ravikovitch's writing they also problematize the assumed secularity of modern law by exposing its structural reliance on the sacred.

The staging of the law as empty and arbitrary, as severed from any ideals, is reinforced by yet another, pivotal biblical allusion implied by the dreaming child's trembling (*ra'ada*). In the book of Job, Eliphaz the Temanite recounts: "Amid disquieting dreams in the night, when deep sleep falls on people, fear and trembling (*ra'ada*) seized me and made all my bones shake. . . . A form stood before my eyes, and I heard a hushed voice: 'Can a mortal be more righteous than God?'"[30] Unaware of committing any sins, the righteous Job never knows and cannot ever know the content of God's law that sentenced him to extreme suffering. An exceptional moment in the Bible, Job's story exposes divine law as completely unknowable and utterly incongruent with the Good. By relating his revelatory dream, Eliphaz, one of Job's consoling friends, attempts to defend God's universally Good law against Job's experience and doubts. He insists that the law is inevitably just, transparent, and universal, and hence any punishment, including Job's, is necessarily indicative of sin—a "classic" juridical reasoning that the condemned Job categorically rejects.[31]

27. Unlike *mishpaṭim*, which are knowable and rational laws; *Bavli* (Babylonian Talmud), Yoma 67b. On ḥaḳḳ (*ḥaqq*) as both legal right and Right—truth, the law of the creator—see Samera Esmeir, *Juridical Humanity: A Colonial History* (Stanford, Calif.: Stanford University Press, 2014), 26–27.

28. G. W. F. Hegel, *Phenomenology of Spirit*, trans. A. V. Miller, rev. ed. (Oxford: Oxford University Press, 1976), 284–89.

29. Kronfeld, *Full Severity of Compassion*, 138–39.

30. Job 4:12–17, NIV.

31. Job 8, 9.

Struggling to decipher the legal logic behind his many punishments, Job is only ever able to read it in his wounds, in the sentence inscribed on his body. He prophesizes, "And after my skin has been destroyed, [from] my flesh I will see God" (*ve-aḥar ʿori nikfu zot; umi-beśari, eḥeze eloha*).[32] Job's affliction thus corroborates Michel de Certeau's argument that every power, including the law, "is written first of all on the backs of its subjects." Precisely because it is abstract and universal, contingent and unknowable, the law must materialize in bodies—fleshed-out examples that, in turn, force it to become specific.[33] Understanding that the law's medium is the body, Job demands that it materialize instead in the form of a trial: "Now that I have prepared my case [*mishpaṭ*: judgment, trial]. . . . Summon me and I will answer, or let me speak, and you reply. . . . How many wrongs and sins have I committed?"[34] But even while pleading for a fair trial (*mishpaṭ*) and a knowable law (*ḥoḳ*), Job is fully aware of their impossibility, sensing that his prosecution is, in fact, in the capricious hands of divine wills. Indeed, when God finally grants Job a hearing, He does nothing but cite His own creation at him, instancing other singular, exceptional phenomena that do not and could not represent any law.[35]

Despite his friends' efforts to subjugate him to God's law, Job is perhaps the first ever to doubt the strict correlation between law and consequences. Seeing his personal suffering, physical and material, as indicative of the arbitrariness of the law, he extrapolates a larger claim about justice: God's justice is not objective; it is merely what the stronger inflicts upon the weaker. "How can I dispute with him?" he asks rhetorically. "Even if I summoned him and he responded, I do not believe he would give me a hearing. He would crush me with a storm and multiply my wounds for no reason."[36] Eventually, the

32. Job 19:26.

33. Michel de Certeau, *The Practice of Everyday Life*, trans. Steven F. Rendall (Berkeley: University of California Press, 1984), 140. Because the Kantian, merely formal law "has no object of knowledge," Gilles Deleuze and Félix Guattari similarly argue, it "is operative only in being stated and is stated only in the act of punishment: a statement directly inscribed on the real, on the body and the flesh; a practical statement opposed to any sort of speculative proposition"; Deleuze and Guattari, *Kafka: Toward a Minor Literature*, trans. Dana Polan (Minneapolis: University of Minnesota Press, 1986), 45.

34. Job 13:18, 22–23.

35. Job 38, 40. According to Jonathan Lamb, while the narratives of Job's adversarial friends tautologize pain—since by a circular logic they equalize it with punishment—God's theophany, his citation of his creation, tautologizes everything, for "everything is because it is; the unique is instanced as unique, put in parallel with itself as an unparalleled phenomenon"; Lamb, The *Rhetoric of Suffering: Reading the Book of Job in the Eighteenth Century* (Oxford: Clarendon; New York: Oxford University Press, 1995), 35.

36. Job 9:14–16.

consoling friends, including Eliphaz, are dismissed as "flatterers," while Job's defiant view is lauded, by both God and the text, as the truth.[37] If not even God is an ideal that may anchor knowable laws, then Job's is a story about the dismissal of the "classic" juridical episteme in favor of a perception of the law as arbitrary and dictated by might. In Ravikovitch's poem, the child's revelation, intertextually aligned with Eliphaz's vision of a universal law, is dismissed as merely a dream, thus critically exposing the law as formal and empty, a weapon wielded by the stronger on the weaker.

This transition from a "classic" to a formal conception of the law was also played out during the trial of the Giv'ati soldiers. Once expert testimonies weakened the causal link between the beating at the house and al-Shami's death, the military judges could not but acquit the defendants of manslaughter. Following the "yes or no" logic of judgment (discussed in Chapter 1), they were only interested in determining whether the beating falls under the category of manslaughter. Yet, in this case, whose uniqueness is emphasized repeatedly throughout their decision, the judges took an active, legislative role and *exceptionally* found the defendants guilty of brutality, ruling that the order to beat non-resisting suspects should have been refused. In a highly unorthodox, utopian move, the court thus examined the legitimacy of the order itself, finding it to be "manifestly illegal."[38]

A "manifestly illegal order" (*peḳuda bilti huḳit ba-'alil*) is a specific legal category in Israeli military law. It designates an order so patently illegal and immoral that soldiers ought to disobey it (while any "merely" illegal order still requires obedience). This category was first introduced by Judge Benjamin Halevy in his decision in the 1957 case of the Kufr Q̱assem massacre, during which an Israeli force, imposing a curfew order on the village, was instructed to shoot all Palestinians found in the streets, even if they had no knowledge of the curfew. Israeli border police thus killed forty-nine villagers returning home from work, unaware of the order. In light of these events, the judge determined that orders whose illegality is essential rather than "merely formal," "piercing the eye and infuriating the heart," must raise a "black flag" and be refused.[39] The Kufr Q̱assem Affair thus created a decisive precedent.

37. Job 42:7.

38. Kassim, "Order to Beat Palestinians," 236.

39. Adi Parush, "Psaḳ ha-Din be-Parashat Kefar Ḳasem: Mivḥan ha-Degel ha-Shaḥor veha-Muśag shel Peḳuda Bilti-Ḥuḳit ba-'Alil." *'Iyune Mishpaṭ* 15, no. 2 (1990): 245–72 (my translation); Itamar Mann, "What Is a 'Manifestly Illegal' Order? Law and Politics after Yoram Kaniuk's Nevelot," in *The Politics of Nihilism: From the Nineteenth Century to Contemporary Israel*, ed. Roy Ben-Shai and Nitzan Lebovic (New York: Bloomsbury, 2014), 177–204.

Relying on this juridical history, the Giv'ati case judges took on an apparently sovereign and innovating stance, placing themselves in an external metaposition from which to evaluate the order's legality. Declaring this specific order exceptionally illegal, the judges did not reestablish a higher principle of moral good beyond the law. Rather, by making an exception, they *fundamentally legalized all other immoral and illegal orders*—including the ones given in the military post, which might have led, according to the ruling itself, to al-Shami's death. As a mechanism of judicial self-correction, the "manifestly illegal order" not only fails to solve the problems inherent in the logic of judgment but also intensifies them.

The Giv'ati case in fact exceptionalized twice: by treating the military order as an extreme instance that categorically differs from all others and by treating the soldiers' wanton violence as anomalous rather than definitive of military conduct norms. By isolating particular incidents of violence, like the murders perpetrated by the Giv'ati soldiers and Azaria, Israeli state institutions present them as exceptional cases (*miḳrim ḥarigim*), executed by a few "rotten apples" (*'aśavim shoṭim*; lit., untamed weeds). In doing so, they essentially cover over and sanction the many other cases that together spell out a silent policy of terrorizing, brutalizing, and murdering Palestinians as well as manufacturing their "slow death."[40] The exception therefore has the power not only to determine the sovereign, as Carl Schmitt has famously contended, but also to normalize violent and discriminatory rule.[41]

This dialectical operation—normalizing and universalizing through the exception—was prevalent in the poetry of the 1948 Generation. In his poem "'Al Zot" (About This, 1948), for instance, Nathan Alterman critically portrayed Zionist acts of violence committed during the 1948 War to expel Palestinians. Alterman's poem, as Hannan Hever argues, consistently frames such violence as isolated and exceptional, even while acknowledging that the particular and the universal, the individual and the nation, form, in Alterman's own words,

40. The term, which refers to the forms of death by attrition produced by capitalist environments, was famously coined by Lauren Berlant. See their "Slow Death (Sovereignty, Obesity, Lateral Agency)," *Critical Inquiry* 33, no. 4 (2007): 754–80.

41. The conception I am tracing here is akin to Giorgio Agamben's reworking of Schmitt's "state of exception." Per Agamben, sovereignty is based not on the power to legislate but rather to suspend the law and to declare someone or some state (namely, bare life itself) an exception to the law. This act of exclusion from the juridical and political realms serves in fact to constitute and sustain their universal rule and to erase the violent exclusion at their origin. See Giorgio Agamben, *Homo Sacer: Sovereign Power and Bare Life*, trans. Daniel Heller-Roazen (Stanford, Calif.: Stanford University Press, 1998).

a "lawful pair" (*tsemed ka-ḥoḳ*).[42] Because the individual is always a synecdoche for the nation in Alterman's poetry, his (*sic*) poetic punishment suffices to purify and absolve the entire nation. The writer's liberal subject position, of the critical individual who opposes societal norms, thus merely reaffirms them. Alterman's protest poem, published by the IDF and circulated to soldiers, offered—like those exceptional cases tried in military courts—the sort of cathartic self-criticism necessary for the military machine to carry on uninhibited.

Through the collage of biblical allusions, Ravikovitch questions the efficacy and ethics of judgment and its universal law, demonstrates its operation through and on bodies, considers the implications of the moment of active judgment in which the law is exposed as formal and empty, and reveals such exceptional moments as in fact sanctioning and normalizing violence. Ravikovitch's heavy reliance on theological sources is unsurprising, given that the target of her criticism is precisely the "messiah complex" of the law, its political theological origins. If Schmitt uses theology to secure the sovereign's authority through the procedure of the exception, then Ravikovitch enlists theology and the exception to challenge that very authority (while also criticizing some of the violence of this theology itself).[43]

"The Poetics of Moderate Physical Pressure"[44]

If matter is the medium of the law that, for this very reason, precedes it, then it might merit further consideration. Responding to the unknowable law that operates by inscribing itself in his flesh, Job conversely demands the inscription of his own words, of the memory of his plight, in matter: "Oh, that my words were recorded, . . . that they were inscribed (*yeḥoḳu*) with an iron tool on lead, or engraved in rock forever!"[45] Is this demand a simple reversal? Given the additional meaning of *yeḥoḳu* as "will be legislated," Job's phrase appears

42. Hever, *Al Tagidu be-Gat*, 9–11.

43. Mimi Haskin, "'Yadenu lo Shafkhu et ha-Dam ha-Ze ṿe-'Enenu lo Ra'u': ''Egla 'Arufa' shel Daliya Raviḳovitch ṿeha-Te'ologia ha-Poliṭit shel Ḳarl Shmiṭ," in *Kitme Or: Ḥamishim Shenot Biḳoret u-Meḥḳar 'al Yetsirata shel Daliya Raviḳovitch*, ed. Hamutal Tsamir and Tamar Hess (Bene Beraḳ: ha-Ḳibutz ha-Me'uḥad, 2010), 507.

44. This is the title of one of Ravikovitch's later poems, which parodies and critiques Israeli security services' use of torture to interrogate Palestinians. It particularly challenges the sort of legalized torture euphemized by the former Supreme Court Justice Moshe Landau as "moderate physical pressure." See further in Stanley Cohen and Daphna Golan, "The Interrogation of Palestinians during the Intifada: Ill-Treatment, 'Moderate Physical Pressure' or Torture?" (Jerusalem: B'Tselem, March 1991). For the poem, see Ravikovitch, 293–94/261–62.

45. Job 19:23–24.

at first as a desire to seize the legislator's seat, to take the place of God. Yet, the insistence on materializing his account points at a certain excess of matter over legal documentary evidence and even over representation as such. Ravikovitch's poetic reworking of this affair similarly strives to exceed mediation and evidentiary procedures through her quotational practice and her focus on the victims' bodies, presented to the reader as almost physical signs, to conjure new forms of interpretation and ethical evaluation.

Direct quotations are the exact opposite of the horizontal, universal, self-grounded, and abstract law. They are always particular, concrete cases that, by the very fact of repetition, are embedded in a vertical tradition, thereby calling for evaluation based on comparisons to their precedents. As examples, quotations do not attempt to represent anything or abstract a universal rule. Instead, they merely present, importing a body of text and positing it before us.

After the middle stanza, Ravikovitch embeds a second quotation of a testimony from the Judgment:

> Another witness, Corporal Teperberg, Haim . . . noticed the deceased, who was walking bending forward and was seated next to the wall. He was leaning against the wall and putting his head on his son's shoulder. At that time, blood was oozing from his mouth.

Accounts of torture, as the Palestinian author and literary scholar Anton Shammas observes, are structurally problematic, even when sympathetic. They involve a twofold translative process: transposing pain into legal discourse and distancing it through the three-point linguistic translation (from Arabic to Hebrew to English). In this complex cultural translation, Shammas stresses, the "original" account is often involuntary, for Palestinians might refuse being translated into the occupier's language and its perception of justice as based on confession and recognition. Translation, he maintains, is therefore always violent.[46] Ravikovitch's carved out translation almost seems like a response to Shammas's critique of such juridical, documentary translations. Ravikovitch's does not represent al-Shami's words or feelings under these circumstances, nor does it admit secondhand reports of them. In quoting from the testimonies, she omits any such mentions, thus aiming to avoid the pitfall of "turning the raw, out-of-control violence into a manageable metaphor" that conceals the victim.[47]

In foregrounding al-Shami's physical suffering, fixating on the bodily aspects of the scene, Ravikovitch excludes precisely the details relevant to the

46. Anton Shammas, "Torture into Affidavit, Dispossession into Poetry: On Translating Palestinian Pain," *Critical Inquiry* 44, no. 1 (2017): 122.

47. Ibid., 120.

questions posed by the judges, with their metaphysics of judgment (whether or not the four Giv'ati soldiers directly caused al-Shami's death; whether or not this was the order; and whether or not it was legal). This selective quotation, eliminating everything but the body, is a desperate attempt to relate to someone else as he is, without imposing her own language on him—without putting words in his mouth, thoughts in his head, or feelings in his gestures. This refusal to "translate" al-Shami fully seems geared at avoiding the narcissistic moral imperialism of analogies discussed in Chapter 1, whereby others' suffering is subsumed under and occluded by one's own.

As a literary venture, having no access to others' bodies, this attempt is certainly destined to fail. This necessary failure, however, does not prevent Ravikovitch from asymptotically aspiring to articulate nothing more than these bodies. The desire for the concrete, the distrust of representation, is key to Ravikovitch's later poetry. For instance, in a poem about a preventable death—of "someone or other" killed on the Israeli-Lebanese border "three and a half minutes before the cease-fire / or a massive artillery barrage / whatever comes first"[48]—Ravikovitch concludes with the words "dead like dead" (*met kemo met*). In her poetic system, linguistic mediation is mocked, discarded as useless. Addressing gratuitous death or loss, the figure, the simile, becomes material, is canceled out, reduced to the tautology of the thing-in-itself. Ravikovitch thus not only avoids turning death into a "manageable metaphor" but appears to kill off figuration itself.

In their materiality, Ravikovitch's quotations also stress the pretentiousness of the legal system's claim to know this incident in its totality and to conclusively judge it. Showcasing the discrepancies between the different witnesses' accounts and between those and her own, Ravikovitch's selective quotations demonstrate the epistemic limitation of the legal system (as well as of the poem), suggesting that all knowledge beyond the mere fact of dead and suffering bodies is foreclosed. Echoing her attempt to thematize the body with as little mediation as possible, Ravikovitch's quotations repeat this gesture on the formal level. In a bid to avoid representation, she does not report on the events of the trial or criticize its proceedings (for critique is still within the realm of

48. By whatever flies out of the barrel of a gun
of someone following an order or his heart's desire.
And someone or other, whatever his name may be,
took leave of his life at eleven o'clock in the morning
not intending to meet up with it again
in any of the possible worlds."
—"Yom Ḥoref Tsefoni" (A Northern Winter's Day); Ravikovitch, 251–52/291–92.

representation). Instead, Ravikovitch selects parts of the trial, importing fragments from the Judgment—almost physically—into her poem. This effort, again, remains merely asymptotic, for any selection involves *some* degree of interpretation. As Ravikovitch's textual selections are primarily focused on corporeal descriptions, however, both form and content here unite in accentuating the law's failure to contend with the body, particularly the shattered body.

In a paraphrase of Benjamin's portrayal of Karl Kraus's quotations as *corpus delicti*, as the body of crime that serves as the satirist's ultimate weapon and proof,[49] we may consider Ravikovitch's practice of quotation a *habeas corpus*—a bringing forth of a body of text, of a textual body, to grant it a hearing. Her selections demand that we look at the specific body before us, leaving behind the legal "yes/no" questions and their universalist logic. Instead, asking "which is the case," "of what type it is," we must actively invent a rule, a logic, that may account for this case and that may allow us to evaluate it.[50]

The immanent rule that Ravikovitch finds for interpreting and evaluating this case is that of *Pietà*—a type she discerns in the bodies' posture. We might also call this type "a lullaby," as the poem is titled. Offering the female-gendered type of the Yiddish lullaby, which already incorporates lamentation, the poem is an audio-verbal variation on the visual icon of the mournful mother. By restaging the same corporeal scene three times and by constructing the poem as a lullaby, Ravikovitch emphasizes this type and insists that we assess the case based on the traditional iconographies it recalls. The lullaby type suggests a sympathetic relation (*Pietà*, *ḥemla*) as its own, inherent evaluative criterion—for, ultimately, a lullaby is nothing but a fictional attempt to relate, from within one's monologue, to someone else who is physically present yet verbally inaccessible.[51]

49. Walter Benjamin, "Karl Kraus," in *Reflections: Essays, Aphorisms, Autobiographical Writings*, trans. Edmund Jephcott (New York: Harcourt, Brace and Jovanovich, 1978), 443.

50. Against Kantian determinative judgment—which is merely interested in the Socratic question "What is x?," or "Is this x?," subsuming particulars under universal categories—Deleuze sets up the notion of a Nietzschean immanent evaluation based rather on the question "Which one?," "Of what type is the case?" While evaluation through types may rely on comparisons to precedents (and is thus somewhat related to the tradition of common law, as opposed to codified civil law), it is more akin to seeking a concrete episteme, limited to a particular era and a particular place. Or, in Deleuze's words, "a type is a reality that is simultaneously biological, psychical, historical, social and political"; *Nietzsche and Philosophy*, 20, 115.

51. This *ḥemla* (sympathy or compassion), which the man in the epigraphic poem lacks, is etymologically related to the Arabic *ḥamala*—meaning to carry, to be responsible for—and is thus linked to childbearing and childrearing.

As a lullaby, the poem seems to assume the perspectives of women and mothers, often neglected in the contexts of war or military violence. Scholars have noted Ravikovitch's recurrent use of her own perspective as a woman and a mother to undermine the Zionist narrative and to cross national boundaries by sympathizing with other "private" women.[52] This description, however, both over- and underestimates her. Ravikovitch never truly transgresses national limits. At the same time, her poetics exceeds personal identification—as a woman, as a mother, or as an orphan. In redoubling the mother, rendering the lullaby an intergenerational affair, Ravikovitch forms a collective female voice and points to the structural, ongoing nature of the injustices lamented. The mirroring of the father and son in the two mothers extricates the case from the (masculine) military post environment, connects it instead to female lamentation traditions, and renders the lullaby scene the context for its evaluation. Ravikovitch does not simply use her "femininity" or "motherhood" to relate to other women or mothers, thus accepting given gender norms. Instead, while recognizing that she has nothing at her disposal other than these norms, she pokes holes in them to relate not only to women, thereby contesting the validity of this very category. (Ravikovitch makes similar use of the category of Jewishness, as we will shortly see.)

Centering bodies in their materiality goes against the main currents of political thought. In the ideal polity—from Plato to Arendt—the body is repeatedly made invisible, relegated to the a- or pre-political realm of the private sphere. Its needs are met "before" politics, in some dark substratum that sustains the polis from below and that, in the Greek polis, was literally made of slavery and female reproductive labor. In Arendt's writing, bodily needs are consigned to the homogeneous, "antipolitical" realm of *labor*, separate from both the politics-adjacent sphere of *work* and the deliberative "space of appearance" that forms the political realm of *action*.[53] Arendt's taxonomy of modes of doing is mirrored in her tripartite distinction of sympathetic affects: *compassion* (too immediate and individualistic), *pity* (too distant and contrived), and *solidarity*.

52. Szobel, *Poetics of Trauma*; Kronfeld, "Shira Poliṭit ke-Omanut Lashon"; Hamutal Tsamir, "ha-Tsofa le-Vet Yiśra'el mibi-Fenim: Daliya Raviḳovitch, ha-Shira ha-Le'umit-Yiśra'elit, ṿeha-Migdar shel ha-Yetsugiyut," in *Kitme Or: Ḥamishim Shenot Biḳoret u-Meḥḳar 'al Yetsirata shel Daliya Raviḳovitch*, ed. Hamutal Tsamir and Tamar Hess (Bene Beraḳ: ha-Ḳibutz ha-Me'uḥad, 2010), 600–45; Dana Olmert, "'Ani lo Kan': Ha-'Emda ha-Poliṭit ṿeha-Iyum 'al ha-Zehut be-Shirat Daliya Raviḳovitch," in *Kitme Or: Ḥamishim Shenot Biḳoret u-Meḥḳar 'al Yetsirata shel Daliya Raviḳovitch*, ed. Hamutal Tsamir and Tamar Hess (Bene Beraḳ: ha-Ḳibutz ha-Me'uḥad, 2010), 416–43.

53. Hannah Arendt, *The Human Condition*, ed. Margaret Canovan (Chicago: University of Chicago Press, 1998), 212–13.

The latter Arendt considers a rational and universalizable principle by which "we" "establish deliberately and, as it were, dispassionately a community of interest with the oppressed and exploited."[54] In her Kantian conception of both solidarity and politics as a dispassionate *sensus communis* "as it were," Arendt, like others, excises the body and its needs, passions and differences, not only from the political realm but also from ethical considerations.[55]

Ravikovitch, by contrast, aims to bring the body to light. If for Arendt "persuasion, negotiation, and compromise . . . are the processes of law and politics," which compassion shuns as it wordlessly and apolitically confronts physical suffering,[56] then for Ravikovitch the body must be pulled out of the shadows of homogeneous privacy and into the public, even if the confrontation is not, strictly speaking, political. Her corporeal poetics refuses the mediating procedures of law and deliberative democracy ("persuasion, negotiation, and compromise"). Instead of universally determining what bodies are or need, it merely underscores the fact that all bodies have *some* needs and may therefore suffer.[57] Even if this suffering might resist representation or, as Elaine Scarry contends, destroy the capacity for speech, Ravikovitch refuses to merely leave it obscure, attempting instead to render it visible with minimal mediation. Pace Scarry's legalistic understanding of pain as private and incommunicable, Ravikovitch's poetics suggests that pain is also a social relationship, whose paradigmatic example might be, according to Talal Asad's critique of Scarry, a mother's response to a child's expression of pain.[58]

Western focus on others' suffering bodies, particularly as evidence of their humanity, has been profusely criticized. Even when well-intentioned, it tends to ontologize and vilify pain, rendering its elimination the sole goal of rights.

54. Hannah Arendt, *On Revolution*, ed. Jonathan Schell (New York: Penguin Classics, 2006), 88–89.

55. In *The Life of the Mind* (ed. Mary Mccarthy [San Diego: Mariner, 1981]), Arendt similarly distinguishes between the passive and wordless soul, associated with immediate bodily needs and sensations, and the mind, the active cognitive capacity for thinking and judging, which involves an internal discursive distance, a sort of "space of appearance" within the self. See Rei Terada, "Thinking for Oneself: Realism and Defiance in Arendt," ELH 71, no. 4 (2004): 839–65.

56. Arendt, *On Revolution*, 86–87.

57. Discussing politics as cohabitation, Judith Butler argues that "perhaps all ethical claims presuppose a bodily life, understood as injurable, one that is not restrictively human"; Butler, "Precarious Life, Vulnerability, and the Ethics of Cohabitation," *Journal of Speculative Philosophy* 26, no. 2 (2012): 147.

58. Elaine Scarry, *The Body in Pain: The Making and Unmaking of the World* (New York: Oxford University Press, 1987), 54; Talal Asad, *Formations of the Secular: Christianity, Islam, Modernity* (Stanford, Calif.: Stanford University Press, 2003), 80–82.

It risks appropriating others' victimization and reproducing their hyper-embodiment—a racialized difference requisite for the emergence of the empathetic, reflexive liberal subject.[59] This criticism is certainly warranted in Ravikovitch's case. In fact, as Chapter 5 demonstrates, the hyper-embodiment of Palestinians and Mizrahi Jews, their perception as fungible bodies, enables not only their disposability and estrangement from each other but also the construction of Ashkenazi society as liberal and divorced from violence. That said, Ravikovitch's poetics of the body and the real, of *ḥaḳḳ*, has three unique characteristics: first, it considers, as mentioned, Palestinian pain as collective rather than individualized; second, it engages the pained body "not by way of a simulated wholeness" but in its shattered form, for, as Saidiya Hartman writes, "It is the ravished body that holds out the possibility of restitution, not the invocation of an illusory wholeness or the desired return to an originary plentitude"[60]; and third, rather than being the terminus, the body is centered in her poetry as a starting point for finding an evaluative type, for thinking and rethinking this case.

In her repetitions, Ravikovitch eliminates all aspects of the scene related to the regime of judgment—the concrete details of the witnesses, of the orders, and of the beatings, all utilized in the ruling to determine, "Is this the case?" Rejecting preexisting laws and even the very logic of critique, she invents instead a new, temporary, evaluative type that she both detects and constructs in and for the case.[61] One possible name for this practice is casuistry, or in Hebrew, *pilpul*—a traditional Jewish interpretative method, whose name suggests both its sharp wit (its "pepper," *pilpel*) and its endless turning of matters from one side to the other (*pal-pal*). Because it existed and changed throughout Jewish history, *pilpul* is difficult to conclusively summarize in such a limited space. That said, it did acquire a more narrow, technical sense in the early modern period as a mode of reasoning that starts from concrete problems (usually of *halakha*, law) and, instead of turning to external sources, engages closely with a localized textual case to tease out its theoretical rationale and

59. See, especially, Asad, *Formations of the Secular*; Saidiya Hartman, *Scenes of Subjection: Terror, Slavery, and Self-Making in Nineteenth-Century America* (New York: Oxford University Press, 1997).

60. Hartman, *Scenes of Subjection*, 74.

61. Deleuze associates such creative, immanent evaluation with the eternal return and contrasts it with judgment by pre-given laws. To clarify the difference, he uses Nietzsche's metaphor of the dice-throw: we may cast the dice over and over, waiting for the winning combination according to the existing rules of the game; or we may reinvent the rules each time the dice fall on the table, affirming the result by extrapolating a rule that would "bring back" the dice throw—that is, spell a "win"; Deleuze, *Nietzsche and Philosophy*, 25–29.

then try it on others. Assuming that Rabbinic literature was written perfectly, the analytic-philological method of *pilpul* (known as *ʿiyyun* among Sephardi Jews) considers any seemingly superfluous scriptural word to require reinterpretation, based on its context and on ever finer conceptual distinctions. Innovation, always renewing the meaning of each Talmudic line, is indeed fundamental to *pilpul*.[62] Ravikovitch's selective quotations approximate this *pilpulistic* creative, evaluative mode, as do her biblical and Talmudic allusions.

"I Am Not Here"

Counterfactual allusions, a second critical building block of Ravikovitch's poetics, are key to the first stanza, to which we now return. They produce countermemory by inserting a certain relief or interruption into Ravikovitch's own tradition. For instance, while the trope of "shining white mothers," their characterization as pure and holy, is a convention of the Yiddish lullaby, the redoubling of the mother in the grandmother exceeds these conventions and frees up their figures to take on other meanings.[63] As the following verses introduce the fatal incident in Jabalya, one way to explain this redoubling is to understand the two mothers as singing each to her own son—that is, the Palestinian child from Jabalya, the mother's son, and his father, the grandmother's son. By redoubling the "holy mother" figure, Ravikovitch opens this convention of the Yiddish lullaby to being potentially occupied by Palestinians as well, thus drawing attention to their possible lament.

Jewish symbols and conventions—such as the "pure mothers" and their shawl (*miṭpaḥat*)—are recurrently enlisted in the poem and opened up to new connotations. This culminates in the sixth line, when we learn that the song to be sung, which presents the Givʿati case, is "an ancient and mournful tune" (*zemer ʿatiḳ ve-nuge*). Not merely a bitter ironic comment on the prevalence of Israeli soldiers' violence, this phrase also intertwines and carves out the titles of two canonical Hebrew poems, "Zemer Nuge" (Mournful Song), written by Raḥel Bluwstein in the 1920s, and "Nigun ʿAtiḳ" (Ancient Tune), written by Nathan Alterman in the 1950s. While these two poems, set to music and therefore widely known in Israel, seem so specifically Israeli, their content, as unrequited love songs, aspires to express universal human experience. Yet,

62. Haim Zalman Dimitrovsky, "ʿAl Derekh ha-Pilpul," in *Sefer ha-Yovel li-Khvod Shalom Baron*, ed. Shaul Lieberman, Hebrew Section (Jerusalem: Ha-Aḳademiya ha-Americaʾit le-Madaʿe ha-Yahadut, 1975), 111–82. In English, see Daniel Boyarin, "'Pilpul': The Logic of Commentary," *Dor LeDor*, no. 3 (1986): 1–25, and the sources therein.

63. Kronfeld, "Shira Poliṭit ke-Omanut Lashon," 522.

this attempt at universality—composing melancholy love songs whose story is as ancient as time, only purely in Hebrew—is itself part and parcel of the Zionist national enterprise. It positions Hebrew poetry as one national corpus amongst others and situates Israel—whose canon, too, now consists of age-old mournful tunes and is thus itself as ancient as time—as a nation like any other.[64] By attributing these poems to the two lamenting mothers, however, Ravikovitch not only carves out space in the Hebrew canon for the long-familiar mournful tune of soldiers brutalizing Palestinians, but also redeems these poems of their universalist aspirations, tying them back to their locality, and precisely thereby exposing their nationalist ambitions.[65]

This approach is central to Ravikovitch's poetics and could be summed up by the declaration "I am not here" (*ani lo kan*), which opens several stanzas of her well-known poem "Reḥifa be-Gova Namukh" ("Hovering at a Low Altitude," 1982). The poem, quoted in the epigraph, depicts a scene of violence against a young Palestinian girl. While seemingly self-negating or representing a willful Israeli blindness, this nonsensical formula, "I am not here," encapsulates in fact the logic of Ravikovitch's self-evacuating intertextuality. It is at once an ironic rendering of an escapist spirit and an expression of sharing one's "here" through a partial self-removal. An "I" that suspends itself from "here" clears space for others to appear; yet, by indexing a "here," as though with its very finger, this "I" clings to the "here," thus exposing complete self-negation as impossible (even when desired).[66] Proposing a relation to others through this aspirational self-removal, through the "not here" of her "I," Ravikovitch's declaration is a poetic stab at decolonization, as unsatisfying as it may be.

The formula, a contrarian denial of the present situation, operates as litotes—a rhetorical figure that broadens the interpretative scope through partial negation. Often used ironically, litotes subtly emphasizes an implied positive through a negative statement (e.g., "not a walk in the park"). By frequently employing litotes in her narration, Ravikovitch tacitly presents a second, counterfactual, implied story behind the one she is telling. Owing to the litotes,

64. Hamutal Tsamir makes similar claims about the Statehood Generation in Hebrew poetry in her book *be-Shem ha-Nof: Le'umiyut, Migdar ve-Subyekṭiviyut ba-Shira ha-Yiśre'elit bi-Shenot ha-Ḥamishim veha-Shishim* (Jerusalem: Keter; Merkaz Heḳsherim, ha-Merkaz le-Ḥeḳer ha-Sifrut veha-Tarbut ha-Yehudit veha-Yiśre'elit, Universitat Ben-Gurion ba-Negev, 2006).

65. In so doing, Ravikovitch also exposes the fiction behind the Zionist imagery of an ancient Hebrew tune, continuously transmitted from biblical times to modern Israel, as well as criticizes the exclusion of Jewish tunes, both Yiddish and Mizrahi, from Zionist history.

66. On the status of the self in "Reḥifa be-Gova Namukh," compare Olmert, "'Ani lo Kan.'" On the grammatical and logical impossibility of the phrase "I am not here," see Kronfeld, "Shira Poliṭit ke-Omanut Lashon," 537.

Ravikovitch's counterfactuals are truly "counter"—not simply a possible road-not-taken but the negated form of the actually depicted narrative. The poem "Ima Mithalekhet" (A Mother Walks Around, 1992), for instance, conveys the aftermath of IDF soldiers' killing of a fetus, still in his mother's womb. Ravikovitch relays this Palestinian woman's experience—the stillbirth of a murdered child and a life lived in his absence—in the future tense and through litotic counterfactuals. She narrates nothing but the events that the child and his mother *will not* experience, yet could have potentially experienced, had he been born.

> . . . and he won't wave his arms about or cry his first cry
> and they won't slap his bottom
> won't put drops in his eyes
> won't swaddle him
> after washing the body.
> He will not resemble a living child.
> His mother will not be calm and proud after giving birth
> and she won't be troubled about his future,
> won't worry how in the world to support him
> and does she have enough milk
> and does she have enough clothing
> and how will she ever fit one more cradle into the room.[67]

Introducing space into her own experiences through litotic negation, the counterfactual narrative does not represent—nor presume exact knowledge of—a Palestinian mother's life. At the same time, however, it gives her center stage.

In "Shir 'Ereś Meturgam mi-Yidish," as well as in Ravikovitch's poetry more broadly, the litotic negation is applied, specifically, to the past and by use of allusions. Jewish history and cultural heritage become the arsenal whose carving out produces counter-memory—a reactivation of the past modified by litotic counterfactuals. Ravikovitch thus seems to relate to Palestinians not by separating herself from the Jewish collective and its history, but rather by making this history, including the colonization of Palestine itself, all the more present. It is by recruiting her heritage to the fullest degree that it becomes the "not here" through which she presents and relates to Palestinians' experiences.

Ravikovitch's counterfactual allusions are central to "Reḥifa be-Gova Namukh," in which a tragic story is narrated by listing everything that the Palestinian girl is not: "She doesn't walk with neck outstretched and wanton

67. Ravikovitch, 214/234.

glances," / She doesn't paint her eyes with kohl. / She doesn't ask, Whence cometh my help."[68] Weaving together a tight biblical referential web, Ravikovitch employs her tradition in a litotic form to highlight the girl's difference from Jewish society, past and present, while also raising questions about Jewish tradition and its sacred texts. Referring to two of the prophets of destruction mentioned earlier, Ravikovitch's litotic allusions indict the "classic" juridical logic they espouse. Because these prophets metaphorized the transgression of God's law in gendered terms—the nation as a wanton woman—and the punishment as justified sexual violence, negating their words rejects the applicability of this framework, both generally and to this particular case of arbitrary sexual violence.[69]

These counterfactual allusions do not subsume others, for their negation serves to mark and acknowledge differences. The Palestinian mothers in "Shir 'Ereś Meturgam mi-Yidish" are not equated with the Jewish mothers of Yiddish lullabies—such a universalizing equation would simply trivialize their pain, turning all suffering into one and the same suffering. Similarly, had she attempted to speak for them, Ravikovitch might have risked erasing their alterity. Instead, it is her own heritage that she repeats selectively, with gaps, according to the procedure of the "I am not here."

In light of this carving out and making room, the labeling of this lullaby a translation seems apt, as these attributes are recurrent in familiar accounts of translation. Perhaps the most famous example is Benjamin's essay "The Task of the Translator," which emphasizes the gap produced in translation: "Whereas content and language form a certain unity in the original, like a fruit and its skin, the language of the translation envelops its content like a royal robe with ample folds . . . and thus remains unsuited to its content, overpowering and alien."[70] Both before and after Benjamin, the distance between original and translation, the translator's incessant negotiation between impossible absolute faithfulness to a source and an equally impossible radical freedom, were ever-present in Western theories of translation. This complexity of translation is often tied to the quandary of ethical relations, as the entire problem is still all too often oriented along an axis that stretches from the extremes of absolute untranslatability—the impossibility of accessing the other in its radical difference—to perfect translatability, the complete reduction of others to

68. Ravikovitch, 174–76/179–81.

69. Kronfeld, "Shira Poliṭit ke-Omanut Lashon," 534.

70. Walter Benjamin, "The Task of the Translator," in *Walter Benjamin: Selected Writings*, ed. Michael William Jennings and Marcus Paul Bullock, trans. Harry Zohn (Cambridge, Mass.: Belknap, 2004), 1:258.

one's own language in the absence of any markers of shared meaning.[71] In postcolonial studies and their critiques of translation, this dichotomy often stems from the scholarly focus on translation's subsumption of indigenous languages into the global English-language market.[72] The fact that translations do exist, however, constantly challenges this assumed impasse, which thus emerges largely as a Western anxiety or as specific to the history of English-language imperialism (particularly in the Indian subcontinent). Indeed, such perceptions of translation are incongruent with Hebrew and Arabic textual traditions—cultures of commentary, of interpretation and reinterpretation, in which, as in the case of *pilpul*, every reading is a rereading and every writing a rewriting, often critical and creative. And this fact, far from producing crisis or existential dread, drives intellectual, aesthetic, and social changes. The question, therefore, should be refocused on *how* translations operate. And that is precisely what Ravikovitch does in her poem, which thus justifies its title to the last degree.

"Their Cry Still Rises Night after Night"[73]

The final stanza begins thus:

> Mama and grandma are singing a song
> so that you sleep without harm, tender child,
> holy mothers are watching over you.
> Here, a twig from above you fell as well.[74]

The sarcastic tone running like a red thread through the poem and condemning the nihilistic attitude of those who "sleep" during such grave injustices,

71. As early as Longinus, intertextuality was articulated in terms of loyalty and freedom; Longinus, *On Sublimity*, trans. D. A. Russell (Oxford: Clarendon, 1965), 19. See also Susan Bassnett, *Translation Studies* (London and New York: Routledge, 2002); Susan Bassnett and André Lefevere, eds., *Constructing Cultures: Essays on Literary Translation* (Clevedon: Multilingual Matters, 1998); Gayatri Chakravorty Spivak, "Can the Subaltern Speak?," in *Marxism and the Interpretation of Culture*, ed. Cary Nelson and Lawrence Grossberg (Urbana: University of Illinois Press, 1988), 271–313.

72. Kronfeld, *Full Severity of Compassion*, 180.

73. This verse is from "Shir 'Ereś," Ravikovitch's second iteration of the poem; Ravikovitch, 219–20/241.

74. *hine gam zalzal me'alekha tsanaḥ*—where *me'alekha* might signify "(from) above you" or "from amongst your leaves." I foreground the first meaning in my translation since it echoes the mothers' protection "from above," as well as the angels', thus relating to Ravikovitch's struggle against transcendental judgment.

culminates here with the holy mothers alleging to sing a protective song. This statement seems rather ironic, almost cruel—as a Palestinian, the child has already been brutalized; as a Jewish Israeli, sheltered from harm in his bed, he requires no protection. Standing in stark contrast to the injured Palestinian child, his utter passivity is thereby disparaged.

Passivity is indeed the target here. It is also implied by the allusion to a famous poem by Haim Nahman Bialik, Israel's national poet, "Tsanaḥ lo Zalzal" (A Twig Fell, 1911). This poem employs an extended metaphor comparing human life to the transformations of a twig throughout the cycle of seasons to lament the expiration of the lyrical self's life and lifeforce. Its eponymous opening verse encapsulates its significance: "A twig fell upon a fence and slumbered" (*tsanaḥ lo zalzal ʿal gader ṿa-yanom*). What leads to demise is this slumber on the fence, for had the twig fallen on either side of it, upon fertile ground—that is, had the subject taken any action instead of merely sleeping or "sitting on the fence"—then it might have avoided being thrown out of the cycle of life. Linking passivity and sleep with death, the twig joins the four angels of the throne in foreshadowing destruction and in calling upon the sleeping children of Israel and Palestine to awaken and act.

The sense of a cyclical return, introduced by the allusion and its seasonal figuration, is reinforced in the next verses:

As you will grow up and become a man,
the anguish of Jabalya you shall never forget
from '48 to '67, from '67 to '88,
the anguish of Jabalya you shall never forget,
and the village of Beita and the village of Ḥawara
and Sajaʿiyya and the village of Silfit.[75]

The plea to never forget clarifies that the poem's critique of the law and its suspension of judgment do not equal an absence of awareness or evaluation. With this plea, Ravikovitch again enlists and interrupts her own heritage, reappropriating and carving out two holocaust commemoration practices. Adopt-

75. In teleological retrospect, Ravikovitch's mention of Sajaʿiyya (usually rendered *Shujaʿiyya*) and Ḥawara add two more instances to the series (1948, 1967, 1988 . . .). During the 2014 Israeli attack on the Gaza Strip, the densely populated neighborhood of Shujaʿiyya was pummeled to the ground. In a single day—Saturday, July 20, 2014—at least 65 Palestinians were killed and 288 wounded. In February 2023, hundreds of Jewish settlers violently attacked the West Bank village of Ḥawara, backed by the IDF, in revenge for the killing of two settler brothers by a Palestinian gunman (though the chronicle of retaliations is, of course, much longer and more uneven). A Palestinian was killed and dozens wounded. The Israeli finance minister Bezalel Smotrich publicly called to "wipe out" Ḥawara.

ing the ceremonial citation of names of towns that endured great suffering, she replaces East European place names with Palestinian ones. Likewise, reclaiming the command to "never forget," she translates it from its established first-person-plural form used for holocaust commemoration, "We shall not forget" (*lo nishkaḥ*), into the second-person imperative, "You shall not forget" (*lo tishkaḥ*). In her counterfactual allusions, Ravikovitch repurposes European Jewish history to observe Palestinian catastrophes by plugging in place names, instead of testifying to Palestinian experiences or fusing those under *the* Palestinian condition, in the singular. The repeated citation of proper names of Palestinian towns and villages is a technique that, like Ravikovitch's quotations, aims to bypass mediation and approximate the real. The litany of concrete sites is redoubled in the litany of years marking specific historical events—the *nakba* of 1948, the war and occupation of 1967,[76] and the incident at Jabalya during the First Intifada in 1988. In the Hebrew original, the sound *aḥ*, an elegiac cry of pain and anguish, concludes the Hebrew years' names and the command to never forget (*mi-tashaḥ le-tashkaḥ, mi-tashkaḥ le-tashmaḥ, / et tsaʿar Jibaliyya lo tishkaḥ*)—an alliteration that intensifies the sense of suffering and lamentation. Insisting on the singularity of concrete places, events, and bodies, and inserting those into her counterfactual allusions, these verses synthesize and maximize Ravikovitch's two poetic methods.

The litany of sites and years also creates a metonymic generalization, expanding the purview by invoking other cases. As opposed to the exceptionalist reasoning of the judges, the repetitive allusion to various atrocities in different places and times refutes the "uniqueness" of the Givʿati Affair, presenting it instead as one among many cases of senseless orders and vicious violence. In Ravikovitch's critical ventriloquy of this cycle, however, the different cases are not reduced to a single, coherent story—they maintain their proper names. Thus, unlike determinative judgment, which subsumes particulars under a universal rule, concept, or category, this generalizable type is attached to the singularities of the particular case. While the concern with the particular seems to align types with Kantian reflective judgment, the

76. The years in this verse are Jewish years. They do not overlap with Gregorian calendar years, and their numerals are represented by the Hebrew alphabet. Translating the year *tashkaḥ* is thus quite a challenge. Mostly coinciding with 1968, its first few months were still part of 1967, which somewhat justifies its translation here as 1967 (even if the 1967 War itself took place during the previous Jewish year, *tashkaz*). A homonym of the word *tishkah* (you will forget), its name both echoes and contradicts the earlier command to never forget, perhaps lamenting how quickly Jewish Israelis forgot about 1967. The homonym also alludes to Yehuda Amichai's poem "Jerusalem 1967," which uses the year name *tashkaḥ* to criticize Israeli forgetfulness of the similarities between the holocaust and the 1967 occupation.

latter aims to generate a universal rule for the singular case, whereas typological generalization remains local and contingent, amassing some resonant cases that might suggest their own immanent criterion of evolution.[77] It thus offers a different, lateral relation between the one and the many that consists in adjoining—putting side by side—concrete places and moments in a series that is both open (to future additions) and circumscribed (geographically, culturally).

At first glance, Ravikovitch seems critical of using particular cases to make more general social or political claims. In her poem "Marina Ḥadad" (Marina Haddad, 2005), Ravikovitch narrates, through litotic counterfactuals, the events that could have taken place had the news reporters bothered visiting the recently deceased Marina Haddad. She contends,

> All the makings were there: bereavement, sorrow,
> the mother a single parent, the state of the nation as metonymy
> for the fate of the individual (especially vice versa)
> . . .
> She was one of a kind,
> call it the luck of a goy that she alone
> was not exploited
> to diagnose the state of the nation
> and forecast the inescapable ramifications.[78]

Despite the "metonymy" label, it is instead synecdoche that Ravikovitch denounces here, for what disconcerts her is the exploitation of an individual for representing the whole—specifically, the organic, personified totality of the nation. Her critique is waged precisely against the Altermanian strategy of the "lawful pair"—using the particular to stand in for, and thus absolve, the national community. The litanizing of proper names of years and towns, by contrast, does not constitute a synecdoche. Instead of universalizing the Giv'ati Affair or effacing differences between various calamities, even within Palestinian history, the list forms a metonymic series, a malleable yet limited generalization, suggesting that this singular case might indeed share similar features with other, adjacent cases, to which it is irreducible.[79]

77. Immanuel Kant, *Critique of Pure Reason*, trans. Werner S. Pluhar (Indianapolis: Hackett, 1996); Immanuel Kant, *Critique of Judgment*, trans. Werner S. Pluhar (Indianapolis: Hackett, 1987).

78. Ravikovitch, 259–60/297–98.

79. A similar metonymic generalization is suggested by Job's singular suffering. Like others, Maimonides wondered whether Job was a real man or a poetic fiction, a symbol (*mashal*, a parable). He first concluded, based on the large number of different interpretations, that Job must be an allegory. Yet, zeroing in on the opening verse of the book—"*Ish haya be'erets 'Uts*"

This metonymic generalization, central to Ravikovitch's poetics and to the ethics it proposes, is born from the combination of litotic allusions (of engraving, *ḥaḳiḳa*) and the *habeas corpus* of quotations (of material reality, *ḥaḳḳ*). It also puts forward a specific mode of comparison between Palestinians and Jewish Israelis. Through the figure of Marina Haddad, for instance, whose name is suggestive of a Christian Palestinian, Ravikovitch's counterfactuals parodically showcase differences in media reporting: while Jewish bereavement and loss are swiftly translated into the usual metaphors, easily universalized as concerning the entire nation, the deceased Palestinian is left alone in her hospital bed. Ravikovitch thus criticizes not only the neglect of others' tragedies but also the synecdochic mediation of loss. Contemplating the unfathomable pain that Marina Haddad's mother must have felt, Ravikovitch both professes its resistance to representation and insists on making it present.[80] Concluding that "heartrending suffering is suffering that rends / the heart of the sufferer / alone,"[81] she both destroys the neat "old metaphor" by exposing its tautology and foregrounds the sufferer in her loneliness, in the incommunicability of her singular pain—so present that it is all but physical.

The lullaby's finale brings Ravikovitch's critical poetics to its most radical peak:

> And all their blood shall be on our heads,
> demand it from us,
> nice child.

The blood "on our heads" refers to the biblical story of Rahab and of the destruction of the Canaanite city of Jericho. Before their invasion of Canaan and the series of battles that ensues, the Israelites' leader, Joshua, sends spies to scout out the land. Rahab, known as "the harlot," hides the spies from their enemies in Jericho. In return, she obtains immunity—an assurance that she and her family will not be harmed in the coming conquest battle, provided they remain within her clearly marked house. Should they stay within the house, their bloodshed would be "on our heads"; should they venture out, it would

("There was a man in the land of Uz")—Maimonides also observed the dual meaning of the word *'uts*, which is both a proper name (as in Gn 22:21: "Uz his firstborn") and the second-person imperative of the verb *la-'uts*, "to consult," "to deliberate," "to decide," by which the text exhorts the readers, he explains, to closely study and evaluate its ideas (*Guide for the Perplexed* III.22). Along these lines, one might say that Job was at once both a singular, existing man and a parable and that the undecidability between the two is necessary for truly reading his book.

80. "And what she endured / I'm at a loss to express / or even to fathom"; Ravikovitch, 259–60/297–98.

81. Ibid.

be "on their heads." Indeed, the promise is kept, and Rahab and her family are saved, while the rest of Jericho's population is massacred.[82] The blood "on our heads" is therefore the bloodshed of the exceptionally sacred, of those who must not be harmed even in a situation of sweeping carnage. However, unlike the occupation of Canaan in the days of Joshua, modern colonization in Palestine spares no one, hence "*all* their blood shall be on our heads."

The blood "on our heads" is indeed the mark of the exception to the violence of colonial occupation, of that rare instance when the order to commit murder would be "manifestly legal." Yet another counterfactual illusion reinforces this reading. The blood demanded from "us"—literally, "from our hands" (*mi-yadenu*)—references the biblical *ḥoḳ* of the beheaded heifer (to which Ravikovitch dedicated a poem, exploring Jewish-Palestinian relations). When a slain body is found beyond municipal limits and the killer's identity is unknown, the elders of the nearest town must behead a heifer and wash their hands over its body, while declaring, "Our hands (*yadenu*) did not shed this blood, nor did our eyes see it done" (Dt 21:7). Intended to purify the community of the shedding of innocent blood, this scapegoating ritual exceptionalizes the violence (implying it was perpetrated by some "rotten apples," not "us"). This time, Ravikovitch forms a counterfactual not by negating through litotes as usual but by omitting instead the original negation in the ritualistic declaration. The blood that *is* "on our hands" suggests the failure of the meta-juridical attempt to abdicate collective responsibility through an exceptionalizing rite—that is, by such mechanisms as the "lawful pair" and the manifestly illegal order, which ultimately normalize colonial violence. Since juridical self-critique is exposed as impossible, true responsibility, blood, must be demanded.[83]

The call on the child and the reader to demand this blood from the Jewish collective in Israel is crucial, and its interpretations are legion. First, it is a call for a re-trial, for a re-evaluation of the case, according to the type provided by the poem. Second, critical of the spurious, exceptionalizing logic of juridical self-critique, the demand calls specifically for a reevaluation of *collective* culpability. This reevaluation, however, is still to come, for an alternative trial never materializes in the poem. It therefore appears that not only juridical self-critique, but also an individual, ethical one, is useless. Third is the simpler message that IDF brutality might lead some Palestinian children to grow up to fight against it, possibly violently. Neither the future temporality of reevalu-

82. Jos 2:19, 6:16–17.

83. On blood as a mechanism of universalizing through exclusion and on its national and racial effects, see Gil Anidjar, *Blood: A Critique of Christianity* (New York: Columbia University Press, 2016), 40–44.

ation or the symmetrical "cycle of revenge" departs greatly from the "shooting and crying" approach. Finally, however, the demand for blood is also a plea for the (self-)destruction of the collective in its current form. Unable to take this supra-critical step herself, Ravikovitch has paved the way for her readers, urging them to move forward with decolonization, with a true removal of the "I" from "here," whereby either the "I" or the "here" must be radically changed to resolve the nonsensical formula that is Israel. In Ravikovitch's poetic attempt to push beyond mediation, beyond the deliberative democracy of *medina/seconda* and its judgment, decolonization appears as the only conclusion. It is precisely this obvious conclusion, and the blood "on our hands" that the legal system works so hard to obscure.

Coda: Mediating History

The Palestinian author and scholar Adania Shibli, born in 1974 in Palestine, holds a Ph.D. in Media and Cultural Studies and currently lives between Berlin and Ramallah. Like Ravikovitch, she seeks to reconsider a murder case exceptionalized by the Israeli military legal system. If Ravikovitch does so by way of self-critique and while responding to a recent affair, then Shibli's historical novel, *Tafṣil Thanawi* (Minor Detail, 2017), presents the wrongdoing of the colonizing enemy and focuses on an affair that took place over seventy years ago, in 1949.[84] Thus, the structural issues with the evidentiary logic of the law—its ethnographic desire for disinterested documentation and its over-reliance on state legal institutions—are exacerbated in Shibli's novel by a dual inaccessibility: the temporal distance of the affair and the classification of state documents.

Shibli's novel, her third, centers on the Nirim Affair, which eerily aligns with Ravikovitch's poem in the epigraph, as it also concerns the rape and murder of a Palestinian girl and the Israeli refusal to contend with it. In August 1949, a patrol of Jewish Israeli soldiers, recently deployed near the Egyptian border, encountered two Palestinian men and a girl (neither her name nor her age is known. Some witnesses reported that she was ten to fifteen years old; others claimed that she was fifteen to twenty years old). After apprehending all three, the soldiers and their commander, Second Lieutenant Moshe, shot in the air to scare off the men and hauled the Palestinian Bedouin girl onto their vehicle. When they arrived back in their outpost, the soldiers locked the girl in a shed. They later undressed her, washed her publicly under a water pipe, burnt her clothes, cut her hair short, and washed it with gasoline. During a festive Friday night dinner, the

84. Adania Shibli, *Minor Detail*, trans. Elisabeth Jaquette (New York: New Directions, 2020). In Arabic: Shibli, *Tafṣil Thanawi* (Beirut: Dar al-Adab li-l-Nashr wa-l-Tawzi', 2017).

platoon commander, Moshe, put forward two options for a vote, entrusting the girl's fate in his soldiers' hands: either use her as a kitchen worker or have sex with her. The soldiers voted overwhelmingly in support of rape. Second Lieutenant Moshe drew up a schedule, divvying up the upcoming nights between the various squads—a timetable for a continuous gang rape. On the first night, the commander, his deputy, and the staff squad (drivers, cooks, medics, squad commanders, etc.) raped the girl. The next morning, deviating from his careful plan, the platoon commander ordered his deputy, Sargent Michael, to execute her. The deputy and a handful of soldiers drove the girl a quarter of a mile out of the outpost, dug a shallow grave in the sand in front of her eyes and, when she attempted to escape, shot her dead. Then they buried her.

David Ben Gurion, the first prime minister of Israel, summed up this affair in his diary: "a horrific atrocity: . . . twenty-two men debated what to do with her: it was decided and executed—they washed her, cut her hair short, raped her and killed her." For fifty-four years, this was the only trace of the rape and murder of the Palestinian girl who disappeared in the Naqab Desert in August 1949. Even though rumors immediately began circulating—some of them quickly led to a military investigation and, subsequently, to trial—the details of the case and the closed-door court-martial proceedings were sealed. In 2003, *Haaretz* journalists gained access to the classified materials and exposed the case in a sensational piece.[85] No one else since, however, was able to access the documents directly. Currently, the only available record is the *Haaretz* piece, on which my earlier summary is based.

The case was first exposed when a researcher examined the records of the 1956 Kufr Qassem massacre trial—the very trial during which Judge Halevy coined the exceptionalist legal notion of the "manifestly illegal order." During the Kufr Qassem trial, the prosecution presented as precedent the classified Judgment from the Nirim Affair, since it rejected the defendants' "merely following orders" line of defense, thus already establishing that some orders must not be obeyed.[86] That the Nirim Affair played a role in the conception of the "manifestly illegal order" is no coincidence, as it was one of a mere handful of cases during which the nature of such murderous orders was even discussed (and thus effectively whitewashed).

The first of *Tafṣil Thanawi*'s two chapters narrates the historical Nirim Affair, while the second, which takes place in the present, follows a Palestinian

85. Aviv Lavie and Moshe Gorali, "'I Saw Fit to Remove Her from the World,'" *Haaretz*, October 29, 2003, https://www.haaretz.com/1.4746524.

86. Moshe Gorali, "'Od Degel Shaḥor," *Haaretz*, October 28, 2003, https://www.haaretz.co.il/misc/1.920418.

woman writer from Ramallah, who ventures to recover its details. The narrative that unfolds in the first chapter is thus logically the fruit of the journey narrated in the second. The discovery of a minor detail, that she herself was born exactly twenty-five years to the day after the murder in Nirim, motivates the protagonist to cross borders and checkpoints in search of information in Israeli archives and museums. Personalizing the affair, this detail stresses its significance to the narrator over its systemic significance. For this reason (as well as others to be soon discussed), the novel belongs to the genre of autofiction—a mostly Anglo-American industry that is increasingly becoming global. Indeed, Shibli's novel is in dialogue with literary trends in the Anglophone world, nodding to J. M. Coetzee and Saidiya Hartman, amongst others.

In a methodically disinterested tone, the first chapter narrates the details of the Nirim Affair based solely on the information found in the *Haaretz* piece. Presented from the perspective of the platoon commander, these events are layered with an added, fictionalized narrative through-line about a dog bite, the ailment that ensues, and the commander's attempts at self-treatment. The landscape is elaborately depicted by the omnipresent narrator. Local plants are described in minute detail and mentioned by name. Human actions, by contrast, are presented in a terse, factual language that seems to aspire to the documentary detachment of legal records. Taking this language to an absurd level, this chapter describes all occurrences as corporeal, sensorial actions severed from any psychological or ideological interiority. This style of *ḥaḳḳ* serves, like Ravikovitch's, to criticize the procedure of the legal system; unlike Ravikovitch, however, the goal is not one of empathy for this suffering body but rather of critically exposing the operation of the ideology driving it. Shibli, too, utilizes subtraction and the chiseling of relief (*ḥaḳiḳa*), avoiding both first-person narration and free indirect speech, thus denying the readers access to the commander's thoughts and feelings. Instead, she offers repeated descriptions of pains and aches, as well as of the officer's obsessive hygienic and medicinal rites. In portraying the commander in this matter-of-fact manner, Shibli seems to critically respond to the deep, conflicted, and speculative protagonist of Zionist literature, explored in Chapter 2 of this book. Like other Palestinian authors (discussed earlier, in Chapter 3), Shibli counters this conflicted Zionist writing by using a surface-level style and staying close to the body. But, while other Palestinian authors did so by utilizing humorous, absurd narrations to document their own history and lives, Shibli's response is dry, almost tedious, and centers on writing that Zionist subject himself. Her documentary style actively deprives him of the reflexive depth that, as we have seen, serves Zionism as an ideological justification for colonization and as a mechanism of overcoming. In fact, the commander's compulsive attempts at overcoming his affliction are depicted as yielding nothing.

The writing technique that Shibli applies to the Zionist protagonist—adhering to a forensic rhetoric that disallows subjective memories or affects—is the same juridical mediating strategy used by Zionism to dismiss Palestinians' legal claims for recognition. Both legal rules of evidence and (still) common methodologies of historical argumentation discount the memories of Palestinian victims of Israeli atrocities, even while such atrocities still structure survivors' lives. Indeed, the state often abuses hearsay rules to privilege its own records and render others inadmissible. Reappropriating this strategy, replicating it to the letter, Shibli applies it to the Jewish actors in the Nirim Affair. Yet, her failure to produce any new historical detail or legal recognition suggests that this procedure only serves those who control the means of production of historical records and determine the standards by which their reliability is judged.

Moreover, even when Palestinian narratives are admitted, as Esmeir argues, most are not considered reliable:

> Memory-based narratives have to manifest a certain order when admitted to modern law, Israeli law in particular. Describing modern law as a Faustian-Cartesian dream of order, Seyla Benhabib calls it "transparent, precise, planned, symmetric, organized and functional." It stands in opposition to the "traditional, chaotic, unclear, lacking symmetry and overgrowing" system.[87]

Historiography, as Esmeir observes, often employs not only the same forensic procedures as the legal system but also its ideological frameworks: the positivist historian entertains "a prosecutional focus" on events and conceives of history as linear and progressive, thus separating past from present, dissecting history into isolated events, and assigning blame to individual actors. By contrast, survivors' testimonies reveal a temporal conception that fuses past and present, stressing the collective terror that governs Palestinians' lives instead of discrete events.[88] Given Palestinians' expulsion and dispersal, such memories are far less likely than state-sanctioned archives or historical research to cohere and fit neatly into the "Faustian-Cartesian" order of law and history. Indeed, a living, continuous community and its institutions are necessary for piecing together and sustaining such memories, for thinking them through in any systemic manner.

87. Samera Esmeir, "1948: Law, History, Memory," *Social Text* 21, no. 2 (2003): 33.
88. Ibid., 36.

The second chapter of *Tafṣil Thanawi* raises the very same critique, as its Palestinian first-person narrator struggles to find anything of value in Israeli museums and archives. The narrator explicitly scorns archives and their trite language, concluding that "official museums . . . really have no valuable information to offer me, not even small details that could help me retell the girl's story."[89] And, for her, it is the small detail—the "fly on the painting," the dust on the desk, everything that escapes the "Faustian-Cartesian dream of order"—that might expose the true story. This narrator, whose anxiety grants her copious depth, also expresses a communal sense of ceaseless terror and the epistemic foreclosure produced by fragmentation. The dust that covers the 1949 Nirim Outpost also adorns the author's desk in her twenty-first-century office in Ramallah as a result of a nearby bombing. Intense dog barks traverse the two parts of the novel. Both motifs challenge the "evental" progressive logic of historiography and thread together various instances of violence, pointing to their ongoing, metonymic, and generalizable nature and to the "ghostly" temporal framework by which a community knows and commemorates them.

It is the novel's finale—spoiler alert!—that truly throws Shibli's critique into relief. While visiting her final destination, the Nirim Outpost, the narrator recognizes that she has been looking in the wrong places all along. As she offers an older Palestinian woman a ride in her car, the narrator suddenly realizes Esmeir's lesson:

> I steal glances at her as I drive, at part of her face, which is lined with sharp wrinkles, then at her hands, which she lets rest in her lap, on the fabric of her black dress, and they seem stronger than any hands I've seen in my life. They're traced with blue veins that recall the lines on the maps I tossed into the back seat when I stopped the car to take her with me. She's probably in her seventies. The girl would have been around the same age now, most likely, if she hadn't been killed. Maybe this old woman has heard about the incident, since incidents like that would have reached the ears of everyone living in the Naqab (*kull ahālī al-naqab*), terrorizing them all (*iyyāhum jamīʿan*), and no one who heard about it would be able to forget.[90]

Yet, the woman leaves the car and "disappears" (*takhtafī*) before the narrator is able to bring herself to talk to her about the incident. Consumed with regret, the narrator exclaims, "How clumsy! It was she, not the military museums or the settlements and their archives, who might hold a detail that could

89. Shibli, *Minor Detail*, 79.
90. Ibid., 102/123.

help me uncover the incident as experienced by the girl. And finally arrive at the whole truth (*al-ḥaḳīḳa*)."[91]

Realizing that the real truth, *al-ḥaḳīḳa*, is the living memories of elderly Palestinians—a collective, oral archive of knowledge, which the colonial state threatens to disappear—the narrator decides to follow the woman into an unpaved side path, unknowingly walking into a military zone. As soon as she notices a group of soldiers, the peril dawns on her. Trying to control her angst, she reaches for the chewing gum in her pocket, which usually helps calm her nerves during interactions with Israeli security personnel. The soldiers shoot her before her hand reaches her pocket. Her shooting is described in the exact same language as that of the anonymous Palestinian girl at the novel's opening—in both cases the gunshot takes effect before its distant sound is heard.[92] The novel thus suggests not only that the *nakba* is continuous, even circular and repetitive, but that the realm of memory, too, is controlled by Israeli state violence, that nothing and no one escapes. Not even history or its writer. Despite her apparent death, however, the narrator had somehow produced the first part of the novel—the retelling of the Nirim Affair. Her efforts are supported at every turn by others: the car and the credit card used for the journey are borrowed from colleagues, and she orients herself in space based on memories others have shared with her about their villages and towns. Like Esmeir, Shibli seems to assert that only a continuous community and its institutions can guard memories against death.

Tafṣil Thanawi has been criticized for its erasure of historical detail and of class disparities, as its ending appears to equate the suffering of the narrator and of the Bedouin girl. While successfully conveying the ongoing nature of colonization, Shibli's aesthetic choices, Bashir abu Manneh argues, also lead her to offer no resistance to Palestinian erasure, in content or in form. The silences—the absence of historical detail, of the archive, and of the girl's voice—thus risk "replicating the erasure the novel seeks to criticize."[93] A possible explanation for these blind spots is Shibli's foregrounding of the personal and its styling within the generic conventions of Anglo-American autofiction. In a world plagued with rapidly intensifying capitalist processes that erode welfare and privatize care, literature plays an instrumental role in the insourcing of care to the self. Autofiction, in particular, serves neoliberal bibliotherapeutic

91. Ibid., 103/124.

92. Ibid., 50, 105.

93. Bashir Abu-Manneh, "The Palestinian Novel after the Era of Mass Revolt," *Jacobin* (blog), January 30, 2022, https://jacobin.com/2022/01/israel-palestine-occupation-nakba-literature-universality.

ends. It is recuperative, either through a narrative overcoming of trauma and adversity or through an anesthetizing and editorializing scripting of such experiences, handing readers a neat theory, a sense that they could rest satisfied in understanding and judging injustices and hardships.[94] Although Shibli's frantic, lost narrator does not enjoy overcoming, the narrative itself is recuperative, as she manages to produce, theoretically, the first half of the novel, the complete and orderly account of the Affair. For the reader, even if not for the narrator, things neatly come to a close, as Shibli's novel not only submits a tidy report but also conceptualizes both the impossibility of recovering history and the necessity of building alternative reservoirs of knowledge (yet without undertaking this positivist work). Forsaking not only historical details, however minor, but also the minor detail as a type—the fly on the painting, the nuanced details that escape ordering and representation—what Shibli offers instead is a systemic theory.

Thus, while producing no new history, the novel does offer a theoretical critique of historiography. Perhaps the narrator's failure and death—the sense of stagnation, of the endless repetition of the *nakba*—are not descriptive but prescriptive by way of negation? Through them, Shibli criticizes the narrator's hesitance to follow the old woman, her failure to realize *in time* that what must be researched and recorded are communal memories and oral histories. In this light, the novel appears less defeatist, suggesting not necessarily that historical knowledge or political resistance are foreclosed but that these should be sought inside the community and outside of state institutions and archives. Although the methodologies of oral history are increasingly embraced by academia, contemporary public and scholarly discourse in Israel suggests that much more work is needed to legitimize and build such archives: Jewish Israelis, including some historians, largely refuse to recognize the 1948 massacre of Palestinians in Tantura (the case at the core of Esmeir's argument) and the affair of the disappeared Yemenite, Mizrahi, and Balkan children (soon to be discussed) because testimonies in these well-documented cases are oral and have not been sanctioned by the state.

It would have been tempting to turn, in the next chapter, to such alternative communal narrations, thus concluding the book on an optimistic note. As Shibli's writing makes clear, however, such optimism is unwarranted in the present reality, as isolation, fragmentation, and hatred have only been amplified. Instead, Chapter 5 explores the rise of severance and hostility within

94. On the contemporary therapeutic narrative and its uses in and though literature, see Eva Illouz, *Saving the Modern Soul: Therapy, Emotions, and the Culture of Self-Help* (Berkeley: University of California Press, 2008).

Palestinian society, within Jewish Israeli society, and between the two populations, focusing on recent technologies of control, on the one hand, and on historical forms of racialization, on the other. Crossing over to Chapter 5 is not only Shibli's writing but also Ravikovitch's ultimately liberal perception of racialized others—Arabs both Palestinian and Jewish—as hyper-embodied, where vulnerability quickly spills over into an exceptional tendency for violence.

5
Inqisām
(Hostile Severance)

And between us there was nothing left
not even the aroma of coffee
thanks to which I was once able to imagine
that there is life
and chatter
and hope.
Now
all that links us
is blood
and blood
and blood.

—SHLOMI HATUKA, "HA-DAM HEḤLIF ET HA-ḲAFE"
(BLOOD FOR COFFEE)

Since the Second Intifada, and even more so since the forced split (*al-inqisām*) between Hamas and Fatah and the Israeli siege of Gaza, the relationship between official Israel and Palestinians in the OPT has been governed by the paradigm of the "no partner for peace" (*'ein parṭner le-shalom*)—a spin phrase coined by the then Israeli prime minister Ehud Barak as a means to refuse negotiation and retrench the status quo.[1] Within Israeli society, a growing political crisis, embodying irreconcilable social rifts, has led to five election rounds in

1. This statement has been exposed as an intentional political spin by several of Barak's former advisors and aides. One of them, Eldad Yaniv, admitted: "There are still people who say, 'We gave them everything at Camp David and got nothing.' That is a flagrant lie. . . . I was

three years (2019–22) and to a sweeping "judicial reform" met with vehement protests (2023). While Israeli opinions regarding the Palestinian question are, according to recent polls, converging toward an impassive "radical center," electoral votes and affiliation groups are increasingly polarizing.[2] This process is driven less by political positions or values and more by shifts in power distribution and affective loyalties. As ideological commitments are becoming murkier and traditional socioeconomic elites are losing *some* power (mostly cultural), a "tribal" mobilization against a threatening other is consolidated—be it the old, liberal Ashkenazi elite, the new religious Zionist one, a rhetorical Mizrahi "second Israel," or, as always, Palestinians.[3] In the Palestinian society of the West Bank, too, social fragmentation abounds, despite the impression of greater national cohesion and sweeping normalization created by rapid integration into global capitalism. Such fragmentation, this chapter argues, is at least partially caused by Israeli technologies of control, which operate through outsourcing and on the border. These severance technologies, unlike other methods and conceptions of separation (such as segregation or apartheid), aim to divide not only colonizer from colonized but also, and especially, the colonized from each other.

I put forward *inqisām*—"severance," with its overt hostility and hostile hospitality—as a figurative concept that might be capacious enough to account for contemporary conditions in Palestine-Israel, despite profound disparities across demographics and settings. It might also name these disparities themselves and their co-constitution. By investigating severance, I do not mean to suggest that relations are primary and are only later disrupted by conflict; rather, I ask why political bonds and solidarities that might seem obvious and expected do *not* form. Seeking to elucidate the current *hostile severance*, this chapter focuses on the knotted role Mizrahi Jews play in its formation. By analyzing the television series *Fauda* (2015–2022), I aim to answer two important yet neglected questions: what inspires hostility toward Palestinians in Jewish Israelis in general and amongst Mizrahi Jews in particular? Is there a specifically Mizrahi hostility, and what are its history and form? To address these, the chapter first traces the historical racialization processes that sharply divided Jewish

one of the people behind this false and miserable spin"; quoted in Peter Beinart, *The Crisis of Zionism* (New York: Picador, 2013), 72.

2. Tamir Sorek, "Ḳiṭuv Medume be-Maḥane ha-ʿElyonut ha-Yehudit," *Teʾoria u-Vikoret* Esh be-Śde ḳotsim: Tiḳ Masot (2021): 1–6.

3. "Tribal" appears here in quotation marks to acknowledge its pejorative baggage and to refer to a specific understanding of the term as a technique of colonial "divide and rule." See note 57 in this chapter.

Arabs from Palestinian Arabs. Through the contemporary works of the Mizrahi poet Shlomi Hatuka and through the history of the Zionist importation of Jewish Yemenite labor and the 1950s "Yemenite, Mizrahi and Balkan Children Affair," I explore the historical *severing assimilation* that folded Mizrahi Jews into the family of the Jewish nation while racializing them as relatively expendable. Assimilating *mizraḥim* by radically severing them from their countries, cultures, and families, the Zionist leadership also placed them in greater physical proximity to Palestinians—on the border and in mixed cities—as both a human bulwark and security personnel. Lastly, the chapter investigates the experience of *internal severance* and hostility prevalent within contemporary Palestinian society. Through the severed poetics of Adania Shibli, whose writing concluded Chapter 4, I examine how Israeli technologies of control from the border (epitomized by the checkpoint) and of security outsourcing (embodied by collaboration) inspire hostility and internal distance amongst Palestinians.

These forms of severance might seem disjointed across both space and time. And, in a way, they are. In yet another way, however, one telescopically impacts the other in cascading effects that this chapter aims to flesh out. If Palestinian internal severance is perpetrated through Israeli border control, then it matters that populating and policing the border are tasks delegated overwhelmingly to Mizrahi Jews, who thus become the executors of state violence and policies. Recall, for instance, the checkpoint execution of Abdel Fattah al-Sharif, discussed in Chapter 4. The exceptional decision of the military legal system to prosecute Elor Azaria, the shooter, is intimately bound to his Mizrahi identity. Azaria's defense team in fact argued, during the appeal stage, that his indictment constituted selective enforcement of the law, since he acted in line with IDF general norms of conduct. Following the logic of *ḥoḳ*, the court rejected this argument and racialized Azaria as exceptionally violent. It thus legally distanced Israeli institutions from the routine violence they exact, reconstituted the collective as moral, and renormalized its foundational colonial violence.[4] Coming from a family of security personnel, Azaria also embodies the selective tracking of *mizraḥim* into law enforcement. Their

4. The sociologist Yehouda Shenhav expressed this dual process succinctly, arguing that Azaria's Mizrahiness was central to the case because the "Mizrahi is [perceived as] not one of us—we are more moral, better"; quoted and translated by Ronit Lentin in *Traces of Racial Exception: Racializing Israeli Settler Colonialism* (London and New York: Bloomsbury Academic, 2018), 4. Lihi Yona and Itamar Mann make a similar argument about the legal system's exceptionalization and racialization of Azaria; Yona and Mann, "ha-Motsi'im la-Po'al: Mizraḥim ṿe-Alimut Ribonit be-Iśra'el," *Mishpaṭ u-Mimshal* 23 (2021): 47–48.

overrepresentation in high-contact roles renders *mizraḥim* more disposable than *ashkenazim* and transforms them into executors of Israeli severance policies that, in turn, render Palestinians disposable. Indeed, the ultimate cost is borne by Palestinians, in physical and societal devastation, a severance greatly accelerated by the very form of border policing—the checkpoint—manned by Mizrahi security personnel like Azaria.

More schematically, the history of the Zionist racialization of Mizrahi Jews, which aimed to integrate them into Israeli society through severance, appears as the mirror image of the Zionist attempt to sever Palestinians from their land and national identity. Palestine was abstracted from Palestinians for the use of Zionism. Conversely, Mizrahi Jews were abstracted from their lands to service the same project as working, settling, policing bodies. The racialization of Palestinians in Israel, as discussed in Chapter 3, passed through their *denationalization*—their othering separation from the Jewish collective but only under a generic, "ethnic" category ("Arabs"), not a national one ("Palestinians"). Conversely, the racialization of Mizrahi Jews passed through their *(de)Arabization*, their assimilation into the Jewish collective but only under a homogenizing, "ethnic" category of *mizraḥim* (or earlier, *ʿedot ha-mizraḥ*, "the ethnic communities of the Orient"), which severed them from their various, mostly Arab, communities and cultures, yet simultaneously "Arabized" them as bodies for use.

Thus, as Shlomi Hatuka writes in the poem featured in the epigraph, all that "links us"—an ambiguous "us," which could be read as Mizrahi Jews and Palestinians or as the Jewish Israeli collective—is "blood/and blood/and blood."[5] The

5. This "us" in Hatuka's poem is indeed highly ambiguous and could also be understood as referring to a personal relationship. My reading is bolstered, however, by the imagery of the coffee's aroma. Not simply an Orientalist trope, it alludes to Mahmoud Darwish's prose poem *Dhakira li-l-Nisyan* (A Memory of Forgetfulness, 1986), which depicts the poet's longing for the fragrance of coffee during the Israeli siege of Beirut. While tying coffee to the everyday of wartime and to Israeli bombardment of Palestinian refugee camps, this imagery is also a self-reference to Hatuka's poem "ʿIsḳa" (A Deal), in which Arab coffee expresses what is shared between Mizrahi Jews and Palestinians and meets an explicit mention of Darwish. It concludes,

And after all this,
just one word by Darwish,
just one car passing through Jaffa
playing Omer Adam or Zehava Ben,
just one passerby
who is confused by my appearance or confuses me with his;
frankly, just sitting across from the *muʿalem* in obligatory silence,
two cups of coffee between us,
is, in that moment, enough for me to unapologetically say:

blood of an essentialized, shared, racial identity, which is all that is left after all other ties—cultural, social, or ideological—are severed; the blood of bloodshed, of war and hostilities, which becomes the only form of relation; and the blood of family ties, through which Israeli (racio)national cohesion is imagined. In this repetition, it is the line break, the severance, that allows "blood" to mean (at least) three different things—that is, to operate as an antanaclasis, a repeated catachresis. It is also this severance that, paradoxically, relates all three.

Assimilating Severance: Racializing Mizrahi Jews

> *Nahilah told Yunes about the sobs they'd heard coming from the moshav the Yemenis had built over al-Birwa and about the mysterious rumors of children dying and disappearing. She said the Yemeni Jewesses would go out into the fields and lament like Arab women and that she'd started to fear for her children. "If the children of the Jews are disappearing, what will happen to ours?"*
>
> —ELIAS KHOURY, *BAB AL-SHAMS*

Written by the Lebanese author Elias Khoury (b. 1948), the monumental novel *Bab al-Shams* (Gate of the Sun, 1998) aims to record and animate the *nakba*, as well as Palestinian survival and resistance. As the quotation demonstrates, the novel toys at times with the dividing line between Jews and Arabs. In one especially sentimental scene, the Palestinian Umm Hassan returns to her stolen home in the Galilee only to find, like Said and Safiyya in Kanafani's novella, a Jewish woman living in it. This time, however, the occupant, Ella Dweik, is Mizrahi. In her professed desire to return to Beirut, Ella is depicted as uprooted from the only place she ever considered home. Without eliding the differences between the two women's conditions—for one is colonizing the home of the other, one remains while the other returns to the refugee camp to die—their conversation suggests both cultural intimacy and a shared experience of displacement.[6] In a novel dedicated to the *nakba*, Khoury finds space for mentioning the severance of *mizraḥim* from the Arab world and their implantation in a foreign, unchosen country. Given a mutual cultural register

---

Explain it to me one more time
because I still don't understand:
where do the Mizrahis end
and the Arabs begin?
—Hatuka, *Mizraḥ Yare'aḥ* (Tel Aviv: Tangier, 2015), 66, my translation.

6. Elias Khoury, *Gate of the Sun*, trans. Humphrey Davies (New York: Picador, 2006), 107–10.

and their shared yet uneven experiences of displacement, what forms the racial line that so neatly separates Jewish Arabs from Palestinian Arabs? How was this racialization entrenched, and how is it perpetuated today?

Through disparate stories, combining patches of self-proclaimed fiction with fragments of documentary evidence (often based on oral testimonies), Khoury's epic also retraces the historical and topological contours of *al-jalīl* (the Galilee), the northern region of Palestine. By so doing, Khoury counteracts an Israeli policy dubbed *yihud ha-galil* (the Judaization of the Galilee), implemented after the 1948 War, whose stated goal was to erase many Galilean Palestinian villages, towns, and neighborhoods, along with their environmental and cultural ecosystems, and to establish new Jewish settlements in their stead. Populating these required importing Jews to this relatively remote and underdeveloped region. While *kibbutzim* welcomed Ashkenazi Jews with free land, and while the later *moshavim* (cooperative agricultural villages) and *mitspim* (exclusive "quality of life" communities) were meant to lure in upper-middle-class Ashkenazi families with serene views and land subsidies, the brunt of the "Judaization" project was borne by Mizrahi Jews, settled in *ma'abarot* (absorption camps), in *'ayarot pitu'aḥ* (development towns), and in former Palestinian neighborhoods in the cities.[7]

This spatial dispersal of *mizraḥim* was underwritten by the demographic and strategic economy of fungible bodies. Bodies were needed for tabulation in the "demographic war" and for barricading the borders against Palestinian "infiltrations"; bodies were needed for holding onto newly colonized areas and preventing Palestinian refugees from returning to them; and bodies were needed as labor power for established industries in *kibbutzim* and *moshavim*. These physical roles—settlement, border security, labor—were largely fulfilled by Mizrahi Jews, who were long perceived, as Hazaz's stories demonstrate, as corporeal and easily content (see Chapter 2). Without the resources, protections, or recognition afforded to the negligible minority of *ashkenazim* who chose to settle the borders, Mizrahi Jews were generally coerced into this tripartite role, and its fulfillment therefore was not considered ideological and heroic; nor did it earn them any social cachet.

7. Israeli public discourse lauded the Ashkenazi *kibbutzim* for braving the task of border protection, yet their small number (about 1.5 percent of the Jewish population) meant that they were unable to achieve it, and the task was delegated, sans its heroism, to *mizraḥim*. These *kibbutzim*—whose members, unlike *mizraḥim*, chose to settle the borders—enjoyed not only recognition and better military protection but also better infrastructure, a much higher quality of life, and free access to sizeable state resources; Ella Shohat, "Sephardim in Israel: Zionism from the Standpoint of Its Jewish Victims," *Social Text*, no. 19/20 (1988): 18.

A small minority of *mizraḥim* formed mono-ethnic *moshavim*, such as the Yemenite religious *moshav* Ahihud (*Aḥihid*), established in 1950 on the expropriated lands of the Palestinian village al-Birwa (mentioned in Chapter 3 as the birthplace of Mahmoud Darwish). Ahihud is the Yemenite *moshav* referenced in the quotation from *Bab al-Shams*, and its story encapsulates the twin processes of the Zionist racialization of *mizraḥim*. The first process constituted Mizrahi Jews as exploitable bodies, easily severed and displaced in the service of "Judaizing" space or of the labor market (in this case, to meet the labor needs of the nearby kibbutz, Yasʿur). Crucially, as both labor and bodies in space, *mizraḥim* were supposed, quite literally, to replace Palestinians—or, at the very least, to compete with them—thus forming a severed, adversarial relation (*inqisām*) to them. By this process, *mizraḥim* were "Arabized," racialized as natural, cheap, unskilled, expendable workers. Simultaneously, Mizrahi Jews were subjected to a second racializing process, their "Judaization" or assimilation through severance and de-Arabization, a forced bearhug into the nation. An extreme case of severing assimilation is the "Yemenite, Mizrahi and Balkan Children Affair" (henceforth, the Affair), whose specter is raised by Nahilah's depiction of the bereaved Jewish Yemenite women, whose children were disappearing. Treated as expendable, thousands of Mizrahi infants and toddlers were systemically severed from their families in the years 1948–54. While the details of the Affair are still highly controversial in Israel, testimonies suggest that some children were then put up for adoption by Ashkenazi families and thus assimilated (more soon).

Both these processes are poetically investigated in the works of Shlomi Hatuka (b. 1978). A third-generation Yemenite Jew, Hatuka has published three poetry collections and is the cofounder of the Amram Association, which is in the process of building an online archive of families' oral testimonies and demands investigation and recognition of the Affair. He was a pillar of the Mizrahi cultural and activist revival of the 2010s, which coalesced, interestingly enough, around a poetry group. In his poem "Ḳufsa Sheḥora" (Black Box), from his first collection *Mizraḥ Yareʾaḥ* (Moon Rise/Moon East, 2015), Hatuka writes:

> I am the black box
> recording Flight 742, 1952,
> and I registered everything
> I wrote down everything.
> I registered the agents' instructions:
> "Leave the Torah scrolls and jewelry behind
> and climb on board naked or else
> the aircraft will not take off";

I registered the plunderers
and the pilots:
"This is the simple, natural worker, able to do any work, without
indignity, without philosophy and without poetry"—huh . . .
. . .
In the mirror, I registered the faces of the enemies
and on the TV screen, the faces that were missing.
In one portrait I registered two women:
my aunt Leah
and her twin sister,
the one who disappeared;
I registered you, my grandmother,
nursing one with milk
and the other with tears.[8]

Writing from the vantage point of the flight recorder, Hatuka insists on the objectivity of his poetic record while problematizing the extreme lengths to which Mizrahi speech must go to be considered reliable. The flight registered is one of the many by which Yemen's Jewish community was airlifted to Israel in an operation titled *Marvad ha-Ḳesamim* (The Magic Carpet, 1949–56), during which its Torah scrolls and other heirlooms were pilfered.[9] By repeating the phrase *rashamti* (I recorded, registered, wrote down), Hatuka alludes to Darwish's famous poem "Biṭaqat Huwiyya" (Identity Card, 1964), with its commanding apostrophe, "write down, I am an Arab" ("write down," *sajjil* in the original, was translated into Hebrew as *tirshom*—a different conjugation of the same verb Hatuka uses).[10] Responding to Darwish's command to record, Hatuka's poem stresses the "Arabness" that Mizrahi Jews might share with Palestinians and that they are simultaneously conditioned to view as a mark of the enemy—a self-severance that underlies their racialization.

8. Hatuka, *Mizraḥ Yare'aḥ*, 35–36, my translation.

9. Shoshana Madmoni-Gerber, *Israeli Media and the Framing of Internal Conflict: The Yemenite Babies Affair* (New York: Palgrave Macmillan, 2009), 36.

10. The poem is one of Darwish's most famous works. It stirred a controversy in Israel in 2016, when the minister of culture and sports, Miri Regev, attempted to censor it for its "anti-Jewish sentiments." In response, the Palestinian singer Tamer Nafar collaborated with the Mizrahi spoken word artist Yossi Zabari in performing Nafar's song "Ana Mish Poliṭi" (I am not political), which quotes the contentious Darwish poem. As the two raised their fists in a Black Power salute, Zabari added a stanza of his own to the song, in direct dialogue with Darwish: "Write down! / I, too, am an Arab / but unlike Darwish, Mahmoud / I am an Arab *min al-yahūd*. (Arabic, "of the Jews"). See Tamer Nafar and Yossi Zabari, "Ana Mish Poliṭi," *YouTube*, September 22, 2016, https://www.youtube.com/watch?v=aIYbJ2NYaQI.

The first of the two racializing processes mentioned earlier, the Arabization of Mizrahi Jews, is central to the poem. Utilizing another form of allegedly objective documentation, Hatuka quotes the early Zionist view of Yemenites that motivated their importation to Palestine. Indeed, given its *capitalist colonial* logic, Zionism regarded Arabs, Jewish or not, as cheap, disposable working bodies.[11] In this process of proletarianization, the "Arabness" of Mizrahi Jews—their exploitability as "natural workers," Orientalistically assumed—was valued. This racializing exploitation has a long history, particularly amongst Yemenite Jews. Early in the twentieth century, Yemenite Jews were already imported to fulfill Jewish landowners' labor needs and to depose Palestinian Arab labor. In accordance with a deliberate plan, confessed by Zalman Shazar in 1920, Yemenite workers were intentionally kept in poor and deprived conditions that would force them to work for low wages and guarantee their continued exploitation.[12] The motivating ideology behind this plan was expressed as early as 1909 in an article in *ha-Zvi* signed by Sh. R.—in all likelihood, Arthur (Shimon) Ruppin, the main architect of the Zionist land purchase project. This article, as quoted in Hatuka's poem, portrays the Yemenite worker as "the simple, natural worker, able to do any work, without indignity, without philosophy and without poetry." Yet the original escalates further:

> And Mr. Marx certainly is not found in his pocket or in his mind. I do not mean to suggest that the Yemenite element must remain in its current uncultivated and barbaric state. . . . The Yemenite workers today are on the same dismal level as the *falaḥim* [Arab peasants, a Hebrew-inflected Arabic word], and in matters of expertise and bodily health they cannot even compare to the *falaḥim*. There is no doubt, however, that these Yemenite workers, who would not expect funds from their home country, Yemen, and whose poverty is immense, will be forced . . . to lift the shovel, the plow, and the horse's reins, their bodies will heal and fortify, and they will gain familiarity with the work and its conditions, becoming the better contenders for every

11. Gershon Shafir, "The Meeting of Eastern Europe and Yemen: 'Idealistic Workers' and 'Natural Workers' in Early Zionist Settlement in Palestine," *Ethnic and Racial Studies* 13, no. 2 (1990): 172–97.

12. On this "Satanic role" and the racializing proletarianization of Yemenite Jews, see Zvi Ben Dor-Benite, "Satan and Labor: Proletarianization and the Racialization of the Mizrahim," in *Race and the Question of Palestine*, ed. Ronit Lentin and Lana Tatour (Stanford, Calif.: Stanford University Press, Forthcoming).

aspect of farming work. The Yemenites will then come to take, and they are indeed *able* to take, the place of the Arabs.[13]

In a perfectly circular reasoning, the author treats the Arabness of Yemenites as both a natural given and a result of an acculturation process, of racialization. Because Yemenite workers are like Arabs, they are assumed to work so naturally. And because, like Arabs, they are poor and cannot rely on European "parents" for funds, they will be forced into Zionist agricultural labor—allegedly more proper, more efficient, *more natural* labor. Finally, through this process of Arabization, they will replace the Palestinian Arabs as *more proper* Arabs, Arab*ized* rather than merely Arabs, Arabs no longer by nature but by form, function, and class.

A second racialization process de-Arabized and "Judaized" *mizraḥim* through severance. Given its *racial colonial* logic, Zionist society was not eager to admit Arabs, Jewish or not, into its ranks, lest they lower its civilizational level or render it "Levantine."[14] Compelled by the obliterating results of the holocaust, however, the Zionist leadership eventually decided to assimilate and "salvage" *some* of the indigenous "Orientals," replicating a common operation of settler colonial states. Just as Australian settlers found fully aboriginal children to be beyond redemption yet elected to assimilate "mixed" children, Zionists chose to assimilate only those "mixed" Arabs, the Jewish Arabs,

13. Sh. R., "'Al ha-Temanim," *ha-Zvi*, January 27, 1909 (my translation). Not only Ruppin's initials led me to believe he is behind this piece but also the nearly identical view he expressed in a speech delivered two years earlier: "Even more primitive is the mode of life of the Yemenite Jew, who is happy to have any sort of home. Nevertheless, these immigrants from Yemen are a valuable element for Palestine, for they are able, by virtue of the fewness of their needs, to compete successfully with the cheap labor of the Arabs. . . . they can easily be transformed into agricultural workers, and from all appearances they will play a considerable role in this field." See Arthur Ruppin, "The Picture in 1907," in *Three Decades of Palestine: Speeches and Papers on the Upbuilding of the Jewish National Home*, New ed. (Westport, Conn.: Praeger, 1975), 4.

14. David Ben Gurion, Israel's first prime minister, proclaimed, "We do not want Israelis to become Arabs. We are in duty bound to fight against the spirit of the Levant, which corrupts individuals and societies." In 1949, at the height of Mizrahi mass immigrations, the journalist Arye Gelblum wrote that these were "people whose primitivism is at a peak, whose level of knowledge is one of virtually absolute ignorance, and worse, who have little talent for understanding anything intellectual. Generally, they are only slightly better than the general level of the Arabs, Negroes, and Berbers in the same regions. In any case, they are at an even lower level than what we knew with regard to the former Arabs of Eretz Israel" and "are totally subordinated to the play of savage and primitive instincts"; both quoted in Shohat, "Sephardim in Israel," 4.

rendering Judaism a tool of what Patrick Wolfe called "deracination."[15] In distinguishing "the 'evil' East (the Moslem Arab) from the 'good' East (the Jewish Arab)," as Ella Shohat contends, "Israel has taken upon itself to 'cleanse' the Sephardim of their Arab-ness and redeem them from their 'primal sin' of belonging to the Orient."[16] Through de-Arabization—through severance from their (mostly) Arab cultures—Mizrahi Jews were able to assimilate into the Jewish majority. This severance, as Shohat demonstrates, involved various vectors of rupture—not only dislocation and displacement but also dismemberment, dischronicity, and dissonance (the split narrative of Zionist modernization).[17]

The racialization of Mizrahi Jews combined this *de-Arabization* with the aforementioned *Arabization*—their construction as natural workers and fungible bodies, further "Arabized" through training—forming a paradoxical racializing mode that might be termed *(de)Arabization*. This mode used severance to force the assimilation of *mizraḥim* into hegemonic Ashkenazi culture and into the nation. An especially brutal case of such severing assimilation is colloquially known as "the Yemenite children disappearance affair," to which Hatuka's poem alludes by recording his family history of a "disappeared" child in yet another form of documentary evidence. The Affair, as mentioned, concerns the mysterious yet systematic separation of thousands of Mizrahi infants and toddlers from their (mostly Arab) families between the years 1948 and 1954. About two-thirds of the children who disappeared in those years from hospitals and from *ma'abarot* nurseries were from the Yemenite Jewish community. State documents that recorded the Affair and its investigations were sealed until 2016, then partially released. Some of the archives have been inexplicably destroyed. Yet, out of the thousands of testimonies of families and healthcare personnel, a consistent method nonetheless emerges: while some children were forcibly removed from their families by nurses and social workers, in most cases parents were told that their healthy children required hospitalization or placement in a nursery for "better" care. Given the chaotic, unhygienic conditions in the *ma'abara* and their inexperience with their new environment, parents often complied. A few days later, they were informed that the child had passed away, yet no proof, death certificate, body, or grave were provided. In a few dozen reported cases, stubborn pleading and loud protests miraculously

15. On the deracination of Arab Jews and its colonial effects on Palestinians, see Patrick Wolfe, *Traces of History: Elementary Structures of Race* (London and New York: Verso, 2016), chap. 8; Lentin, *Traces of Racial Exception*, chap. 4.

16. Shohat, "Sephardim in Israel," 7–8.

17. Ella Shohat, "Rupture and Return: The Shaping of a Mizrahi Epistemology," *Hagar: International Social Science Review* 2, no. 1 (2001): 63.

brought the child back from the dead. Families have been searching for seven decades but, despite repeated appeals to state institutions and law enforcement agencies, most were not able to locate their children or obtain their bodies or proof of death.[18]

Families, activists, and a growing number of scholars assume that adoption was one end goal of this systemic severance. Indeed, this hypothesis is supported by records of illegal and semi-legal adoptions, of de facto adoptions and forged documents, that quite explicitly attest to trafficking in children. When missing children were eventually found years later, it was in adoptive Ashkenazi families.[19] This hypothesis is also bolstered by the well-documented racist attitude of Israeli healthcare personnel at the time: their expressed beliefs that Mizrahi parents were unqualified to care for their children and that the size of Mizrahi families alone meant that their children were easily replaceable—fungible bodies in a political economy of reproduction.[20]

For about seventy years, this affair has been treated as marginal—a minute moral blemish on the otherwise successful project of Mizrahi Jews' assimilation. Over the years, as a result of persistent pressure from affected families, three commissions were convened to investigate the Affair—in 1967–68 (Bahlul-Minkowski), in 1984–88 (Shalgi) and in 1995–2001 (Kedmi). Despite missing archives and their inability to establish the fate of dozens of children, all three commissions confidently concluded that the rest were "probably" dead. Their work, however, appears slapdash at best and an empty ritual at

18. For critical accounts of the Affair, see Naama Katiee, "Why Is the Left Silent on the Kidnapping of Mizrahi Babies?," *+972 Magazine* (blog), June 21, 2015, http://972mag.com/why-is-the-left-silent-on-the-kidnapping-of-mizrahi-children/108028/; Madmoni-Gerber, *Israeli Media and the Framing of Internal Conflict*; Nathan Shifriss, *Halakh le-An?: Parashat Yalde Teman; ha-Ḥaṭifa yeha-Hakhḥasha* (Tel-Aviv: ʻAliyat ha-Gag; Yediʻot Aḥaronot; Ḥemed, 2019). For an archive of families' testimonies, see "Amram Association: The Yemenite, Eastern and Balkan Children Affair," *Amram Association* (blog), https://www.edut-amram.org/en/.

19. Hanna Gibori, the head of the Northern District Adoption Services in those years, testified before the commission: "Physicians handed over babies for adoption straight out of the hospital, without the official adoption agencies being involved." In a Knesset plenary in 1959, MK Ben-Tzion Harel stated that a considerable percentage of children "are adopted straight from the hospital or maternity center. In some cases, this is done in unacceptable ways, in a manner that borders on trafficking." Quoting these, Shlomi Hatuka concludes that the records "are filled with testimonies by nurses and caregivers who describe the 'underground adoption railroad' in the 1950s"; Hatuka, "The Tragedy of the Lost Yemenite Children: In the Footsteps of the Adoptees," *Ha-ʻOkets* (blog), January 25, 2014, https://enghaokets.wordpress.com/2014/01/25/the-tragedy-of-the-lost-yemenite-children-in-the-footsteps-of-the-adoptees/.

20. Nathan Shifriss collated such expressions by healthcare professionals from the Kedmi Commission report in *Yaldi Halakh le-An*, 52–54.

worse; they regularly smoothed over incriminating evidence, creating an illusion of oversight while this whole affair was largely swept under the rug.[21]

Not at all marginal, however, the Affair is in fact constitutive, I argue, not only of the Zionist racialization of *mizraḥim* but also of *inqisām* in Palestine-Israel more broadly. Indeed, this affair crystalizes the two processes of racializing *mizraḥim* mentioned earlier. It Arabized the abducted children, treating them as expendable bodies because of their supposed inferior Arabness, while also forcibly de-Arabizing them, severing them from their families and radically assimilating them.[22] This severing assimilation impacted not only the children but also their families, as well as *mizraḥim* more broadly. A crucial effect of such severances was that any Ashkenazi child—and, later, any Ashkenazi adult—encountered by families of the disappeared could theoretically be (as long as gender and age happened to fit) their lost relative, who had been adopted.[23] Severing assimilation racialized *mizraḥim* by pressing them into the "one big Jewish family" that is Israeli society. National cohesion in Israel, imagined as familial, was thus forged precisely by splitting families apart.

As suggested by Hatuka's verse "In the mirror, I registered the faces of the enemies," anger and resentment inspired by the Affair were easily redirected toward "Arabs," already marked as enemies in Israel. The affective web of imagined family ties fabricated throughout the nation by the Affair, the presumed benevolence behind Zionist "civilizing missions," and state representatives'

21. The commissions failed to entertain, as Boaz Sangero demonstrates, "an epistemology of suspicion" toward the state and its institutions. Their work is thus questionable even within the debatable juridical logic that governs their work; Sangero, "be-En Ḥashad en Ḥaḳira Amitit: 'Duaḥ Ṿa'adat ha-Ḥaḳira ha-Mamlakhtit be-'Inyan Parashat He'almutam shel Yeladim mi-Bene 'Ole Teman,'" *Te'oria u-Vikoret* 21 (2002): 47–76.

22. Severance and abduction of children are common colonial assimilation methods, not at all unique to Israel. In Australia, from the late nineteenth century to the 1970s, the government and church missions removed children of Aboriginal and Torres Strait Islander descent from their homes, placing them in institutions and in foster or adoptive families to assimilate them into white society. Similarly, during the nineteenth century and the first half of the twentieth, Native American children in the U.S. and Canada were forcibly removed from their families and placed in boarding schools, purportedly for the sake of their assimilation and "civilization." In Réunion, a French colonial island territory, in 1963–82, 2,150 children were stolen and transported to France in an official attempt to strengthen and repopulate the French countryside. Some children were officially adopted, while others lived as free labor on farms. Comparing the Affair to the cases of the "stolen generations" or of *l'affaire des Enfants de la Creuse* stresses its racialized colonial nature.

23. The testimonies collected by the Amram Association, like many of the declassified testimonies in the state archive, reflect families' continued tendency to search for the disappeared in others' faces. See *Amram Association*.

repeated gaslighting insistence that nothing had happened save for a little disorder in record-keeping—all complicated the possibility of directing rage at its rightful target. Both the Affair and the process of Arabizing Mizrahi Jews drove home the realization that *mizraḥim*, like Palestinians, are highly expendable when their bodies are not needed. Because the idea to import *mizraḥim* originated in the Zionist desire to replace Palestinian workers, the meaning of their racial difference was born in this context, encompassing both their similarity to Palestinian labor and their role as its easily portable uprooters. Given the then recent history of the *nakba* as an exemplar of expendability, Mizrahi Jews quickly recognized the expediency of expressing ardent national loyalty to avoid sinking once more to the level of bodies for use and to distinguish themselves from the competition. Indeed, Palestinian and Mizrahi rivalry over unorganized, unskilled labor (organized labor, by contrast, was conquered by Ashkenazi Jews through the *Histadrut*) lasted for decades, with ebbs and flows. A major ebb took place following 1967, when Palestinian laborers flooded the Israeli market and *mizraḥim* leveraged this opportunity to advance to the ranks of middlemen and contractors.[24] Since then, a Mizrahi middle class has increasingly formed and is now all the more invested in safeguarding its socioeconomic success. Unsurprisingly, the contemporary legacies of assimilating severance have intensified expressions of national loyalty into overt forms of hostility, hatred, and violence toward Palestinians.

Hostile Severance: Mizrahi Jewish Hostility toward Palestinians

During the 2014 Israeli attack on Gaza, an anecdotal news story drew international attention, particularly amongst Western leftist circles. Near the largely Mizrahi border town of Sderot, located less than a mile from the Gaza Strip, Jewish Israelis regularly climbed onto a hilltop, carrying plastic chairs and battered car seats, to watch Hamas's rocket fire and the Israeli Air Force's bombardment of Gaza. The Danish correspondent who broke the story captured this ritual on camera, captioning his photograph "cinema Sderot" and portraying the spectators as cheering on the Israeli attack. Indeed, it was quite a distasteful display of hatred and hostility, very unpalatable to liberal political correctness.

In singling out the residents of Sderot, however, media and leftists ignored the historical processes that wedged this Mizrahi population there. In the 1950s, in order to "Judaize the Negev," recent Kurdish, Iranian, and North African

24. Hillel Cohen, *Śon'im: Sipur Ahava* (Tel Aviv: 'Ivrit, 2022), chap. 4.

immigrants were coercively settled in Sderot—a *maʿabara* turned development town, planted on the stolen lands of the Palestinian village Najd. Like Mizrahi Jews elsewhere, they were lodged there to "strengthen the borders" and to serve as an available labor reserve for nearby *kibbutzim*. The hilltop spectatorship thus points to the greater proximity of this population to political violence relative to the Israeli population at large and exposes this proximity as imposed by the Zionist project of territorial "Judaization." The focus on the politically incorrect spectatorship, however, drew attention away from the pilots bombarding Gaza—and from the generals and politicians initiating, devising, and ordering such attacks—and reoriented it toward the spectators, thus rendering Sderot a cinema, both a spectacle and a screen. Veering political culpability away from the largely Ashkenazi establishments of the military and the government—with their allegedly measured, and hence liberal, state violence—the news story rendered *mizraḥim* in Sderot an exemplar of "bad" Zionist violence, unapologetic and illiberal. Yet their hateful opinions, however unsavory, have far less direct impact on the violence in Gaza. Or, as the Palestinian MK Jamal Zahalka put it in 2007 (and again in 2015), "The *ashkenazim* took away Palestine, not the *mizraḥim*. Not those who shout 'death to the Arabs' took our lands but those who said 'we bring peace upon you.'"[25]

Indeed, some Mizrahi writers and activists emphasize the empty rhetoric of Mizrahi hate for "Arabs," while others argue that it is largely exaggerated, even fabricated by the media to detract attention from the liability of a hegemonic Ashkenazi political and military elite.[26] While there is some truth to both arguments, it is also crucial to acknowledge the existence of Mizrahi animosity toward Palestinians, its contemporary intensification, and its diffusion throughout the Jewish Israeli population in what has become a "post-Mizrahi" moment. If we treat *mizraḥim* as true political subjects, and not simply as incited by Ashkenazi puppet masters, then this hostility requires careful consideration. Is there a specifically Mizrahi animosity, and how did it come to be? If Mizrahi Jews share forms of racialization with Palestinians and thus economic

25. In Rachel Leah Jones (dir.), *Ashkenaz*, Trabelsi Productions, Israel, 2007.

26. Mizrahi Jews are often blamed, for instance, for sustaining the nationalist *Likud* party. According to Alona Miryam Illuz, however, Ashkenazi votes for *Likud* surpass Mizrahi ones, even relative to their share of the population. Her numbers are based on governmental reports of the 2015 elections; Illuz, "Lama Mizraḥim Mamshikhim leha-Tsbiʿa la-Likud?," *Ha-ʿOkets*, February 8, 2019, https://www.haokets.org/2019/02/08/-מזרחים-למה-לליכוד-להצביע-ממשיכים/. Shohat cites similar numbers from the 1981 elections. She further argues that the Mizrahi vote for Likud is not necessarily related to the latter's policies toward Palestinians and is often "a minimal and even misplaced expression of Sephardi revolt against decades of Labor oppression"; Shohat, "Sephardim in Israel," 27–28.

and political interests, why is there so little cooperation and so much overt Mizrahi hatred at the moment?[27] Without assuming that Mizrahi violence is more common, we still must ask: why did some *mizraḥim* go into the streets of al-Lydd (Lydda, Lod) to beat on Palestinians during the events of May 2021?[28]

Such urgent questions are rarely considered through the prism of cultural production. Yet, looking to forms of Mizrahi self-representation that engage recent events might provide distinct answers. One example of such self-representation—broadly understood, within the limits of the economic and ideological pressures of the television industry—is the contemporary action series *Fauda* (2015–2022), created by two Mizrahi men, Lior Raz (b. 1971) and Avi Issacharoff (b. 1973).[29] Picked up by Netflix in 2016, *Fauda* (*fauḍā*, Arabic for "chaos") is one of the most successful Israeli shows ever produced. It follows a special IDF "counterterrorism" unit whose members operate undercover, infiltrating the OPT disguised as Palestinians to conduct "targeted assassinations," high-risk surveillance and arrest operations, and various other forms of warfare that push against—and often cross—the bounds of legality.

As Jewish Arabic speakers operating by emulating Palestinians, members of this and similar units are known in Israel as *mista'arvim*—"those who Arabize themselves" (based on the Arabic *musta'ribīn*).[30] Here, as in the case of the Yemenite workers, the racialized role of Mizrahi Jews involves both the assumption of a natural Arabness as a point of departure (to be transcended)

27. This is not to erase a long history of Mizrahi-Palestinian collaborations, from the Ottoman era, through the binational communist party and the Mizrahi Black Panthers, to contemporary Palestinian-Mizrahi cultural projects that often work around and with BDS limitations.

28. As has happened before in other mixed cities. For a history of this violence and a somewhat different explanation of its origins, see Cohen, *Śon'im*.

29. Representations of Mizrahi violence have become very common on Israeli screens in recent years. In 2019 alone, Israeli television and cinema have produced the drama miniseries *ha-Ne'arim* (Our Boys), based on the true story of the kidnapping and murder of the Palestinian teenager Mohammed Abu Khdeir by Yossef Haim Ben-David and his minor nephews; the series *Eli* (in English, *The Spy*), inspired by the life of the Mossad spy Eli Cohen; the documentary film *Yamim Nora'im* (Days of Awe, released in English as *Incitement*), about the life of Yigal Amir, the assassin of Yizhak Rabin; and the feature *Mami* (released in English as *Red Fields*), whose fictional plot follows a young Mizrahi woman who becomes the leader of a warmongering party. *Fauda* is unique amongst these in being created by Mizrahi Jews.

30. Jewish use of the term preceded the Israeli state. When Sephardi Jews migrated to North Africa and the Middle East following the Christian conquest of the Iberian Peninsula, they used *musta'ribūn/musta'ribīn* to refer to the older Jewish communities in these regions, which had long adopted Arab customs. See Yigal Shalom Nizri, "Die Stimme Jaakobs Stimme, Die Haende Essaws Haende," in *Frequency-Modulated Scenario*, ed. Eran Schaerf (Berlin: Archive, 2015), 336.

and a process of training by which Arab Jews become Arab*ized*, more proper Arabs, readied for this labor.[31] Because the IDF, post-Oslo, no longer keeps regular troops on the ground in West Bank urban centers, such special units have drastically increased their operation scope, contributing to greater distrust and hostility within Palestinian society (to be soon discussed).

Themselves former members of an IDF *mista'arvim* unit, the creators of *Fauda* were open in interviews about basing its plot on their military service (Issacharoff is also a journalist specializing in "Palestinian and Arab Affairs").[32] Based on the insinuated autobiographical component, some have classified the show as part of the Israeli "shooting and crying" genre discussed in Chapter 2.[33] But *Fauda* does not conform to this genre's conventions. It eschews self-criticism and exhibits very little crying or regret—for the fate of either Palestinians or Israeli combatants and their morality.[34] Its only motor is endless violence. This is partly because this is an action show, whose genre demands ever accelerating, exhilarating, enthralling fighting. *Fauda* meets this demand by staging a perpetual "cycle of violence" and by personifying it. In constructing "well-rounded" figures embedded in close-knit communities, the show aims to entice the audience to emotionally invest in their fates.

Let there be no mistake: *Fauda* is a highly ideological show. It engages in the kind of forced epistemic disappearance examined earlier in Chapter 3. The show, whose writers, creators, directors, producers, and editors are all Jewish Israelis, does not reflect Palestinian reality or experiences.[35] It rarely discloses the Israeli occupation in the West Bank or the colonial conditions in Palestine-Israel more broadly. Its rendition of the landscape allows no Separation Wall, no queues or abuse at checkpoints, no settlements, no refugees, no siege, and

31. On the longer history of *mista'arvim* in the Zionist secret services and its reliance on (de) Arabizing Mizrahi Jews, see Yonatan Mendel, "Re-Arabizing the De-Arabized: The Mista'aravim Unit of the Palmach," in *Debating Orientalism*, ed. Ziad Elmarsafy, Anna Bernard, and David Attwell (London: Palgrave Macmillan, 2013), 94–116.

32. For instance, Helen Mann, "An Interview with Lior Raz: 'Fauda' Co-Creator and Star, Lior Raz, Brings the Israeli-Palestinian Conflict to Netflix," *CBC*, January 4, 2017, https://www.cbc.ca/radio/asithappens/as-it-happens-wednesday-edition-1.3920983/fauda-co-creator-and-star-lior-raz-brings-the-israeli-palestinian-conflict-to-netflix-1.3920988.

33. Rachel Shabi, "The Next Homeland? The Problems with Fauda, Israel's Brutal TV Hit," *Guardian*, May 23, 2018, https://www.theguardian.com/tv-and-radio/2018/may/23/the-next-homeland-problems-with-fauda-israel-brutal-tv-hit.

34. Cf. Ari Folman (dir.), *Vals 'im Bashir* (released in English as *Waltz with Bashir*) (Sony Pictures Classics, 2008).

35. As the Palestinian journalist Ziyad Abul Hawa charitably argues, "If the writers are all Israeli, no matter how good the intentions are, they are not realistically showing what is happening in Palestinian areas"; Shabi, "Next Homeland?"

no large-scale aerial attacks. While it employs Palestinian actors and brings their dialect to the screen, *Fauda* constructs a depoliticized perception of Palestinian-Jewish relations in Israel as cyclical violent retributions.[36] Yet, despite and with its distortions, this ideological drift renders *Fauda* more useful here, for it exposes common attitudes amongst Jewish Israelis that are often sublimated or sidestepped in official discourse. Indeed, *Fauda*'s political stance, as the Palestinian novelist Sayed Kashua argues, is prototypical—reminiscent of ideas exhibited in many Israeli films.[37] To better understand current Jewish Israeli hatred, these unspoken attitudes, which are nonetheless expressed on the screen, must be investigated.

Fauda could also be viewed as a text by which Mizrahi men reflect on the significant role assigned to them in the Israeli economy of violence and morals. Treated as expendable bodies, *mizraḥim* were indeed used as a "security belt" against Palestinians, settled along the borders, in mixed cities and, more recently, in West Bank settlements—into which, since the 1980s, Israeli welfare has largely migrated, sweeping its dependents with it.[38] While Mizrahi Jews are thus more vulnerable to violent interactions with Palestinians than *ashkenazim*, their role on the stage of violence is not merely passive. Mizrahi men, in particular, have long served in close-contact positions in the Israeli security system—the police, border police, intelligence, and other security apparatuses.[39] They therefore become, as the legal scholars Lihi Yona and Itamar

36. Israeli media celebrated the fact that, with *Fauda*, the Palestinian vernacular was finally featured on Israeli television; however, its Jewish actors speak Arabic with a noticeable accent that bespeaks estrangement and carelessness.

37. Sayed Kashua, "'Fauda' Creators Think Arabs Are Stupid," *Haaretz*, January 12, 2018, https://www.haaretz.com/opinion/.premium-fauda-creators-think-arabs-are-stupid-1.5730664.

38. Danny Gutwein, "The Settlements and the Relationship between Privatization and the Occupation," in *Normalizing Occupation: The Politics of Everyday Life in the West Bank Settlements*, ed. Marco Allegra, Ariel Handel, and Erez Maggor (Bloomington: Indiana University Press, 2017), 21–33.

39. Since the turn of the century, "peripheral" populations (*mizraḥim*, as well as Ethiopian Jews, migrants from the former USSR, Druze Arabs, and certain religious Jews) have gradually taken over combat roles in the IDF. Respectively, the IDF social architecture has been restructured, as Lihi Yona and Itamar Mann argue, so that the higher a soldier's socioeconomic position is, the greater his distance from the enemy. Thus, Mizrahi Jews, as well as other "peripheral" populations, tend to be positioned in roles requiring greater contact with Palestinian fighters and civilians; Yona and Mann, "ha-Motsiʾim la-Poʿal," 47. Yet, Mizrahi complicity with Israeli "security" has a longer history. In the preface to his book on Arab Jews, Shenhav, whose parents migrated to Israel from Iraq, reflects on the involvement of his father and his fathers' friends in Israeli intelligence in the 1950s: "How ironic that their very entry into the Israeli collective—through their intelligence work—demanded that they remain part of the Arab world against which they worked. Such is the logic of the Israeli state: top-heavy with contradictions";

Mann astutely observe, "the executors of sovereign violence"—whether lawful or unlawful, officially sanctioned by the state or merely inspired by its interests. What consigns Mizrahi Jews to this "executors class," Yona and Mann contend, is their historical racialization as morally inferior and naturally prone to violence, as well as their status as the "internal others" of Israeli society, which allows the regime to distance itself from the spectacle of violence. The view of "Orientals" as predisposed to violence colors the perception of Palestinians as well, thus rationalizing in turn the violence inflicted on them.[40] As in Sderot, then, by "front-lining" *mizraḥim* as executors (*motsiʾim la-poʿal*, also "executioners"), Israeli hegemony and state officials secure their personal safety, reinforce social hierarchies, constitute *mizraḥim* as subservient and obedient, and morally elevate themselves above violence, as though it were not perpetrated in their name and under their orders.

Crucially, however, the proximity to Palestinians renders *mizraḥim* not only more likely to execute visible violence and more vulnerable to blame and injury, but also capable of imagining the "enemy" as equal. The "Arabization" of Mizrahi Jews is responsible for this geographical proximity, which generates both closer familiarity and increased fear. It is also responsible for the aforementioned historical labor competition between *mizraḥim* and Palestinians—a rivalry that further contributes to the imagining of parity. Thus, while the colonial attitude of historical Zionism, inflected through a supremacist Orientalist lens, treated Palestinians as inferior—and therefore as either deserving of oppression or in need of civilization—the current Mizrahi hostility assumes equality of sorts.

While the symmetry suggested by the concept of conflict with which this book has opened is structurally false, for it dominates in the name of the lawless violence it mythologizes, contemporary *mizraḥim*, I argue, presume real symmetry between (Jewish) Israelis and Palestinians, even if this presumption does not reflect reality or translate to a demand for political equality. Indeed, in its portrayal of violence as a series of retaliatory actions, *Fauda* reflects and reproduces this imagined symmetry. In the show's pre-history, Doron Kabilio (played by Lior Raz) and his undercover unit had executed Taufiq Hammed, usually known by his *kunya*, abu Ahmed, who is presented as a Hamas leader and an "arch-terrorist" responsible for the death of 116 Israelis. Following this

---

Shenhav, *The Arab Jews: A Postcolonial Reading of Nationalism, Religion, and Ethnicity* (Stanford, Calif.: Stanford University Press, 2006), 3. See also Gil Eyal, *The Disenchantment of the Orient: Expertise in Arab Affairs and the Israeli State* (Stanford, Calif.: Stanford University Press, 2006).

40. Yona and Mann, "ha-Motsiʾim la-Poʿal," 5–6.

operation, Doron retires from service to mend his marriage, starting a vineyard in hope of peaceful domesticity. *Fauda* opens by disrupting this idyllia: learning that abu Ahmed is in fact alive, Doron promptly returns to service. He joins his unit in an undercover operation to capture abu Ahmed by infiltrating his brother's wedding. In the chaos (*fauḍā*) that erupts when their covers are blown, the agents kill abu Ahmed's brother, Bashir. In retaliation, Bashir's widow, Amal, plants a bomb in a Tel Aviv bar frequented by Doron's colleague and brother-in-law, Boaz, thus killing Boaz's girlfriend while committing suicide. Predictably, Boaz attempts to avenge his girlfriend's death by going after abu Ahmed.

Things escalate quickly. Capturing Boaz and planting a bomb inside his body, abu Ahmed turns him into an involuntary suicide bomber—a deeply phantasmatic form of symmetry. The unit then ventures on an unauthorized mission to kidnap Sheikh Awadalla, a local leader and abu Ahmed's friend, hoping to use him as leverage in bargaining over Boaz's return. The first season climaxes with a face-off between the two teams, during which both Boaz and the Sheikh are blown up. The second season could be summed up as the revenge journey of Sheikh Awadalla's son—Nidal Awadalla, known as al-Makdasi—whose only life goal is to avenge his father's death by killing Doron (he is also depicted, for added dramatic effect, as puppeteered by ISIS). The imagined symmetry is taken to a whole new level when al-Makdasi forms a unit of *mityahadim*—Hebrew-speaking undercover Palestinian agents meant to "pass" as Jews and operate within 1948-Israel.[41]

Although the series currently stretches over four seasons, this short recap suffices to reveal the "cycle of revenge" at its core and to showcase its effects. Symmetrizing the actions and conditions of both groups, the endless retributions depoliticize those actions and conditions by rendering all violence criminal, personal, and intra- and interfamilial, in a style reminiscent of the long-time trope of Jews and Arabs as cousins or half-brothers, as in the biblical Abrahamic myth.[42] The retributions also dehistoricize by presenting "the conflict" as primordial and necessarily endless and distort temporality by employing a preemptive security logic.

A myriad of plot lines and formal parallels reinforce the sense of symmetry in the show. For instance, insubordination within Hamas is mirrored

41. On the trope of Palestinian "passing" and its literary history, see Chapter 3—especially note 45 and the sources it cites.

42. On the Abrahamic myth, its segmentary logic, and its effects in the context of Palestine-Israel, see Matan Kaminer, "The Abrahamic Ideology: Patrilineal Kinship and the Politics of Peacemaking in the Contemporary Middle East," *Millennium*, forthcoming.

by insubordination within the *mista'arvim* unit, and Doron's wife's sexual "infidelity" is mirrored by the actions of the wife of Walid, a key Hamas leader in Season Two. In acting outside the rule of law, much like Elor Azaria, the protagonists supposedly become "just like" their Palestinian counterparts (they also conform, however, to the conventions of certain subgenres of action shows—"outlaw," "mafia"—in which, to catch the criminal, the policeman must himself [*sic*] become a criminal, blurring the line of legality).[43]

The creators of *Fauda* have repeatedly clarified that the symmetry is intentional. In an interview, Raz claimed that he strove to show "both sides" and that there are obvious similarities between the Palestinian and Israeli protagonists.[44] Diana Buttu, a Palestinian-Canadian human rights lawyer, criticized *Fauda* for obscuring the deeply asymmetrical nature of occupation: "If you're not careful, you find yourself drawn into the assassinations, you get lured into the cat and mouse" of two teams endlessly retaliating against one another.[45] Such critiques of the show's pretense to evenhandedness are perfectly warranted, given the stark power imbalance. But what if the symmetry that the show constructs is not simply or only propagandist—a rationalizing self-justification or an intentionally advertised lie, such as the Ministry of Foreign Affair's statement explored in the Introduction?

When the imagined symmetry in *Fauda* is considered as a genuine fantasy, it reveals a less supremacist view of Palestinians as possessing some similarity to, or at least parity with, Jewish Israelis—an equality that, in Hobbesian fashion, itself underlies violence. One possible explanation for this view is the greater proximity of *mizraḥim* to Palestinians. Another is their joint Arab past, a common history that the show thematizes as the grounds for intimate and kind relations across national borders (notable examples are the conversation between Doron's Iraqi father and the Palestinian doctor, Shireen, as well as Captain Ayub's close friendships with informants, PA officials, and their families). A third, perhaps less generous explanation is that *Fauda* is a product of its time. First aired during "the knives intifada" (2015–16) and following the 2014 Israeli attack on Gaza, the show reflects an Israeli longing for a clear, easily vilified culprit. Such a political imaginary presided over the previous intifadas, when Israeli discourse, centering on "terrorist organizations," easily

43. Omri Ben Yehuda similarly observes that *Fauda* established a symmetry and a continuum "between 'proper' Israel and its 'Territories,' through which Hamas is rendered legitimate and equated with Israel in what seems like a fight between clans"; Ben-Yehuda, "The Retribution of Identity: Colonial Politics in Fauda," *AJS Review* 44, no. 1 (2020): 12.

44. Mann, "An Interview with Lior Raz."

45. Shabi, "Next Homeland?"

pinned responsibility for acts of violence on Palestinian political organizations (the PLO, Hamas, and others) with clear hierarchies, ideologies, and leaderships. This framework allowed Israeli officials to prosecute, punish, and execute offenders and to preempt attacks through surveillance, arrests, and assassinations. In the time of *inqisām*, however, such an organized culpable party is more difficult to manufacture: first, because the massive attacks on Gaza exposed the stark imbalance of power; second, because attacks by Palestinians in the West Bank and within 1948-borders Israel are increasingly carried by individuals untethered from political organizations, thus becoming sporadic, more difficult to preempt or prosecute.[46] In its mirroring and parallels, therefore, *Fauda* fictionally reconstructs that bygone legally liable enemy, easily identifiable and vilifiable, to which Israelis had grown accustomed.

The symmetry in *Fauda*, however, differs from that of the concept of conflict not only because it is sincerely believed while the latter is structurally false, but also because its form is vastly different. Taking the form of a confrontation or a duel, it involves two binary sides and avoids the legal setting of judgment. The tertiary mediating figure of the judge disappears, along with the entire system of philosophical enquiry, with its dialogue, persuasion, negotiation, and search for solutions. Michel Foucault describes this competition model as Homeric (as well as feudal and Germanic) and explicitly contrasts it with the litigation model of the state, with its deliberation, inquiries, and obsession with property, which he depicts as Oedipal (as well as Roman and modern). In the duel, fighters face off against each other to establish not the truth or a new set of laws, but rather who is stronger and therefore right. It is a binary logic of self or other, of winning or losing, of survival and domination or death and subjugation. Unlike conflict as judgment, the duel does not aim to transcend the "state of nature"; to the contrary, its political form develops based on the assumed egalitarianism of that mythic state, rendering the fight itself—a ritualized gesture of vengeance—into juridical proof and the law, into a ritual of war.[47]

Above all, symmetry is produced in the show through the core narrative force of the "cycle of revenge." While revenge presents itself as rooted in the

46. On this shift in imagining the Palestinian enemy, see Liron Mor, "Resistance into Incitement: Translation, Legislation, 'Early Detection' and the Palestinian Poet's Intention," *Arab Studies Journal* 27, no. 1 (2019): 118–54.

47. Michel Foucault, "Truth and Juridical Forms," trans. Lawrence Williams and Catherine Merlen, *Social Identities* 2, no. 3 (1996): 327–42. In the procedure of competition, Foucault writes, "there is neither judge, nor sentence, nor truth, nor investigation, nor testimony to find out who has told the truth." The role of deciding is "left to the fight, or to the challenge, or to the risks each opponent would take" (327–28).

clear linearity of cause and effect, the show exposes its circular, dehistoricizing, and preemptive temporality, which distorts both history and causality. The revenge subplot, ubiquitous in recent Israeli cinema, attests to a perception of violence in Palestine-Israel as a never-ending, cyclical conflict[48] (thus also flattering Western audiences, who may easily condescend to both sides). When violence is wrested out of history and made personal, its context and rationale disappear. It emerges instead as eternal and essential—materializing with no cause or motive other than its own compulsion. In an asymmetrical context like the one in Palestine-Israel, such de-historicization delinks Palestinian uprising from the Israeli colonial actions and policies that it attacks, thus mystifying the causes of violence and exculpating Israel. The cyclicity of revenge also places both parties in some antediluvian time—a time before the law and civilization. After all, in the West, a defining feature of a civilized society is the sublation of personal revenge by an impersonal universal system of law. This is, famously, Hegel's reading of *Antigone*, in which Antigone's entombing embodies the "civilizing" transition from and sublation of a divine, family-based law of personal commitments (represented by Antigone) toward the universal civic law of the polis (represented by its ruler, Creon).[49]

Allegedly responding to a past injury, revenge also anticipates the retribution for the retribution. In a preemptive logic, it uses hypothetical future violence, which may or may not strike, to further justify violence in the present. And because this reasoning is tautological, vindication is guaranteed. Preemptive circularity suffuses Israeli discourse (a paradigmatic example is the sloganized idea that Palestinians "want to throw Israelis into the sea" and should therefore be disenfranchised). It is also all-pervasive in *Fauda*, in which Israeli reactions to past violence are regularly conflated with preemption of future attacks. For instance, after a failed operation in Season Two, Nurit, the sole female agent, confronts Doron, claiming that all this violence is merely about him and his vendettas. Doron responds angrily: "My vendettas? They are *our* vendettas! So that they don't kill me, you, and your friend over here!" The ease with which Doron repurposes revenge as preemptive defense is revealing. Indeed, threats of future attacks repeatedly serve as the explicit pretext for "targeted assassinations" of Palestinian figures, even while revenge for past killings repeatedly surfaces as the immediate motive. Relating the preemptive circularity in *Fauda* to collective trauma, the film scholars Nurith Gertz and Raz Yosef describe the

48. Ben-Yehuda, "Retribution of Identity," 9, referencing Raya Morag, *Waltzing with Bashir: Perpetrator Trauma and Cinema* (London and New York: I. B. Tauris, 2013), 152.

49. G. W. F. Hegel, *Phenomenology of Spirit*, trans. A. V. Miller, rev. ed. (Oxford: Oxford University Press, 1976), 284–89.

Israeli "cycle of violence" as producing trauma whose sources are both "rooted in the past and return from the future." The dual temporality of this anxiety creates a sense of vulnerability in Israeli society, by which "Israel's defensive national unity is solidified."[50] At once stemming from and perpetuating the victimized logic of "never again," preemption in Israel drives the "cycle of violence" and forms its discursive, legal, and technological grammar.

Central to *Fauda* and the Israeli imagination, the "cycle of violence" as a series of personal vendettas depoliticizes actions and policies in Palestine-Israel, presenting all violence as nothing but feuds between individuals. In the show, those individuals are in turn all tangled together, embroiled in romantic and familial webs. Doron's team member Boaz is his wife's brother; Doron's wife has an affair with another team member, Naor; the only woman on the team, Nurit, has an illicit relationship with its commander, Mickey Moreno, and later with a new member; Herzl, yet another team member, marries Moreno's sister.

Indeed, the family is the main theatre of violence in *Fauda*. As the aforementioned plot summary suggests, many acts of violence involve close relatives of both the protagonists and the antagonists. In the show, the family is also the key arena of Israeli power play, of that manipulative and subjugating violence that forces collaboration. In Season Three, for instance, after Doron infiltrates a Palestinian man's family and turns him into an unwitting collaborator, the man, Bashar, and his father venture to seek spectacular revenge. Similarly, Captain Ayub, the Shin Bet operative assigned to the unit, paternalistically treats Palestinian informants like his own children. To gather intelligence and pressure Palestinian combatants, he regularly threatens, seduces, interrogates, coordinates with, and helps their family members.

The trope of blood feuds, of familial violence and segmentary societies, not only symmetrizes the Palestinian-Israeli context but also empties violence of ideological commitments, rendering it personal and criminal rather than communal and political. No motivations are provided for the Jewish characters' investment in warfare save for their personal vendettas (or pathologies, as later episodes sometimes suggest).[51] So much so that Doron is repeatedly recruited back to the unit with the argument that, precisely because of his personal loss, only he could ever hunt down the current culprit. Palestinian characters, too, are portrayed as motivated solely by a personal drive for revenge, as the Hamas

50. Nurith Gertz and Raz Yosef, "Trauma, Time, and the 'Singular Plural': The Israeli Television Series Fauda," *Israel Studies Review* 32, no. 2 (2017): 3.

51. In the background, however, some specters nonetheless insist that the Palestinian characters are also motivated by ideological commitments, while the Israeli ones, by contrast, execute violence as a source of income.

or ISIS ideologies that presumably inspire their operations are never presented. So much so that al-Makdasi's major operation is dubbed "the first terrorist attack committed on personal grounds." When he stages an ISIS-style execution, this attitude is literalized. In the moment of the ISIS liturgy that introduces the ideology behind the execution, al-Makdasi simply states, "Let the Zionist enemy know that this is 'an eye for an eye and a tooth for a tooth'" (reciting the biblical quotation in Hebrew). Breaking with the habitual rhetoric of the "war on terror," *Fauda* thus suggests that primitive revenge is the *only* motive Jewish Israelis are able to ascribe to Palestinian political violence.

Fauda manifests a national tendency for imagining collective cohesion by sanctifying the family and by employing familial tropes. The family was, as demonstrated, a key site of the efforts to assimilate Mizrahi immigrants and bind them to the nation. To this day, Israel's fixation on maintaining Jewish "demographic superiority" translates into an aggressive pro-natalist agenda, which centers on the family. Israeli preoccupation with fertility yielded what is considered one of the most developed assisted reproductive technology industries in the world. In its "political economy of fertility," the Israeli national health care system covers the costs of artificial insemination, ova donations, and in vitro fertilization (IVF) (but not of birth control). It also conducts the highest number of IVF treatments per capita in the world.[52] Israel was the first country to legalize surrogacy—first, for heterosexual couples and single mothers and, later, for same-sex couples and single fathers. Although abortions are legal, they are conditioned upon approval from a designated medical committee.[53] Finally, Jewish Israeli society perceives and preserves itself through the figure of the family. Discussing the nation-family-army triad, Gertz and Yosef mention that, when young Israelis were asked in a recent survey "what they liked best about Israel," the most common replies were "the country gives [one] a sense of family" and "Israelis come together during times of crisis."[54]

In *Fauda*, however, the family emerges as a retroactive justification for a sense of belonging to a collective whose demarcation lines are capricious. In its constant mirroring, *Fauda* testifies to both the strictness and the arbitrariness

52. Jasbir K. Puar, *The Right to Maim: Debility, Capacity, Disability* (Durham, N.C.: Duke University Press, 2017), 111–12.

53. Yael Hashiloni-Dolev, A *Life (Un)Worthy of Living: Reproductive Genetics in Israel and Germany* (Dordrecht: Springer, 2007); Israel Ministry of Health, "Fertility Treatments and Surrogacy," *Israel Ministry of Health Website*, accessed November 14, 2021, https://www.health.gov.il/English/Topics/fertility/Pages/default.aspx; Ruth Levush, *Israel: Reproduction and Abortion: Law and Policy* (Washington D.C.: Law Library of Congress, Global Legal Research Center, 2012).

54. Gertz and Yosef, "Trauma, Time, and the 'Singular Plural,'" 6.

of the division between Mizrahi Jews and Palestinians. The very first episode of the series showcases this paradox in an elaborate changing room scene depicting the unit members readying themselves for an undercover operation. In a voyeuristic montage of cosmetic tasks, performed by men in front of mirrors, the agents paint their beards a darker shade of brown, use makeup to cover over tattoos, and dress up in cheap distressed clothes to "Arabize" themselves (see figure 5). The sheer volume of fuss in the changing room suggests that a change is indeed necessary, that to pass as Palestinians the Jewish agents must dramatically transform themselves. These agents, however, are themselves Arabs—as *mizraḥim*, their families originated in Arab countries and are perceived as such in Israel.[55] The drama of this conversion therefore seems quite exaggerated. As yet another example of the racializing process of (de)Arabization, this scene shows how Arab Jews are Arabized, turned into more useful Arabs, better at working for the state and executing its policies. Through this process, Arab Jews are made Arab in form and function alone, severed from Arab history or "content" and turned against it.

While this theatrical transformation—the process of *hista'arvut*, of self-Arabization—stages racial and national lines as essential, the cinematography destabilizes them by generating confusing symmetries. This montage alludes to Gillo Pontecorvo's famous changing room transformation in *The Battle of Algiers* (1966), where, by contrast, female indigenous fighters disguise themselves as French colonists—a pathos-filled transformation that enables revolutionary violence *against the colonizers*. Moreover, throughout the montage in *Fauda*, the director also planted shots of abu Ahmed laboring to disguise himself as an elderly man in preparation for secretly attending his brother's wedding (see figure 6). He, too, is captured in front of a mirror, painting his beard with a toothbrush just as painstakingly as the *mista'arvim* (only in a lighter shade, to form the illusion of greys).[56] Underscoring the performative aspect of identity and drawing these symmetrical parallels, including the mirroring of mirrors themselves, the scene seems to muddle the racial line.

In fact, *Fauda* regularly reveals how close Mizrahi Jews and Palestinians are and how forced their separation is. For instance, during an undercover opera-

55. Two of the agents are named Herzl and Eli—first names that are generally associated with *mizraḥim*. Both Moreno and Kabilio are Sephardi last names. Ayub's parents, according to him, hail from Lebanon and Egypt.

56. On mirroring Palestinians as a legal technique of Jewish settlers, who thus work both inside and outside the rule of law (much like the *Fauda* team), see Kareem Rabie, *Palestine Is Throwing a Party and the Whole World Is Invited: Capital and State Building in the West Bank* (Durham, N.C.: Duke University Press, 2021), chap. 9.

Figure 5. "Changing Room Scene: Avihi," *Fauda*, season 1, episode 1, directed by Assaf Bernstein, written by Lior Raz, Avi Issacharoff, Michal Aviram, Assaf Beiser, and Liora Kamintzky. Ṭender Hafaḳot, Kasṭina Tiḳshoret, aired February 15, 2015, on Yes TV. Screenshot.

Figure 6. "Changing Room Scene: abu Ahmad," *Fauda*, season 1, episode 1, directed by Assaf Bernstein, written by Lior Raz, Avi Issacharoff, Michal Aviram, Assaf Beiser, and Liora Kamintzky. Ṭender Hafaḳot, Kasṭina Tiḳshoret, aired February 15, 2015, on Yes TV. Screenshot.

tion, Doron, disguised as a Palestinian called Amir, develops a romantic relationship with abu Ahmad's female doctor, Shireen. This highly phantasmic cross-national love affair survives Shireen's marriage to a Hamas leader and recovers, even climaxes, after she learns of Doron's true identity. Confessing that he feels more at ease in Shireen's culture, when he is on "their" turf (*hunāk, ʿindkum*), Doron insists that his identity as the Palestinian Amir is not a lie; "It feels real." Later, Doron's father tells Shireen over ʿ*idje* that he identifies as a Jewish Arab (ʿ*arabī yahūdī*) and that in his birthplace, Baghdad, "Arabs and Jews all lived together." Indeed, the two quickly become close, using familial terms of endearment (e.g., *bintī*). Ayub's lifelong intimate relationship with abu Maher, a PA official, also blurs the lines, as the two not only coordinate security operations but also closely follow each other's lives. This familial relationship culminates when Ayub extricates abu Maher's son from prison, manipulating the father-son relationship to unsettle the young man and turn him into a collaborator.

So, what makes Arab Jews Jewish? In *Fauda*, very little. The agents speak Arabic and sing in Arabic in their most intimate moments—at weddings, memorials, even while having sex. Facing death, Doron uses an Islamic prayer, in Arabic, until his executioner demands that he pray to his own god. In contemporary Israel, *Fauda* seems to suggest, group identity, with its patriotism and racist hatred, is nearly random, a sort of belonging that was once described as "tribal" or "clannish"—the tautological loyalty one might feel for a soccer club. Often, such arbitrary political identities, whereby the very fact of belonging dictates hatred for other groups, correlate to longer cultural, linguistic, or religious traditions, thus appearing historical, even ancient.[57] In the Israeli case, however, such identifications are not continuous with the past. The histories of Mizrahi populations are heterogeneous, amongst themselves and in relation to *ashkenazim*, whose cultures are themselves varied. Since Jewish society in Israel comprises diverse forms of secularism, religiosity, and "traditionalism," Jewish religion, too, cannot serve as a clear identity anchor (even while religious Zionism is pushing for it to become one).

What distinguishes the two groups, in fact, is merely power. Dominance—strength, supremacy, resources—emerges as the sole content of Jewish collective difference in Israel and as the motivation behind Mizrahi hostile severance. The power imbalance, the fact of Israeli domination, is inadvertently exposed in *Fauda* through occasional aerial shots that mimic Israel's surveillance

57. Mahmood Mamdani calls this mode of define and rule "tribalism" and claims that "as an administrative practice and as the currency of political competition [it] has endured and today been taken to its absurd extreme"; Mamdani, *Neither Settler nor Native: The Making and Unmaking of Permanent Minorities* (Cambridge, Mass.: Belknap, 2020), 30.

technologies and thus nearly literalize its upper hand—its control of the sky, the air, and infrastructures, as well as information and communication technologies (see figures 7 and 8).[58] Other mise en abyme shots, of security personnel in the command room following operations through screens, are nearly unprecedented in exposing the magnitude of the Israeli surveillance system and the vast resources, both economic and human, that are invested in it (see figures 9 and 10). Such "one-way mirrors" are also a formal expression of *inqisām*, of severance from Palestinians as a means for sustaining their "inclusion" under Israeli control as excluded non-citizens. Attachment to this domination—to always having the upper hand in the duel and thus being proven right—translates into blind, arbitrary loyalty to the nation, whose boundaries are fortified with racialized hatred, particularly by those most economically and socially vulnerable, those most at risk for misrecognition—a risk that, despite decades of severing assimilation, remains real.

By "hatred," I refer here to an affect consonant with Sara Ahmed's definition of hate as an "againstness" feeling, which is unconscious—an amalgamation of displacements that do not originate in a single psyche. It is affected by the story and animates it, rather than being its cause or explanation. By circulating through signs, by stringing "figures of hate" into a common threat, hate accumulates emotional value—an "affective economy" with material, social, and psychic effects. This circulation, Ahmed writes, "produces a differentiation between 'us' and 'them,' whereby 'they' are constituted as the cause of 'our' feeling of hate." Perceived here no longer as coming from inside and directed toward preexisting external others, hate generates instead the very distinction between inside and outside and negotiates the boundaries between communities. A border phenomenon, hate is closely tied to proximity: the appearance of imagined others as a threat in "our" sphere, their close presence or touch, is experienced as an injury, as a violent negation of both self and nation, precisely because they cannot be fully excluded.[59] The conversion of feelings of injury into hate for others, read as its cause, miraculously inverts the positions of those in power and those threatened and victimized, just as its rhetoric often converts hatred (of others) into love (of the nation, the race, our own).

In the Israeli context, such bare hatred could be seen, as the anthropologist Matan Kaminer argues, as the result of the receding horizon of ideology—the

58. Often highlighting its verticality, Eyal Weizman discusses this mode of spatial control in *Hollow Land: Israel's Architecture of Occupation* (London and New York: Verso, 2017).

59. Sara Ahmed, *The Cultural Politics of Emotion*, 2nd ed. (New York: Routledge, 2014), 48. While presented as universal, Ahmed's definition of hate is articulated within the specific racialized contexts of Euro-American anti-migrant rhetoric and discussions of "hate crimes."

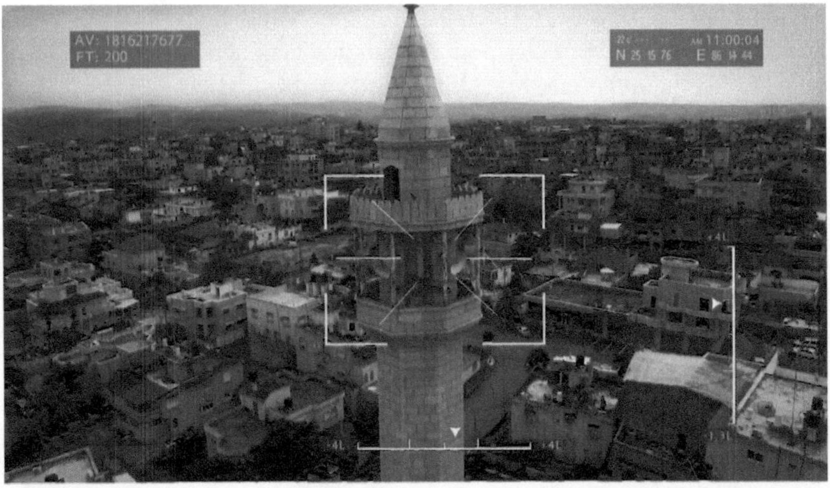

Figure 7. "Aerial Shot," *Fauda*, season 1, episode 1, directed by Assaf Bernstein, written by Lior Raz, Avi Issacharoff, Michal Aviram, Assaf Beiser and Liora Kamintzky. Ṭender Hafaḳot, Kasṭina Tiḳshoret, aired February 15, 2015, Yes TV. Screenshot.

Figure 8. "Aerial Shot: Nablus," *Fauda*, season 2, episode 11, directed by Rotem Shamir, written by Lior Raz, Avi Issacharoff, and Amir Mann. Ṭender Hafaḳot, Kasṭina Tiḳshoret, aired March 11, 2018, Yes TV. Screenshot.

Figure 9. "Command Room Screens: Interrogation," *Fauda*, season 2, episode 9, directed by Rotem Shamir, written by Lior Raz, Avi Issacharoff, and Amir Mann. Ṭender Hafaḳot, Kasṭina Tiḳshoret, aired February 25, 2018, Yes TV. Screenshot.

Figure 10. "Command Room Screens: Operation," *Fauda*, season 4, episode 12, directed by Omri Givon, written by Lior Raz, Avi Issacharoff, and Noah Stollman. Ṭender Hafaḳot, Kasṭina Tiḳshoret, aired September 28, 2022, Yes TV. Screenshot.

purging of Zionism of all values. If in the past, hating Arabs was a means to some "lofty" Zionist ends, however ill-perceived—realizing socialist ideals (for some), establishing a Jewish-only sovereign state—then today the ends have evaporated, and hatred is all that remains.[60] Kaminer's description of the present moment in Israel is apt (though it discounts religious, messianic ideals, which are increasingly becoming a significant motor), but it does not explain how or why this moment came to be. The explanation I attempted here showcases two aspects of Mizrahi society, as exemplified by *Fauda*, which together helped crystallize Zionist patriotism into today's hostile severance, or *inqisām*. The first, which stems from the "Arabization" of *mizraḥim* as expendable, is their proximity to Palestinians and their greater vulnerability to, and execution of, violence. The combination of increased vulnerability and uncredited sacrifices could be seen to form the perfect storm stirring *mizraḥim* to perform the spectacle of violent hatred even more visibly and loudly—a rather vicious cycle. A second, correlated aspect is the Mizrahi tendency to imagine Palestinians, for better or worse, as equal—a worthy opponent in this fantastically symmetrical soccer match (whereas Israeli governments historically held a condescending view, regarding Palestinians as exceptionally violent and their violence as exceptionally unlawful). It is this combination of greater proximity and imagined equivalency, I contend, that motivates Mizrahi Jews to seek and protect Jewish dominance through hatred. Given their assimilating severance—the cultural de-Arabization of Mizrahi Jews and their pressing into familial bonds with the nation—neither this form of loyalty nor its emptiness is surprising.

While driven by a largely Mizrahi experience, this mode of inward loyalty and outward hostility is no longer limited to *mizraḥim*. What coheres Jewish Israeli identity today is a victimized fear of (a future, imagined) injury and a fantasy of an equal enemy, both of which fashion Israeli Jewish hatred out of "familial" love for the nation and aid in maintaining the status quo. Indeed, the Jewish Israeli collective's self-image as a perpetual victim is sustained in and through the Mizrahi periphery, with its greater exposure. Israeli society thus turns places like Sderot into a synecdoche for the nation (a trope whose problematic implications Chapter 4 considered). This attitude is so prevalent that it has even etched itself into the agenda of the marginal Jewish anti-war left. During the past four Israeli military campaigns against Gaza (2008, 2012, 2014, 2021), a recurrent chant in anti-war demonstrations had been, "In Gaza and in Sderot, children want to live" (*be-'Aza ve-Śderot, yeladot rotsot li-ḥyot*). While Gaza is the name of the entire Strip and is indeed consumed by Israeli

60. Matan Kaminer, "li-Śno 'Aravin ze 'Arakhim: Teḥilat ha-Sof shel ha-Ḳolonyalizem ha-Yiśra'eli?," *'Atidot* (blog), July 7, 2014, https://atidot.wordpress.com/2014/07/07/hating-arabs/.

violence, Sderot serves here as a synecdoche for Israeli suffering more broadly. This popular slogan, whose parallel structure inadvertently perpetuates a false symmetry, suggests that a sense of both vulnerability and fantastic symmetry suffuses Jewish Israeli society.

Since these processes now affect Israeli society more broadly, I label the current moment "post-Mizrahi." The musicologist Oded Erez employs the term to describe the recent "Mizraḥization" of Israeli popular music, insisting that it implies neither "that contemporary Israel is a 'post-racial' . . . utopia" nor "that Mizrahi Jews have achieved equality or have ceased to suffer from bias." Instead, it designates a process of transvaluation and diffusion of Mizrahiness, its becoming more acceptable in Israeli society, even aesthetically desirable, but at the price of commodification—being reduced to easily digestible, reified, and unthreatening markers of authentic experience, consumable by all.[61] Indeed, the diffusion of Mizrahi national loyalty is supported by this aesthetic, cultural shift.

When Palestinians are finally featured on Israeli TV as "well-rounded" figures and *mizraḥim* are allowed to be Arabs, their relationships are reduced to familial conflicts—personal, libidinal, primordial blood feuds and retributions that take place between and within families. Such representations of political violence reflect Jewish Israeli perceptions and desires better than official discourse. Depoliticizing and dehistorizing, they mask the Israeli colonial disappearance of Palestinians and instead reinforce common Israeli fantasies of symmetry and of indigeneity. The Jewish Israeli collective derives these fantasies from and fulfills them through its Mizrahi population.

By focusing on the structural processes that have racialized *mizraḥim* as both executors and expendable bodies and by claiming that hatred is unconscious precisely because it is collective, I do not mean to erase Mizrahi Jews' complicity or ignore their colonial privileges. Similarly, the aim of criticizing this racializing structure is not simply to call for bettering the Mizrahi position within the Israeli settler state, but rather to challenge the racial mechanisms that render both Mizrahi Jews and Palestinians expendable and exploitable. Although a whole edifice is invested in separating them and concealing their codependence, these mechanisms converge under the racial language of a single colonial regime, whose shifting imperatives regarding the two populations produce its diverging idioms. This convergence, neither consensual nor equitable, is perhaps best exhibited by the security roles *mizraḥim* fulfill, as a

61. Oded Erez, "Bass and Silsulim: Israeli Music after Muzika Mizrahit," in *Routledge Handbook on Contemporary Israel*, ed. Guy Ben-Porat et al. (London and New York: Routledge, 2022), 476–88.

result of which they, like the men in *Fauda*, coerce Palestinians into becoming collaborators, a treason that puts Palestinians at risk of both social isolation and death (a historical irony, perhaps, since "treason" was precisely how Palestinians of older generations regarded the Mizrahi complicity in the Israeli security apparatus).[62]

Internal Inqisām: *Palestinian Severing Hostility*

The year 2007 marks the violent split (*al-inqisām*) between the Gaza Strip and the West Bank. After Hamas won the 2006 Palestinian legislative election, political relations between Hamas and Fatah—which still controlled most administrative and security apparatuses in the West Bank—became strained. This clash, as well as Hamas's subsequent seizure of power in Gaza, served as a pretext for Israel to impose a blockade on the Gaza Strip, thus effectively transforming a political split into a geographical one. Following the Split, as the political theorist Nasser Abourahme puts it, "Hamas eventually settled for a besieged and ostracized fiefdom in Gaza, and a self-disciplining Fatah in the West Bank re-integrated into the global-imperial political order. Priorities shifted, and the national lost further traction in the face of renewed factionalism and the engineering of an internal enemy."[63] Persistently transfusing Palestinian society with suspicion and hostility, these last two effects of *al-inqisām*—increased fracturing and fabricated internal enemies—form the subject of this section. What technologies contribute to this fracturing? And how might Palestinian literature make poetic sense of communal severance?

In this post-*inqisām* time, the border has become the main site in and through which Israeli security apparatuses exercise control, as the Gaza blockade regrettably demonstrates. Since the Split, Israeli border technologies—checkpoints and other crossings, surveillance and biopolitical apparatuses, walls and fences clad in security machinery—are proliferating, becoming more automated, systemic, and permanent-looking. Increasing the distance between Israeli soldiers and Palestinians passing through, they render distance a marker of both progress and status. These technologies are emblematized by the checkpoint—central to Israeli control since the First Intifada—and especially by the more recent large "terminals," first introduced in 2005 and "perfected"

62. Cohen, *Śon'im*, chap. 4.

63. Nasser Abourahme, "The Productive Ambivalences of Post-Revolutionary Time: Discourse, Aesthetics, and the Political Subject of the Palestinian Present," in *Time, Temporality and Violence in International Relations*, ed. Anna M. Agathangelou and Kyle D. Killian (London: Routledge, 2016), 135.

in the biometric crossings of 2019. The Israeli desire for distance and severance, for governing Palestinians while limiting direct engagement, couples border control with the outsourcing of policing to the Palestinians themselves—a strategy I here term "insourcing."

Indeed, the experience of checkpoints and border crossings remains paradigmatic for most Palestinians, especially in the West Bank.[64] This is still the case despite the increasing integration of the West Bank into the global economy, which the PA has led since the mid-2000s, aiming to form an image of normalcy by turning to the market instead of politics.[65] Checkpoint experiences of isolation, alienation, and hostility thus still abound and are foregrounded in cinematic and literary works as recent as Farah Nabulsi's short film *al-Hadiyya* (The Present, 2020), Isabella Hammad's *Enter Ghost* (2023), and Adania Shibli's novel *Tafṣil Thanawi* (Minor Detail 2017), discussed in Chapter 4.[66]

Here, I focus on Shibli's earlier short story "al-Tala'ub bi-l-'Adid min Dharrat al-Ghubar" ("The Manipulation of Many Dust Particles," 2002; published in English as "Dust," 2007),[67] which detects and depicts the hostility infused into Palestinian society by Israeli colonization and its distanced control, outsourced to the checkpoint and to collaborators. Revolving around the Qalandia checkpoint and its spatial-temporal-affective ontology, the story explores the checkpoint as both a material technology and a metaphor

64. "Crossing barriers is perhaps the single most definitive experience in contemporary Palestinian life," writes Abourahme. Indeed, the exiled Palestinian intellectual and politician Azmi Bishara named the OPT "the land of checkpoints," and the Palestinian scholar Rashid Khalidi claimed that the shared anxiety of Palestinians at the checkpoint "proves that they are a people, if nothing else does." See Abourahme, "Spatial Collisions and Discordant Temporalities: Everyday Life between Camp and Checkpoint," *International Journal of Urban and Regional Research* 35, no. 2 (2011): 453; Bishara, *al-Hajiz: Shazaya Riwaya, al-Kitab al-Awwal: Wajd fi Bilad al-Hawajiz* (Haifa: Metaphora, 2004); Khalidi, *Palestinian Identity: The Construction of Modern National Consciousness* (New York: Columbia University Press, 2009), 5.

65. On these shifts, see Rabie, *Palestine Is Throwing a Party*; Lisa Taraki, "Urban Modernity on the Periphery: A New Middle Class Reinvents the Palestinian City," *Social Text* 26, no. 2 (2008): 61–81.

66. Other recent examples include Suad Amiry's *Nothing to Lose But Your Life: An 18-Hour Journey with Murad* (2010), Mourid Barghouti's memoir *Wulidtu Hunak, Wulidtu Huna* (2009; *I Was Born There, I Was Born Here*, 2012), Rabai al-Madhoun's novel *al-Sayyida min Tall Abib* (2009; *The Lady from Tel Aviv*, 2013), and Rashid Masharawi's film *Eid Milad Laila* (*Laila's Birthday*, 2008).

67. Adania Shibli, "al-Tala'ub bi-l-'Adid min Dharrat al-Ghubar," *al-Karmel Faṣliyya Thakqafiyya*, no. 70–71 (2002): 300–309; released in English as "Dust," trans. Yasmeen Hanoosh, *Iowa Review* 37, no. 2 (2007).

for the fragmentation of Palestinians' lifescapes. Although "al-Tala'ub" slightly predates *al-inqisām*, its articulation of checkpoint experiences prefigures the hostile severance of this period.

With more than a glimmer of humor, Shibli reveals the profound onto-epistemological uncertainty that the checkpoint produces, as well as its severing effect on society: her unnamed narrator complains about her friends being chronically late because of the checkpoints, so "Why should I always arrive on time, wait, and suffer doubts about time, place, day, and the notion of clarity itself?"[68] Indeed, as both concrete technology and literary trope, the checkpoint operates in "al-Tala'ub" on three key levels, which together form the very coordinates of being and the conditions of possibility of knowledge—space, time, and subjectivity (including intersubjectivity).

First, then, the checkpoint has a decimating effect on Palestinian space. While foregrounding the narrator's inner world, Shibli's story also reifies the checkpoint experience by giving it a spatial, physical form—that of dust. Neither an allegory nor a symbol, dust in "al-Tala'ub" is an indexical sign that physically participates in and is directly affected by the phenomenon it represents.[69] "Dust. This is how the tragedy is able to engulf us all."[70] Like Israeli surveillance, dust is ubiquitous, inescapable: "Every movement, even the slightest, stir[s] up terrible dust storms." It clings on, both in the checkpoint and beyond it, so that no amount of "comprehensive cleaning campaigns" ever gets rid of it entirely.[71] Shibli's dust also forms an insulating layer, a cloistering shell, amidst the checkpoint. It thus conveys both the individual psychological isolation produced by ubiquitous control and the collective claustrophobia of the Palestinian geography, dissected into enclaves by land theft, walls, and checkpoints. Expressed here by the dust, this *inqisām* might be seen as referring to and condensing a somewhat longer history of Israeli severance of Palestinian space.[72]

In Shibli's work, checkpoint severance permeates Palestinians' lives more broadly. Trading the "big" historical and political Palestinian issues for

68. Shibli, "Dust," 95.

69. I am thinking here with Charles Sanders Peirce's definition of indexical signs. See Richard J. Parmentier, "Peirce Divested for Nonintimates," in *Signs in Society: Studies in Semiotic Anthropology* (Bloomington: Indiana University Press, 1994), 3–22.

70. Shibli, "Dust," 95/302, translation modified.

71. Ibid., 100.

72. Already in 2005, Sari Hanafi labeled this systemic destruction of space in the OPT "spacio-cide" and claimed that, by targeting the very grounds of Palestinians' lives, it aims to make inevitable their "voluntary" transfer; Hanafi, "Spacio-Cide and Bio-Politics: The Israeli Colonial Conflict from 1947 to the Wall," in *Against the Wall: Israel's Barrier to Peace,* ed. Michael Sorkin (New York: New Press, 2005), 251–61.

psychosomatic depth and detail, her writing colors nearly every aspect of life, every situation, with the same affective qualities that characterize her treatment of the checkpoint—existential dread, social isolation, disempowerment. Shibli's second novel, *Kulluna Ba'id bi-Dhat al-Miqdar 'an al-Ḥubb* (We are All Equally Far from Love, 2004), rarely mentions obvious instances of Israeli colonialism, sketching instead isolated portraits of paralyzed and alienated individuals. Although unstated, Shibli attests, the fragmented and claustrophobic "Palestinian landscape has designed the novel in the very inability of the characters to move."[73] Tracing sensorial poetic snapshots of a young girl's experiences, her first novel, *Masas* (Touch, 2002) is even less explicit about its location. Both works, however, carefully explore the temporal, spatial, corporeal, and affective implications of Palestinian social and geographic severance, employing the same trapped, estranged, and anxious voice as "al-Tala'ub."

Second, the checkpoint disrupts Palestinian time. Indeed, much has been written on the spatiotemporal effects of Israeli barriers and checkpoints—their constitutive distortion of space and time, their rendering of distance unpredictable and of space less usable or knowable, their so-called temporization of Palestinians, and their formation of radically disjointed timescapes within Palestinian society.[74] "Al-Tala'ub" explores this disrupted temporality by zeroing in on the formative Palestinian experience of waiting, on that stagnation and suspense of time produced by the checkpoint. A tangible metaphor for waiting, dust particles pile on top of one another and amass on bodies: even in just fifteen minutes at the checkpoint, the narrator reports, "many dust storms have no option but to accumulate on me." The inert, actionless passage of time is thus presented not as empty but as a burden, recorded cumulatively in matter. A corporal, pain-adjacent burden: "Maybe I can bear pain, but I do not want to bear the dust on top of it."[75]

Like many before her, Shibli's narrator asserts that "waiting has become a lifestyle" for Palestinians.[76] Indeed, ever since Edward Said (always the first to

73. José García, "Adania Shibli on Writing Palestine from the Inside," *Literary Hub* (blog), February 6, 2017, https://lithub.com/adania-shibli-on-writing-palestine-from-the-inside/.

74. Abourahme, "Spatial Collisions and Discordant Temporalities"; Ariel Handel, "Where, Where to, and When in the Occupied Territories: An Introduction to Geography of Disaster," in *The Power of Inclusive Exclusion: Anatomy of Israeli Rule in the Occupied Palestinian Territories*, ed. Adi Ophir, Michal Givoni, and Sari Hanafi (New York and Cambridge, Mass.: Zone, 2009), 179–222; Amal Jamal, "Conflict Theory, Temporality, and Transformative Temporariness: Lessons from Israel and Palestine," *Constellations* 23, no. 3 (2016): 365–77; Helga Tawil-Souri, "Checkpoint Time," *Qui Parle* 26, no. 2 (2017): 383–422.

75. Shibli, "Dust," 95–96.

76. Ibid., 96.

articulate the problem) diagnosed the Palestinian predicament as a crisis of contemporaneity, an impasse born of temporal severance, similar diagnoses have proliferated, depicting the Palestinian condition as a suspended present, stagnant transience, an abeyance of history.[77] Shibli's short piece of autofiction, "Out of Time" (2006), literalizes this temporality of waiting. As the narrator is withheld and searched by a security guard at the Israeli airport, her wristwatch simply freezes, suggesting a temporal suspense so radical that time measurement standards become meaningless. She then muses, "Maybe my watch was only trying to comfort me by making me believe that all that search and delay had lasted zero minutes. As if nothing had happened. Or perhaps it simply refuses to count the time that is seized from my life, a time whose only purpose is to humiliate me and send me into despair." Regarding the paused time as a protective mechanism intended to "obscure the time of pain," the narrator nonetheless emphasizes the humiliation and despair of the wait, revealing its punitive nature.[78] Indeed, the checkpoint wait is often evocative of carceral time, "a temporal nothingness that exists purely as a sentence, a punishment."[79]

Crucially, Shibli links this disjointed, carceral temporality to communal severance. In the tragicomic, absurdist voice that traverses Palestinian literature, the narrator of "al-Tala'ub" discloses, "I have three friends left at the most, after making some cutbacks to the list. I visit them once a week during the same trip in order to pass the checkpoint as little as possible. So my visits to them turned into a race with time."[80] Tired of waiting and of doubting space, time, and perception itself, she actively severs social relations. Moreover, even when connecting with friends, as when the narrator finally arrives at her destination, all the despair, self-loathing, and anger, which accumulated like dust during her trip, erupt. She unexpectedly loses her temper with a little boy who is simply trying to help wash her dust-filled hair. Running out of time, she is unable

77. Edward W. Said, *Reflections on Exile and Other Essays* (Cambridge, Mass.: Harvard University Press, 2000), 47. Amal Jamal writes, for instance, that the common post-*nakba* experience of Palestinians is one of "suspended time, an attenuated existence over which there is no control, and the lack of normal continuity. All Palestinian communities, wherever located . . . share a festering sense of temporariness, the suspension and emptying of time, of waiting"; Jamal, "The Struggle for Time and the Power of Temporariness: Jews and Arabs in the Labyrinth of History," in *Men in the Sun*, ed. Tal Ben Zvi and Hanna Farah (Herzliya: Herzliya Museum of Contemporary Art, 2009), E19–20, and the sources in note 74 in this chapter.

78. Adania Shibli, "Out of Time," in *A Map of Absence: An Anthology of Palestinian Writing on the Nakba*, ed. Atef Alshaer (London: Saqi, 2019), 193–94.

79. Tawil-Souri, "Checkpoint Time," 402.

80. Shibli, "Dust," 96.

to atone by reading him a story.[81] The checkpoint, with its spatiotemporal distortion, is thus revealed to have significant social costs. Based on ethnographic research of the same checkpoint, Qalandia, Helga Tawil-Souri similarly observes that co-evalness, the sharing of time, is a necessary precondition for functional communication, for a community.[82]

Third, then, the checkpoint is a technology for fracturing Palestinian society. Its severing of intersubjective relations begins with its severing effects on Palestinian subjectivity. Shibli's narrators repeatedly profess feeling it necessary to neutralize emotions, especially at the checkpoint. In "al-Tala'ub," when depicting a successful casual crossing of the checkpoint, the narrator claims that it was accomplished only by "freezing" all her feelings.[83] In *Tafṣil Thanawi*, the narrator attempts to quell her turbulent emotional world every time she nears a checkpoint by yawning and chewing gum—a procedural tic that both puts up a front of arrested feelings and serves as a ritual for conjuring emotional stillness.[84]

Despite such proclamations of neutralized emotions, however, "al-Tala'ub" is in fact bursting with fierce, intense feelings. One emotion is particularly prominent. Hostility. It is everywhere. When the narrator meets neighbors in the market, who "ask where [she had] disappeared to," the young woman confesses that she "can no longer stand them." Hostility is so diffused that it becomes disembodied, impersonal. Walking through the market, the woman hears someone calling her name, cursing her; she turns around but sees no one. When others express hostile behavior, the narrator appears incapable of understanding its source. On her way home, a passing boy mimes shooting at her with his finger. She comments, "I do not know how I have offended him."[85] Yet, hostility is most pronounced at and around the checkpoint, which propagates an entire ecosystem of taxi shuttles, petty vendors, coffee and food stalls, and youngsters selling knickknacks and offering car-cleaning services. The narrator's patience is repeatedly tested by honking taxi drivers. In the shuttle taxi from the checkpoint to Ramallah, another passenger tries to strike a conversation, but she ignores him, brooding to herself: "Who does he think I am, talking to me! He asked me about the checkpoint and I said there was some shooting. He said something else and I, *filled with hostility, could not even hear him*."[86]

81. Ibid., 95–96.

82. Tawil-Souri, "Checkpoint Time," 391.

83. Shibli, "Dust," 101.

84. Adania Shibli, *Minor Detail*, trans. Elisabeth Jaquette (New York: New Directions, 2020).

85. Shibli, "Dust," 103.

86. Ibid., 99, emphasis mine.

Hostility, or self-severance, thus appears as both a result of the social severance imposed by checkpoints and an affective self-preservation technique against it. Shibli's narrator contemplates, for instance, a friend from Nablus who, prohibited by the checkpoints from traveling to see her family, "does not allow herself to miss them too much."[87] In this sense, *inqisām*—self-severance and social hostility—operates by affectively distancing oneself, much like the emotional neutralization deemed by Shibli's narrators the best method for crossing the checkpoint without a nervous breakdown.[88] This self-distancing, from oneself and from one's community, inversely correlates to the border technologies that distance Israeli soldiers from Palestinians.

Like the dust particles in Shibli's story, which cling to one's body well beyond the checkpoint, *inqisām* too saturates Palestinian society, flooding every realm of life. Shibli expresses this all-pervasiveness by constructing a waiting scene at a post office in Jerusalem that parallels the checkpoint waiting scenes and is thus formally continuous with them. In line at the post office, the narrator notices that the Palestinian customers speaking to the teller are baffled by the latter's Hebrew. Although proficient in Hebrew, the young woman does not offer to mediate. She rationalizes: "I do not help them because they did not turn to me. . . . I am silent; I hear all their efforts and remain silent. I deny them. I am not one hundred percent sure that the teller is racist but I am afraid. I fear that my box will not arrive at its desired destination on time because I am an Arab."[89] Through the narrator's fear and her withholding of help, Shibli suggests the spilling over of severance and hostility from the checkpoint to more mundane, demilitarized spaces.

The checkpoint severs not only by generating disconnected geographic and temporal cells but also by physically isolating individuals from one another and by inducing competition between them. "Al-Tala'ub" opens with a portrayal of the car queue waiting to cross the checkpoint, demonstrating that what separates Palestinians in this setting is not only motorized metal frames but also the competition ignited by the wait. While stuck, watching the other cars, the narrator allows her mind to distractedly ponder, "Is the driver a man or a woman? If it is a woman, is she wearing a headcover or not? What is her age and level of attraction? And if it is a man, does he wear sunglasses? Is he cute? Is there a wedding ring on his finger? Is he returning glances?" She provides this wealth of detail, however, only to dramatize how quickly one forgets all about these other drivers, even the targets of romantic speculation, "at the

87. Ibid., 100.
88. Ibid., 93.
89. Ibid., 97.

slightest indication that your car line has moved," suggesting that competition dominates all other concerns.[90] In documenting the hostile rivalry inspired by the checkpoint amongst male Palestinian laborers, Tawil-Souri similarly reports that "there is no solidarity between them while here. The checkpoint might close or the turnstile be frozen for an inordinate amount of time. Every person wants to—*needs* to—make sure that he or she is ahead. There is no sense of togetherness: these atomized beings are a mass inevitably about to get fragmented by the turnstiles."[91]

Since "al-Tala'ub" was first published, the atomizing effect of the checkpoint has only intensified. Starting in the mid-2000s, Israel has developed and introduced a series of new technologies—fenced corridors, automatic gates and turnstiles, metal detectors, ID card sensors, and biometric iris and fingerprint scanners—that deepen checkpoint *inqisām*. These technologies desocialize Palestinians, abstracting each into a single, solitary unit, bureaucratically, biopolitically, and physically. These technologies introduce distance not only amongst Palestinians but also between them and the Israeli guards operating the checkpoint, and thus hostility emerges as the result not only of competition and individuation but also of the inaccessibility of Israeli security personnel and the unknowability of their procedures.[92]

While Israeli power often invisibilizes its modes of operation (as Chapter 3 demonstrates), at the checkpoint this self-distancing has the added effect of imposing calibrated chaos and deliberate uncertainty. Crossing the checkpoint by foot, the narrator of "al-Tala'ub" finds herself caught in a tumultuous shooting scene, as youths are preparing to throw stones and drivers honk at her to signal imminent danger. The narration of this chaotic checkpoint scene is itself intensely confused, as though muffled by the narrator's hands covering over her ears to shut out the mayhem. Because of the disorder, the narrator seems to forget all concerns and aspirations save for the desire to cross safely. She actively dissociates from everyone, whether honking drivers or a child asking her to watch him attempt to throw a stone.[93]

Shibli thus displays the checkpoints' aptitude for undermining epistemic certainty and ontological security. Perhaps most paradigmatic are the "flying checkpoints," whose sole purpose is all too often to introduce disorder, to disrupt the normal expectations of everyday life and reestablish the army's

90. Ibid., 93/301, translation modified.

91. Tawil-Souri, "Checkpoint Time," 398.

92. As Tawil-Souri reports, the "consequence of indirect interaction with soldiers is that people increasingly take out their frustrations on each other" (ibid., 405).

93. Shibli, "Dust," 98.

omnipresence.[94] At the time of Shibli's writing, checkpoints entertained no regular structure, no consistent routine, no knowable rules. Each checkpoint was constructed differently and contingently, depending on the terrain and on the random materials and technologies available. Its procedures and layout often changed with each personnel change—a regular occurrence in the military. If the unpredictability of the checkpoint and its ways might have been coincidental effects of a heterogeneous system at first, they are now integral to the structure of Israeli control.[95] Checkpoint procedures remain deeply obscure even after the "civilianization" (*izru'aḥ*)—a 2005 policy shift intended to rebrand checkpoints as demilitarized, systemic, and neutral "border crossings." To improve "customer service," security in some of the so-called terminals was outsourced to private companies. Since a single checkpoint could now be operated simultaneously by the IDF, the Border Police, and private security (although all draw their personnel largely from the same racialized proletariat), authority and its responsibility become diffused and obscured. Meanwhile, greater automation casts the administration of the checkpoint as technical, impartial, and impersonal, yet decisions on whether to allow a person to cross, on whether to search, detain, or humiliate them, still ultimately rest with the security guards and are, too often, arbitrary.[96] The twin processes of privatization and automation, however, make Israeli power representatives increasingly unavailable to Palestinians, thus eliminating opportunities for direct communication, explanations, or appeals and rendering the capricious checkpoint processes even more opaque and frustrating.

The epistemic foreclosure of checkpoint procedures deepens an already growing sense of hostility and self-severance. Indeed, the *inqisām* caused and manifested by the checkpoint seems easy to internalize. As always, Shibli's narrator literalizes this effect. Clarifying that visits to friends, with the burden of dust and hostility, have become "a duty, and in part a defiance of checkpoints,"

94. Based on an interview I conducted, on the condition of anonymity, on March 6, 2008, with a platoon commander who operated checkpoints for two years. IDF soldiers, he explained, are furnished with a flying checkpoint kit, consisting of rudimentary tools for halting movement—two folding spike strips and a mobile stop sign—that they are required to keep in their vehicle at all times, ready to be deployed.

95. "Unpredictability is the new norm," as "control through the creation of calibrated chaos, the changing of rules and procedures with no warning or explanation, is enacted daily at checkpoints"; Julie Peteet, *Space and Mobility in Palestine* (Bloomington: Indiana University Press, 2017), 58.

96. Irus Braverman, "Checkpoint Watch: Bureaucracy and Resistance at the Israeli/Palestinian Border," *Social & Legal Studies* 21, no. 3 (2012): 297–320; Weizman, *Hollow Land*, chap. 5.

she also wonders, "but what else do I defy, if these checkpoints are now set up inside me!"[97] Indeed, expressions of self-loathing abound in "al-Tala'ub." On her return trip, despite her carefully thought-out commitment to riding only older taxis of drivers from Ramallah, and only if they are elderly and cool-headed, she ends up on "a new car with a yellow license plate, carrying the symbol 'IL' [for Israel], and its driver is a [young] gangster. All of this is to declare that I hate myself." And as though this statement were not explicit enough, she soon adds, "Living, it seems, asks nothing more of me than self-destruction."[98] Being regularly forced to act against one's own desires and interests appears as self-destructive, producing psychological fissures and internal walls.

Shibli's "al-Tala'ub" further ties this self-destruction to a sense of collaborating with the enemy. It confidently identifies collaboration as another key cause of Palestinian severance. Shibli's narrator reports refraining from writing during a shuttle taxi ride to avoid raising the other passengers' suspicion that she is gathering intelligence. Later, while walking home through the market, paranoia creeps in. The woman develops the sense that "too many eyes are staring at [her]," that a young man who suddenly stands up, or another who momentarily blocks her path, is going to shoot her, and that the coffee vendor avoids touching her hand when returning her change because they all believe she is a collaborator. On the endless way home, her eyes kept to the ground, she musters all her energy just to "continue walking casually, as if [she] were not a collaborator."[99] So intensely internalizing the fear of collaborators, the fear of *being* a collaborator, Shibli's narrator eventually asserts outright, "I am a collaborator. I hesitate to leave my house. I am filled with horror to the point of suffocating." Secluding herself, she asserts that the only way to terminate her horror would be to self-destruct, to cut off her own head. This self-distrust saps the narrator's life force and generates her hostility toward herself and her neighbors.[100]

The Israeli security apparatus, and specifically Mizrahi middlemen as its executors, often resort, as mentioned, to pressuring Palestinians into collaboration. Knowing from experience that the racialized term "Arabs" designates those who are disposable, they "recruit" Palestinians in blatant disregard for the grave dangers wrought by collaboration. In *Fauda*, the societal results of being suspected of collaboration are perhaps most obvious in Bashar and his

97. Shibli, "Dust," 96.
98. Ibid., 99–100.
99. Ibid., 101–2.
100. Ibid., 102–3.

father's self-destructive quest, in their family's severance from its community, and in the hostile, ever distrustful factionalism of Palestinian combatants. Indeed, as Shibli's narrator's insulating and self-destructive response implies, collaboration and its attendant suspicion are a crucial source of *inqisām* in Palestinian society.

There is, however, no reason to suspect the narrator of collaboration. In fact, she herself identifies the dust on her shoes as a burden that is proof—proof of walking through the checkpoint like everyone else.[101] Why, then, is she so anxious about being suspected? An answer is suggested in the penultimate scene. It is nighttime, and the narrator is stopped by soldiers. One of them inquires why she is carrying a passport instead of an ID card, and she repeatedly answers, "Because I'm free." Then,

> He asks me to step aside. I scream and scream and scream. Just like that. I do nothing but scream. I scream like a mad woman. I scream because I am not a collaborator. The officer comes and hands me my passport as he finds no reason to detain me. But I am still screaming and he asks me politely to leave. And I do not know why he is speaking to me politely. What if someone passed by and saw the officer speaking to me politely, and what if this officer returned and spoke to me politely next time, and what if he memorized my name and called me by it while I am crossing with hundreds of others, to ask me how I was doing that day! What will I say to the passersby! I will scream again, and instead of saying I am a collaborator, they will say I am mad.[102]

If any smooth or nonconfrontational interaction with Israeli powers might be read as a sign of collaboration, then the coveted successful crossing of the checkpoint becomes incriminating. At checkpoints, you're damned if you do and damned if you don't: if your passage is denied, life is irrevocably disrupted; if your passage is uneventful, you might become suspect. More dramatically still, any successful crossing necessarily renders the narrator a collaborator, in a sense, for it entails accepting Israel's authority to set and operate barriers.

Collaboration refers not only to individuals' actions but also to the very relationship between Israel and the PA. Israel's main project since Oslo has been the replacement of its direct policing of the OPT with indirect control, largely by forming a Palestinian National Authority with a limited derivative sovereignty over bantustanized Palestinian territories. Its "security coordination" with the PA, which has intensified since the Split, unburdens Israel of its legal

101. Ibid., 101.
102. Ibid., 103–4.

obligations as an occupying power and effectively outsources most on-the-ground enforcement to Palestinians. Israeli control thus remains behind the scenes, or at the border. Outsourcing security—more accurately dubbed *in*-sourcing, since it recruits the local population rather than outside labor—is a long-honored colonial tradition. British-style "indirect rule" delegates limited power to an elite indigenous class to reorient both culpability and hostility toward it and away from the colonizers.[103] Ruling with no to little trust, such dependent governments rely on violence and thus, in a cyclical manner, further increase mistrust. Checkpoints are, in a sense, a physical expression of the collaboration between Israel and the PA and of the PA's limited authority. By exercising control only from the perimeter, checkpoints maintain the mirage of a functioning Palestinian autonomy within its enclaves, while allowing Israel to retain ultimate control.

Internal severance, *inqisām* in the Palestinian context, might be the most dialectical concept this book proposes. Or, rather, it exhibits a "frozen dialectics."[104] Israeli attempts to maximize distance within Palestinian society have been taken up, since 2007, by Palestinian coalitions openly working, according to Kareem Rabie, "to cultivate that distance and enhance stability to produce common sense around practices of investment, privatization, and state building."[105] At the same time, the Israeli efforts to increase Palestinian fragmentation, the immensity of the checkpoint system, and the brutality of the Gaza blockade all dialectically testify to the growing collective power against which they push. The name of the recent Palestinian uprising, the Unity Intifada (*intifādat al-waḥda*, 2021), even if it emerged amongst limited classes and locales, expresses an aspiration for reconstituting collective cohesion in defiance of fragmentation, checkpoints, and borders. "Al-Tala'ub" manifests this struggle in the narrator's repeated braving of checkpoints for the sake of friendships. Shibli's *Kulluna Ba'id bi-Dhat al-Miqdar 'an al-Ḥubb* more explicitly reflects the dialectics of love and hate, of community and severance: although each and every one of its protagonists is "far from love," isolated and immobile, they all strive for this love and share an "equal" distance from it.

Inqisām is also dialectical because it severs in order to connect and control, because it includes by way of exclusion, and vice versa—an effect that is not necessarily achieved or desired by other apparatuses of separation (e.g., "divide and rule," segregation, separation walls). The miraculous border alchemy

103. Mamdani, *Neither Settler nor Native*, 3.

104. George Ciccariello-Maher, *Decolonizing Dialectics* (Durham, N.C.: Duke University Press, 2017), 28–29.

105. Rabie, *Palestine Is Throwing a Party*, 4.

of *inqisām* is captured by the word itself, whose root also implies acts of conjuring and divination (in Arabic), as well as straight-up magic (in Hebrew). Relating back to the first conflictual concept introduced in Chapter 1, *inqisām* inside-outs juridico-political conflict by constantly producing the separation and egalitarianism that the latter assumes as given and by using state control to evoke the lawless violence it purports to manage.

With Open Eyes

Hatuka's poem "Be'eynayyim Peḳuḥot" (With Open Eyes, 2014) engages Palestinian colonial oppression in relation to Mizrahi marginalization. The poem's epigraph ("If the children of the Jews are disappearing, what will happen to ours?") quotes part of the earlier long quotation from Khoury's *Bab al-Shams*, thus responding to a literary invitation extended by Khoury, who had already critically related the effects of Zionism on Palestinians and on Mizrahi Jews. Through a series of rhetorical questions, Hatuka explores these linked yet divergent effects:

> And if that has been done to our children,
> what is being done to their children,
> and if that has been done to our parents,
> what is being done to their parents,
> and if that has been done to our grandparents,
> what is being done to their grandparents?
>
> And if we calculate our money
> on our walk down to the grocery store,
> and if for us this short walk turns
> into soul-searching,
> into rage,
> then what do their steps turn into?
>
> . . .
>
> Listen up, Moroccan men,
> whose grandfathers, when they were young,
> were shot in their heads with four hundred rad of X-rays
> instead of being speckled over by rays of sun;
> Listen up, Yemenite women,
> whose grandmothers, when they were mothers,
> had their babies snatched from their embrace
> as though removing the sun from the world;
>
> . . .

After the eyelids are unburdened by the stories
and the eyes are cleansed of tears
victims, too,
are witnesses.[106]

Neither equating the two injustices nor subordinating one to the other, Hatuka reverses Khoury's formula to ask: if this is what hegemonic Israel is capable of doing to Mizrahi Jews—who were assimilated, however painfully, into the Jewish collective—then what might it be capable of doing to Palestinians, severed from their land without assimilation? Like Ravikovitch, Hatuka illuminates Palestinian hardships by elaborating on his own personal and familial experiences, without speaking for Palestinians or making epistemic claims about their experiences. In adopting the Rabbinic hermeneutical method of *ḳal va-ḥomer* (lit., lenient and strict)—reasoning a fortiori, "from the stronger case"—his rhetorical questions not only strengthen the link between Mizrahi and Palestinian oppression but also consistently stress that, even if we do not know *exactly* what Palestinian conditions are, we do know that they must be worse.

In the final stanza, after attending to wrongs suffered by *mizraḥim*—the disappeared children affair and the Irradiations Affair[107]—Hatuka insists that "victims, too, / are witnesses." This ambiguous claim could be understood as arguing that the severed children's families are not only victims but also witnesses to the injustice committed against them. But what have they witnessed, exactly? Typically, abductions were perpetrated in their absence. Instead, the poem might be read as calling upon the Mizrahi victims of these two affairs (and, metonymically, of other modes of marginalization and oppression), befogged as they are by their own pain, to serve as witnesses to injustices perpetrated against Palestinians—a reading that is supported by the comparative structure of the poem. While "witnesses" might imply passivity and noninvolvement—which Mizrahi Jews, as executors, simply cannot claim—it might also suggest responsibility, at the very least, for making an injustice seen. Since the severing assimilation of Mizrahi Jews was accomplished at the expense of Palestinians, who are the direct targets of Mizrahi "execution" and of the Zionist project of "Judaizing the territory," *mizraḥim* are undeniably complicit in this violence. Between these two binary interpretations—a Mizrahi responsibility for attaining justice solely for

106. Hatuka, *Mizraḥ Yare'aḥ*, 68–70, my translation.

107. This affair (1948–60) refers to the systemic treatment of tens of thousands (possibly hundreds of thousands) of Mizrahi Jews with ionizing radiation for *tinea capitis*, a minor skin condition that recedes on its own. The irradiation increased the risk of cancerous and noncancerous growths of the head and neck among a sizable portion of those subjected to it.

themselves versus their responsibility for attaining justice for Palestinians as well—lies the choice of *mizraḥim* today.

In a sense, the main conflict in "severance"—and the crux of this chapter—is precisely the tension between agency and structure, between intentional choices and compelled or unconscious actions. For, the question remains: who is it that racializes? The severance apparatuses surveyed here offer valuable lessons on agency. The automated and outsourced checkpoint is emblematic of modes of control that structurally erase traces of agency, thus serving precisely those responsible for its violence. Racism is often thought of in similar terms, as an independently existing structure that individuals merely man or not. Yet, observing the checkpoint from outside clarifies that such real abstractions are operated by people. The Affair demonstrates, conversely, that racializing processes often unfold in the absence of direct orders or institutional guiding hands. Racialization is often shaped rather by a structure formed out of the cumulative acts of individuals, who are, for this very reason, not without agency. This agential structure is also—and especially—true for the executionary positions assumed by *mizraḥim*.

Some might suggest "ethnicization" as a more accurate name for the racialization of *mizraḥim*, who were constructed as "Oriental" but still "Jewish" by eliminating the raciality of their Arabness. As their Arabness is no longer expressed as an immutable racial category—out of which it is impossible to convert, as is the case of Palestinians—it becomes an ethnic one, which is difficult but not impossible to transcend, because it depends, to some degree, on practices and on socioeconomic class. While stressing an important asymmetry between the two groups, this conceptualization maintains, however, the usual cognitive mapping whereby Palestinians are complete victims, fully trapped in the structure, and *mizraḥim* are conscious actors, even if loosely oppressed. Moreover, not only is "Arabness" a racialized category whose meaning—expendable, exploitable bodies—is shared by both, but it was also born only out of this dynamic: it is because it delegated exposure and unorganized labor to others that Ashkenazi society in Israel racialized them and built itself as white and socialist-liberal; it is because *mizraḥim* had to shed "Arabness" that it became definitive of disposability; and it is because Mizrahi Jews could be (de)Arabized that Palestinians could not. What severance severs, and thus conceals, is the co-constitutive nature of the racializing structures that expendabilize, rendering one's children abductable, one's body exploitable in executing violence, and one's—another's?—body even more disposable, subjected to this very same violence.

Postscript

On Societies of Management

In September 2022, the Israeli army piloted a new technology in the West Bank city of Hebron "in preparations for confronting those disturbing the order"—a remotely operated crowd dispersal system, capable of firing tear gas, stun grenades, and sponge-tipped bullets (which, despite their legalization and sugar-coated name, have caused severe injuries over the years). The technology was installed in a highly populated area, with considerable foot traffic, over a checkpoint on Shuhada Street (not far from where Elor Azaria shot Abdel Fattah al-Sharif—an incident discussed in the last two chapters). The developer of this technology, a company named "Smart Shooter," prides itself on creating systems that, based on artificial intelligence and image processing, are capable of monitoring and remotely "hitting" human targets.[1]

Similar technologies have boomed in recent years. Instead of soldiers, Israeli military drones now carry out surveillance operations and fire tear gas and live ammunition; facial recognition cameras are installed in many checkpoints and correspond to a rapidly expanding biopolitical database (as discussed in Chapter 5); platform surveillance is on the rise, as Palestinians' activity on

1. Hagar Shezaf, "Israeli Army Installs Remote-Control Crowd Dispersal System at Hebron Flashpoint," *Haaretz*, September 24, 2022, https://www.haaretz.com/israel-news/2022-09-24/ty-article/.premium/israeli-army-installs-remote-control-crowd-dispersal-system-at-hebron-flashpoint/00000183-70c4-d4b1-a197-ffcfb24f0000.

social media is monitored by algorithmic systems.[2] Indeed, such technologies reflect the use of Palestine and Palestinians as row data and an experimentation lab for Israeli warfare and security technologies, whose "tried and tested" status drives up profits (a form of extraction considered in Chapter 3).

While it is often the hi-tech and novel nature of such technologies that draws attention, my interest lies elsewhere. These technologies—as well as more mundane others—are also deployed to cover over, to make invisible and disavow, "the conflict" in its normative sense. They do so either by "preempting" and "defusing" Palestinian violence before it ever materializes—obviating the question of *whether* it would have ever materialized—or by veiling Israeli violence, and especially those who execute it, behind automated, detached, and "neutral" technologies of control. Or rather, of management. Indeed, this is the stuff of what Israeli politicians and generals call "conflict management": it not only minimizes the human, economic, and political costs of Israeli colonization, thus allowing it to continue unchanged, but also hides it behind the benevolent- and impartial-looking facade of bureaucracy, surveillance, automation, algorithmic calculations, and expert decision making.[3]

Although it might appear new, a post-Oslo phenomenon, the Israeli use of management or administration (both termed *nihul* in Hebrew) as a means of control has a long history. Since 1967, administrative orders (*tsavim minhaliyim*)—despotic ad hoc acts of legislation issued by Israeli General Commanders in the OPT—have effectively created a separate, convoluted, ever-changing legal code for Palestinians in those territories. Also since 1967, administrative detentions (*ma'atsarim minhaliyim*) serve to incarcerate thousands of Palestinians routinely and invisibly for indefinite periods of time, without trial or charge, as all evidence is classified. The Civic Administration (*ha-minhal ha-ezraḥi*), established in 1981 under the command of the Ministry of Defense and later of the army, controls every aspect of Palestinian lives in the OPT not directly associated with security (in Gaza, its operation ended in 2005). The Civic Administration and administrative orders have colluded to facilitate, for instance, the 1980s Israeli land grab project, during which vast tracts of Palestinian land were expropriated as "state lands" by legal means, which concealed the violence of dispossession.

2. I elaborate on Israeli platform policing systems in "Resistance into Incitement: Translation, Legislation, 'Early Detection' and the Palestinian Poet's Intention," *Arab Studies Journal* 27, no. 1 (2019): 118–54.

3. See, for instance, Yael Berda, *Living Emergency: Israel's Permit Regime in the Occupied West Bank* (Stanford, Calif.: Stanford University Press, 2017); Eyal Weizman, *The Least of All Possible Evils: Humanitarian Violence from Arendt to Gaza* (London and New York: Verso, 2011).

Such concealment or disavowal of "conflict," a key effect of *nihul*, appears to be in tension with my opening argument, which suggested that Zionist discourse not only assumes but also promotes a perception of the Palestinian-Israeli context as a juridico-political conflict—that is, as a zero-sum legal dispute between two symmetrical parties over land, which should be juridically decided or else risk the eruption of lawless pre-political violence. (Recall the announcement of the Israeli Foreign Affair Ministry from the Introduction: "the PA and Palestinian terror groups are presenting a real-estate dispute between private parties, as a nationalistic cause, in order to incite violence in Jerusalem.")

How to reconcile this tension? Some of the figurative concepts presented in this book offer possible explanations. Through the lens of *ikhtifā'*, for instance, it becomes evident that, in eliminating, segregating, exploiting, and racializing Palestinians, Israeli colonialism has always aimed to erase this erasure itself—to negate its own violent negation, to deny the denial.[4] In this sense, the normative concept of conflict is itself a veil for Israeli colonial violence. The various "managing" techniques mentioned earlier are geared toward the same end. By taking the perspectives of *ishtibāk* and *inqisām* we might see, moreover, that the distance introduced by management—especially when it is technology-based—severs communication and bars that clashing engagement between the neck and the sword, whose other-than-political, noncommunicative communication depends on the intimate proximity between body and blade.

The explanation, however, could be much simpler. At its core, *nihul*—administration, management—is an approach still based in, and fully compatible with, the *medina/madīna* concept of conflict (explained in Chapter 1). Israeli officials mask their violence behind impartial policing precisely because they regard conflict as judgment and thus, among other things, as symmetrical and as yoked to a forever deferred future solution. Indeed, the very opposition between unlawful violence and law enforcement, whose violence is made invisible by its legality, is integral to the normative perception of conflict. And however much Israeli administration strives to hide it, juridico-political conflict is patently still its telos and motor. *Nihul* operates in the

4. Saree Makdisi's *Tolerance Is a Wasteland: Palestine and the Culture of Denial* (Oakland: University of California Press, 2022) makes—and centers—a similar argument. For instance: "Palestinian presence in and claim to Palestine (as well as Zionism's role in violently attempting to negate that claim) are . . . occluded in such a way that that act of denial is itself denied by being expressed not in negative terms but through the positive affirmation of various wonderful virtues" (2).

name of that conflict, for what it claims to administer is nothing other than what Michel Foucault once termed "race wars"—zero-sum conflicts between identity groups, formed of the eternal war rumbling underneath politics. The biopolitical state then conducts its conflict through population management, consigning enemy races to a "letting die" in order to safeguard the survival and prosperity of the one race that matters.

"Conflict management"—like Foucault's notion of biopolitics or governmentality or Gilles Deleuze's society of control—is thus not at all opposed to juridico-political conflict; it is, instead, its sinister modulation. Under the garb of norming and automation, expert knowledge and computerized calculations, it still "manages"—or, rather, inflicts—violence, whose necessity is derived precisely from the assumption of political conflict. Indeed, its technocrats and officials constantly exercise sovereign judgment, for someone must always interpret algorithmic data, just as someone must decide when, how, and to what extent to operate those remote technologies. (What this framework does expose, however, is the fact that Israeli institutions "manage" *all* the populations between the river and the sea, at least to some extent.)

Nihul thus still functions within the juridico-political framework of conflict, while obfuscating this very fact and obscuring the role of the judge. It seemingly abdicates sovereign judgment to individual experts or to technology, dethroning the philosopher judge, with its internal tribunal, deliberative search for truth, and power of decision. Yet it is still this sovereign judgment that keeps operating from behind or under the seat of power. As "conflict management" conceals violence and judgment, what it truly manages right out of sight is interiority, of either subjected others—reduced to data, statistical threats, and geographic interruptions—or the authorities that operate it. It is thus judgment without the judge; judgment without the dialogue that subtends it. By circumventing interiority and seemingly eliminating decision-making, it facilitates the continuation of colonization while eliminating both culpability and engagement. This is indeed a whole other problem, which I hope to take up elsewhere.

The 2023 judicial coup or overhaul, still ongoing as this book is nearing completion, demonstrates both the operation of *nihul* and its limits. While it is conducted in the name of the populace and presents itself as a democratic and authentic reform, most of its proposed policies and bills were in fact written by experts in a think tank funded by anonymous Americans donors with a neoliberal, messianic agenda—the Kohelet Forum. In contradiction to this surreptitious *nihul*, however, some right-wing politicians involved in the coup explicitly call for putting an end to both "conflict management" and the "two sides" modus operandi, by unapologetically establishing Jewish superiority. For instance, openly expressing his distaste for both *nihul* and political solutions, the Israeli finance minister Bezalel Smotrich has devised a "plan of determination"—in Hebrew, *hakhra'a*, both "decision" and "subjugation." This plan proposes a future in which Israel takes over mandatory Palestine in its entirety, where Jews "win" and they alone have national rights in the land. Palestinians will be faced with three options: subjugation (i.e., forgoing national claims and living without citizenship rights in autonomous bantustans), emigration (i.e., transfer), and fight (i.e., being subdued by unchecked military power). While this is presented as a future plan—and a decisive one at that, departing from "conflict management"—this apartheid-style one state is already our present, at least to an extent, for Palestinians in the OPT are currently living the "option" of subjugation. Although purportedly offered to Palestinians, the other two "options" are in fact prospects that Smotrich desires for himself. As far as his political milieu is concerned, the situation should continue as is, only with the added powers to settle the OPT, expel Palestinians, and use indiscriminate military might—all without judicial oversight, or *nihul*. Exhibiting the contradictory form of *levaṭim* (examined in Chapter 2), the contradiction between *nihul* and *hakhra'a* might prove to be productive.

Ours is a time when conflict is played both up and down. On the one hand, conflict as judgment—the opposition between politics as war and pre-political multitudinal violence—appears amplified at the moment. In Palestine-Israel, news outlets report on increasing sectarianism and communal fragmentation, while repeated failed Israeli elections and the mass protests against the judicial coup attest to sharp social divides (taking place over the heads of Palestinians and to their exclusion). Globally, class disparities are at an all-time high as twentieth-century-style war was dusted off and brought back by Russia and the Trump era intensified the impression of a U.S. partisan culture war. On the other hand, especially in the Atlantic world, conflict is often camouflaged by *nihul* as lives are technocratically administered by experts, special advisors, and governmental offices that aim to conceal decision making, as well as societal fault lines at home and colonial wars abroad. Even in our personal lives, we might be subjected, depending on location, to the liberal command to avoid conflict at all costs. (When I first moved to the United States, I experienced the liberal aversion to conflict as quite a culture shock). The disavowal of juridico-political conflict, however, does not preclude its operation; it merely makes it more difficult to detect and critique. It is still the paradigm that perpetuates an ongoing race war, in the metaphoric and literal sense; that yokes our lives to the exclusive property relation of "possessive individualism"; and that sustains an imperial economic and environmental war against the world's poor, racialized, or (post)colonized.

More than anything, perhaps, the burdens of climate change, becoming clearer and heavier with each passing day, are borne unequally along racial, imperial, and (post/neo)colonial lines, increasingly dividing those with grounds to inhibit from those without. This disaster is currently perceived and "managed" as a juridico-political conflict—within the framework of rights, whose administration evades historical and present liability and whose solutions are juridical and nation-based (as even international rights or coordination presuppose the national). At the risk of speculation, however, I find it quite plausible that the sheer magnitude of both disaster and displacement might soon destabilize the juridico-political framework, forcing a dramatic transformation of the fundamental coordinates of sociality, communication, and subsistence. Indeed, when seeking instances that trouble the juridico-political ontology of Palestine-Israel I often think of environmental phenomena: the sewage water of Gaza—untreated as a result of Israeli restrictions on building materials and electric power—that pollutes the sea that flows straight to Israel's southern shores; or the sinkholes that gape open because of Israeli over-extraction of West Bank resources. These, it appears, cannot be managed nor subjugated nor resolved.

On Political Terms

This book has offered a set of figures conceptualizing the workings of conflictual mechanisms in Palestine-Israel. As the previous discussion suggests, however, there are other, more established prisms through which to consider this context. Why not simply utilize the political concepts already in circulation—occupation, colonization, settler colonialism, apartheid, genocide, biopolitics, siege? These largely juridical terms are all powerful analytics, especially when pushed to intersect with one another, and I, too, employed them throughout this study. Indeed, scholars have put these comparativist terms to great use, shedding light on current and historical facets of Palestine-Israel and, specifically, on Israeli methods of violence and dispossession. This focus on Israeli actions already hints at one of the main reasons for my hesitation to subordinate the conversation to these terms. But there are other reasons, too.

In the year 2020, the renowned academic Achille Mbembe was vehemently attacked in Germany for comparing Israeli practices in Palestine to "the reviled model of apartheid." Yet, looking at Mbembe's texts—especially, his essay "The Society of Enmity," which was at the heart of this controversy—one finds that whenever he uses the term "apartheid" in the context of Palestine-Israel Mbembe is quick to clarify that "the metaphor of apartheid does not fully account for the specific character of the Israeli separation project." This is not because this project is somehow more humane but rather, according to Mbembe, because of Zionism's theological qualities, its hi-tech infrastructure, its lesser dependence on indigenous labor, and its ability to transform itself into "an instrument of strangulation."[5] Elsewhere, too—in his famous "Necropolitics" and in a preface to an essay collection titled *Apartheid Israel: The Politics of an Analogy*—whenever Mbembe refers to the Palestinian condition as apartheid, he describes it also as an extractive laboratory, as genocide, as siege, and even as somehow similar to Jim Crow and to slavery as a form of death-in-life.[6] Why does Mbembe resort to an entire catalogue of theoretical frames when talking about this case? Calling attention to the shortcomings of his comparison, which does not quite capture the situation, Mbembe faces up to this failure by citing additional theoretical models in an ever-expanding list.

I find Mbembe's phrasing useful for three reasons that also underlie my decentering of existing paradigms. First, he uses apartheid explicitly as a metaphor, rather than an analogy, rendering the comparison intentionally imperfect, so that neither case covers over the other and future connections to other cases remain possible. While pointing out fundamental differences, Mbembe nonetheless forms a comparative metaphor, thus undermining Israel's claim for exceptionalism, associating the Palestinian case with other indigenous struggles around the globe, increasing legibility, and inviting solidarity. To allow the specificities of the Palestinian-Israeli case to shine through instead of being subordinated to analogical terms, I similarly utilize metaphors, keeping these open to future reuses and imperfect comparisons, which might in turn boost the legibility of and solidarity with other, future contexts.

Second, the issue with the available models, in Mbembe's diagnosis, is that none of them fits perfectly nor exhausts all the key aspects of coloniality in Palestine. Certainly, no comparison ever fully captures its "target" case in all its nuances. In the context of Palestine-Israel, however, this inherent problem is entwined with yet another: each of the existing concepts is often helpful in representing the conditions of only one segment of the Palestinian population—Palestinians in the West Bank, or in Gaza, or in the diaspora, or in refugee camps, or within 1948 Israel. These concepts thus tend to split Palestinian society along the same "divide and conquer" lines that were colonially drawn in 1948, 1967, or 1993. They even reinforce and reinscribe those lines.

5. Achille Mbembe, "The Society of Enmity," *Radical Philosophy*, no. 200 (2016): 23–24.

6. Achille Mbembe, "Foreword: On Palestine," in *Apartheid Israel: The Politics of an Analogy*, ed. Sean Jacobs and Jon Soske (Chicago: Haymarket, 2015), vii–viii; Achille Mbembe, "Necropolitics," trans. Libby Meintjes, *Public Culture* 15, no. 1 (2003): 11–40.

Third, these concepts are limited not only because they fail to comprehensively address all the various aspects of Zionist colonization but also because, in their focus on Israeli actions, they tend to neglect Palestinian anti-colonialism and, simply put, Palestinian lives. Mbembe's recourse to amassing several (mostly imported) conceptual frameworks demonstrates that—despite the vast, brilliant, and meticulous sociological, economic, historical, and political studies of Palestine and Palestinians—more work is necessary for comprehending the colonial conditions, anti-colonial struggles, aesthetic contributions, and everyday phenomenologies of Palestine *under their own proper names*. I was curious to see what new prisms might emerge once established concepts do not take precedence, once attention is reoriented instead toward this context and its literatures. I was especially curious to see whether, by focusing on the literary archive, concepts might arise that do not simply criticize the current political order but might also push against its axioms or shift the focus elsewhere entirely. The success or failure of this endeavor is up to the reader to judge. Or evaluate.

For these reasons, the book centered on conceptual figures suggested by literary works, insisting on gathering conflictual concepts local not only to the Palestinian-Israeli context but specifically to its poetics. Occasionally, this study also referred to those other paradigms—especially the broadest one, colonialism—in order to harness their analytical force and to maintain their comparative edge. As long as differences and inadequacies are marked, as Mbembe does by inventorying, such comparative procedures might enable concepts, including the ones proposed here, to resonate with other contexts, people, and cultures. I hope that the reader finds ways to make use of them.

Acknowledgments

Academic acknowledgments often invoke an image of a robust, close-knit intellectual community. I am hesitant to create such an illusion. Much of this book has in fact been written in isolation, which was only partly caused by a global pandemic. It was also the result of an arbitrary and shrinking academic job market. Due to this arbitrariness, I was lucky to land an academic position that afforded me the institutional support necessary for writing and publishing this book. For the same reason, however, I also lost a cohort of stimulating, supportive, and creative colleagues. And we all lost the contributions of their potential scholarship.

Nevertheless, this book owes its existence to the wisdom, generosity, and support of many teachers, colleagues, and friends. I am forever indebted to the no-longer-anonymous readers of the manuscript, Chana Kronfeld and Nasser Mufti, whose exceptionally perceptive, attentive, and meticulous readings have made this book a thousand times better. Their ability to see what I meant, even when I failed to convey it, was both astounding and encouraging. My deepest gratitude to Fordham University Press, and especially to the acquisitions editor, Tom Lay, for his patient and expert assistance and to Kem Crimmis and Aldene Fredenburg for their skilled help in the production process. Special thanks also to the exquisite word seamster Curtis Brown for copy edits and to my meticulous friend Kahlid Hadeed for his help with proofreading the manuscript.

Phenomenal teachers and mentors have made my academic path feel slightly less wobbly. I am especially thankful to Adi Ophir and Ariella Azoulay, who introduced me to critical theory and conceptual writing and who impressed upon me the importance of locally inflected political thought.

Formative conversations with Elias Khoury at the beginning of the writing process, and with Ella Shohat and Anton Shammas at its end, have benefited this book tremendously. Zvi Ben-Dor Benite, my unofficial mentor, regularly shed light on the often-opaque workings of academia and valiantly read drafts of countless proposals. Bruno Bosteels and Deborah Starr accompanied the early stages of this project with verve and commitment. Special thanks to my doctoral advisor, Neil Saccamano, for his close, careful guidance and for an ongoing conversation that was always kind, insightful, and witty in equal measures.

For an unforgettable year, I am indebted to Cornell's Society for the Humanities and to the Society Fellows. My research was also supported by an Anne Tanenbaum Postdoctoral Fellowship at the Center for Jewish Studies at the University of Toronto, Canada. I am grateful to my students and hosts there—in particular, to Yigal Nizri, Anna Shternshis, and Ato Quayson. A Junior Faculty Manuscript Workshop Grant from the University of California Humanities Research Institute (UCHRI) was instrumental in developing the book's argumentative core. I would like to thank UCHRI and the participants of the workshop—Gil Anidjar, Gil Hochberg, Chana Kronfeld (again!), Jacques Lezra, Jeff Sacks, and Rei Terada. The final stages of writing were supported by a Faculty Seed Grant from the UCI Center for Global Peace and Conflict Studies and by a Publication Support Grant from the UCI Humanities Center. I am extremely grateful to both.

The book has been informed by conversations held at various venues, where participants' comments and questions have challenged me to refine thoughts and arguments. I am indebted to the participants and to the organizers—especially to Ziad Dallal for a MESA panel on Arabic poetry; to Veli Yashin for a priceless conference at UC Riverside; to Ella Elbaz-Nir and Ahmad Diab for their ACLA panel on conflict in Israel-Palestine; to Reʿee Hagay and Deborah Starr for a workshop on Mizrahi culture at Cornell University; to David Theo Goldberg for a workshop on civil war; and to the Frankel Institute Fellows, whom I met just as work on this manuscript was wrapping up and who proved to be the most collegial, most inspiring interlocutors. Finally, I am grateful to extraordinary journal editors and special issue conveners—Michael Allan, Elisabeth Anker, Almog Behar, Yuval Evry, and Sherine Seikaly—whose input and kindness have truly benefitted my work.

At the University of California, Irvine, I was fortunate to find a warm and welcoming home in the Department of Comparative Literature and in adjacent programs. For conversations, insights, meals, and moral support, I thank

Yousuf al-Bulushi, Eyal Amiran, Houri Berberian, Tamara Beauchamp, Alicia Carroll, Herschel Farbman, Ben Garceau, Simcha Gross, Sherine Hamdy, Adriana Johnson, Zoe Klemfuss, George Lang, Matthias Lehmann, Christophe Litwin, Andrej Luptak, Julia Lupton, Catherine Malabou, Miriam Mora-Quilon, Susan Morrissey, Jane Newman, Nasrin Rahimieh, Gabriele Schwab, Chelsea Shields, John Smith, Tiffany Willoughby-Herard and, again and especially, Rei Terada. I am particularly grateful to the brilliant graduate students in my seminars on conflict, orientalism, and the Palestinian novel—especially, Danah Alfailakawi, Ashley Call, Daniel Carnie, Mehra Gharibian, Lillian Goldberg, Zainab Hussein, Gayatri Mehra, Yassaman Rahimi, Rebecca Sacks, and Henry Ward.

Dear friends and comrades have accompanied this project from its inception. For early conversations on related topics, I thank Adam Aboulafia, Merav Amir, Naama Katiee, Shachar (Freddy) Kislev, Tehila Sasson, and Roy Wagner. This book would not have existed without the friendship of, and heated debates with, Diana Allan, Shir Alon, Danielle Drori, Elik Elhanan, Lorenzo Fabbri, Amit Gilutz, Aaron Hodges, Gal Katz, Roni Masel, Sarah Pickle, Hadass Svirsky, Assaf Tamari, Pioter Shmugliakov, and Tatiana Sverjensky. Many thanks to my various early-days reading groups, especially TRG and the antediluvian Plato-Hegel group; to the members of Cornell's Students for Justice in Palestine, who truly sustained me, in more ways than one (thanks for the pasta, Max and Mario!); and to the feminist colloquium for so collegially thinking out loud about writing. Special thanks to Nasser Abourahme, for the smallest yet most impactful writing group ever and for his indispensable feedback on each and every one of the chapters of this study.

Annie McClanahan and Ted Martin, family of choice and sustainers of the heart and mind, have shown me unmatched generosity throughout the writing process and gave this book its title. I owe them more than words could express, not least because my words could never match their superb style. Oded Erez, Matan Kaminer, Itamar Mann, and Shira Shmuely—first and last readers, forever interlocutors, middle of the night reassurers—have proven that some conversations are measured in decades and yet might still amaze. For this quenching water that is thicker than blood I am forever grateful.

Finally, I would like to thank my family—Moshe, Ronit, Tom, Maayan, and Yuval Mor, as well as Dalia Ayache, Nava Shimoni, Yotam Ben Bassat, and my nieces and nephew—whose warm support and innumerable objections have kept me going. Very special thanks to my partner, James Robertson, for endless drafts read, miles traveled, shit talked, and exquisite cocktails crafted. Quite literally, I could not have done this without him. Rania, my life and soul, was born during the writing process and gave it renewed purpose and zest. Despite the grim subject of this book, I dedicate it to her, with the hope that her generation will no longer have any use of it.

Brief portions of Chapter 3 have appeared as "Humor and the Law of Rights: Voltaire's Cosmopolitan Optimism and Emile Habiby's Dissensual Pessoptimism," in *Comparative Literature* (2019). An early iteration of part of Chapter 4 appeared as "Nihilism and Repetition: Dahlia Ravikovitch's Reiterations as Critique," in *The Politics of Nihilism: From the Nineteenth Century to Contemporary Israel*, edited by Nitzan Lebovic and Roy Ben Shai (Continuum/Bloomsbury, 2014). I thank the publishers, Duke University Press and Bloomsbury Academic, an imprint of Bloomsbury Publishing, for permissions to reprint.

Bibliography

Abdel-Malek, Kamal. *The Rhetoric of Violence: Arab-Jewish Encounters in Contemporary Palestinian Literature and Film.* New York: Palgrave Macmillan, 2005.

Abourahme, Nasser. "'Nothing to Lose but Our Tents': The Camp, the Revolution, the Novel." *Journal of Palestine Studies* 48, no. 1 (2018): 33–52.

——. "The Productive Ambivalences of Post-Revolutionary Time: Discourse, Aesthetics, and the Political Subject of the Palestinian Present." In *Time, Temporality and Violence in International Relations*, edited by Anna M. Agathangelou and Kyle D. Killian, 129–55. London: Routledge, 2016.

——. "Spatial Collisions and Discordant Temporalities: Everyday Life between Camp and Checkpoint." *International Journal of Urban and Regional Research* 35, no. 2 (2011): 453–61.

Abu Remaileh, Refqa. "Narratives in Conflict: Emile Habibi's *al-Waqa'i al-Ghariba* and Elia Suleiman's *Divine Intervention*." In *Narrating Conflict in the Middle East: Discourse, Image and Communications Practices in Lebanon and Palestine*, edited by Dina Matar and Zahera Harb, 85–108. London: I. B. Tauris, 2013.

Abu-Ghazaleh, Adnan Mohammed. *Arab Cultural Nationalism in Palestine during the British Mandate.* Beirut: Institute for Palestine Studies, 1973.

Abulhawa, Susan. *Mornings in Jenin.* New York: Bloomsbury Publishing, 2010.

Abu-Manneh, Bashir. "The Palestinian Novel after the Era of Mass Revolt." *Jacobin* (blog), January 30, 2022. https://jacobin.com/2022/01/israel-palestine-occupation-nakba-literature-universality.

——. *The Palestinian Novel: From 1948 to the Present.* Cambridge and New York: Cambridge University Press, 2016.

Agamben, Giorgio. *Homo Sacer: Sovereign Power and Bare Life.* Translated by Daniel Heller-Roazen. Stanford, Calif.: Stanford University Press, 1998.

——. *Stasis: Civil War as a Political Paradigm.* Stanford, Calif.: Stanford University Press, 2015.

Ahmed, Sara. *The Cultural Politics of Emotion*. 2nd ed. New York: Routledge, 2014.

Alcalay, Ammiel. *After Jews and Arabs: Remaking Levantine Culture*. Minneapolis: University of Minnesota Press, 1992.

Al-Haj, Majid. *Education, Empowerment, and Control: The Case of the Arabs in Israel*. Albany: State University of New York Press, 1995.

Allan, Diana. *Refugees of the Revolution: Experiences of Palestinian Exile*. Stanford, Calif.: Stanford University Press, 2013.

Allan, Michael. "How Adab Became Literary: Formalism, Orientalism and the Institutions of World Literature." *Journal of Arabic Literature* 43, no. 2/3 (2012): 172–96.

Alon, Shir. "No One to See Here: Genres of Neutralization and the Ongoing Nakba." *Arab Studies Journal* 27, no. 1 (2019): 92–119.

Al-Shaikh, Abdul-Rahim. *Qalb Ḥimar: Sharon bayna Majaz al-Maḥkama wa-Maḥkamat al-Majaz*. Ramallah: Palestinian House of Poetry, 2007.

Alter, Robert. "Introduction (to 'Rahamim')." In *Modern Hebrew Literature*, edited by Robert Alter, 253–56. New York: Behrman House, 1975.

Amram Association. "Amram Association: The Yemenite, Eastern and Balkan Children Affair." *Amram Association* (blog). https://www.edut-amram.org/en/.

Anidjar, Gil. *Blood: A Critique of Christianity*. New York: Columbia University Press, 2016.

———. *The Jew, the Arab: A History of the Enemy*. Stanford, Calif.: Stanford University Press, 2003.

———. *Semites: Race, Religion, Literature*. Stanford, Calif.: Stanford University Press, 2007.

Apter, Emily. *Unexceptional Politics: On Obstruction, Impasse, and the Impolitic*. Brooklyn: Verso, 2018.

Arendt, Hannah. *The Human Condition*. Edited by Margaret Canovan. Chicago: University of Chicago Press, 1998.

———. *The Life of the Mind*. Edited by Mary Mccarthy. San Diego: Mariner, 1981.

———. *On Revolution*. Edited by Jonathan Schell. New York: Penguin Classics, 2006.

Aristotle. *On Rhetoric: A Theory of Civic Discourse*. Translated by George A. Kennedy. 2nd ed. New York: Oxford University Press, 2006.

———. *Poetics*. Translated by S. H. Butcher. New York: Hill and Wang, 1961.

Asad, Talal. *Formations of the Secular: Christianity, Islam, Modernity*. Stanford, Calif.: Stanford University Press, 2003.

Ashkenaz. Directed by Rachel Leah Jones. Trabelsi Productions, Israel, 2007.

Asmar, Ahmad, and Marik Shtern. "*Mi-Ba'ad le-Tiḳrat ha-Zekhukhit: Falasṭinim ṿe-Yiśra'elim be-Shuḳ ha-Ta'asuḳa bi-Yrushalayim*." Jerusalem: Mekhon Yerushalayim le-Meḥḳare Mediniyut, 2017.

Ayalon, Ami. *Reading Palestine: Printing and Literacy, 1900–1948*. Austin: University of Texas Press, 2004.

Azem, Ibtisam. *The Book of Disappearance*. Translated by Sinan Antoon. Syracuse, N.Y.: Syracuse University Press, 2019.

——. *Sifr al-Ikhtifa'*. Beirut: al-Jamal, 2014.

Azoulay, Ariella. *From Palestine to Israel: A Photographic Record of Destruction and State Formation, 1947–1950*. Translated by Charles S. Kamen. London: Pluto, 2011.

Azoulay, Ariella, and Adi Ophir. *The One-State Condition: Occupation and Democracy in Israel/Palestine*. Stanford, Calif.: Stanford University Press, 2012.

Bachner, Andrea. *The Mark of Theory: Inscriptive Figures, Poststructuralist Prehistories*. New York: Fordham University Press, 2018.

Balibar, Étienne. "What's in a War? (Politics as War, War as Politics)." *Ratio Juris* 21, no. 3 (2008): 365–86.

Barakat, Rana. "Writing/Righting Palestine Studies: Settler Colonialism, Indigenous Sovereignty and Resisting the Ghost(s) of History." *Settler Colonial Studies* 8, no. 3 (2018): 349–63.

Bargad, Warren. *Ideas in Fiction: The Works of Hayim Hazaz*. Chico, Calif.: Scholars Press, 1982.

——. "Realism and Myth in the Works of Hayim Hazaz: 1933–1943." In *From Agnon to Oz: Studies in Modern Hebrew Literature*, 85–94. Atlanta: Scholars Press, 1996.

Barzel, Hillel, ed. *Ḥayim Hazaz: Mivḥar Ma'amre Biḳoret 'al Yetsirato*. Tel Aviv: 'Am 'Oved, 1978.

Bashir, Bashir, and Amos Goldberg, eds. *The Holocaust and the Nakba: A New Grammar of Trauma and History*. New York: Columbia University Press, 2018.

Bassnett, Susan. *Translation Studies*. London and New York: Routledge, 2002.

Bassnett, Susan, and André Lefevere, eds. *Constructing Cultures: Essays on Literary Translation*. Clevedon: Multilingual Matters, 1998.

Behar, Moshe, and Zvi Ben-Dor Benite, eds. *Modern Middle Eastern Jewish Thought: Writings on Identity, Politics, and Culture, 1893–1958*. Waltham, Mass.: Brandeis University Press, 2013.

Beinart, Peter. *The Crisis of Zionism*. New York: Picador, 2013.

Ben Dayan, Ortal. "Kakh Shoded ha-Ma'arav et ha-'Itsuvim ha-Yelidiyim." *Śiḥa Meḳomit* (blog), July 18, 2016. https://www.mekomit.co.il/-האופנה-וקניין-תרבותי-תעשיית/.

Ben Dor-Benite, Zvi. "Satan and Labor: Proletarianization and the Racialization of the Mizrahim." In *Race and the Question of Palestine*, edited by Ronit Lentin and Lana Tatour. Stanford, Calif.: Stanford University Press. Forthcoming.

Benjamin, Walter. "Critique of Violence." Translated by Edmund Jephcott. In *Walter Benjamin: Selected Writings*, edited by Michael William Jennings and Marcus Paul Bullock, 1:236–52. Cambridge, Mass.: Belknap, 2004.

——. "Karl Kraus." In *Reflections: Essays, Aphorisms, Autobiographical Writings*, translated by Edmund Jephcott, 239–73. New York: Harcourt, Brace and Jovanovich, 1978.

——. "The Task of the Translator." In *Walter Benjamin: Selected Writings*, edited by Michael William Jennings and Marcus Paul Bullock, translated by Harry Zohn, 1:253–64. Cambridge, Mass.: Belknap, 2004.

———. "Theses on the Philosophy of History." In *Illuminations: Essays and Reflections*, edited by Hannah Arendt, translated by Harry Zohn, 253–64. New York: Harcourt, Brace & World, 1968.

———. "Trauerspiel and Tragedy." In *Walter Benjamin: Selected Writings*, edited by Michael William Jennings and Marcus Paul Bullock, translated by Harry Zohn, 1:55–58. Cambridge, Mass.: Belknap, 2004.

Ben-Yehuda, Omri. "The Retribution of Identity: Colonial Politics in *Fauda*." *AJS Review* 44, no. 1 (2020): 1–21.

Berda, Yael. *Living Emergency: Israel's Permit Regime in the Occupied West Bank*. Stanford, Calif.: Stanford University Press, 2017.

Berlant, Lauren. "Slow Death (Sovereignty, Obesity, Lateral Agency)." *Critical Inquiry* 33, no. 4 (2007): 754–80.

Bhandar, Brenna. *Colonial Lives of Property: Law, Land, and Racial Regimes of Ownership*. Durham, N.C.: Duke University Press, 2018.

Bishara, Azmi. *Al-Hajiz: Shazaya Riwaya, al-Kitab al-Awwal: Wajd fi Bilad al-Hawajiz*. Haifa: Metaphora, 2004.

Bloch, Chana, and Chana Kronfeld. "Dahlia Ravikovitch: An Introduction." *Prooftexts* 28, no. 3 (2008): 249–81.

Boyarin, Daniel. "'Pilpul': The Logic of Commentary." *Dor LeDor*, no. 3 (1986): 1–25.

Boyarin, Daniel, Daniel Itzkovitz, and Ann Pellegrini, eds. *Queer Theory and the Jewish Question*. New York: Columbia University Press, 2003.

Braverman, Irus. "Checkpoint Watch: Bureaucracy and Resistance at the Israeli/Palestinian Border." *Social & Legal Studies* 21, no. 3 (2012): 297–320.

Brenner, Rachel Feldhay. *Inextricably Bonded: Israeli Arab and Jewish Writers Re-Visioning Culture*. Madison: University of Wisconsin Press, 2010.

Brown, Wendy. *Walled States, Waning Sovereignty*. New York and Cambridge, Mass.: Zone, 2010.

B'Tselem. *The Occupation's Fig Leaf: Israel's Military Law Enforcement System as a Whitewash Mechanism (Report)*. Jerusalem: B'Tselem, May 2016.

Buck-Morss, Susan. "Aesthetics and Anaesthetics: Walter Benjamin's Artwork Essay Reconsidered." *October* 62 (1992): 3–41.

Busbridge, Rachel. "Israel-Palestine and the Settler Colonial 'Turn': From Interpretation to Decolonization." *Theory, Culture & Society* 35, no. 1 (2018): 91–115.

Butler, Judith. "Precarious Life, Vulnerability, and the Ethics of Cohabitation." *Journal of Speculative Philosophy* 26, no. 2 (2012): 134–51.

Campbell, Ian. "Blindness to Blindness: Trauma, Vision and Political Consciousness in Ghassan Kanafani's 'Returning to Haifa.'" *Journal of Arabic Literature* 32, no. 1 (2001): 53–73.

Campos, Michelle. *Ottoman Brothers: Muslims, Christians, and Jews in Early Twentieth-Century Palestine*. Stanford, Calif.: Stanford University Press, 2010.

Certeau, Michel de. *The Practice of Everyday Life*. Translated by Steven F. Rendall. Berkeley: University of California Press, 1984.

Chronicle of a Disappearance [Arabic: *Sijill Ikhtifa*]. Directed by Elia Suleiman. International Film Circuit, 1996.
Ciccariello-Maher, George. *Decolonizing Dialectics*. Durham, N.C.: Duke University Press, 2017.
Cicero, Marcus Tullius. *Rhetorica ad Herennium*. Edited by Harry Caplan. Loeb Classical Library. Cambridge, Mass.: Harvard University Press, 1954.
Cohen, Hillel. *Śon'im: Sipur Ahava*. Tel Aviv: 'Ivrit, 2022.
Cohen, Stanley, and Daphna Golan. "The Interrogation of Palestinians during the Intifada: Ill-Treatment, 'Moderate Physical Pressure' or Torture?" Jerusalem: B'Tselem, March 1991. https://www.btselem.org/sites/default/files/sites/default/files2/the_interrogations_of_palestinians_during_the_intefada_ill_treatment_moderate_physical_pressure_or_torture_march_1991.pdf.
Cohen, Uri S. *Ha-Nusaḥ ha-Biṭḥoni ve-Tarbut ha-Milḥama ha-'Ivrit*. Jerusalem: Mosad Bialiḳ, 2017.
Colebrook, Claire. *Irony in the Work of Philosophy*. Lincoln: University of Nebraska Press, 2002.
Darwish, Mahmoud. *Fi ḥaḍrat al-Ghiyab*. Beirut: Riyaḍ al-Rayyis li-l-Kutub wa-l-Nashr, 2006.
da Silva, Denise Ferreira. "No-Bodies." *Griffith Law Review* 18, no. 2 (2009): 212–36.
Deleuze, Gilles. "Coldness and Cruelty." In *Masochism*, translated by Jean McNeil, 9–138. New York: Zone, 1991.
——. "How Do We Recognize Structuralism?" In *The Two-Fold Thought of Deleuze and Guattari: Intersections and Animations*, translated by Charles J. Stivale and Melissa McMahon. New York: Guilford, 1998.
——. *Nietzsche and Philosophy*. Translated by Hugh Tomlinson. London and New York: Continuum, 2002.
——. *Proust and Signs*. Translated by Richard Howard. Minneapolis: University of Minnesota Press, 2000.
Deleuze, Gilles, and Félix Guattari. *Kafka: Toward a Minor Literature*. Translated by Dana Polan. Minneapolis: University of Minnesota Press, 1986.
de Man, Paul. "The Concept of Irony." In *Aesthetic Ideology*, edited by Andrzej Warminski, 163–84. Minneapolis: University of Minnesota Press, 1996.
——. "The Epistemology of Metaphor." *Critical Inquiry* 5, no. 1 (Autumn 1978): 13–30.
——. "The Rhetoric of Temporality." In *Blindness and Insight: Essays in the Rhetoric of Contemporary Criticism*, 2nd ed., rev., 7:187–228. Minneapolis: University of Minnesota Press, 1983.
Derrida, Jacques. "Force of Law: The 'Mystical Foundation of Authority.'" In *Deconstruction and the Possibility of Justice*, edited by Drucilla Cornell, David G. Carlson, and Michael Rosenfield, translated by Mary Quaintance, 3–67. Routledge, 1992.
——. "White Mythology: Metaphor in the Text of Philosophy." In *Margins of Philosophy*, translated by Alan Bass, 207–71. Chicago: University of Chicago Press, 1986.

Diamond, Eitan. "Crossing the Line: Violation of the Rights of Palestinians in Israel without a Permit." *B'Tselem* (blog), March 2007. https://www.btselem.org/publications/summaries/200703_crossing_the_line.

Dimitrovsky, Haim Zalman. "'Al Derekh ha-Pilpul." In *Sefer ha-Yovel li-Khvod Shalom Baron*, edited by Shaul Lieberman, Hebrew Section:111–82. Jerusalem: Ha-Aḳademiya ha-America'it le-Mada'e ha-Yahadut, 1975.

Ebileeni, Maurice. *Being There, Being Here: Palestinian Writings in the World*. Syracuse, N.Y.: Syracuse University Press, 2022.

El-Ariss, Tarek. *Trials of Arab Modernity: Literary Affects and the New Political*. New York: Fordham University Press, 2013.

Elbaz-Nir, Ella. "A-Voiding the Void." *Tel Aviv Review of Books* (blog), April 28, 2021. https://www.tarb.co.il/a-voiding-the-void/.

Epstein, Yitzhak, and Alan Dowty. "'A Question That Outweighs All Others': Yitzhak Epstein and Zionist Recognition of the Arab Issue." *Israel Studies* 6, no. 1 (2001): 34–54.

Erez, Oded. "Bass and Silsulim: Israeli Music after Muzika Mizrahit." In *Routledge Handbook on Contemporary Israel*, edited by Guy Ben-Porat, Yariv Feniger, Dani Filc, Paula Kabalo, and Julia Mirsky, 476–88. London and New York: Routledge, 2022.

Erez, Oded, and Arnon Yehuda Degani. "Songs of Subordinate Integration: Music Education and the Palestinian Arab Citizens of Israel during the Mapai Era." *Ethnic and Racial Studies* 44, no. 6 (2021): 1,008–29.

Erez, Oded, and Nadeem Karkabi. "Sounding Arabic: Postvernacular Modes of Performing the Arabic Language in Popular Music by Israeli Jews." *Popular Music* 38, no. 2 (2019): 298–316.

Esmeir, Samera. "1948: Law, History, Memory." *Social Text* 21, no. 2 (2003): 25–48.

———. *Juridical Humanity: A Colonial History*. Stanford, Calif.: Stanford University Press, 2014.

———. "The Time of Engagement, Zaman al-Ishtibak." *Law, Culture and the Humanities* 10, no. 3 (2014): 397–407.

Eyal, Gil. *The Disenchantment of the Orient: Expertise in Arab Affairs and the Israeli State*. Stanford, Calif.: Stanford University Press, 2006.

Eze, Emmanuel Chukwudi. "The Color of Reason: The Idea of 'Race' in Kant's Anthropology." In *Postcolonial African Philosophy: A Critical Reader*, 103–40. Lewisburg, Pa.: Blackwell, 1997.

Farsakh, Leila. *Palestinian Labour Migration to Israel: Labour, Land and Occupation*. Abingdon and New York: Routledge, 2005.

Fauda. Seasons 1–4. Created by Lior Raz and Avi Issacharoff. Ṭender Hafaḳot, Kasṭina Tiḳshoret, 2015–22. Yes TV.

Foucault, Michel. *"Society Must Be Defended": Lectures at the Collège de France, 1975–1976*. Translated by David Macey. New York: Picador, 2003.

———. "Truth and Juridical Forms." Translated by Lawrence Williams and Catherine Merlen. *Social Identities* 2, no. 3 (October 1996): 327–42.

Freud, Sigmund. *Jokes and Their Relation to the Unconscious.* Translated by James Strachey. New York: Norton, 1960.

García, José. "Adania Shibli on Writing Palestine from the Inside." *Literary Hub* (blog), February 6, 2017. https://lithub.com/adania-shibli-on-writing-palestine-from-the-inside/.

Gertz, Nurith, and Raz Yosef. "Trauma, Time, and the 'Singular Plural': The Israeli Television Series *Fauda*." *Israel Studies Review* 32, no. 2 (2017): 1–20.

Ghanem, As'ad. *The Palestinian-Arab Minority in Israel, 1948–2000: A Political Study.* Albany: State University of New York Press, 2001.

Ghanim, Honaida. "'Hekhan Kulam!': Di'alektika shel Mehika u-Veniya ba-Proyekt ha- Kolonyali ha-Tsiyoni." *Zmanim*, no. 138 (2017): 102–15.

Glissant, Édouard. *Poetics of Relation.* Translated by Betsy Wing. Ann Arbor: University of Michigan Press, 1997.

Gluzman, Michael. "ha-Kina ha-'Oletset: 'Al Shene Shirim shel Daliya Ravikovitch 'al Yona Volakh." In *Kitme Or: Hamishim Shenot Bikoret u-Mehkar 'al Yetsirata shel Daliya Ravikovitch*, edited by Hamutal Tsamir and Tamar Hess, 173–82. Bene Berak: ha-Kibutz ha-Me'uhad, 2010.

Gorali, Moshe. "'Od Degel Shahor." *Haaretz*, October 28, 2003. https://www.haaretz.co.il/misc/1.920418.

Govrin, Nurit. "Sipure ha-Mahapekha ke-Sug Sifruti." In *Me'asef: Mukdash li-Yetsirat Hayim Hazaz*, edited by Dov Sadan and Dan Laor, 236–56. Jerusalem: Agudat ha-Sofrim ha-'Ivrim be-Yiśra'el ve-Agudat Shalem, 1978.

Graham-Brown, Sarah. *Palestinians and Their Society, 1880–1946.* London and New York: Quartet, 1980.

Grassiani, Erella. "Between Security and Military Identities: The Case of Israeli Security Experts." *Security Dialogue* 49, no. 1–2 (2018): 83–95.

Grunebaum, G. E. von. "Bayān." In *Encyclopaedia of Islam*, 2nd ed., edited by P. Bearman, Th. Bianquis, C. E. Bosworth, E. van Donzel, and W. P. Heinrichs. Leiden: Brill, 2012. Accessed online: http://dx.doi.org/10.1163/1573-3912_islam_SIM_1298.

Gutwein, Danny. "The Settlements and the Relationship between Privatization and the Occupation." In *Normalizing Occupation: The Politics of Everyday Life in the West Bank Settlements*, edited by Marco Allegra, Ariel Handel, and Erez Maggor, 21–33. Bloomington: Indiana University Press, 2017.

Habiby, Emile. *The Secret Life of Saeed: The Pessoptimist.* Translated by Salma Khadra Jayyusi and Trevor LeGassick. New York: Interlink, 2002.

———. *al-Waqa'i' al-Ghariba fi Ikhtifa' Sa'id abi al-Nahs al-Mutasha'il.* Beirut: Dar Ibn Khaldun, 1974.

Hajjar, Lisa. *Courting Conflict: The Israeli Military Court System in the West Bank and Gaza.* Berkeley: University of California Press, 2005.

Halper, Jeff. "The Palestinians: Warehousing a 'Surplus People.'" *ICAHD* (blog), May 23, 2019. https://icahd.org/2019/05/23/the-palestinians-warehousing-a-surplus-people/.

Hanafi, Sari. "Spacio-Cide and Bio-Politics: The Israeli Colonial Conflict from 1947 to the Wall." In *Against the Wall: Israel's Barrier to Peace*, edited by Michael Sorkin, 251–61. New York: New Press, 2005.

Handel, Ariel. "Where, Where to, and When in the Occupied Territories: An Introduction to Geography of Disaster." In *The Power of Inclusive Exclusion: Anatomy of Israeli Rule in the Occupied Palestinian Territories*, edited by Adi Ophir, Michal Givoni, and Sari Hanafi, 179–222. New York and Cambridge, Mass.: Zone, 2009.

Harlow, Barbara. "Return to Haifa: 'Opening the Borders' in Palestinian Literature." *Social Text*, no. 13/14 (1986): 3–23.

Hartman, Saidiya. *Scenes of Subjection: Terror, Slavery, and Self-Making in Nineteenth-Century America*. New York: Oxford University Press, 1997.

Hashash, Yali. *Bat shel Mi At: Drakhim le-Daber Feminizem Mizraḥi*. Tel Aviv: ha-Ḳibuts ha-Me'uḥad, 2022.

Hashiloni-Dolev, Yael. *A Life (Un)Worthy of Living: Reproductive Genetics in Israel and Germany*. Dordrecht: Springer, 2007.

Haskin, Mimi. "'Yadenu lo Shafkhu et ha-Dam ha-Ze ṿe-'Enenu lo Ra'u': "Egla 'Arufa' shel Daliya Raviḳovitch ṿeha-Te'ologia ha-Poliṭit shel Ḳarl Shmiṭ." In *Kitme Or: Ḥamishim Shenot Biḳoret u-Meḥḳar 'al Yetsirata shel Daliya Raviḳovitch*, edited by Hamutal Tsamir and Tamar Hess, 498–511. Bene Beraḳ: ha-Ḳibutz ha-Me'uḥad, 2010.

Hatuka, Shlomi. *Mizraḥ Yare'aḥ*. Tel Aviv: Tangier, 2015.

———. "The Tragedy of the Lost Yemenite Children: In the Footsteps of the Adoptees." *Ha-'Okets* (blog), January 25, 2014. https://enghaokets.wordpress.com/2014/01/25/the-tragedy-of-the-lost-yemenite-children-in-the-footsteps-of-the-adoptees/.

Hawari, Mahmoud. "The Citadel of Jerusalem: A Case Study in the Cultural Appropriation of Archaeology in Palestine." *Present Pasts* 2 (2010): 89–95.

Hazaz, Aviva, and Haim Hazaz. "'U-Ven 'Av le-Ḥavero Ma'afilim ha-Shamayim, Sheḥore-Sheḥorim.'" *Haaretz*, April 16, 2014. https://www.haaretz.co.il/literature/prose/.premium-1.2295687.

Hazaz, Haim. "ha-Derasha." In *Sipurim Nivḥarim*, 184–202. Tel-Aviv: Devir la-'Am, 1952.

———. "Harat-'Olam." In *Avanim Rotḥot*, 137–52. Tel-Aviv: 'Am 'Oved, 1965.

———. "ha-Tayar ha-Gadol." In *Reḥayim Shevurim: Sipurim*, 223–39. Tel Aviv: 'Am 'Oved, 1941.

———. *Mishpaṭ ha-Ge'ula*. Edited by Aviva Hazaz. Tel Aviv: 'Am 'Oved, 1977.

———. "Rahamim." In *Modern Hebrew Literature*, edited by Robert Alter, translated by I. M. Lask, 257–64. New York: Behrman House, 1975.

———. "Raḥamim." In *Sipurim Nivḥarim*, 158–66. Tel-Aviv: Devir la-'Am, 1970.

———. "Raḥamim ha-Sabal." In *Reḥayim Shevurim: Sipurim*, 215–22. Tel Aviv: 'Am 'Oved, 1941.

———. "The Sermon." In *Modern Hebrew Literature*, edited by Robert Alter, translated by Ben Halpern, 271–87. New York: Behrman House, 1975.

Hegel, G. W. F. *Phenomenology of Spirit*. Translated by A. V. Miller. Rev. ed. Oxford: Oxford University Press, 1976.

Hever, Hannan, ed. *Al Tagidu be-Gat: ha-Nakba ha-Falastinit ba-Shira ha-ʿIvrit, 1948–1958: Asupat Shirim*. Tel Aviv: Zokhrot; Parhesyah; Pardes, 2010.

———. *Producing the Modern Hebrew Canon: Nation Building and Minority Discourse*. New York: NYU Press, 2001.

———. "Sug ha-Omets she-Ḥaser le-Samekh Yizhar." *Haaretz*, April 7, 2020. https://www.haaretz.co.il/literature/study/.premium-1.8748400.

———. "The Crisis of Responsibility in S. Yizhar's 'The Prisoner.'" In *Hebrew Literature and the 1948 War: Essays on Philology and Responsibility*, 78–104. Leiden: Brill, 2019.

Hever, Shir. "Exploitation of Palestinian Labour in Contemporary Zionist Colonialism." *Settler Colonial Studies* 2, no. 1 (2012): 124–32.

———. *The Privatisation of Israeli Security*. London: Pluto, 2017.

Hilal, Jamil. "Imperialism and Settler Colonialism in West Asia: Israel and the Arab Palestinian Struggle." *UTAFITI: Journal of the Arts and Social Sciences* 1, no. 1 (1976): 51–70.

Hirsch, Dafna. "'Hummus Is Best When It Is Fresh and Made by Arabs': The Gourmetization of Hummus in Israel and the Return of the Repressed Arab." *American Ethnologist* 38, no. 4 (2011): 617–30.

Hobbes, Thomas. *Leviathan*. Edited by Richard Tuck. Cambridge and New York: Cambridge University Press, 1996.

Hochberg, Gil Z. *Becoming Palestine: Toward an Archival Imagination of the Future*. Durham, N.C.: Duke University Press, 2021.

———. "From 'Shooting and Crying' to 'Shooting and Singing': Notes on the 2019 Eurovision in Israel." *Contending Modernities* (blog), May 17, 2019. https://contendingmodernities.nd.edu/global-currents/shooting-and-singing/.

———. *In Spite of Partition: Jews, Arabs, and the Limits of Separatist Imagination*. Princeton, N.J.: Princeton University Press, 2010.

———. "'The Mediterranean Option': On the Politics of Regional Affiliation in Current Israeli Cultural Imagination." *Journal of Levantine Studies* 1, no. 1 (Summer 2011): 41–65.

———. "To Be or Not to Be an Israeli Arab: Sayed Kashua and the Prospect of Minority Speech-Acts." *Comparative Literature* 62, no. 1 (2010): 68–88.

———. *Visual Occupations: Violence and Visibility in a Conflict Zone*. Durham, N.C.: Duke University Press, 2015.

Holt, Elizabeth M. "Resistance Literature and Occupied Palestine in Cold War Beirut." *Journal of Palestine Studies* 50, no. 197 (2021): 3–18.

Iḥsan, ʿAbbas, Fadi al-Naqib, and Elias Khoury, eds. *Ghassan Kanafani: Insanan wa-Adiban wa-Munaḍilan*. Beirut: al-Ittiḥad al-ʿAmm li-l-Kuttab wa-l-Ṣuḥufiyyin al-Filasṭiniyyin, 1974.

Illouz, Eva. *Saving the Modern Soul: Therapy, Emotions, and the Culture of Self-Help*. Berkeley: University of California Press, 2008.

Illuz, Alona Miriam. "Lama Mizraḥim Mamshikhim leha-Tsbi'a la-Likud?" *Ha-'Okets*, (blog), February 8, 2019. https://www.haokets.org/2019/02/08/-לליכודלמה-מזרחים -ממשיכים-להצביע/.

Ince, Onur Ulas. *Colonial Capitalism and the Dilemmas of Liberalism*. New York: Oxford University Press, 2018.

Israel Foreign Ministry. "Regrettably, the PA and Palestinian Terror Groups Are Presenting a Real-Estate Dispute between Private Parties, as a Nationalistic Cause." Twitter, May 7, 2021. https://twitter.com/IsraelMFA/status /1390632182398529536.

Israel Ministry of Health. "Fertility Treatments and Surrogacy." Israel Ministry of Health Website. Accessed November 14, 2021. https://www.health.gov.il/English /Topics/fertility/Pages/default.aspx.

Jabra, Jabra Ibrahim. *al-Baḥth 'an Walid Mas'ud*. Beirut: Dar al-Adab, 1978.

Jacobson, Abigail. *From Empire to Empire: Jerusalem between Ottoman and British Rule*. Syracuse, N.Y.: Syracuse University Press, 2011.

Jacobson, Abigail, and Moshe Naor. *Oriental Neighbors: Middle Eastern Jews and Arabs in Mandatory Palestine*. Waltham, Mass.: Brandeis University Press, 2016.

Jamal, Amal. "Conflict Theory, Temporality, and Transformative Temporariness: Lessons from Israel and Palestine." *Constellations* 23, no. 3 (2016): 365–77.

———. "The Struggle for Time and the Power of Temporariness: Jews and Arabs in the Labyrinth of History." In *Men in the Sun*, edited by Tal Ben Zvi and Hanna Farah, E8–23. Herzliya: Herzliya Museum of Contemporary Art, 2009.

Jameson, Fredric. "Antinomies of the Realism-Modernism Debate." *Modern Language Quarterly* 73, no. 3 (2012): 475–85.

Jiryis, Sabri. "Domination by the Law." *Journal of Palestine Studies* 11, no. 1 (1981): 67–92.

Kaminer, Matan. "The Abrahamic Ideology: Patrilineal Kinship and the Politics of Peacemaking in the Contemporary Middle East." *Millennium*, forthcoming.

———. "Li-Śno 'Aravin ze 'Arakhim: Teḥilat ha-Sof shel ha-Ḳolonyalizem ha- Yiśra'eli?" *'Atidot* (blog), July 7, 2014. https://atidot.wordpress.com/2014/07/07/hating -arabs/.

Kanafani, Ghassan. " 'A'id ila Hayfa." In *al-Athar al-Kamila*, 1:337–409. Beirut: Mu'assasat Ghassan Kanafani al-Thaqafiyya: Dar al-Tali'a, 1980.

———. *All That's Left to You: A Novella and Other Stories*. Translated by May Jayyusi and Jeremy Reed. Northampton, Mass.: Interlink, 2005.

———. *'An al-Rijal wa-l-Banadiq*. Beirut: Mu'assasat al-Abḥath al-'Arabiyya, 1968.

———. *Fi al-Adab al-Ṣihyuni*. Beirut: Munaẓẓamat al-Taḥrir al-Filasṭiniyya, Markaz al-Abḥath, 1967.

———. "Ma Tabaqqa Lakum." In *al-Athar al-Kamila*, 1:153–234. Beirut: Mu'assasat Ghassan Kanafani al-Thaqafiyya: Dar al-Tali'a, 1980.

———. "Men in the Sun." In *Men in the Sun, and Other Palestinian Stories*, translated by Hilary Kilpatrick, 21–74. Boulder, Colo.: Lynne Rienner, 1999.

——. "Returning to Haifa." In *Palestine's Children: Returning to Haifa and Other Stories*, translated by Barbara Harlow and Karen E. Riley, 149–96. Arab Authors. Boulder, Colo.: Lynne Rienner, 2000.

——. "Rijal fi al-Shams." In *al-Athar al-Kamila*, 1:29–152. Beirut: Mu'assasat Ghassan Kanafani al-Thaqafiyya: Dar al-Tali'a, 1980.

Kant, Immanuel. *Critique of Judgment*. Translated by Werner S. Pluhar. Indianapolis: Hackett, 1987.

——. *Critique of Pure Reason*. Translated by Werner S. Pluhar. Indianapolis: Hackett, 1996.

Karkabi, Nadeem. "The Impossible Quest of Nasreen Qadri to Claim Colonial Privilege in Israel." *Ethnic and Racial Studies* 44, no. 6 (2021): 966–86.

Kashua, Sayed. *'Aravim Rokdim*. Moshav Ben-Shemen: Modan, 2002.

——. "'Fauda' Creators Think Arabs Are Stupid." *Haaretz*, January 12, 2018. https://www.haaretz.com/opinion/.premium-fauda-creators-think-arabs-are-stupid-1.5730664.

——. *Guf Sheni Yaḥid*. Jerusalem: Keter, 2010.

——. "Hertsel Ne'elam be-Ḥatsot." *Haaretz*, March 10, 2005. https://www.haaretz.co.il/misc/1.1048468.

——. "Why Sayed Kashua Is Leaving Jerusalem and Never Coming Back." *Haaretz*, July 4, 2014. https://www.haaretz.com/.premium-for-sayed-kashua-co-existence-has-failed-1.5254338.

Kassim, Anis F., ed. "The Order to Beat Palestinians: Justice *à la* Israel." *Palestine Yearbook of International Law* 5 (1989): 184–241.

Katiee, Naama. "Why Is the Left Silent on the Kidnapping of Mizrahi Babies?" *+972 Magazine* (blog), June 21, 2015. http://972mag.com/why-is-the-left-silent-on-the-kidnapping-of-mizrahi-children/108028/.

Keshev (Klugman), Shabtai. "Ele sh-En Tiḳva le-Yaldehem.'" *Davar*, March 3, 1950.

Khalidi, Rashid. *Palestinian Identity: The Construction of Modern National Consciousness*. New York: Columbia University Press, 2009.

Khazzoom, Aziza. "The Great Chain of Orientalism: Jewish Identity, Stigma Management, and Ethnic Exclusion in Israel." *American Sociological Review* 68, no. 4 (2003): 481–510.

Khoury, Elias. *Bab al-Shams*. Beirut: Dar al-Adab, 2017.

——. *Gate of the Sun*. Translated by Humphrey Davies. New York: Picador, 2006.

——. "Rethinking the Nakba." *Critical Inquiry* 38, no. 2 (2012): 250–66.

——. "The Mirror: Imagining Justice in Palestine." *Boston Review*, July 1, 2008.

Kierkegaard, Søren. *The Concept of Irony / Schelling Lecture Notes: Kierkegaard's Writings*. Vol. 2. Translated by Howard V. Hong and Edna H. Hong. Repr. ed. Princeton, N.J.: Princeton University Press, 1992.

Kilpatrick, Hilary. "Tradition and Innovation in the Fiction of Ghassān Kanafānī." *Journal of Arabic Literature* 7 (1976): 53–64.

Klein, Ernest. A *Comprehensive Etymological Dictionary of the Hebrew Language for Readers of English*. Jerusalem: Carta, 1987.

Klein, Menachem. "Arab Jew in Palestine." *Israel Studies* 19, no. 3 (2014): 134–53.

Klein, Naomi. "Gaza: Not Just a Prison, a Laboratory." *Nation*, June 15, 2007. https://www.commondreams.org/views/2007/06/15/gaza-not-just-prison-laboratory.

Kotef, Hagar. *The Colonizing Self: Or, Home and Homelessness in Israel/Palestine.* Durham, N.C.: Duke University Press, 2020.

——. *Movement and the Ordering of Freedom: On Liberal Governances of Modernity.* Durham, N.C.: Duke University Press, 2015.

Kotef, Hagar, and Merav Amir. "Between Imaginary Lines: Violence and Its Justifications at the Military Checkpoints in Occupied Palestine." *Theory, Culture and Society* 28, no. 1 (2011): 55–80.

Kronfeld, Chana. *The Full Severity of Compassion: The Poetry of Yehuda Amichai.* Stanford, Calif.: Stanford University Press, 2015.

——. "Shira Poliṭit ke-Omanut Lashon be-Yetsirata shel Daliya Ravikovitch." In *Kitme Or: Ḥamishim Shenot Biḳoret u-Meḥḳar ʿal Yetsirata shel Daliya Raviḳovitch*, edited by Hamutal Tsamir and Tamar Hess, 514–43. Bene Beraḳ: ha-Ḳibutz ha-Meʾuḥad, 2010.

Lamb, Jonathan. *The Rhetoric of Suffering: Reading the Book of Job in the Eighteenth Century.* Oxford: Clarendon; New York: Oxford University Press, 1995.

Lane, Stanley. *Arabic-English Lexicon.* New York: F. Ungar, 1874.

Laor, Dan, ed. *Ḥayim Hazaz, ha-Ish ṿi-Yetsirato: Devarim she-Neʾemru bi-Melot ʿEśer Shanim li-Feṭirato.* Jerusalem: Mosad Bialiḳ, 1984.

——. "me-'ha-Derasha' le-'Ketav el ha-Noʿar ha-ʿIvri': Heʿarot le-Muśag 'Shelilat ha-Gola.'" In *ha-Maʾavaḳ ʿal ha-Zikaron: Masot ʿal Sifrut, Ḥevra ṿe-Tarbut*, 233–49. Tel Aviv: ʿAm ʿOved, 2009.

Lavie, Aviv, and Moshe Gorali. "'I Saw Fit to Remove Her from the World.'" *Haaretz*, October 29, 2003. https://www.haaretz.com/1.4746524.

Lebovic, Nitzan. *Zionism and Melancholy: The Short Life of Israel Zarchi.* Bloomington: Indiana University Press, 2019.

Lentin, Ronit. *Traces of Racial Exception: Racializing Israeli Settler Colonialism.* London and New York: Bloomsbury Academic, 2018.

Leshem, Noam. *Life after Ruin: The Struggles over Israel's Depopulated Arab Spaces.* Cambridge and New York: Cambridge University Press, 2016.

LeVine, Mark. *Overthrowing Geography: Jaffa, Tel Aviv, and the Struggle for Palestine, 1880–1948.* Berkeley: University of California Press, 2005.

Levush, Ruth. *Israel: Reproduction and Abortion: Law and Policy.* Washington D.C.: Law Library of Congress, Global Legal Research Center, 2012.

Levy, Lital. *Poetic Trespass: Writing between Hebrew and Arabic in Israel/Palestine.* Princeton, N.J.: Princeton University Press, 2014.

——. "'You Just Can't Compare': Holocaust Comparisons and Discourses of Israel-Palestine." In *Israel-Palestine: Lands and Peoples*, edited by Omer Bartov, 58–77. New York: Berghahn, 2021.

Levy, Lital, and Allison Schachter. "Jewish Literature / World Literature: Between the Local and the Transnational." *PMLA* 130, no. 1 (2015): 92–109.

Lewin-Epstein, Noah, and Yinon Cohen. "Ethnic Origin and Identity in the Jewish Population of Israel." *Journal of Ethnic and Migration Studies* 45, no. 11 (2019): 2,118–37.

Li, Darryl. "The Gaza Strip as Laboratory: Notes in the Wake of Disengagement." *Journal of Palestine Studies* 35, no. 2 (2006): 38–55.

Locke, John. *An Essay Concerning Human Understanding*. Edited by Peter H. Nidditch. Oxford and New York: Oxford University Press, 1979.

———. *Two Treatises of Government*. Edited by Peter Laslett. Cambridge: Cambridge University Press, 2003.

Lockman, Zachary. *Comrades and Enemies: Arab and Jewish Workers in Palestine, 1906–1948*. Berkeley: University of California Press, 1996.

Longinus. *On Sublimity*. Translated by D. A. Russell. Oxford: Clarendon, 1965.

Lyotard, Jean-François. *The Differend*. Translated by Georges Van Den Abbeele. Minneapolis: University of Minnesota, 1989.

———. *Enthusiasm: The Kantian Critique of History*. Translated by Georges Van Den Abbeele. Stanford, Calif.: Stanford University Press, 2009.

———. "The Sign of History." In *The Lyotard Reader*, edited by Andrew Benjamin, 393–411. Oxford and Cambridge, Mass.: Wiley-Blackwell, 1991.

MacDonald, D. B., and E. E. Calverley. "Ḥaḳḳ." In *Encyclopaedia of Islam*, 2nd ed., edited by P. Bearman, Th. Bianquis, C. E. Bosworth, E. van Donzel, and W. P. Heinrichs. Leiden: Brill, 2012. Accessed online: http://dx.doi.org/10.1163/1573-3912_islam_SIM_2639.

Madmoni-Gerber, Shoshana. *Israeli Media and the Framing of Internal Conflict: The Yemenite Babies Affair*. New York: Palgrave Macmillan, 2009.

Mahamid, Hatim. "History Education for Arab Palestinian Schools in Israel." *Journal of Education and Development* 1, no. 1 (2017): 37–47.

Maharmeh, Ihab. "Israel's Violations of Palestinian Workers' Rights: COVID-19 and Systemic Abuse." *Al-Shabaka* (blog). July 15, 2021. https://al-shabaka.org/briefs/israels-violations-of-palestinian-workers-rights-covid-19-and-systemic-abuse/.

Makdisi, Saree. *Tolerance Is a Wasteland: Palestine and the Culture of Denial*. Oakland: University of California Press, 2022.

Mamdani, Mahmood. *Neither Settler nor Native: The Making and Unmaking of Permanent Minorities*. Cambridge, Mass.: Belknap, 2020.

Mann, Helen. "An Interview with Lior Raz: 'Fauda' Co-Creator and Star, Lior Raz, Brings the Israeli-Palestinian Conflict to Netflix." *CBC*, January 4, 2017. https://www.cbc.ca/radio/asithappens/as-it-happens-wednesday-edition-1.3920983/fauda-co-creator-and-star-lior-raz-brings-the-israeli-palestinian-conflict-to-netflix-1.3920988.

Mann, Itamar. "What Is a 'Manifestly Illegal' Order? Law and Politics after Yoram Kaniuk's *Nevelot*." In *The Politics of Nihilism: From the Nineteenth Century to Contemporary Israel*, edited by Roy Ben-Shai and Nitzan Lebovic, 177–204. New York: Bloomsbury, 2014.

Mansour, Atallah. *Be-Or Ḥadash.* Tel Aviv: Ḳarni, 1966.

Maoz, Eilat. *Ḥoḳ Ḥay: Shiṭur ve-Ribonut taḥat Kibush.* Bene Beraḳ: ha-Ḳibuts ha-Me'uḥad, Van Leer, 2020.

Masalha, Nur. *Expulsion of the Palestinians: The Concept of "Transfer" in Zionist Political Thought, 1882–1948.* Washington, D.C.: Institute for Palestine Studies, 1992.

———. "On Recent Hebrew and Israeli Sources for the Palestinian Exodus, 1947–49." *Journal of Palestine Studies* 18, no. 1 (1988): 121–37.

Masoud, Ahmed. *Vanished: The Mysterious Disappearance of Mustafa Ouda.* Cyprus: Rimal, 2015.

Massad, Joseph. "Zionism's Internal Others: Israel and the Oriental Jews." *Journal of Palestine Studies* 25, no. 4 (1996): 53–68.

Mbembe, Achille. "Foreword: On Palestine." In *Apartheid Israel: The Politics of an Analogy*, edited by Sean Jacobs and Jon Soske, vii–viii. Chicago: Haymarket, 2015.

———. "Necropolitics." Translated by Libby Meintjes. *Public Culture* 15, no. 1 (2003): 11–40.

———. "The Society of Enmity." *Radical Philosophy*, no. 200 (2016): 23–35.

Mendel, Yonatan. "Forced To . . ." *LRB* (blog), July 25, 2014. https://www.lrb.co.uk/blog/2014/july/forced-to.

———. "Re-Arabizing the De-Arabized: The Mista'aravim Unit of the Palmach." In *Debating Orientalism*, edited by Ziad Elmarsafy, Anna Bernard, and David Attwell, 94–116. London: Palgrave Macmillan, 2013.

Miron, Dan. *ha-Sifriyya ha-'Iyeret: Proza Me'orevet.* Tel Aviv: Yedi'ot Aḥaronot and Ḥemed, 2005.

———. *Ḥayim Hazaz: Asupat Masot.* Merhavia: Sifriyat Po'alim, 1959.

Mor, Liron. "At Af Pa'am lo Ḥozeret, at Holekhet: Re'ayon 'im Elias Khoury," *Erets ha-Emori* (blog), July 25, 2013. https://haemori.wordpress.com/2013/07/25/khoury/.

———. "Humor and the Law of Rights: Voltaire's Cosmopolitan Optimism and Emile Habiby's Dissensual Pessoptimism." *Comparative Literature* 71, no. 2 (2019): 171–93.

———. "Resistance into Incitement: Translation, Legislation, 'Early Detection' and the Palestinian Poet's Intention." *Arab Studies Journal* 27, no. 1 (2019): 118–54.

———. "Zionist Speculation: Colonial Vision and Its Sublime Turn." *Theory & Event* 26, no. 1 (2023): 154–85.

Morag, Raya. *Waltzing with Bashir: Perpetrator Trauma and Cinema.* London and New York: I. B. Tauris, 2013.

Morefield, Jeanne. *Empires without Imperialism: Anglo-American Decline and the Politics of Deflection.* Oxford: Oxford University Press, 2014.

Mouffe, Chantal. *Agonistics: Thinking the World Politically.* London and New York: Verso, 2013.

———. "Deliberative Democracy or Agonistic Pluralism?" *Social Research* 66, no. 3 (1999): 745–58.

Mufti, Nasser. *Civilizing War: Imperial Politics and the Poetics of National Rupture.* Evanston, Ill.: Northwestern University Press, 2017.

Nafar, Tamer, and Yossi Zabari. "Ana Mish Poliṭi." *YouTube* (blog), September 22, 2016. https://www.youtube.com/watch?v=aIYbJ2NYaQI.

Nasrallah, Ibrahim. *Barari al-Ḥumma.* Amman and Beirut: Mu'assasat al-Abḥath al-'Arabiyya, 1985.

Nassar, Maha. *Brothers Apart: Palestinian Citizens of Israel and the Arab World.* Stanford, Calif.: Stanford University Press, 2017.

Nietzsche, Friedrich Wilhelm. "On Truth and Lies in a Nonmoral Sense." In *Philosophy and Truth: Selections from Nietzsche's Notebooks of the Early 1870s,* translated by Daniel Breazeale, 79–91. Atlantic Highlands, N.J.: Humanities, 1999.

Nizri, Yigal Shalom. "Die Stimme Jaakobs Stimme, Die Haende Essaws Haende." In *Frequency-Modulated Scenario,* edited by Eran Schaerf, 332–42. Berlin: Archive, 2015.

Ó Murchú, Niall. "Coloring Palestine: The Flag Device and Cinematic Motivations in Narrative Movies." *Journal of Palestine Studies* 52, no. 1 (2023): 21–42.

Olmert, Dana. "'Ani lo Kan': Ha-'Emda ha-Poliṭit ṿeha-Iyum 'al ha-Zehut be-Shirat Daliya Raviḳovitch." In *Kitme Or: Ḥamishim Shenot Biḳoret u-Meḥḳar 'al Yetsirata shel Daliya Raviḳovitch,* edited by Hamutal Tsamir and Tamar Hess, 416–43. Bene Beraḳ: ha-Ḳibutz ha-Me'uḥad, 2010.

———. "Ma Hitgala le-Gnessin be-Vet Saba?" *Ot* 5 (2015): 93–108.

Ophir, Adi. *'Avodat ha-Hoṿe: Masot 'al Tarbut Yiśre'elit ba-Zeman ha-Ze.* Tel Aviv: ha-Ḳibuts ha-Me'uḥad, 2001.

Oppenheimer, Yochai. *Me'ever la-Gader: Yitsug ha-'Aravim ba-Sifrut ha-'Ivrit veha-Yiśra'elit, 1906–2005.* Tel Aviv: 'Am 'Oved, 2008.

Pappé, Ilan. *The Ethnic Cleansing of Palestine.* Oxford: Oneworld, 2007.

Parmentier, Richard J. "Peirce Divested for Nonintimates." In *Signs in Society: Studies in Semiotic Anthropology,* 3–22. Bloomington: Indiana University Press, 1994.

Parush, Adi. "Psaḳ ha-Din be-Parashat Kefar Ḳasem: Mivḥan ha-Degel ha-Shaḥor ṿeha-Muśag shel Peḳuda Bilti-Ḥuḳit ba-'Alil." *'Iyune Mishpaṭ* 15, no. 2 (1990): 245–72.

Parush, Iris, and Brakha Dalmatzky-Fischler. "'Ma Anaḥnu 'Osim Kan?' ('Od Ḳeri'a be-'ha-Derahsa')." *'Iyunim be-Teḳumat Iśra'el* 16 (2006): 1–40.

Perry, Menahem, and Meir Sternberg. "The King through Ironic Eyes: Biblical Narrative and the Literary Reading Process." *Poetics Today* 7, no. 2 (1986): 275–322.

Peteet, Julie. *Space and Mobility in Palestine.* Bloomington: Indiana University Press, 2017.

Puar, Jasbir K. *The Right to Maim: Debility, Capacity, Disability.* Durham, N.C.: Duke University Press, 2017.

———. "Spatial Debilities: Slow Life and Carceral Capitalism in Palestine." *South Atlantic Quarterly* 120, no. 2 (2021): 393–414.

Quijano, Anibal. "Coloniality of Power, Eurocentrism, and Latin America." *Nepantla: Views from South* 1, no. 3 (2000): 533–80.

Quintilian. *The Orator's Education*. Edited by D. A. Russell. Vols. III, IV. Loeb Classical Library 124–127, 494. Cambridge, Mass.: Harvard University Press, 2002.

R., Sh. "ʿAl ha-Temanim." *ha-Zvi*, January 27, 1909.

Rabie, Kareem. *Palestine Is Throwing a Party and the Whole World Is Invited: Capital and State Building in the West Bank*. Durham, N.C.: Duke University Press, 2021.

Radi, Mohamed. "Les échos du silence dans 'Retour à Haïfa' de Ghassan Kanafani." *Thélème: Revista Complutense de Estudios Franceses* 26 (2011): 273–83.

Rancière, Jacques. *Dissensus: On Politics and Aesthetics*. Translated by Steven Corcoran. London and New York: Bloomsbury Academic, 2010.

Ranta, Ronald, and Yonatan Mendel. "Consuming Palestine: Palestine and Palestinians in Israeli Food Culture." *Ethnicities* 14, no. 3 (2014): 412–35.

Ravikovitch, Dahlia. "ha-Ṭribunal shel ha-Ḥofesh ha-Gadol." In *Mavet ba-Mishpaḥa*, 34–65. Tel Aviv: ʿAm ʿOved, 1976.

———. *Hovering at a Low Altitude: The Collected Poetry of Dahlia Ravikovitch*. Edited by Chana Bloch and Chana Kronfeld. New York: W. W. Norton, 2009.

———. *Kol ha-Shirim*. Edited by Giddo Ticotsky and Uzi Shavit. Tel Aviv: ha-Ḳibuts ha-Meʾuḥad, 2010.

Raz-Krakotzkin, Amnon. "Exile, History and the Nationalization of Jewish Memory: Some Reflections on the Zionist Notion of History and Return." *Journal of Levantine Studies* 3, no. 2 (Winter 2013): 37–70.

———. "Exile within Sovereignty: A Critique of 'The Negation of Exile' in Israeli Culture." In *The Scaffolding of Sovereignty: Global and Aesthetic Perspectives on the History of a Concept*, edited by Zvi Ben-Dor Benite, Stefanos Geroulanos, and Nicole Jerr, 393–420. New York: Columbia University Press, 2017.

———. "Zionist Return to the West and the Mizrachi Jewish Perspective." In *Orientalism and the Jews*, edited by Ivan Davidson Kalmar and Derek J. Pensler, 162–81. Waltham, Mass.: Brandeis University Press, 2005.

Reinert, B., J. T. P. de Bruijn, and J. Stewart Robinson. "Madjāz." In *Encyclopaedia of Islam*, 2nd ed., edited by P. Bearman, Th. Bianquis, C. E. Bosworth, E. van Donzel, and W. P. Heinrichs. Leiden: Brill, 2012. Accessed online: http://dx.doi.org/10.1163/1573-3912_islam_COM_0605.

Ricoeur, Paul. *The Rule of Metaphor: Multi-Disciplinary Studies of the Creation of Meaning in Language*. Translated by Robert Czerny. Toronto and Buffalo: University of Toronto Press, 1977.

Ross, Andrew. *Stone Men: The Palestinians Who Built Israel*. London and Brooklyn: Verso, 2019.

Rothberg, Michael. "From Gaza to Warsaw: Mapping Multidirectional Memory." *Criticism* 53, no. 4 (2011): 523–48.
Rouhana, Nadim N., and Areej Sabbagh-Khoury. "Memory and the Return of History in a Settler-Colonial Context: The Case of the Palestinians in Israel." *Interventions* 21, no. 4 (2019): 527–50.
———. "Settler-Colonial Citizenship: Conceptualizing the Relationship between Israel and Its Palestinian Citizens." *Settler Colonial Studies* 5, no. 3 (2015): 205–25.
Rousseau, Jean-Jacques. *Discourse on the Origin of Inequality.* Edited by Patrick Coleman. Translated by Franklin Philip. Oxford and New York: Oxford University Press, 2009.
———. *Essay on the Origin of Language.* Chicago: University of Chicago Press, 1986.
———. *The Social Contract, Or Principles of Political Right.* Translated by Maurice Cranston. Harmondsworth: Penguin Classics, 1968.
Ruppin, Arthur. "The Picture in 1907." In *Three Decades of Palestine: Speeches and Papers on the Upbuilding of the Jewish National Home*, New ed., 1–34. Westport, Conn.: Praeger, 1975.
Sa'di, Ahmad H. "Incorporation Without Integration: Palestinian Citizens in Israel's Labour Market." *Sociology* 29, no. 3 (1995): 429–51.
———. "Israel's Settler-Colonialism as a Global Security Paradigm." *Race & Class* 63, no. 2 (2021): 21–37.
Sadan, Dov. *Ben Din le-Ḥeshbon: Masot ʿal Sofrim u-Sefarim.* Tel Aviv: Devir, 1963.
Said, Edward W. *Orientalism.* New York: Vintage, 2003.
———. *The Question of Palestine.* New York: Vintage, 1980.
———. *Reflections on Exile and Other Essays.* Cambridge, Mass.: Harvard University Press, 2000.
———. "Zionism from the Standpoint of Its Victims." *Social Text*, no. 1 (1979): 7–58.
Salamanca, Omar Jabary, Mezna Qato, Kareem Rabie, and Sobhi Samour. "Past Is Present: Settler Colonialism in Palestine." *Settler Colonial Studies* 2, no. 1 (2012): 1–8.
Samour, Sobhi. "Covid-19 and the Necroeconomy of Palestinian Labor in Israel." *Journal of Palestine Studies* 49, no. 4 (2020): 53–64.
Sanbar, Elias, and Gilles Deleuze. "The Indians of Palestine" [1982]. Translated by Timothy S. Murphy. *Discourse: Journal for Theoretical Studies in Media and Culture* 20, no. 3 (2013): 25–29.
Sangero, Boaz. "Be-En Ḥashad en Ḥaḳira Amitit: 'Duaḥ Vaʿadat ha-Ḥaḳira ha-Mamlakhtit be-ʿInyan Parashat Heʿalmutam shel Yeladim mi-Bene ʿOle Teman.'" *Teʾoria u-Vikoret* 21 (2002): 47–76.
Sayegh, Fayez Abdullah. *Zionist Colonialism in Palestine.* Beirut: Research Center, Palestine Liberation Organization, 1965.
Sayigh, Rosemary. "On the Exclusion of the Palestinian Nakba from the 'Trauma Genre.'" *Journal of Palestine Studies* 43, no. 1 (2013): 51–60.

Scarry, Elaine. *The Body in Pain: The Making and Unmaking of the World.* New York: Oxford University Press, 1987.

Schlegel, Friedrich. *Philosophical Fragments.* Translated by Peter Firchow. Minneapolis: University of Minnesota Press, 1991.

Schmitt, Carl. *The Concept of the Political.* Expanded ed. Translated by George Schwab. Chicago: University of Chicago Press, 2007.

———. *Political Theology: Four Chapters on the Concept of Sovereignty.* Translated by George Schwab. Chicago: University of Chicago Press, 2010.

Segev, Tom. *The Seventh Million: The Israelis and the Holocaust.* New York: Hill and Wang, 1994.

Seikaly, Sherene. *Men of Capital: Scarcity and Economy in Mandate Palestine.* Stanford, Calif.: Stanford University Press, 2015.

Seikaly, Sherene, and Max Ajl. "Of Europe: Zionism and the Jewish Other." In *Europe after Derrida: Crisis and Potentiality,* edited by Agnes Czajka and Bora Isyar, 120–33. Edinburgh: Edinburgh University Press, 2014.

Setter, Shaul. "S. Yizhar, Sipur she-lo Nigmar: 'Al Ḳol Tse'aḳa shel Ḳahal Yehudi-Falasṭini be-'Sipur Ḥirbat Ḥiz'a.'" *Ot* 6 (2016): 191–213.

Shabi, Rachel. "The Next Homeland? The Problems with *Fauda,* Israel's Brutal TV Hit." *Guardian,* May 23, 2018, https://www.theguardian.com/tv-and-radio/2018/may/23/the-next-homeland-problems-with-fauda-israel-brutal-tv-hit.

Shafir, Gershon. *Land, Labor and the Origins of the Israeli-Palestinian Conflict, 1882–1914.* Berkeley: University of California Press, 1996.

———. "The Meeting of Eastern Europe and Yemen: 'Idealistic Workers' and 'Natural Workers' in Early Zionist Settlement in Palestine." *Ethnic and Racial Studies* 13, no. 2 (1990): 172–97.

Shammas, Anton. *'Arabesḳot.* Tel Aviv: 'Am 'oved; Maiḳelmarḳ, 1986.

———. "Torture into Affidavit, Dispossession into Poetry: On Translating Palestinian Pain." *Critical Inquiry* 44, no. 1 (2017): 114–28.

Shavit, Ari. "Top PM Aide: Gaza Plan Aims to Freeze the Peace Process." *Haaretz,* October 6, 2004. https://www.haaretz.com/1.4710372.

Shenhav, Yehouda. *The Arab Jews: A Postcolonial Reading of Nationalism, Religion, and Ethnicity.* Stanford, Calif.: Stanford University Press, 2006.

Shezaf, Hagar. "Israeli Army Installs Remote-Control Crowd Dispersal System at Hebron Flashpoint." *Haaretz,* September 24, 2022. https://www.haaretz.com/israel-news/2022-09-24/ty-article/.premium/israeli-army-installs-remote-control-crowd-dispersal-system-at-hebron-flashpoint/00000183-70c4-d4b1-a197-ffcfb24f0000.

———. "Within Two Months, 20 Palestinians Were Shot by Israel While Trying to Cross from West Bank." *Haaretz,* December 23, 2019. https://www.haaretz.com/israel-news/.premium-within-two-months-20-palestinian-were-shot-while-trying-to-cross-from-west-bank-1.8298644.a

Shibli, Adania. "al-Tala'ub bi-l-'Adid min Dharrat al-Ghubar." *Al-Karmel Faṣliyya Thaqafiyya,* no. 70–71 (2002): 300–309.

——. "Dust." Translated by Yasmeen Hanoosh. *The Iowa Review* 37, no. 2 (2007): 93–104.
——. *Minor Detail*. Translated by Elisabeth Jaquette. New York: New Directions, 2020.
——. "Out of Time." In *A Map of Absence: An Anthology of Palestinian Writing on the Nakba*, edited by Atef Alshaer, 191–94. London: Saqi Books, 2019.
——. *Tafṣil Thanawi*. Beirut: Dar al-Adab li-l-Nashr wa-l-Tawziʿ, 2017.
Shifriss, Nathan. *Yaldi Halakh le-An?: Parashat Yalde Teman; ha-Ḥaṭifa veha-Hakhḥasha*. Tel-Aviv: ʿAliyat ha-Gag; Yediʿot Aḥaronot; Ḥemed, 2019.
Shohat, Ella. "The Invention of the Mizrahim." *Journal of Palestine Studies* 29, no. 1 (1999): 5–20.
——. *Israeli Cinema: East/West and the Politics of Representation*. Revised ed. London and New York: I. B. Tauris, 2010.
——. "Rupture and Return: The Shaping of a Mizrahi Epistemology." *HAGAR: International Social Science Review* 2, no. 1 (2001): 61–92.
——. "'Sant al-Tasqit': Seventy Years since the Departure of Iraqi Jews." *Jadaliyya* (blog), January 14, 2021. https://www.jadaliyya.com/Details/42239.
——. "Sephardim in Israel: Zionism from the Standpoint of Its Jewish Victims." *Social Text*, no. 19/20 (1988): 1–35.
Siddiq, Muhammad. *Man Is a Cause: Political Consciousness and the Fiction of Ghassan Kanafani*. Seattle and London: University of Washington Press, 1984.
Skinner, Quentin. "Hobbes and the Purely Artificial Person of the State." *Journal of Political Philosophy* 7, no. 1 (1999): 1–29.
Somekh, Sasson. "Falestinaʾi she-Hetsits ve-lo Nifgaʿ." *Ofek* 2 (1972): 145–51.
Sorek, Tamir. "Ḳiṭuv Medume be-Maḥane ha-ʿElyonut ha-Yehudit." Teʾoria u-Vikoret: Esh be-Śde ḳotsim: Tiḳ Masot (2021): 1–6.
Spivak, Gayatri Chakravorty. "Can the Subaltern Speak?" In *Marxism and the Interpretation of Culture*, edited by Cary Nelson and Lawrence Grossberg, 271–313. Urbana: University of Illinois Press, 1988.
——. *Outside in the Teaching Machine*. New York: Routledge, 1993.
Stoler, Ann Laura. *Along the Archival Grain: Epistemic Anxieties and Colonial Common Sense*. Princeton, N.J.: Princeton University Press, 2010.
Swirski, Shlomo. "The Price of Occupation: The Cost of the Occupation to Israeli Society." *Palestine-Israel Journal of Politics, Economics, and Culture* 12, no. 1 (2005). https://pij.org/articles/335/the-price-of-occupation—the-cost-of-the-occupation-to-israeli-society.
Szobel, Ilana. *A Poetics of Trauma: The Work of Dahlia Ravikovitch*. Waltham, Mass.: Brandeis University Press, 2013.
Tageldin, Shaden M. *Disarming Words: Empire and the Seductions of Translation in Egypt*. Berkeley: University of California Press, 2011.
Taharlev, Itamar. "ha-Brit ha-Ashkenazo-Falasṭinit." *Erets ha-Emori* (blog), May 6, 2013. https://haemori.wordpress.com/2013/05/06/alliance/.

Tamari, Salim. *Mountain against the Sea: Essays on Palestinian Society and Culture.* Berkeley: University of California Press, 2008.

———. "What the Uprising Means." *Middle East Report*, no. 152 (1988): 24–30.

Taraki, Lisa. "Urban Modernity on the Periphery: A New Middle Class Reinvents the Palestinian City." *Social Text* 26, no. 2 (2008): 61–81.

Tatour, Lana. "The Israeli Left: Part of the Problem or the Solution? A Response to Giulia Daniele." *Global Discourse* 6, no. 3 (2016): 487–92.

Tawil-Souri, Helga. "Checkpoint Time." *Qui Parle* 26, no. 2 (2017): 383–422.

Terada, Rei. "Thinking for Oneself: Realism and Defiance in Arendt." *ELH* 71, no. 4 (2004): 839–65.

The Ancestral Sin [Hebrew: *Salah, Po Ze Erets Iśra'el*]. Directed by David Deri, Reshet 2017. Documentary series.

The Dupes [Arabic: *al-Makhdu'un*]. Directed by Tawfiq Saleh. Arab Film Distribution, 1972.

The Lab. Directed by Yotal Feldman. Cinephil, 2013.

The Time That Remains [Arabic: *al-Zaman al-Baqi*]. Directed by Elia Suleiman. Le Pacte, 2009.

Totry Jubran, Manal. "'Arim Me'oravot be-Hithayut: Ben ha-Peraṭi la-Tsiburi." *Din u-Devarim* 10 (2017): 17–68.

Tsamir, Hamutal. *be-Shem ha-Nof: Le'umiyut, Migdar ṿe-Subyeḳṭiviyut ba-Shira ha-Yiśre'elit bi-Shenot ha-Ḥamishim ṿeha-Shishim.* Jerusalem: Keter; Merkaz Heḳsherim, ha-Merkaz le-Ḥeḳer ha-Sifrut ṿeha-Tarbut ha-Yehudit ṿeha-Yiśre'elit, Universitat Ben-Gurion ba-Negev, 2006.

———. "ha-Tsofa le-Vet Yiśra'el mibi-Fenim: Daliya Raviḳovitch, ha-Shira ha-Le'umit-Yiśra'elit, ṿeha-Migdar shel ha-Yetsugiyut." In *Kitme Or: Ḥamishim Shenot Biḳoret u-Meḥḳar 'al Yetsirata shel Daliya Raviḳovitch,* edited by Hamutal Tsamir and Tamar Hess, 600–45. Bene Beraḳ: ha-Ḳibutz ha-Me'uḥad, 2010.

Tzfadia, Erez, and Haim Yacobi. *Rethinking Israeli Space: Periphery and Identity.* London and New York: Routledge, 2011.

Tsur, Reuven. "Ḳeri'a be-'Raḥamim.'" In *Me'asef: Muḳdash li-Yetsirat Ḥayim Hazaz,* edited by Dov Sadan and Dan Laor, 257–72. Jerusalem: Agudat ha-Sofrim ha-'Ivrim be-Yiśra'el ṿe-Agudat Shalem, 1978.

Veracini, Lorenzo. "Introducing Settler Colonial Studies." *Settler Colonial Studies* 1, no. 1 (2011): 1–12.

———. "The Other Shift: Settler Colonialism, Israel, and the Occupation." *Journal of Palestine Studies* 42, no. 2 (2013): 26–42.

Waltz With Bashir [Hebrew: *Ṿals 'im Bashir*]. Directed by Ari Folman. Sony Pictures Classics, 2008.

Wazner, Michal. "Ze Ken la-Proṭoḳol: 'ha-Derasha' me'et Ḥayim Hazaz ke-Ṭeksṭ Proṭoḳoli." *Mikan* 9 (2008–9): 42–56.

Weber, Max. *Rationalism and Modern Society.* Translated by Tony Waters and Dagmar Waters. New York: Palgrave Macmillan, 2015.

Wehr, Hans, and J. Milton Cowan. *Arabic-English Dictionary: The Hans Wehr Dictionary of Modern Written Arabic*. 4th ed. Ithaca, N.Y.: Spoken Language Services, 1993.

Weizman, Eyal. *Hollow Land: Israel's Architecture of Occupation*. London and New York: Verso, 2017.

——. *The Least of All Possible Evils: Humanitarian Violence from Arendt to Gaza*. London and New York: Verso, 2011.

Who Profits. "Exploited and Essential: Palestinian Labour under COVID-19 (Flash Report)." *Whoprofits* (blog), June 2020. https://whoprofits.org/wp-content/uploads/2020/06/Exploited-and-Essential-Palestinian-Labour-under-Covid-19-2.pdf.

——. "Industrial Zones in the Occupied Palestinian Territory." *Whoprofits* (blog). June 2019. https://www.whoprofits.org/dynamic-report/industrial-zones.

——. "Proven Effective: Crowd Control Weapons in the Occupied Palestinian Territories." *Whoprofits* (blog), April 2014. https://www.whoprofits.org/wp-content/uploads/2018/06/old/weapons_report-8.pdf.

Wolfe, Patrick. "Settler Colonialism and the Elimination of the Native." *Journal of Genocide Research* 8, no. 4 (2006): 387–409.

——. *Traces of History: Elementary Structures of Race*. London and New York: Verso, 2016.

Yona, Lihi, and Itamar Mann. "Ha-Motsiʾim la-Poʿal: Mizraḥim ve-Alimut Ribonit be-Iśraʾel." *Mishpaṭ u-Mimshal* 23 (2021): 1–57.

Zayad, Luma. "Systematic Cultural Appropriation and the Israeli-Palestinian Conflict." *DePaul Journal of Art, Technology and Intellectual Property Law* 28, no. 2 (2017–18): 81–125.

Zertal, Idith, and Akiva Eldar. *Lords of the Land: The War Over Israel's Settlements in the Occupied Territories, 1967–2007*. New York: Nation, 2009.

Index

1948 Generation *(Dor Tashaḥ)*, 71, 159, 159n13, 169
1948 War, 5, 26–27, 31, 37, 63, 69, 109, 113, 116–117, 119, 169
1967 War, 19, 28, 63, 69n2, 118, 183, 208. *See also* Six Day War

Abourahme, Nasser, 33n16, 228, 229n64
Absentees' Property Law, 117, 155
Abu Khdeir, Mohammed, 210n29
Abu Manneh, Bashir, 192
Abul Hawa, Ziyad, 211n35
Abulhawa, Susan, 123n45
Adab al-Muqawama fi Filasṭin al-Muḥtalla (Resistance Literature in Occupied Palestine) (Kanafani), 26
adoptions, 19, 201, 205–207, 206n19
African Americans, 109n1, 249
Agamben, Giorgio, 3, 23, 169n41
Ahavat Tapuaḥ ha-Zahav (The Love of an Orange) (Ravikovitch), 158
Ahihud, 201
Ahmed, Sara, 223, 223n59
"'A'id ila Ḥayfa" (Returning to Haifa) (Kanafani), 19, 25–26, 28, 31–33, 31n12, 32n13, 33n16, 37–41, 43–49, 45n47, 46n49, 49–53, 52n64, 54–56, 59–65, 60n84, 68–69, 122–123
Alcalay, Ammiel, 11
"All That's Left to You" (Kanafani). *See* "Ma Tabaqqa Lakum"
Allan, Diana, 119
Alter, Robert, 95n80, 96
Alterman, Nathan, 70n4, 159n13, 169–170, 177
Amichai, Yehuda, 159n12, 183n76
Amiry, Suad, 229n66
Amram Association, 201, 207n23
analogy, 44–49
'An al-Rijal wa-l-Banadiq (Of Men and Rifles) (Kanafani), 42–43
Anidjar, Gil, 8, 11
Anti-Boycott Law, 31
anticolonial struggle, 14, 19, 27, 33, 42–44, 58, 140–149, 220. *See also* resistance
apartheid, 58, 65, 111–112, 127, 196, 247–249. *See also* segregation
appropriation, 20, 39, 47–48, 94, 94n78, 110–111, 117, 126–140
Apter, Emily, 3
Arab Jews, 6, 9, 125, 138, 211, 212n39, 220, 222
Arab Job (television series). See *'Avoda 'Aravit*
Arab League, 118
"Arab schools," 124–125
'Arabeskot (Arabesques) (Shammas), 110
Arabic language, 9–12, 23n 26, 31n12, 36, 45n47, 55–56, 112, 118, 125, 133, 134n80, 156–157, 165–166, 173n51, 210, 212n36, 222, 240
Arabic literature, 5, 9–11, 46n49, 53–54, 114, 161n18, 180–181
'Aravim Rokdim (Dancing Arabs) (Kashua), 124
Arendt, Hannah, 36, 43, 80n36, 157, 174–175, 175n55
Aristotle, 12n18, 48, 54

Asad, Talal, 175
Ashkenazi Jews, 9, 96, 98, 102, 104–105, 123n45, 124n49, 128, 137–138, 148, 176, 196, 198, 200–201, 205–209, 209n26, 242
assimilation, 88–89, 122–123, 123n45, 125–126, 197, 199–208
Australia, 207n22
autofiction, 189, 192
'Avoda 'Aravit (Arab Job) (television series), 150
Azaria, Elor, 154, 197–198, 243
Azem, Ibtisam, 20, 108–111, 112n8, 120–121, 125–126, 131, 138–139, 141
Azoulay, Ariella, 11

Bab al-Shams (Gate of the Sun) (Khoury), 9, 22, 138, 199–200, 240
al-Baḥth 'an Walid Mas'ud (In Search of Walid Masoud) (Jabra), 110
Balibar, Étienne, 3
Barak, Ehud, 195, 195n1
Barari al-Ḥumma (Prairies of Fever) (Nasrallah), 110
Barghouti, Mourid, 229n66
Battle of Algiers, The (film), 220
bayān, 53–54
BDS. *See* Boycott, Divestment, and Sanctions (BDS)
Ben Gurion, David, 188, 204n14
Benjamin, Walter, 15n21, 86, 86n54, 91, 142, 173, 180
Berdichevsky, Micha Yosef, 71–72, 98
Bergmann, Hugo, 80n36
Be-Or Ḥadash (In a New Light) (Mansour), 122–123
"Be'eynayyim Peḳuḥot" (With Open Eyes) (Hatuka), 240–242
Bhandar, Brenna, 94n78
Bialik, Haim Nahman, 71, 182
Bible, 31, 95n81, 164, 166–167, 170–171, 184n79
Bishara, Azmi, 229n64
"Biṭaqat Huwiyya" (Identity Card) (Darwish), 202
"Black Box" (Hatuka). *See* "Ḳufsa Sheḥora"
"Blood for Coffee" (Hatuka). *See* "ha-Dam Heḥlif et ha-Ḳafe"
Bluwstein, Raḥel, 177
Book of Disappearance, The (Azem). See *Sifr al-Ikhtifa'*
border control technologies, 197, 228–229, 239, 243–244
Boycott, Divestment, and Sanctions (BDS), 31, 58
Brenner, Rachel Feldhay, 148n112
Brenner, Yosef Haim, 71–73, 72n9
Brit Shalom, 80, 80n36
Brown, Wendy, 39
Buber, Martin, 80n36
Burke, Edmund, 56n77
Butler, Judith, 175n57

calendar, Jewish, 183n76
Canaanism, 76n20
captialism, 5, 73, 122n42, 129, 142, 151, 192, 196, 203
catachresis, 19, 28–30, 30n11, 50, 53, 57, 66, 199
censorship, 114, 144, 202n10
checkpoints, 21, 131, 146, 189, 197–198, 228–239, 243
children, 22, 121, 138, 151, 199, 201, 204–207, 207n22, 226, 240–241
Chronicle of a Disappearance (film). See *Sijill Ikhtifa'*
Ciccariello-Maher, George, 3, 239n104
Civic Administration, 244
civil war, 3
Coetzee, J. M., 189
Cohen, Eli, 210n29
Cohen, Hillel, 123n45, 210n28
colonialism: children and, 207n22; concealment and, 115–121; in conceptions of conflict, 3–4; dialectics of destruction and affirmation and, 113–114; disappearance and, 111–112, 115–121, 123, 151; dispossession and, 39–40, 116; education and, 124–125; elimination and, 111, 115–121; internal, 6n3; Jewish Israeli ignorance of, 113n13; *levaṭim* and, 73, 92–95, 100–101; liberalism and, 40; Mizrahi Jews and, 6–8, 115, 136–139, 213; segregation and, 126n57; settler, 111–113, 120, 126–127, 136; and symmetry, 5, 13–14, 33, 48, 213–218, 220, 226–227; systemic, 14; Zionism and, 42, 94, 112–114, 189–190, 213; Zionism as, 5
coloniality, 114–115
colonization, of Palestine, 5, 94
concealment, 112–113, 115–121
conflict: definition, 1–2, 32–33; dispute and, 13–17; as duel or confrontation, 216, 223; Enlightenment conception of, 33–34; figurative concepts of, 2; in Foucault, 3, 15,

216; in Hobbes, 14–15, 34–39, 44–45; as *ishtibāk*, 18–19, 27–29, 42–44, 67, 245; judgment and, 17–19, 30–42; juridico-political concept of, 15, 30–42, 213, 245–248; law and, 14–15; in Lyotard, 2, 17, 41, 56–57; Oedipal and Homeric, 216; pre-political, 14–18, 33–35; property and, 14–15, 38–40, 216; scholarly interest in, 2–4; sovereignty and, 33–35; state of nature and, 19, 33–35, 216; as term, 1, 13, 17–18. *See also* Israeli-Palestinian conflict
conflict management, 1–2, 14, 243–248
conflict resolution, 1–2, 14, 31, 71, 248
conflictual modes, 18
conversion, to Judaism, 126, 126n57
COVID-19 pandemic, 130
Critique of Judgment (Kant), 56–57, 57n77, 92n69, 93n71, 184n77
Critique of Pure Reason (Kant), 37, 56, 184n77
cuisine, 132–134, *134*, 136–137
cultural appropriation, 126–136

da Silva, Denise Ferreira, 38n27
"ha-Dam Heḥlif et ha-Ḳafe" (Blood for Coffee) (Hatuka), 195, 198–199, 198n5
Dancing Arabs (Kashua). See *'Aravim Roḳdim*
Darwish, Mahmoud, 111, 198n5, 201, 202
Day of Absence (Ward), 109n1
"A Deal" (Hatuka). *See* "'Isḳa"
de Certeau, Michel, 167
de Man, Paul, 29, 29n9, 82, 91–92, 91n65
decolonization, 58, 115, 141n93, 149, 178, 187
deconstruction, 12, 23, 29, 66, 85
Degani, Arnon Yehuda, 122n43
Deir Yassin, 119
Deleuze, Gilles, 38, 44, 62, 64, 146, 146n108, 164, 167n33, 176n61, 246
"ha-Derasha" (The Sermon), 74–95, 75n16, 104, 104n105, 105–107
Derrida, Jacques, 29, 29n9, 54
Dhakira li-l-Nisyan (A Memory of Forgetfulness) (Darwish), 198n5
diasporic Jews, 49, 78, 83–84, 86, 88
Differend, The (Lyotard), 2, 17n24
Different Drummer, A (Kelley), 109n1
disappearance, 50, 109–114, 150–152, 155–156, 227; as anticolonial resistance, 140–149; as appropriation, 126–140; as colonial elimination and concealment, 115–121; as colonial segregation, 122–126; as exploitation, 126–140; as racialization, 136–140. See also *ikhtifā'*
dispossession, 20, 39–40, 65, 116–117, 119, 244, 248
dispute, 13–17, 30, 33, 42–43, 57, 245
disregard, 149–152
Dissensus (Rancière), 3, 52n63
Dor ha-Medina (the Statehood Generation), 159, 159n12, 178
Dor ha-Teḥiya (the Revival Generation), 71–72
Dor Tashaḥ (1948 Generation), 71, 159, 159n13, 169
Druze, 212n39
Dussel, Enrique, 3
"Dust" (Shibli). *See* "al-Tala'ub bi-l-'Adid min Dharrat al-Ghubar"

El-Ariss, Tarek, 10
Eli (the Spy) (televsion series), 210n29
elimination, 111–112, 115–121, 126–127, 138, 149
Emerson, Ralph Waldo, 55
Enlightenment, 19, 33–34, 37, 44, 88
Enter Ghost (Hammad), 229
Entry into Israel Law, 31
episodism, 26n2, 28, 63–64
Epstein, Yitzhak, 115–116
erasure, 109, 111–113, 116n23, 116n25, 117, 126, 137, 139–143, 158, 180, 192, 200, 242, 245
Erez, Oded, 122n43, 125n54, 227
Esmeir, Samera, 42–43, 65, 158, 190–193
ethnic cleansing, 13, 109, 119, 120. *See also* genocide
exile, 62, 73, 75–83, 85–89, 90–91, 93–95, 101, 122, 140; negation of, 75–83, 97
Exodus, 68n1, 69n3
exploitation, 111, 114, 126–141, 201, 203
Eze, Emmanuel Chukwudi, 93n72

Fanon, Frantz, 3
Fatah, 195, 228
Fauda (television series), 21, 210–228, 210n29, 212n36, *221*, 224–225, 237–238
Fi al-Adab al-Ṣihyuni (On Zionist Literature) (Kanafani), 26, 46n49
Fi Ḥadrat al-Ghiyab (In the Presence of Absence) (Darwish), 111
First Intifada, 129, 160, 183, 228
"flying law," 146, 155
food, 41, 59, 132–134, *134*, 136–137, 145

Foucault, Michel, 3, 6n3, 15, 36–37, 216, 216n47, 246
Freud, Sigmund, 146, 146n108

Gate of the Sun (Khoury). See *Bab al-Shams*
genocide, 121, 248–249. *See also* ethnic cleansing
Gertz, Nurith, 217–219
Ghanim, Honaida, 113
Giv'ati Affair, 160, 160n16, 162, 164, 168–169, 172, 183
Glissant, Eduard, 143–145
Gnessin, Uri Nissan, 71, 72n9
Goldmann, Nahum, 102
Gordon, Neve, 130
Green Line, 116–118, 149, 152
Guf Sheni Yaḥid (Second Person Singular) (Kashua), 128

Habiby, Emile, 20, 108, 110, 114n16, 123–124, 128–129, 139, 142–144, 147–149, 155
al-Hadaf (The Goal) (magazine), 26
al-Hadiyya (The Present) (film), 229
al-Haj, Majid, 124
Hanafi, Sari, 230n72
Hamas, 195, 213–216, 215n43, 216, 218, 228
Hammad, Isabella, 229
"Harat-'Olam" (The World's Conception) (Hazaz), 77n22, 89n59
Hartman, Saidiya, 47, 176, 189
Hatuka, Shlomi, 22, 195, 197–199, 198n5, 201–203, 206n19, 207–208, 240–242
Hazaz, Aviva, 104n105
Hazaz, Haim, 9, 19–20, 71–107, 72n9, 74n12–14, 75nn15–17, 76n19, 76n21, 77n22, 89n59, 100n94, 103n102, 104n108, 200
Hebrew language, 9–11, 36, 76n20, 78, 88, 93, 116n23, 124, 128, 145, 156–157, 161, 176, 183, 214, 240, 244, 247
Hebrew literature, 5, 10–11, 19, 68, 71–72, 83, 141n95, 159, 166, 177–178, 181; European context and, 5n3; "rootless" theme in, 72n8; styles in, 98; Yeshurun on, 68; Zionism and, 72–73, 98, 189. *See also specific works*
Hegel, Georg, 15, 77, 96, 166, 217
"Hertsel Ne'elam be-Ḥatsot" (Herzl Disappears at Midnight) (Kashua), 110, 140
"Herzl Disappears at Midnight" (Kashua). *See* "Hertsel Ne'elam be-Ḥatsot"
Hever, Hannan, 69, 70n4, 169
Hilal, Jamil, 112
"Ḥirbet Ḥiz'a" (Khirbet Khizah) (Yizhar), 69, 69n3
historiography, 89, 157–158, 190–191, 193
Histadrut, 122, 122n43, 128
hitlabṭut, 71,72, 96
Hobbes, Thomas, 14–15, 34–36, 37n26, 39, 44–45, 45n46, 56n77, 215
Hochberg, Gil Z., 11, 123–124, 143
ḥoḳ, 20–21, 156–157, 156n5–6, 165–167, 171, 176, 185–186, 189, 192, 197. *See also* law
holocaust, 31–32, 44–50, 121, 159, 161n19, 182–183, 183n76, 204
hostility, 196–197; as a mode of severance, 208–228; within Palestinian society, 228–240
"Hovering at a Low Altitude" (Ravikovitch). *See* "Reḥifa be-Gova Namukh"
humor, 124, 143–144, 146–147, 146n108, 147–149

Ibn al-Mu'tazz, 54
IDF. *See* Israeli Defense Forces (IDF)
Ikhtifā', 2, 20, 110, 114–115, 117, 121, 139–141, 145, 149, 245. *See also* disappearance
'ilm al-bayān, 2, 53–54
"Ima Mithalekhet" (A Mother Walks Around) (Ravikovitch), 179
imperialism, 5, 19, 26, 48, 63, 73, 98, 181
improvement, 94, 102
inqisām, 2, 21–22, 195–196, 201, 207, 216, 223, 228–240, 245
intellectualism, 79–80, 79n35, 97
Intifada, 129, 153–154, 160, 183, 195, 215, 228, 239. *See also* First Intifada; Knives Intifada; Second Intifada; Unity Intifada
invisibilization, 112, 115, 117–118, 128, 139, 143, 147, 235
irony, 2, 77, 82, 82n41, 83, 85, 85n49, 89, 90, 90n61, 91n65, 92, 92n68, 94n75
Irradiations Affair, 241, 241n107
ishtibāk, 2, 18–19, 27–29, 42–44, 65, 67, 245
"'Isḳa" (A Deal) (Hatuka), 198n5
isolation, 117–119, 139, 228–231
Israel: ambiguities and contradictions as foundation of, 70–71, 70n6, 73; apartheid in, 58, 65, 111–112, 127, 196, 247–249; censorship in, 114, 202n10; establishment of, 5, 19, 45, 62, 71–72, 79, 115, 121, 159, 226; Palestine-Israel, as term, 9; population of Mizrahi Jews in, 6–7, 6n5, 7n6; segregation in, 111, 122–126, 140, 149, 196. *See also* Zionism
Israeli Defense Forces (IDF), 70n5, 132, 155, 160, 186, 197, 210–211, 212n39

Mann, Itamar, 197, 212–213, 212n39
Mansour, Athallah, 122–123
"Marina Ḥadad" (Marina Haddad) (Ravikovitch), 184–185
martial law, 70n4, 117, 146, 155. *See also* Military Rule
Marvad ha-Ḳesamim (The Magic Carpet), 202
Marx, Karl, 36, 203
Masas (Shibli), 231
Masharawi, Rashid, 229n66
Masoud, Ahmed, 110
"Ma Tabaqqa Lakum" (All That's Left to You) (Kanafani), 58–59, 63
Ma'na al-Nakba (The Meaning of the Nakba) (Zurayk), 65
Mbembe, Achille, 248–250
Meaning of the Nakba, The (Zurayk). See *Ma'na al-Nakba*
mediating law, 153–194
medina, 36–37, 66, 187, 245
Meir, Golda, 121
Messiah, 83–86, 89n59, 101, 145, 170, 226, 246
metaphor, 12–13, 12n18, 19–20, 26, 28–30, 43–46, 49–54, 55–57, 60–67, 144, 171–172, 185, 229, 232, 248–250
metonymic generalization, 156, 183–185
middle class, 150–151, 208
military-industrial complex, 132
Military Rule, 20. *See also* martial law
Minor Detail (Shibli). See *Tafṣil Thanawi*
Miron, Dan, 76n21, 85–86, 101, 104n108
Mizrahi Black Panthers, 210n27
Mizrahi Jews, 6–7, 9, 21–22, 196; Arabization of, 139, 201–205, 208, 210–211; assimilation of, 123n45, 137–138, 197–198, 199–208; in Azem, 137–139; colonialism and, 115; contradictions with, 70n6; de-Arabization of, 201, 205, 226; Hazaz and, 96, 98, 105; hostility of, toward Palestinians, 208–228; integration of, 138n83; Judaization and, 200–201, 204, 208–209, 241; labor and, 128, 137, 138–139, 200–201, 203–204, 208–209, 211; Likud party and, 209n26; *moshavim* and, 201; population of, 6n5; racialization of, 105, 136, 198–208, 242; Shohat on, 7n6, 9, 139, 205; Zionism and, 70n6, 102, 137, 198, 203, 204n14, 240
modernism, 26n2, 27
moral imperialism, 19, 48
"A Mother Walks Around" (Ravikovitch). *See* "Ima Mithalekhet"
Moses (Bible), 47, 68n1
moshavim, 199–201
Mossad, 26–27, 210n29
Mouffe, Chantal, 3, 57
Mufti, Nasser, 3
"Mul ha-Ya'arot" (Facing the Forests) (Yehoshua), 141n95
al-Mutasha'il (The Pessoptimist) (Habiby). *See* al-Waqa'i' al-Ghariba fi Ikhtifa' Sa'id abi al-Naḥs al-Mutasha'il
mysticism, Oriental, 92n68

Nabulsi, Farah, 229
Nafar, Tamer, 202n10
Nahḍa, 5
al-nakba, 5, 28, 44–49, 65, 109, 113, 116–119, 125, 141, 150, 159, 192–193, 199, 232n77
al-nakba al-mustamirra (the ongoing nakba), 13, 65, 109, 192
Nakba Law, 31, 118, 141
Nasrallah, Ibrahim, 110
Nassar, Maha, 116–117
nationalism, 5, 9, 78, 78n28, 89, 151, 178, 209n26, 245
Nation State Law, 118, 141, 155
Native Americans, 35, 207n22
ha-Ne'arim (Our Boys) (television series), 210n29
"Necropolitics" (Mbembe), 249
Nietzsche, Friedrich, 51, 165, 173n50, 176n61
"Nigun 'Atiḳ" (Ancient Tune) (Alterman), 177
Nirim Affair, 187–189, 191–193
Noy, Menashe, 145

occlusion, 112n9
Occupied Palestinian Territories (OPT), 9
October Revolution, 74
Of Men and Rifles (Kanafani). *See* 'An al-Rijal wa-l-Banadiq
ongoing nakba, the. See *al-nakba al-mustamirra*
opacity, 143–145
Orientalism, 8, 12, 61, 96–97, 132, 198n5, 203
Otsma Yehudit (Jewish Power), 13
Ottoman Empire, 5, 10, 146, 210n27
"Out of Time" (Shibli), 232

Palestine: Canaanism and, 76n20; history of, 4, 7–9, 11–13, 17, 28, 65, 113–114, 125–126, 142, 144, 184, 187–194; resistance in, 14, 42–44, 140–149, 220; as term, 9; Zionism and, 5, 7, 13, 20, 45, 73, 84, 89, 94, 94n78, 95, 101, 103, 113, 115–116, 121, 137, 149, 198.

Palestine-Israel, as term, 9
Palestine Studies, 3–4, 113
Palestinian Authority, 16, 238–239
Palestinian Jews, 8
Palestinian literature, 4, 20, 23, 25, 110, 111, 112n8, 114, 115, 123, 141–143, 228, 232, 250. *See also specific works*
Palestinian Liberation Organization (PLO), 216
Palestinian nationalism, 5
Palestinians: censorship of, 114, 202n10; cuisine of, 132–133; elimination of, 109, 115–119; Green Line and, 116–117, 152; hostility of Mizrahi Jews toward, 208–228; invisibility of, 112, 115, 117–118, 128, 133, 143–144, 147; isolation of, 117–119; labor exploitation of, 127–131, 130n67; middle class, 150–151; social fragmentation among, 196, 229–230, 239, 247; as term, 8–9
pan-Arabism, 26, 116n25
ha-Pardes (The Orchard) (Tammuz), 141n95
Peirce, Charles Sanders, 230n69
Pessoptimist, The (Habiby). See *al-Waqa'i' al-Ghariba fi Ikhtifa' Sa'id abi al-Naḥs al-Mutasha'il*
PFLP. *See* Popular Front for the Liberation of Palestine (PFLP)
pilpul, 2, 21, 176–177
Plato, 30, 96, 164, 173n50, 174
PLO. *See* Palestinian Liberation Organization (PLO)
poetry, 111, 155–156, 158–187. *See also* Darwish, Mahmoud; Hatuka, Shlomi; Ravikovitch, Dahlia
Pontecorvo, Gillu, 220
Popular Front for the Liberation of Palestine (PFLP), 26, 41
possessive individualism, 39, 247
postcolonial theory, 29–30, 30n11
present absentees, 65, 117, 146
"Prisoner, The" (Yizhar). *See* "ha-Shavuy"
property, conflict and, 14–15, 38–40, 216
Puar, Jasbir K., 121n42

qaḍiyya, 54–56, 66
Qadri, Nasreen, 126n57
al-Qasrawi, Ramzi Aziz al-Tamimi, 154
Question of Palestine, The (Said), 114n16, 133n78
Quintilian, 29n9, 90n61

Rabie, Kareem, 220n56, 239
Rabin, Yitzhak, 160n16, 210n29
racialization, 8–9, 92, 136–140, 242; adversarial 21, 105, 137; of Azaria, 197; coloniality and, 115, 136–140, 203–205; conversion to Judaism and, 126n57; disappearance and, 111, 136–140; Israel and, 126, 136–140, 242; *levaṭim* and, 90–105; of Mizrahi Jews, 105, 136, 197–208, 203–205, 213, 242; nature and, 93, 105; property and, 40, 247; segregation and, 122; severance and, 198, 199–208; of Yemenite Jews, 203–205, 203n12; Zionist, 93–95, 126, 136–140, 148, 197–198, 201–205, 207, 213
racism, 45–46, 206, 222, 234, 242
Radi, Mohamed, 60n84
"Raḥamim ha-Sabal" (Rahamim the Porter) (Hazaz), 74–75, 95–105, 95n80
Rancière, Jacques, 3, 23, 52, 57
Ravikovitch, Dahlia, 21, 153, 155–156, 158–187, 158n10, 189
Raz, Lior, 21, 210, 213
Raz-Krakotzkin, Amnon, 88
realism, 26, 26n2, 27, 108–109
Regev, Miri, 202n10
"Reḥifa be-Gova Namukh" (Hovering at a Low Altitude) (Ravikovitch), 153, 178
resistance, disappearance as, 140–149
retribution, 217–218
"Returning to Haifa" (Kanafani). *See* "'A'id ila Ḥayfa"
Réunion Island, 207n22
revenge, 187, 214, 216–219
Revival Generation *(Dor ha-Teḥiya)*, 71–72
Ricoeur, Paul, 54, 66
Rousseau, Jean-Jacques, 14–15, 33–34
Ruppin, Arthur (Shimon), 203, 204n13
Russia, 74, 74n12, 95

Sa'di, Ahmad, 122
Said, Edward, 63, 112, 114n16, 117n27, 133n78, 231–232
Samour, Sobhi, 126–127
Sanbar, Elias, 113, 149–150
Sangero, Boaz, 207n21
Sayegh, Fayez A., 112
Scarry, Elaine, 175
Schlegel, Friedrich, 90, 90n61, 91n65
Schmitt, Carl, 15, 78n28, 169, 169n41, 170
Scholem, Gershom, 80n36
Scott, James C., 148n112
SCT. *See* settler colonial theory (SCT)

Sderot, 208–209, 213, 226–227
Second Intifada, 129, 195
Second Person Singular (Kashua). See *Guf Sheni Yaḥid*
segregation, 20, 111–112, 122–126, 122n43, 126n57, 133, 140, 148–149, 196, 239, 245. *See also* apartheid
Seikaly, Sherene, 3–4
separation paradigm, 10–11, 130
Sephardi, 6, 88–89, 96, 98, 100, 104, 205, 210n30. *See also* Mizrahi Jews
"Sermon, The" (Hazaz). *See* "ha-Derasha"
settler colonialism, 5, 7, 58, 100, 111–115, 119–120, 126–127, 136, 204, 248
settler colonial theory (SCT), 111–115, 119–122, 126–127, 133, 136, 139, 141n93, 248
severance, 21–22, 196–198; assimilative, 199–208; hostile, 208–240; internal, 228–240
Shafir, Gershon, 127, 139
al-Shaikh, Abdul-Rahim, 117
Shammas, Anton, 110, 117, 171
al-Shami, Hani, 160, 163
al-Sharif, ʿAbdel Fattah, 154, 243
"*ha-Shavuy*" (The Prisoner) (Yizhar), 69
Sheikh Jarrah, 13, 16–17, 151
Shekhol ve-Khishalon (Breakdown and Bereavement) (Brenner), 72n9
Shenhav, Yehouda, 197n4, 212n39
Shibli, Adania, 21, 157–158, 187–194, 197, 229–240
Shifriss, Nathan, 206n20
"Shir ʿEreś Meturgam mi-Yidish" (A Lullaby Translated from the Yiddish) (Ravikovitch), 155–156, 158–187
Shohat, Ella, 7n6, 9, 137, 139, 200n17, 205, 209n26
"shooting and crying," 69–71, 69n2, 70n4, 83n44, 187, 211
Shovrim Shtiḳa (Breaking the Silence) (NGO), 70n5
Sifr al-Ikhtifa' (The Book of Disappearance) (Azem), 108–112, 112n9, 120–121, 125–126, 131–132, 138–139, 141–142
Sijill Ikhtifa' (Chronicle of a Disappearance) (film), 110, 133–136, 134–136, 143, 145–146
Six Day War, 69. *See also* 1967 War
Smotrich, Bezalel, 182n75, 247
social contract, 34, 39, 51
speculation, 92, 94, 98–101, 107; in literature, 109n1, 234
Spivak, Gayatri, 29–30
Statehood Generation *(Dor ha-Medina)*, 159, 159n12, 178
state of nature, 14, 15n21, 19, 33–35, 39, 216
Stoler, Ann Laura, 150
stream of consciousness, 26n2
subjectivity, 38, 73, 77, 82n41, 83–84, 92, 147, 230, 233
Suleiman, Elia, 20, 110, 125, 133–136, 134–136, 142–147, 151
surveillance, 117, 127, 130, 131n72, 132, 136, 143, 145–147, 210, 216, 222–223, 224–225, 230, 243–244
Swirski, Shlomo, 130
symmetry, 5, 13–14, 24, 33, 45, 48, 190, 213–218, 220, 226–227

Tafṣil Thanawi (Minor Detail) (Shibli), 21, 157–158, 187–194, 229
Taharlev, Itamar, 138n83
"al-Talaʿub bi-l-ʿAdid min Dharrat al-Ghubar" ("The Manipulation of Many Dust Particles") (Shibli), 229–240
Tamari, Salim, 103n101, 129–130
Tammuz, Benjamin, 141n95
Tantura, 119, 193
ha-Tasriṭa'i (The Screenwriter) (television series), 150
Tawil-Souri, Helga, 233, 235, 235n92
"ha-Tayar ha-Gadol" (The Great Wanderer) (Hazaz), 103, 103n102
Tchernichovsky, Shaul, 71
teḥiya, 5
terrorism, 16, 18, 210, 213, 215, 219
Time that Remains, The (film). *See* al-Zaman al-Baqi
"Tinoḳ lo Horgim Paʿamayim" (You Can't Kill a Baby Twice) (Ravikovitch), 163n23
torture, 131, 143, 170n44, 171
"ha-Ṭribunal shel ha-Ḥofesh ha-Gadol" (The Summer Break Tribunal) (Ravikovitch), 158n10
tropes, 12n18, 48, 53–54, 90, 101, 109, 132, 219
Tsamir, Hamutal, 178n64
"Tsanaḥ lo zalzal" (A Twig Fell) (Bialik), 182
Tsur, Reuven, 99n93, 103n104

Unity Intifada, 151–152, 239

Vanished: The Mysterious Disappearance of Mustafa Ouda (Masoud), 110
Veracini, Lorenzo, 114–115, 120

violence: and anticolonial struggle, 13–14, 19, 27, 33, 42–44, 142, 220; in Benjamin, 15n21, 142; colonial, 14, 21, 46, 68, 69, 73, 113, 120–123, 155–156, 186, 197, 239, 245; constitutive, 15–16, 33, 35, 113; cycle of, 21, 183, 211, 214–218; defusion of, 144, 244; diffusion of, 209; exceptional, 155, 156, 169–170, 183, 186, 197, 226; individual attacks, 153–154; Israeli construal of, 13–14; judgment and, 17–19, 33–39, 41–43, 170, 245–246; and law, 14–18, 15n21, 21, 27, 33–38, 142–144, 146, 153–194, 197, 213–217, 226, 254; as law destroying, 142; as law preserving, 15, 15n21; lawless, 14, 17, 31, 33, 226, 240, 245, 247; literature and, 10–13, 27–28, 68, 70, 70n4, 123, 148–149, 228; Mizrahi Jews and, 197–198, 209–210, 210n29, 212–213, 220, 227; sovereign, 35, 213; state, 14–19, 21, 33–35, 113, 192, 197, 209, 213, 217, 226–227, 244. *See also* terrorism; torture; Giv'ati Affair

al-Waqa'i' al-Ghariba fi Ikhtifa' Sa'id abi al-Naḥs al-Mutasha'il (The Strange Circumstances of the Disappearance of Saeed the Ill-Fated Pessoptimist) (Habiby), 110, 123–124, 128–129, 137, 142–143, 147–149
Ward, Douglas Turner, 109n1
We are All Equally Far from Love (Shibli). See *Kulluna Ba'id bi-Dhat al-Miqdar 'an al-Ḥubb*
Weber, Max, 16n23
Weisglass, Dov, 127n59
"With Open Eyes" (Hatuka). *See* "Be'eynayyim Pekuḥot"
Wittgenstein, Ludwig, 57
Wolfe, Patrick, 111, 205
World Zionist Organization, 102

Ya 'ish (four volumes) (Hazaz), 74
Yehoshua, A. B., 141n95
Yemenite, Mizrahi and Balkan Children Affair, 138, 201, 205–208, 241–242
Yemenite Jews, 74, 138, 197, 201–206, 203n12, 240–242
Yeshurun, Avoth, 68
Yiddish language, 78, 88, 161
Yizhar, S., 69–70, 70n4, 141n95
"Yom Ḥoref Tsefoni" (A Northern Winter's Day) (Ravikovitch), 172n48
Yona, Lihi, 197, 212–213, 212n39
Yosef, Raz, 217–218
ha-Yoshevet ba-Ganim (Thou That Dwellest in the Gardens) (Hazaz), 74

Zabari, Yossi, 202n10
Zahalka, Jamal, 209
al-Zaman al-Baqi (The Time that Remains) (film), 125, 141
"Zemer Nuge" (Mournful Song) (Bluwstein), 177
Zionism, 3–5, 48, 69–73, 94n78; appropriation and, 94, 94n78; Arabness and, 203–205; Brit Shalom and, 80n36; Canaanism and, 76n20; Christianity and, 89n59; colonialism and, 42, 94, 112–114, 189–190, 213; cultural appropriation and, 113, 126–136; diasporic Jews and, 49, 78, 86; disappearance and, 109, 115–116, 149; ethnic cleansing and, 13; exile and, negation of, 75–83; exploitation and, 126–136; imperialism and, 98; Jewish history and, 78–79, 79n35, 83–89; Judaism and, 73, 75, 77–80, 82, 93, 104–105; Judaization and, 116, 209; *levaṭim* and, 84–107; Mizrahi Jews and, 102, 137–139, 196–198, 201–205, 204n14, 208–209, 213; mythology of, 47; negation and, 111; Palestinians and, 198; racism and, 45–46
Zionists, as term, 8–9
"'Al Zot" (About This) (Alterman) 169–170
Zurayk, Constantin, 65

www.ingramcontent.com/pod-product-compliance
Lightning Source LLC
Chambersburg PA
CBHW020357080526
44584CB00014B/1064